'Abdu'l-Bahá in Their Midst

This book is dedicated to

'Abdu'l-Bahá

for His example and inspiration

It is also dedicated to my wife, Sharon O'Toole,
who brought me into the Faith of Bahá'u'lláh,
thus allowing me to discover 'Abdu'l-Bahá.
She also encouragingly put up with my endless hours
of research and writing,
then patiently proof-read the results.
For over three decades, she has been my best friend.

# 'Abdu'l-Bahá in Their Midst

Earl Redman

GEORGE RONALD
OXFORD

George Ronald, Publisher
Oxford
www.grbooks.com

© Earl Redman 2011
All Rights Reserved

Reprinted 2012, 2019

A catalogue record for this book is available from the British Library

ISBN 978-0-85398-557-0

Cover design: Steiner Graphics

# CONTENTS

| | | |
|---|---|---|
| Preface | | vii |
| 1 | Who is 'Abdu'l-Bahá? | 1 |
| 2 | 'Abdu'l-Bahá's Travels to the West | 3 |
| 3 | A Delay in Egypt | 8 |
| 4 | Arrival in the West<br>*Thonon-les-Bains – London – Bristol – Byfleet – London – Paris* | 17 |
| 5 | Egypt and an Atlantic Crossing<br>*Alexandria* | 50 |
| 6 | Greeting the Statue of Liberty<br>*New York* | 55 |
| 7 | 'White and Black Sitting Together'<br>*Washington, DC* | 89 |
| 8 | The Mother Temple of the West<br>*Chicago – Cleveland, Ohio and Pittsburgh – Washington, DC* | 107 |
| 9 | The City of the Covenant<br>*New York – Boston – New York – Philadelphia – New York* | 125 |
| 10 | Summer Travels<br>*Montclair and West Englewood – New York – Boston – Dublin – Green Acre – Malden* | 145 |

11  North to Canada                                                  179
    *Montreal*

12  California Bound                                                 189
    *Buffalo and Niagara Falls – Chicago – Kenosha –
    Minneapolis/St Paul – Omaha and Lincoln – Denver –
    Glenwood Springs – Salt Lake City*

13  'Your Love Drew Me to You'                                       211
    *San Francisco and Oakland – Pleasanton – San Francisco –
    Los Angeles – San Francisco – Sacramento*

14  The Last Days in America                                         243
    *To Chicago – Cincinnati – Washington, DC – Baltimore,
    Maryland and Philadelphia – New York*

15  Return to the United Kingdom                                     273
    *Liverpool – London – Oxford – London – Edinburgh –
    Bristol – London*

16  From Paris to Budapest and Back                                  307
    *Paris – Stuttgart – Esslingen – Stuttgart – Bad Mergentheim –
    Budapest – Vienna – Stuttgart – Paris*

17  Home Again                                                       326
    *Port Said, Ismailia, Alexandria and Ramleh – Haifa*


Bibliography                                                          339
References                                                            345
Index of Names                                                        365

# PREFACE

*The day is not far off when the details of 'Abdu'l-Bahá's missionary journeys will be admitted to be of historical importance. How gentle and wise he was, hundreds could testify from personal knowledge, and I, too could perhaps say something . . .*[1]

In March of 2007, I entered the House of the Master while on pilgrimage. I'd been there before, but wasn't sure what to expect this time. After our guide had given a brief talk, my feet led me to 'Abdu'l-Bahá's room, where I tucked myself into a corner. My feelings were very different from my first visit to this room, which had been more akin to a history lesson. This time I was drawn to 'Abdu'l-Bahá by an irresistible force and felt impelled to pray. Following what seemed to be a short time, I raised my head and opened my eyes. The room was empty. A glance at my watch showed that 45 minutes had passed, mysteriously fleeting. I have been drawn to 'Abdu'l-Bahá ever since.

On 30 August 2010, I received an email from the Bahá'í World News Service with a link to a new story about the travels of 'Abdu'l-Bahá to the West. It stated that 100 years previously, the Master had left Haifa and begun His three-year, history-making journey to the West. Then a friend sent me an email with a long string of photos taken of 'Abdu'l-Bahá in America, England, France and Germany. I found myself mesmerized by both the story and the photos.

My interest piqued, I pulled two books on 'Abdu'l-Bahá's travels from our bookshelves: *Mahmúd's Diary* (an account of those travels by one who was there) and *239 Days* by Allan Ward. Both are solely about the Master's journey through America and both contained bits and pieces of stories about which I wanted to know more. Using the references in the books, a pile of volumes began to rise on my desk, but it didn't take long before the pile spilled off onto the floor into another pile. And then two piles. Then three! There were the obvious books about the life of 'Abdu'l-Bahá and books of remembrances of 'Abdu'l-Bahá. Then there were the biographies of those well-known Bahá'ís who had been involved with 'Abdu'l-Bahá's travels. The *Star of the West*, in its completely unindexed glory, was a treasure trove of stories so long as one had the patience to scan all of its thousands of stories and articles with an eye calibrated to discover key words such as London, Bristol, Paris, New York, Chicago, Green Acre, Stuttgart, Ahmad Sohrab (one of 'Abdu'l-Bahá's secretaries on His travels), Juliet Thompson, Louis Gregory, Lady Blomfield, and Hippolyte Dreyfus-Barney.

The biographies of well-known Bahá'ís were a great source of inspirational personal stories about their interactions with the Centre of the Covenant. It was surprising, however, that a number of dedicated believers who contributed significantly to the progress of the Faith were not represented in my literary cordillera. So, I turned to the internet and started typing in the names of people mentioned in some of the stories. This search uncovered many fascinating stories by or about Fred Mortensen, Ali Yazdi, Hippolyte Dreyfus-Barney, Howard MacNutt, Sachiro Fujita, Muriel Ives Barrow Newhall, Elaine Lacroix Hopson, and Louis Gregory, as well as leading me to the published diaries of Juliet Thompson and Agnes Parsons. Strangely, these sources were heavily American. In searching for information about Ali-Kuli Khan, I discovered that Marzieh Gail was his daughter and so discovered another treasury in her family history, *Arches of the Years*.

The books and internet sites I read contained the most amazing stories, filled with awe-inspiring accounts of souls in contact with Bahá'u'lláh's designated Interpreter and His conduit to the world. They were so revealing, so inspiring and so tear-provoking that I was constantly in danger of dripping tears onto my keyboard. The stories illustrated the spiritual powers of 'Abdu'l-Bahá, the Servant of Bahá (Bahá'u'lláh). Time after time, I read of the arrival of a guest whom none had expected except 'Abdu'l-Bahá; of how often 'Abdu'l-Bahá would delay His departure to catch a train, meet 'important people' or attend a meeting, to the consternation and frustration of those around Him, because He 'knew' someone who needed to see Him was coming. Many times the 'someone' was unknown and poor or roughly dressed, but 'Abdu'l-Bahá would wait for them, then surround them with His love. There were also stories of those who thought themselves important,

PREFACE

but who were reduced to wordlessness in the presence of the Master.

I began to collect some of the stories to share with others. Then one day, while trying to get information about the Irish Bahá'í winter school, I found myself volunteering to do two sessions at the school about 'Abdu'l-Bahá's travels. By the time I had exhausted my initial sources, I had compiled 54 pages of stories to tell. Some of the anecdotes were related to others that occurred at different times so, in order to have a clearer picture of how some people interacted with 'Abdu'l-Bahá and how they were filled with the fire of the love of God and were spiritually impelled to rush into the field of service, I began to convert all those pages of discrete tales into a narrative. That process led to this book.

What fascinated me about 'Abdu'l-Bahá on His travels were not the public talks He gave, though many of those are truly inspiring, but what people remembered about Him. This volume is therefore the narrative of how 'Abdu'l-Bahá affected and transformed those He met, described by using their own words. It also includes many quotations from Him as each individual remembered them later. Sometimes, what 'Abdu'l-Bahá said was written down within hours, but often it was days, weeks, months or even years later. Therefore, almost all of the words quoted in this book as being from 'Abdu'l-Bahá are not authenticated and they should be taken in the spirit of pilgrim's notes.

In a letter written by Edward Getsinger, he specifically refers to this matter of authenticity:

> By the way . . . when a question comes up regarding meetings, feasts, explanations, it was said by 'Abdu'l-Bahá in my presence that the written word or tablet must be taken as guidance, and not the spoken word, for 'have I not said on the steamer in [New York] that they will say he said so and so, but pay only attention to the Tablets written with my signature and seal,' He said . . . so it is with all matters, those who claim authority for this and that he said 'have they a Tablet to that effect?'[2]

Rather ironically, this quotation is itself a pilgrim's note, but it gets the point across. Shoghi Effendi, Guardian of the Bahá'í Faith, rather emphatically made the same point:

Much of the confusion that has obscured the understanding of the believers should be attributed to this double error involved in the inexact rendering of an only partially understood statement. Not infrequently has the interpreter even failed to convey the exact purport of the inquirer's specific questions, and, by his deficiency of understanding and expression in conveying the answer of 'Abdu'l-Bahá, has been responsible for reports wholly at variance with the true spirit and purpose of the Cause. It was chiefly in view of the misleading nature of the reports of the informal conversations of 'Abdu'l-Bahá with visiting pilgrims, that I have insistently urged the believers of the West to regard such statements as merely personal impressions of the sayings of their Master, and to quote and consider as authentic only such translations as are based upon the authenticated text of His recorded utterances in the original tongue.[3]

What you will read here, then, is what people remembered Him saying, but not necessarily exactly what 'Abdu'l-Bahá said or what He may have actually meant.

# ACKNOWLEDGEMENTS

First and foremost, I have to gratefully thank my wife, Sharon O'Toole, for allowing me to disappear into great piles of books for long periods of time and for bringing me coffee so I could stay there. She was also my first editor and checked every page with her eye for the details I always miss. I also greatly appreciate the help of Lewis Walker, of the National Bahá'í Archives of the United States, and Lesley Taherzadeh and Manijeh Afnan-Murray, of the Bahá'í Archives Team of the United Kingdom. Lewis, with Archivist Roger Dahl, though claiming to be simple 'table-setters . . . for the feast that researchers . . . provide the public', contributed many fascinating pages of pilgrims' notes about 'Abdu'l-Bahá's visit that added spice to the story. Lesley and Manijeh supplied me with scans of English newspaper stories from 'Abdu'l-Bahá's 1911 and 1913 visits to the United Kingdom. To Ann O'Sullivan and Sarah Sabour-Pickett, I must express my appreciation for strongly suggesting that the book be published. Maurice Sabour-Pickett carefully went through the manuscript at an early stage and offered many constructive suggestions. I also thank Ilse Kiebler for her help in translating my German references. And finally, I must gratefully acknowledge the many helpful and illuminating comments and suggestions from May Hofman, and for all the painstaking editorial work she did to ensure accuracy throughout. She suggested additions, subtractions and modifications that, in the end, turned all the pages of my manuscript into an actual book.

# I

# WHO IS 'ABDU'L-BAHÁ?

Though bent with age, though suffering from ailments resulting from the accumulated cares of fifty years of exile and captivity, 'Abdu'l-Bahá set out on His memorable journey across the seas to the land where He might bless by His presence, and sanctify through His deeds, the mighty acts His spirit had led His disciples to perform. The circumstances that have attended His triumphal progress through the chief cities of the United States and Canada my pen is utterly incapable of describing. The joys which the announcement of His arrival evoked, the publicity which His activities created, the forces which His utterances released, the opposition which the implications of His teachings excited, the significant episodes to which His words and deeds continually gave rise – these future generations will, no doubt, minutely and befittingly register. They will carefully delineate their features, will cherish and preserve their memory, and will transmit unimpaired the record of their minutest details to their descendants.[1]

Who is 'Abdu'l-Bahá and why should we strive to follow the example of His life? Why is it important to see how He interacted with and affected those around Him? To help clarify the station of 'Abdu'l-Bahá, Shoghi Effendi wrote:

> Whether in the Kitáb-i-Aqdas, the most weighty and sacred of all the works of Bahá'u'lláh, or in the Kitáb-i-'Ahd, the Book of His Covenant, or in the Súriy-i-Ghuṣn (Tablet of the Branch), such references as have been recorded by the pen of Bahá'u'lláh – references which the Tablets of His Father addressed to Him mightily reinforce – invest 'Abdu'l-Bahá with a power, and surround Him with a halo, which the present generation can never adequately appreciate.

He is, and should for all time be regarded, first and foremost, as the Centre and Pivot of Bahá'u'lláh's peerless and all-enfolding Covenant, His most exalted handiwork, the stainless Mirror of His light, the perfect Exemplar of His teachings, the unerring Interpreter of His Word, the embodiment of every Bahá'í ideal, the incarnation of every Bahá'í virtue, the Most Mighty Branch sprung from the Ancient Root, the Limb of the Law of God, the Being 'round Whom all names revolve,' the Mainspring of the Oneness of Humanity, the Ensign of the Most Great Peace, the Moon of the Central Orb of this most holy Dispensation – styles and titles that are implicit and find their truest, their highest and fairest expression in the magic name 'Abdu'l-Bahá. He is, above and beyond these appellations, the 'Mystery of God' – an expression by which Bahá'u'lláh Himself has chosen to designate Him, and which, while it does not by any means justify us to assign to Him the station of Prophethood, indicates how in the person of 'Abdu'l-Bahá the incompatible characteristics of a human nature and superhuman knowledge and perfection have been blended and are completely harmonized.[2]

Uniquely in religious history, a Manifestation of God had unequivocally appointed a successor, One who would be able to unerringly interpret His Revelation and His Word. Bahá'u'lláh, in His own hand, wrote in the Kitáb-i-'Ahd that upon His passing, all Bahá'ís were to turn to 'Abdu'l-Bahá, Whom He designated as the Centre of His Covenant. 'Abdu'l-Bahá was the son of Bahá'u'lláh and was born on the very night that the Báb, the Manifestation of God Who preceded and announced the coming of Bahá'u'lláh, declared His Own mission. 'Abdu'l-Bahá was the first to believe in His Father's station as a Manifestation of God. Repeatedly throughout His travels in the West, 'Abdu'l-Bahá insisted that He was not a Prophet and did not hold the same station as His Father. He claimed simply to be the Servant of Bahá'u'lláh, albeit a servant Who had been given the gift of infallibility in the interpretation of His Father's Will.

# 2

# 'ABDU'L-BAHÁ'S TRAVELS TO THE WEST

'Abdu'l-Bahá's journey to the West was a monumental event in the life of the young Bahá'í Faith. As described by Shoghi Effendi in *God Passes By*:

> So momentous a change in the fortunes of the Faith was the signal for such an outburst of activity on His part as to dumbfound His followers in East and West with admiration and wonder, and exercise an imperishable influence on the course of its future history. He Who, in His own words, had entered prison as a youth and left it an old man, Who never in His life had faced a public audience, had attended no school, had never moved in Western circles, and was unfamiliar with Western customs and language, had arisen not only to proclaim from pulpit and platform, in some of the chief capitals of Europe and in the leading cities of the North American continent, the distinctive verities enshrined in His Father's Faith, but to demonstrate as well the Divine origin of the Prophets gone before Him, and to disclose the nature of the tie binding them to that Faith.[1]

Elaine Lacroix Hopson writes in her book, *'Abdu'l-Bahá in New York*, that:

> The primary purpose of 'Abdu'l-Bahá's journey to America was to officially proclaim His Station as the Centre of the Covenant, to rally the unity of the Bahá'í Community, and to establish the strong foundation of love and integrity upon which the future of the Faith of Bahá'u'lláh would stand and progress. With complete disregard for His frail physical condition, the Master gave most of His time in

America to the friends, to their spiritual needs, to turn their weaknesses into springboards for future greatness, to weave a web of love connections between them.[2]

Many of those whose names today are the bright lights of Western Bahá'í history had their lives changed by meeting 'Abdu'l-Bahá on His travels. Some, whom He met for the first time, included the future Hands of the Cause of God Dorothy Baker, John Hyde and Clara Dunn, Paul Haney, Horace Holley, Leroy Ioas and Mary Maxwell (Amatu'l-Bahá Rúḥíyyih Khánum). Others He met included future Hands of the Cause of God Corinne True, Louis Gregory, Sutherland Maxwell, Martha Root and Roy Wilhelm, and other notables such as Lady Blomfield, Hippolyte and Laura Dreyfus-Barney, Sarah Farmer (of Green Acre), Isabel Fraser, Edward and Lua Getsinger, Joseph and Pauline Hannen, Marion Jack, Howard Colby Ives, Ali Kuli Khan and his family, Edward and Carrie Kinney, Alma Knobloch, May Maxwell, Fred Mortensen, Grace and Harlan Ober, Agnes Parsons, Ethel Rosenberg, Juliet Thompson, Miriam Thornburgh-Cropper and Jane Whyte.

'Abdu'l-Bahá was released from prison in 1908 because of the revolt of the Young Turks against the Ottoman Emperor 'Abdu'l-Ḥamíd. Almost immediately, Western believers began petitioning Him to visit their countries. The Americans, in particular, were eager for 'Abdu'l-Bahá to visit their shores, but He made it plain that He would not visit there until the Bahá'í community was united.

The American Bahá'í community was suffering from three ailments during those early years of the century: Covenant-breaking, the cult of the individual and racism. The first problem was due to Ibrahim Kheiralla. He learned of the Bahá'í Faith in Cairo, then went to America in 1892 to teach the new faith, settling in Chicago. Kheiralla was an effective teacher and, together with Thornton Chase, the first American Bahá'í he taught, raised up a community of a few hundred spiritually-enlightened souls. Kheiralla's teaching, unfortunately, included many of his own beliefs, including reincarnation, dream interpretation and occultism.

This great success, however, quickly inflated Kheiralla's already overlarge ego and resulted in him hoping to split the leadership of the Bahá'í world with 'Abdu'l-Bahá. From Kheiralla's viewpoint, since he was so successful in America, it seemed only right that he be the one to guide and administer the Faith there, while 'Abdu'l-Bahá could lead the rest of the world's Bahá'í community. Meeting 'Abdu'l-Bahá in Haifa in 1898 was a huge blow to Kheiralla because it became obvious that 'Abdu'l-Bahá would have no part in his desire for leadership. That frustration led him to Mírzá Muḥammad-'Alí, 'Abdu'l-Bahá's half-brother and Arch-breaker of Bahá'u'lláh's Covenant. Mírzá Muḥammad-'Alí sent his eldest son, Shu'á'u'lláh, to America to aid Kheiralla. Kheiralla had written a book which was theoretically about the Faith, but also included his superstitions and mistaken ideas. When 'Abdu'l-Bahá told him not to publish his book, he did so anyway, resulting in a split in the American Bahá'í community.[3]

The great majority of the American believers remained steadfast and quickly fled from Kheiralla, rallied by Thornton Chase, Anton Haddad, Mírzá Abu'l-Faḍl and Ali-Kuli Khan, but a few weaker ones followed the charismatic doctor and broke the Covenant. There was much confusion in the Bahá'í community about how to deal with the Covenant-breakers and this was still affecting the community between 1908 and 1911.

The second problem was basically ego. The earliest American believers were truly independent thinkers, which was why they were able to recognize and follow this new faith whose founder had such an unusual name. Since there was little Bahá'í literature in English at that time, there were differences of opinion about what, exactly, the Faith believed and how it should be taught. There were many clashes between strong-willed individuals that resulted in contention and alienation.

Tossed into this mix was the fact that most of the early American believers were either wealthy, or at least well off, and white. The barrier of racial unity was one that stood high in front of the early upper-class Bahá'ís. Their social standing simply didn't allow them to associate with black people, whether they were Bahá'ís or not.

While on pilgrimage in Haifa in 1909, Alice Breed asked 'Abdu'l-Bahá: 'If we build the Temple [the American House of Worship] quickly and send a ship for You, will You come to America?' 'Abdu'l-Bahá responded: 'I will come of My own volition to America if they build the Mashriqu'l-Adhkár quickly. But,' (sadly and very gently) 'they will not build it quickly.'[4] Then in April of 1911, 'Abdu'l-Bahá wrote to the American Bahá'ís:

> If the friends and the maid-servants of the Merciful long for the visit of 'Abdu'l-Bahá, they must immediately remove from their midst differences of opinion and be engaged in the practice of infinite love and unity . . . If ye are yearning for my meeting, and if in reality ye are seeking my visit, ye must close the doors of difference and open the gates of affection, love and friendship . . . Verily, verily, I say unto you, were it not for this difference amongst you, the inhabitants of America . . . would have, by now, been attracted to the Kingdom of God . . . Is it meet that you sacrifice this most glorious Bounty for worthless imaginations?[5]

The Master amplified this with Tablets to individual believers such as Isabella Brittingham:

> If the believers of God in New York and other cities of America establish, in a befitting manner, union and harmony with spirit, tongue, heart and body, suddenly they shall find 'Abdu'l-Bahá in their midst. Unless this union is brought about, the Breath of the Holy Spirit shall not have any effect, for the physical body must find capacity, so that the life of the Spirit can breathe through it. If the Beloved of the union of the friends and the harmony of the believers become manifest, the East and the West of America shall be perfumed through the sweet fragrance of the Paradise of Abhá . . .[6]

## Departure from Haifa

Sydney Sprague was on pilgrimage in Haifa in September 1910. One afternoon, 'Abdu'l-Bahá had come and visited with Mr Sprague and the other pilgrims. Everything seemed normal. But that evening 'as usual, the believers gathered before the house of 'Abdu'l-Bahá to receive that blessing, which every day is ours, of being in his presence, but we waited in vain, for one of the sons-in-law came and told us that 'Abdu'l-Bahá had taken the Khedivial steamer to Port Said.' Sprague wrote from Haifa: 'I have a very big piece of news to tell you. 'Abdu'l-Bahá has left this Holy Spot for the first time in forty-two years, and has gone to Egypt . . . Everyone was astounded to hear of 'Abdu'l-Bahá's departure, for no one knew until the very last minute that he had any idea of leaving . . . after forty-two years in this cage, the Divine

Bird has spread His wings and in perfect freedom flown away.'[7]

When asked about His abrupt departure, 'Abdu'l-Bahá's attendant, Siyyid Asadu'lláh-i-Qumí, wrote: "Abdu'l-Bahá did not inform anyone that he was going to leave Haifa. The day he left he visited the Holy Tomb of the Báb on Mt Carmel and when he came down from the mountain of the Lord, he went direct to the steamer. This was the first anyone knew about the matter... The only persons who accompanied 'Abdu'l-Bahá to Egypt were Mirza Moneer Zain and Abdul Hossein.'[8]

When 'Abdu'l-Bahá left Haifa, He called upon the one person in whom He had complete trust and confidence – His sister, Bahíyyih Khánum, the Greatest Holy Leaf, but she may not have known about His intentions until she received a Tablet from Him written, probably, when He was already sailing toward Egypt. In this Tablet, the Master left her in charge of the Bahá'í community:

> O thou my sister, my dear sister!
>
> Divine wisdom hath decreed this temporary separation, but I long more and more to be with thee again. Patience is called for, and long-suffering, and trust in God, and the seeking of His favour. Since thou art there, my mind is completely at rest.
>
> In recent days, I have made a plan to visit Egypt, if this be God's will. Do thou, on my behalf, lay thy head on the sacred Threshold, and perfume brow and hair in the dust of that Door, and ask that I may be confirmed in my work; that I may, in return for His endless bounties, win, if He will, a drop out of the ocean of servitude.[9]

'Abdu'l-Bahá continued to write to Bahíyyih Khánum and to His wife, Munírih Khánum, all through His travels.

# 3

# A DELAY IN EGYPT
*September 1910–August 1911*

With 'Abdu'l-Bahá's departure, the Covenant-breakers moved quickly in an attempt to take advantage of the situation. Mírzá Muḥammad-'Alí quickly began spreading the rumour that 'Abdu'l-Bahá had been forced to flee the Holy Land. A cleric friendly with the Covenant-breaker telegraphed one of his supporters in Jaffa to board 'Abdu'l-Bahá's ship and see if He was indeed aboard. The man boarded the ship and came face to face with 'Abdu'l-Bahá. Another of the cleric's supporters did the same thing in Port Said.[1] Because of this scheming, 'Abdu'l-Bahá wrote to Muníríh Khánum that:

> Should people enquire about My whereabouts, tell them that certain prominent Americans and Europeans have repeatedly sought and received promises that I would make a trip to those areas . . . be evasive as much as possible . . . The less said the better it would be. Tell Dr Fallscheer [the Holy Family's doctor in Haifa] also not to divulge the truth, and thou shouldst not divulge either as far as possible.[2]

After arriving in Port Said, 'Abdu'l-Bahá had initially planned to continue immediately to Europe, but His poor health forced Him to stay in Port Said for a month. While there, He asked Siyyid Asadu'lláh-i-Qumí: 'Do you realize now the meaning of my statement when I was telling the friends that there was a wisdom in my indisposition? . . . Well, the wisdom was that I must always move according to the requirements of the Cause.'[3]

After the month in Port Said, 'Abdu'l-Bahá, as He had in Haifa, suddenly and without warning, boarded a ship bound for Europe. His cruise, however, was very short because His health forced Him back onshore at Alexandria on the other side of the Nile Delta.

Ali Yazdi, who was a lad of 11 years, lived in Ramleh, an eastern suburb of Alexandria, when 'Abdu'l-Bahá arrived. He wrote that:

> ... I heard the news of the coming of 'Abdu'l-Bahá to Ramleh. I heard that suddenly, without warning, He had left Haifa on a steamer bound for Europe, that He had stopped in Port Said because of ill health and fatigue, and that He was coming to Alexandria. Then the news came that *He was coming to Ramleh!*
>
> ... All I knew about him was what I had heard my father tell us. No one in the family that I knew except Father and Grandfather had seen Him. There were no pictures then, except an early one taken when He was a young man in Adrianople. He was a prisoner beyond our reach – a legendary and heroic Figure ...
>
> A crowd gathered in front of the Hotel Victoria for His arrival. Suddenly there was a hush, a stillness, and I knew that He had come. I looked. There He was! Then He walked through the crowd – slowly, majestically, smiling radiantly as he greeted the bowed heads on either side. I could only get a vague impression of Him, as I could not get near Him. The sound of the wind and the surf from the nearby shore drowned out His voice so I could hardly hear Him. Nevertheless, I went away happy.
>
> A few days later a villa was rented for Him and His family not far from the Hotel Victoria. It was in the best residential section, next to the beautiful Mediterranean and the beaches. Like all the villas in that area, it had a garden with flowers and flowering shrubs. It was there that 'Abdu'l-Bahá chose to receive a great variety of notables, public figures, clerics, aristocrats and writers – as well as poor and despairing people.
>
> I went there often, sometimes on the way home from school, sometimes on weekends. I spent most of my time outside of school in His garden. I would wait to get a glimpse of Him as He came out for His customary walk or conversed with pilgrims from faraway places. To hear His vibrant and melodious voice ringing in the open air and to see Him exhilarated me and gave me hope. Quite often He came to me and smiled and talked. There was a radiance about Him, an almost unlimited kindness and love that shone from Him. Seeing Him infused me with a feeling of goodness. I felt humble and at the same time exceedingly happy.

I also had many opportunities to see the Master . . . at meetings and festive occasions. I especially remember the first time He came to our house to address a large gathering of believers. The friends were all gathered, talking happily, waiting. All of a sudden there was quiet. I could hear from the outside the voice of 'Abdu'l-Bahá – very resonant, very beautiful – before He entered the room. Then He swept in, with His robe flowing.

He was straight as an arrow. His head was thrown back. His silver-grey hair fell in waves to His shoulders. His beard was white. His eyes were keen; His forehead, broad. He wore a white turban around an ivory-coloured felt cap. He looked at everyone, smiled and welcomed all with *Khushámadíd! Khushámadíd!* (Welcome! Welcome!)

I had been taught that in the presence of 'Abdu'l-Bahá I should sit or stand with my hands crossed in front of me and look down. I was so anxious to see Him that I found myself looking up furtively now and then.

He spoke often and on many subjects. For nine months it seemed like paradise. Then He left us and, after three months in Cairo, sailed for Europe. How dismal everything became.

. . . He spoke to me on several occasions. He always called me 'Sheikh-Ali', the name He Himself had given me, after my uncle . . . who was the first member of the family to join the Faith. When 'Abdu'l-Bahá spoke to me, I would look into his eyes – blue, smiling, full of love.[4]

It didn't take long for 'Abdu'l-Bahá to attract attention. In November 1910 an Englishman, Wellesley Tudor-Pole, spent nine days with 'Abdu'l-Bahá in Alexandria. Tudor-Pole had first heard of the Bahá'í Faith and 'Abdu'l-Bahá when he was in Constantinople in 1908. Back in England, he became active in the Bahá'í community and hosted 'Abdu'l-Bahá at his guest house in Clifton, Bristol, when the Master was in the United Kingdom in both 1911 and 1913. Tudor-Pole described 'Abdu'l-Bahá:

Although Abdu'l Bahá (who was always known to his family, followers and friends in affectionate reverence as 'The Master') would often quote his father's sayings and relate various incidents from his life, he never gave descriptions of his personality, and we are told that the pictures which have come down to us give a very poor impression of his father's stature and dignity.

He wished to be remembered not by his person or his human frame, but by his teachings, and his actions. In this respect, one is sure that Abdu'l Bahá, too, would not wish his personality, his physical aspect, to obscure the inspiration of his teachings and the example of his life. I was in close contact with him on many occasions, in Palestine, Egypt, Paris, London and Bristol, and although I retain a dear picture of his gracious and dignified personality, it would not be easy to translate such a picture into adequate words.

The most abiding impression I received from intimate contact with him was his immense breadth of outlook, permeated with the spirit of deep and loving kindness. Whatever the topic under discussion – ranging from religion to the weather, from sunsets to the flowers, from ethics to personal behaviour, Abdu'l Bahá always struck the universal note, the note of Oneness as between the Creator and all His creation, great or small.[5]

During the First World War, Tudor-Pole played a notable role in the protection of 'Abdu'l-Bahá when the leader of the Ottoman Turks threatened His life. After the passing of the Master, Tudor-Pole drifted away from the Faith, unable to find a connection between the organization of the Faith being created by Shoghi Effendi with his interest in 'spiritual regeneration', rather than a new religion.

In Alexandria, Tudor-Pole reported that 'Abdu'l-Bahá's health was much improved and that He looked strong and vigorous. According to Tudor-Pole, 'Abdu'l-Bahá 'spoke much of the work in America, to which he undoubtedly is giving considerable thought. He also spoke a good deal about the work that is going forward in different European centres as well as in London, and he expects great things from England during the coming year . . .'[6]

Shortly after 'Abdu'l-Bahá settled in Ramleh, 13-year-old Shoghi Effendi arrived and stayed with his grandfather. Shoghi Effendi and the 11-year-old Ali Yazdi both attended the French Brothers' School there and became friends. Like his Grandfather, Shoghi Effendi, who was always full of energy and the love of life, usually called his younger companion Sheikh-Alí.[7]

Shoghi Effendi was commonly 'Abdu'l-Bahá's translator for talks with Tudor-Pole. One day, Shoghi Effendi was not present and 'Abdu'l-Bahá spoke to Tudor-Pole in Persian. Completely amazed, Tudor-Pole found that he could understand and reply to what the Master was saying. The ability to understand Persian vanished the moment Shoghi Effendi returned.

Tudor-Pole had planned to return to England overland via Palestine and Turkey, but 'Abdu'l-Bahá said he should return by ship to Marseilles. This change of plans upset him because all his tickets were arranged, but he didn't know how to say no to the Master. The next day he was ready to depart for the ship when 'Abdu'l-Bahá asked him to do Him a favour in Paris. Unhappily, he agreed and was told to find a nearly blind Persian student, Tamaddunu'l-Mulk, give him some money and tell him to go to 'Abdu'l-Bahá in Alexandria. Then Tudor-Pole was told that the student's address was not known.

Arriving grumpily in Paris, Tudor-Pole went to the Persian Embassy, but they had never heard of the student. He spent a whole day in the area where students lived, but again had no success. Realizing that being upset was probably hindering any spiritual guidance, Tudor-Pole cleared his mind and went to collect his baggage at the train station. Crossing the Pont Royal, he spotted a young man of apparent Eastern origin using a stick to tap his way down the street. Dodging through traffic, Tudor-Pole managed to catch the youth and discovered that he was, indeed, the student mentioned by 'Abdu'l-Bahá. Tudor-Pole gave the youth the money and the instructions, which the young man gleefully carried out.

Tudor-Pole continued to London the next day. When he arrived at his office, he found that he was only just in time to avert a serious crisis. Had he stuck with his original overland travel plans, he would have had grave difficulties.[8]

Initially, the Egyptian newspapers were not friendly. Some of the more incendiary would send their papers where Bahá'í visitors would see them. At first, a few of the Bahá'ís wanted to respond and correct the lies, but 'Abdu'l-Bahá simply said, 'These are the heralds of the Kingdom. God is using them to inform the people of our arrival. Let them write anything they like. They will come to investigate, realize the truth and themselves make answer.'[9]

Things happened just as the Master had predicted. In March 1911, a daily newspaper called *The Valley of the Nile* contained a full-page article about 'Abdu'l-Bahá, describing His life and His teachings. The paper also noted that 'all the prominent people of Egypt are beginning to feel his spiritual presence and call upon him to receive instruction'.[10] A Persian weekly called *Chihrih-Nimá*, whose editor had previously been distinctly unfriendly towards 'Abdu'l-Bahá and the Bahá'ís, changed its attitude and began reporting on 'Abdu'l-Bahá's travels and showed great respect and admiration.[11] A variety of other Cairo newspapers similarly printed laudatory accounts of Him.

Louis Gregory, the future Hand of the Cause of God, made a six-day pilgrimage to visit 'Abdu'l-Bahá at Ramleh, at the direct invitation of the Master, from the 10th to the 16th of April. As soon as possible after his arrival, Gregory went to a store run by Mírzá Ḥasan Khurásání (Khorassani), where he met several of the local Bahá'ís. He had a letter of introduction from Edward Getsinger, that had been translated into Persian, which he gave to Muḥammad Yazdí. Yazdí asked: '"You want to see our Lord?" . . . Upon giving my assent, he agreed to act as guide . . . I reasoned that . . . I had no wish to take him away from his business. But he put my objections aside, saying, "This is spiritual business!"'[12] Louis Gregory was taken to 'Abdu'l-Bahá's meeting where he met several others including Louisa Mathew, an English woman who would figure prominently in his future. Like many others, he wrote a pen-portrait of 'Abdu'l-Bahá:

> Viewed with the outer eye, he seemed about the medium height, with symmetrical features. His lineaments indicate meekness and gentleness, as well as power and strength. His colour is about that of parchment. His hands are shapely, with the nails well manicured. His forehead is high and well rounded. His nose is slightly aquiline; his eyes light blue and penetrating; his hair is silvery, and long enough to touch the shoulders; his beard is white. His dress was the Oriental robes, graceful in their simplicity. On his head rested a light tarbush, surrounded by a white turban. His voice is powerful, but capable of producing infinite pathos and tenderness. His carriage is erect and altogether majestic and beautiful . . .
>
> On the rational plane, his wisdom is incomparable. During the time of my visit persons of culture were present from different parts of the world. But people of acquired learning are but as children

to 'Abdu'l-Bahá. They were reverent in their attitude toward him and one of them, an Oxford man, praised his wisdom with much enthusiasm . . .[13]

Gregory describes 'Abbás Effendi, as 'Abdu'l-Bahá was known to the general public, as being

> seen walking about the streets. Ofttimes he would ride upon the electric tramway, making change and paying his fare in the most democratic fashion. His reception room was open to believers and nonbelievers alike . . . Thus . . . thousands of persons had opportunity to see 'Abbás Effendi; but among these how few perceived 'Abdu'l-Bahá! [14]

On his way home from Egypt, Louis Gregory spent four days in London. Arthur Cuthbert, when meeting the future Hand of the Cause of God, said:

> To meet such a great soul, so filled with the true Bahai spirit in any man is an inspiration; but when this man is a negro, and wise enough to be proud of his colour, then it is a revelation impressive with great significance as one contemplates the difficult problems existing between the white and black populations. How such problems can be changed by a few such men aflame with God's Word![15]

One day 'Abdu'l-Bahá was visited by two ladies who were not believers. They were very impressed with Him and, as they were leaving, offered an amount of money to be used for the poor. 'Abdu'l-Bahá told them that it would be better if they distributed the money themselves. Their comment as they left was that He was 'A very extraordinary man!'[16]

On another day, 'Abdu'l-Bahá spoke of meeting some Protestants in Haifa. They invited Him to a school exhibition where one person read a Bible lesson from the first chapter of John, 'In the beginning was the Word,' after which 'Abdu'l-Bahá was invited to speak. 'Abdu'l-Bahá proceeded to give them an explanation of the Word which pleased everyone. They said that never before had they heard so clear and beautiful an explanation. But one from among them suddenly understood the reality of 'Abdu'l-Bahá's explanation and said, '"When He speaks of the Word He does not mean Christ, but Bahá'u'lláh!" Then they became angry.'[17]

'Abdu'l-Bahá was especially concerned with racial unity, or the lack of it, in America. One day when Louisa Mathew was present, 'Abdu'l-Bahá asked Louis Gregory, who was black:

> 'Are the coloured and white believers entirely united?' Referring to the friends, I answered that there was not entire unity, but that there were earnest souls of both races who desired closer unity and hoped that He would point out to them the means of attaining it. He said: 'The best means is to accept this Cause. All differences must fade among believers. In the present antagonism there is great danger to both races. Intermarriage is a good way to efface racial differences. It produces strong, beautiful offspring, clever and resourceful . . .
>
> 'The coloured people must attend all the unity meetings. There must be no distinctions. All are equal. If you have any influence to get the races to intermarry, it will be very valuable.'[18]

It was here that 'Abdu'l-Bahá planted a seed in the hearts of Louisa Mathew and Louis Gregory that blossomed into the first interracial marriage in the American Bahá'í community only a year later.

Muḥammad Yazdí wrote to the American Bahá'ís from Egypt, before 'Abdu'l-Bahá left, to address the fears of many Americans that the Master would face a hostile press and antagonistic people. In his letter, he reassured the Americans that all would be well:

> Some people have expressed anxieties and fears because of Abdul-Baha's possible visit to America; they think that the newspapers will write sensational articles and ridicule the Cause. Such people are very short-sighted. They have not realized deeply, nor superficially, the force of Abdul-Baha's presence. Neither have they dreamed of the magnetic influence of his Highness . . . He is a man whose very appearance will solve all the perplexed anxieties of the visionaries of disaster . . . Should we be afraid to receive the One who is the source of all our inspiration and all our light? . . . Future historians will record the coming of Abdul-Baha to America as a great and momentous event. Broaden your vision and look into the future, when the nations of America shall celebrate, from one end of the

continent to the other, the anniversary of the day when Abdul-Baha set foot upon 'the land of the brave and the home of the free!'. . . He does not want your houses and palaces, but your hearts. Prepare your hearts, purify your hearts, cleanse your hearts, that he may find a place therein.[19]

Shortly after Louis Gregory left Ramleh for Haifa, 'Abdu'l-Bahá moved to Cairo where He stayed for almost three months. While in Cairo, He was interviewed by many prominent people attracted by His wisdom and knowledge. On 22 July, 'Abdu'l-Bahá returned to Ramleh, where He stayed for three weeks. Finally, on 11 August, 'Abdu'l-Bahá sailed for Europe, arriving first in Marseilles, France.

# 4

# ARRIVAL IN THE WEST

*August–December 1911*

## THONON-LES-BAINS, FRANCE

Hippolyte Dreyfus-Barney met 'Abdu'l-Bahá upon His arrival at Marseilles and had the privilege of escorting him to Thonon-les-Bains, a quiet town on the French part of Lake Geneva. The Master thoroughly enjoyed the train ride through the verdant country they traversed. During the following two weeks, 'Abdu'l-Bahá rested in the scenic splendour of the Alps, giving few formal talks and meeting informally with an increasing number of Bahá'ís who travelled across Europe to see Him. Writing to His wife, Munírih K͟hánum, 'Abdu'l-Bahá described the area as 'truly a delightful place. The mildness of the weather, the freshness of the grass and fields, the lushness and pleasantness of the hills, as well as the beauty of the scenery are most perfect. From the day I left Iran until now I had not seen such a place.'[1]

Juliet Thompson was deeply attached to 'Abdu'l-Bahá. When she had departed from Haifa after her pilgrimage in 1909, 'Abdu'l-Bahá had promised that they would meet again. On 13 July she received a letter from Ahmad Sohrab enclosing a Tablet from 'Abdu'l-Bahá. In the Tablet, 'Abdu'l-Bahá summoned her to meet Him in London, where Ahmad Sohrab said He would be addressing the Universal Races Congress a week later. Juliet 'leaped over every "hindrance" . . . and within the week . . . boarded the Lusitania.'[2] A few days later, she was in London, but 'Abdu'l-Bahá was not. He cabled that she should wait in London. It wasn't until 22 August that Juliet received a telegram that said simply 'COME HERE. HOTEL PARC. ABDUL BAHA.'[3]

Juliet, along with Tamaddunu'l-Mulk, was on the train the next day. When they arrived in Geneva, they barely had time to catch the next train and no time to inform anyone of their impending arrival in

Thonon-les-Bains, so the station was empty of friends when they arrived. When there appeared to be no one to take them to the hotel, they appropriated a wheelbarrow for their luggage and pushed it up to the hotel. She then describes the Hotel du Parc where 'Abdu'l-Bahá was staying:

> A great white hotel. At its entrance, two oleander trees in bloom. Inside, high ceilings, white walls, glass doors, rose-coloured carpets, rose-coloured damask furniture. Beyond the green terrace with its marble balustrade, Lake Geneva. Behind the hotel, two mountains overhung with clouds. In the halls and strolling through the grounds: gay, artificial, dull-eyed people. Passing among these silently with His indescribable majesty, His strange Power and His holy sweetness, the Master –'Abdu'l-Bahá – unrecognized but not *unfelt*. As He passes, the dull eyes follow Him, lit up for a moment with wonder.[4]

## Juliet Thompson

Juliet Thompson was a New York artist and painter who, at one point, lived across the street from Kahlil Gibran. She discovered the Faith about 1898, then went to Paris in 1901 where she met Thomas Breakwell, another early Bahá'í. The following year, Juliet went back to New York where she became a successful painter. Her first pilgrimage was in 1909, after which she was in thrall to 'Abdu'l-Bahá.

Juliet attracted marriage proposals from Roy Wilhelm and John Bosch and was, at one point, engaged to Mason Remey. The love of her life, however, was Percy Grant, a Unitarian minister, whom 'Abdu'l-Bahá said she could marry, but only if he became a Bahá'í. He didn't and she remained single throughout her life.

When 'Abdu'l-Bahá began His travels to the West, He called her to join Him at Thonon-les-Bains. She spent as much time as possible in His company when He arrived in America and painted His portrait. In 1926, Juliet made a second pilgrimage and in the 1940s she made several long teaching trips into Mexico.

'Abdu'l-Bahá was particularly fond of her because of her total honesty. When the Guardian asked her what she thought of the design for the American House of Worship near Chicago, she said that she didn't like it because 'it looks like a wedding cake'.

Juliet's *Diary* is one of the most intimate books about 'Abdu'l-Bahá's interactions with one of His followers. With her artistic eye and writing style she left a mesmerizing memoir of her time with the Master.

## Hippolyte and Laura Dreyfus-Barney

Also staying at the hotel were Hippolyte and Laura Dreyfus-Barney.

Hippolyte Dreyfus learned about the Faith from May Maxwell about 1900. Coincidentally, he also met Laura Barney, his future wife, at May's apartment. Many of the first translations of the Writings into French were made by Hippolyte because his linguistic skills, which included Persian and Arabic, enabled him to translate the Kitáb-i-Aqdas into French from Arabic. Because of his background in law, Hippolyte was of great value to Shoghi Effendi after the ascension of 'Abdu'l-Bahá. He was instrumental in the early stages of attempting to regain possession of Bahá'u'lláh's house in Baghdad in the 1920s and he helped pave the way for the emancipation of Bahá'ís in Egypt in 1925.[5]

Laura Barney was an American, daughter of painter Alice Barney and sister of the notorious Natalie. Laura found the Faith in Paris. On her return to America, she was mocked in a Washington gossip magazine, but convinced her mother of the truth of the Faith. Though she was away from Paris between 1901 and 1906, Laura made several trips to see 'Abdu'l-Bahá in the Holy Land. In 1905, she travelled with Hippolyte Dreyfus and Madame Lachenay to Iran at the request of the Master, the first Western Bahá'ís to do so. They visited Tabriz, Maku and Ashqabad, where the first Bahá'í House of Worship had been built. During Laura's many visits to 'Abdu'l-Bahá, she compiled what became the book *Some Answered Questions*. She, like her future husband, became fluent in Persian

Laura and Hippolyte were married in 1911 and spent much of the rest of the year travelling with 'Abdu'l-Bahá in Europe. They also were with the Master in Washington, DC and in London and Paris in 1913.

* * *

On the morning of 24 August Juliet finally was reunited with the Master. His first words to her were: 'Are you happy, Juliet?' He greeted her with those same words the next morning. That short phrase became

'Abdu'l-Bahá's common greeting during His long journey throughout the West.

That evening at dinner, He asked Juliet if she had expected to be in Thonon with him. The following conversation about disunity ensued:

'No indeed I did not! May we all be in just such a gathering with You in New York!'

'I have made a pact with the American friends. If they keep the pact I will come.'

'The believers are much better friends than they were.'

'I shall have to *know* that! Bahá'u'lláh,' the Master continued, 'was bound with a chain no longer than the distance from here to that post.' With a sudden terrific agitation He rose and pointed to a column close to the table. 'He could scarcely move. Then He was exiled to Baghdad, to Adrianople, to Constantinople, to 'Akká – four times! He bore all these hardships that unity might be established among you. But if, among themselves, the believers cannot unite, how can they hope to unite the world? Christ said to His disciples: "Ye are the salt of the earth, but if the salt has lost its savour, wherewith shall it be salted?"' . . .

'If I had done my whole duty I might have accomplished more toward unity.'

'I hope you will become perfect. *Inshá'lláh*, through the help of Bahá'u'lláh, you will be perfect. When you return to America, Juliet, I want you to do your best to bring about unity.'

'I will do my utmost to carry out every suggestion you make to me, my Lord. I will work, not alone for the sake of the believers, but for the sake of others who would follow You if they could see You.'

'Had it not been for these divisions,' said our Lord, 'the Cause would have made great progress by now in America.'[6]

The next day, Hippolyte Dreyfus-Barney was on the terrace of the hotel while 'Abdu'l-Bahá paced back and forth a distance away. As he stood there, a man he recognized from Persia approached him. The man was Ẓillu's-Sulṭán, the grandson of Náṣiri'd-Dín Sháh, during whose reign the Báb had been executed and Bahá'u'lláh imprisoned and exiled. Ẓillu's-Sulṭán himself had been responsible for the deaths of 'The King of the Martyrs', Mírzá Muḥammad-Ḥasan; 'The Beloved of the Martyrs',

Mírzá Muḥammad-Ḥusayn; and many others. The prince greeted Hippolyte and asked: 'Who is that Persian nobleman?'

'That,' answered Hippolyte, 'is 'Abdu'l-Bahá.'
And now Ẓillu's-Sulṭán spoke very humbly.
'Take me to Him,' he begged.
Hippolyte told me all about it: 'If you could have seen the brute, Juliet, mumbling out his miserable excuses! But the Master took him in His arms and said: "All those things are in the past. Never think of them again." Then He invited Ẓillu's-Sulṭán's two sons to spend a day with Him.'
And so it was that Prince Bahrám came to lunch.
A beautiful boy – Prince Bahrám – like a Persian miniature. His skin is as smooth as ivory, his straight features finely chiselled, his eyebrows meet in a thin, black line across His nose. But being so young he is wholly unawakened spiritually, and he hasn't any manners at all! After lunch, assuming the privileges of a royal prince and Muhammadan, he stalked out of the room ahead of Laura and me – when the Master, in spite of our protests, had insisted on our preceding Him. However the Master said later: '*Bahrám Mírzá bad níst*,' (Prince Bahrám is not bad) so I can afford to be tolerant![7]

After Ẓillu's-Sulṭán left, Laura, Hippolyte, Juliet and the Master went for an automobile ride. They stopped at a small inn for tea where 'Abdu'l-Bahá was surrounded by about fifteen children selling bunches of violets. He, of course, bought all the flowers.
Leaving the children, 'Abdu'l-Bahá walked into the woods to see the Devil's Bridge, which Hippolyte had told him was especially beautiful. When they returned, so did the children, hoping for more money. Laura quickly shooed them away, but the Master called over one specific child saying 'But to this *little* one I have not given.'[8]
As they returned to Thonon, they passed a particularly beautiful waterfall. The Master walked to the edge of the precipice, gazing at the cascade, then He sat on a rock hanging over the deep abyss. Juliet remembers seeing 'that Figure of quiet Power perilously poised above the precipice, that still, rapt Face delighting in some secret way in the beauty of the waterfall.'[9]
'Abdu'l-Bahá thoroughly enjoyed the drive, animatedly pointing out

the bright green fields and hills, the villages and the mountains. At one point, He asked:

> 'If I come to America, Juliet, will you invite Me to see such waterfalls?'
>
> 'I will invite You to Niagara if You will come to America! But surely, my Lord, Your coming doesn't depend on my invitation.'
>
> 'My invitation to America will be the unity of the believers.'
>
> 'Louise Stapfer asked me to give You her love and beg *You* to come and unite us. Otherwise, she said, we will never be united.'
>
> 'No, you must do that yourselves. See in what perfect harmony we are now! You are not complaining of one another. But if I should go to America they would *all* be complaining of one another and . . . I would fly away!'
>
> Once, breaking a silence, He said: 'There was no one in the world who loved trees and water and the country so much as Bahá'u'lláh.'
>
> So sad was His voice that it was like a sigh and I seemed to feel what He was thinking. *He* was free at last to travel about the world and see all the beauties of nature, which He too loved, while the Blessed Beauty had lived for long years walled up in that treeless city, 'Akká, and died still a prisoner.[10]

The next day, 26 August, that disunity that kept 'Abdu'l-Bahá from going to America came to Thonon. Annie Boylan arrived and came into the Dreyfuses' room where Hippolyte, Laura, and Juliet were sitting. She was 'in a state of suppressed fury and almost immediately boiled over with the most revolting slander against Mr MacNutt. *This*, she said, she intended to lay before the Master to prove that Mr MacNutt was unfit to serve the Cause.' But hours passed before the Master finally arrived at the door. Juliet wrote that He looked very tired and worn. After warmly greeting Annie Boylan, He spoke before anyone else could:

> 'In this Cause, hundreds of families have sacrificed themselves. There have been more than twenty thousand martyrs. The breast of His Highness the Báb was riddled by dozens of bullets; Bahá'u'lláh suffered years and years in prison; and We have had all these difficulties and borne all these trials that the canopy of Oneness might be uplifted in the world of humanity, that Love and Unity might

be established amongst mankind, until all countries become as one country, all religions be merged into one religion, all the continents be connected and between all hearts a perfect understanding and love may appear.

'The people of Bahá must be the cause of uniting all the nations. They must dispel inharmony and dispute. So now we must consider deeply how the Bahá'ís must really be, what characteristics they must have and what actions they must perform.

'And if there is not this love and harmony among Bahá'ís how can they cause it to appear among the inhabitants of the earth? How can an ill man nurse others? . . . the first thing the Bahá'ís must do is to feel love and unity in their hearts before they can spread it among others.

'Is it possible to conceive that all the troubles, all the trials of Bahá'u'lláh and the martyrs have been without result? Surely you will not have it so! If you would all act entirely in accordance with the Teachings of Bahá'u'lláh no discord would ever appear. Then all disagreements will vanish, and be certain that the pavilion of Unity will be hoisted in the world of man . . .

'I know you would not have all these trials and difficulties produce nothing. Therefore I am waiting and expecting to hear that love and harmony have blossomed in the hearts of all the Bahá'ís in America.

'Now the Bahá'ís must be occupied in spreading the Cause of God and furthering the instructions of Bahá'u'lláh, and not spend their time in disputing with one another. If they do the first, all will be happy; they will be assisted by the Breath of the Holy Spirit and become the beloved of His Heart.'

While the Master was speaking [Annie Boylan] continued to bristle, jarring the whole room as she seethed with her bottled-up 'proof', which now of course she dare not 'lay before the Master'. She couldn't even mention Mr MacNutt! I saw her as an embodiment of the discord in New York, and those terrific vibrations, *blasting* into the Master's happy holiday (the first one in all His life), nearly killed me.[11]

Hippolyte told Juliet that they would go to Vevey, Switzerland on 4 September if 'Abdu'l-Bahá felt well enough. Early that morning, they were awakened by a buoyant 'Abdu'l-Bahá saying in English, 'I want to go!' Juliet then noted that the Master stood at the door of Tamaddunu'l-Mulk calling 'Mademoiselle!' Apparently the diminutive Persian had begun to wear corsets to improve his figure.[12]

The happy party, which included Laura and Hippolyte Dreyfus-Barney, Juliet Thompson and five Persians, drove to the ferry in a large stationwagon. While waiting for the boat, 'Abdu'l-Bahá wandered through a wood near the landing and then along the beach by some drying fishing nets. When they boarded the boat, Juliet noted that 'All the people on the landing stared at Him as He moved quietly forward with that strange power and that holy sweetness.'

Juliet described the boat ride to Vevey:

> To be with Him in a boat on this lake so like the Sea of Galilee! He sat with His bronze 'abá around Him, His hands hidden in its full sleeves . . . The mist-veiled Alps were His background and His Majesty so dominated them that they appeared as no more than a filmy drop-curtain. The mist thickened, almost blotting out the mountains, blending them into the lake, and I felt that we had left earth with Him and our boat was sailing through ether. Just as I was thinking this, He said: 'Others are passing from an immortal to a mortal kingdom, but the Bahá'ís are journeying in the Ark of the Covenant, from a mortal to an immortal world . . .'[13]

In Vevey, they visited Edith Sanderson, her mother and two of their friends, one of whom was an agnostic. When the ladies asked 'Abdu'l-Bahá about immortality, He gave a short talk on the spiritual world, summarizing by saying:

> The unborn child would deny the existence of this world for the reason that he knows nothing of it and the best condition to him is the world of the womb, the best food his nourishment there. He could not visualize this world. But when he is born and arrives at understanding, he sees what a beautiful world this is.
>
> So with the spiritual kingdom. The people of this world cannot comprehend the conditions of that immortal world, but, when they reach it, they see that this, in comparison, is just like the world of the womb. The unborn child says: 'This is the best world. I am quite satisfied with it. I must not leave it.'[14]

While 'Abdu'l-Bahá and His companions were crossing Lake Geneva, Lillian Kappes and Elizabeth Stewart arrived in Thonon from America on their way to assist Dr Susan Moody in building up the Tarbíyát school in Tehran. The women only spent two days with 'Abdu'l-Bahá; on the first evening 'he told several humorous stories, but the second all his talk was pointed to us and of the Kingdom . . . We went out with "I am sending you forth as Jacob sent Joseph of old" – and I could say nothing but "Ya-Baha'ul-Abha! Ya-Baha'ul-Abha!" he echoing it back and repeating while he held us fast at either hand going forward toward the doorway. And so we went forth.'[15]

Horace Holley and his wife, Bertha, were living in Italy when 'Abdu'l-Bahá arrived in Thonon; Hippolyte Dreyfus informed them of the Master's presence and they lost no time in seeking Him. They arrived on the afternoon of 29 August and Horace wrote:

> I saw among them a stately old man robed in a cream-coloured gown, his white hair and beard shining in the sun. He displayed a beauty of stature, an inevitable harmony of attitude and dress I had never seen nor thought of in men. Without having ever visualized the Master, I knew that this was He. My whole body underwent a shock. My heart leaped, my knees weakened, a thrill of acute, receptive feeling flowed from head to foot . . . From sheer happiness I wanted to cry – it seemed the most suitable form of self-expression at my command . . . My questions answered themselves. I yielded to a feeling of reverence which contained more than the solution of intellectual or moral problems. To look upon so wonderful a human being, to respond utterly to the charm of His presence – this brought me continual happiness. I had no fear that its effects would pass away and leave me unchanged. I was content to remain in the background . . . Patriarchal, majestic, strong, yet infinitely kind, he appeared like some just king that very moment descended from his throne to mingle with a devoted people . . . 'Abdu'l-Bahá restores man to his state a little lower than the angels.[16]

## Horace Holley

Horace Holley was born in Connecticut and heard about the Bahá'í Faith when, as a young man, he left America in 1909 for a summer holiday in Europe. On the crossing he met Bertha Herbert, who had introduced the Baháʾí Faith to Lady Blomfield two years earlier. Horace quickly became a Baháʾí and, with Bertha, a married man and didn't return to America until the outbreak of the First World War. The marriage didn't last but the Faith did. In 1919, he married Doris Pascal.

Horace was a poet and soon after his first meeting with ʿAbdu'l-Bahá also wrote a book about the Faith, *Bahaism: The Modern Social Religion*. As soon as it was published in London he sent a copy to the Master and received a Tablet from Him commending the book and saying: 'Thank thou God that thou art confirmed and assisted; thy aim is to render service to the Kingdom of Abhá, and thy object is the promotion of the teachings of Baháʾu'lláh.' This Horace continued to do for the rest of his life.

Back in the United States, he became widely known as editor, writer and translator, and was the impetus for the creation of the Baháʾí Publishing Committee. But his unique contribution was in the establishment of the Baháʾí Administrative Order. He was a member of the National Spiritual Assembly of the United States and Canada for 36 years and its secretary for 34 of those years. He was of assistance to Shoghi Effendi in the publication of the Guardian's works, and his own writings were highly esteemed by the Guardian, who wrote: 'I greatly value your presentation of the various aspects of the Cause, for whose expansion, consolidation and defence you have, for so many years, laboured so indefatigably and served with such distinction.' Horace was appointed a Hand of the Cause of God in 1951 and in 1959 was called to serve at the World Centre of the Faith, where he died a year later.[17]

\* \* \*

ʿAbdu'l-Bahá relied on Hippolyte Dreyfus-Barney to arrange his stays in France and his journeys to and from England. He called upon him not only to interpret into French an address He gave in Pasteur Wagner's noted church in Paris, but also to interpret into English the words he spoke to the congregations of some of the outstanding churches in London.[18]

At one point, before He departed Lake Geneva, ʿAbdu'l-Bahá looked out across the lake and said 'slowly and impressively: "There is much work to be done around the lake."'[19] In 1925, this work began with the establishment of the International Bahá'í Bureau in Geneva, an office designed to promote the affairs of the Faith in Europe. The Bureau was recognized by the League of Nations and Shoghi Effendi wrote that it was to act as an intermediary between Haifa and other Bahá'í centres.

When 'Abdu'l-Bahá left Thonon, he stayed overnight at the Hôtel de la Paix in Geneva before continuing on to London.

## LONDON, ENGLAND

Lady Blomfield, in hopes of having 'Abdu'l-Bahá stay in her London flat at 97 Cadogan Gardens, had written Him an invitation. And one day she received a telegram that read: "ABDU'L-BAHÁ ARRIVING IN LONDON 8TH SEPTEMBER. CAN LADY BLOMFIELD RECEIVE HIM?'[20] Of course she could, even when He arrived four days early, on 4 September.

### Lady Blomfield

Sara Louisa, Lady Blomfield was a prominent member of the Bahá'í community in the United Kingdom. Born near Limerick in Ireland, her mother was Catholic and her father was Protestant.[21] She first learned about the Bahá'í Faith from Bertha Herbert. Bertha directed her to Hippolyte Dreyfus and Ethel Rosenberg in Paris, who helped her see the greatness of Bahá'u'lláh, whose station she accepted in 1907. In England, she discovered Mary Virginia (Maryam) Thornburgh-Cropper, and with her and Ethel Rosenberg continued the work begun by Ethel, Maryam and her mother Harriet Thornburgh of raising up a Bahá'í community in England.

Lady Blomfield was a humanitarian, involved with the Save the Children Fund and the Declaration of Geneva for the salvation of the world's starving and refugee children. She compiled the talks that 'Abdu'l-Bahá gave while He was in Paris into the book *Paris Talks*, and participated in compiling those he gave in London in 1911 into the book *'Abdu'l-Bahá in London*. Her reminiscences of His two visits to London, as well as her conversations with the ladies of the Holy Family during her visits to 'Akká and Haifa, are recounted in her book *The Chosen Highway*. As World War I drew to its close she was instrumental in bringing the threats made against 'Abdu'l-Bahá to the attention of the authorities, and later facilitated the National Spiritual Assembly of the British Isles in acquiring corporate status with the League of Nations.

## Ethel Rosenberg

Ethel Rosenberg became a Bahá'í in about 1899 and went on her first pilgrimage in 1901. While with the Master, she carefully wrote down everything He said to help her teach the Faith on her return. Later that year, she travelled to the United States to help the Americans spread the Faith. Mírzá Abu'l-Faḍl was also in America at that time and Ethel Rosenberg learned much from him. She was able to visit 'Abdu'l-Bahá again in 1904. In 1907 while in Paris, she was introduced to Lady Blomfield. Upon returning to London she worked tirelessly with Lady Blomfield and Mrs Thornburgh-Cropper to raise up the English Bahá'í community. She visited 'Abdu'l-Bahá again in 1909.

When 'Abdu'l-Bahá arrived in London, Ethel Rosenberg became His social secretary, ensuring that all who wished to meet the Master were able to do so. She was also instrumental in helping people to understand His station.

Ethel Rosenberg followed 'Abdu'l-Bahá to Paris where He began establishing a precursor of the Bahá'í administrative order in the United Kingdom. He asked Ethel Rosenberg, Maryam Thornburgh-Cropper, Jane Whyte, Alice Buckton, Lady Blomfield, Wellesley Tudor-Pole and Gabrielle Enthoven to form a committee to decide what to do about collecting funds and publishing Bahá'í books. Their first published book was *'Abdu'l-Bahá in London.*

Ethel Rosenberg made her third pilgrimage in November 1921, but arrived just after 'Abdu'l-Bahá's passing. She stayed in Haifa long enough to meet Shoghi Effendi, who sent her home with instructions to call for the election of a spiritual assembly, a body that would within a year become the first National Spiritual Assembly of the British Isles and on which Ethel served.[22]

In 1926, she returned to Haifa at the request of Shoghi Effendi to serve as his secretary. When she left a year later, she carried back a gift to the British Bahá'í community from the young Guardian – a robe worn by Bahá'u'lláh. She passed away in 1930.[23] Shoghi Effendi named her as an Apostle of 'Abdu'l-Bahá.

\* \* \*

'Abdu'l-Bahá left Thonon-les-Bains and Geneva and arrived in London on 4 September 1911. Like many others, Lady Blomfield wrote a pen-portrait of the Master:

> He arrived! And who shall picture Him?
>
> A silence as of love and awe overcame us, as we looked at him; the gracious figure, clothed in a simple white garment, over which was a light coloured Persian *'abá*; on His head He wore a low-crowned *táj*, round which was folded a small, fine-linen turban of purest white; His hair and short beard were of that snowy whiteness which had once been black; his eyes were large, blue-grey with long, black lashes and well-marked eyebrows; His face was a beautiful oval with warm, ivory-coloured skin, a straight finely-modelled nose and firm, kind mouth . . .
>
> His figure was of such perfect symmetry, and so full of dignity and grace, that the first impression was that of considerable height. He seemed an incarnation of loving understanding, of compassion and power, of wisdom and authority, of strength and of a buoyant youthfulness, which somehow defied the burden of His years; and such years!
>
> One saw, as in a clear vision, that he had so wrought all good and mercy that the inner grace of Him had grown greater than all outer sign, and the radiance of this inner glory shone in every glance, and word, and movement as he came with hands outstretched.[24]

She also recorded his first words to them:

> 'I am very much pleased with you all. Your love has drawn me to London. I waited forty years in prison to bring the Message to you. Are you pleased to receive such a guest?'
>
> I think our souls must have answered, for I am not conscious that anyone uttered an audible word . . .
>
> Oh, these pilgrims, these guests, these visitors! Remembering those days, our ears are filled with the sound of their footsteps – as they came from every country in the world! Every day, all day long, a constant stream.[25]

Wellesley Tudor-Pole wrote that many of London's newspapers carried stories about His arrival and noted that most of the coverage was 'restrained and dignified in tone' and that there had been 'a welcome absence of sensationalism' in the descriptions of 'Abdu'l-Bahá or His life, though most were surprised that more than forty years of imprisonment had left so few visible marks. 'Abdu'l-Bahá allowed many reporters to interview Him, all of whom left 'greatly impressed by his noble dignity and spiritual simplicity'. He was commonly called the 'Persian Prophet', but a few more correctly reported Him as 'the Son of a Prophet' and accurately pointed questioners to the teachings and life of Bahá'u'lláh.

Tudor-Pole described a typical day for 'Abdu'l-Bahá:

> He rises about 5 a.m. and works for some hours at his correspondence. Interviews commence soon after 9 a.m. and last until midday. After lunch he takes a short rest and then usually drives out into the parks or to visit various people who are deeply interested in his work. Gatherings of the friends take place nearly every evening and he has given some wonderful discourses at such times . . . He is quite vigorous and looks both well and cheerful.[26]

Two days after His arrival, 'Abdu'l-Bahá began a series of meetings with believers and seekers in the homes of London Bahá'ís. Maryam Thornburgh-Cropper held her 'At Home' meetings on 6 and 12 September, with 45 to 60 people in attendance. Lady Blomfield hosted a small gathering on the 8th, and on the 22nd Marion Jack and Elizabeth Herrick organized a meeting with 'Abdu'l-Bahá for 80 people at 137A High Street, Kensington. In all of these gatherings, the Master asked if everyone was happy and spoke of unity among the friends.[27] At one meeting, Abdu'l-Bahá asked Emmeline Pankhurst, the suffragist:

> 'Give me your reasons for believing that woman today should have the vote?'
>
> Answer: 'I believe that humanity is a divine humanity and that it must rise higher and higher; but it cannot soar with only one wing.' 'Abdu'l-Bahá expressed His pleasure at the answer, and smiling, replied: 'But what will you do if one wing is stronger than the other?' Answer: 'Then we must strengthen the weaker wing . . .'

'Abdu'l-Bahá smiled and asked: 'What will you say if I prove to you that woman is the stronger wing?'

The answer came in the same bright vein, 'You will earn my eternal gratitude!'[28]

At another meeting with the friends, 'Abdu'l-Bahá said:

> To most men who have not heard the message of this teaching, religion seems an outward form, a pretence, merely a seal of respectability. Some priests are in holy office for no other reason than to gain their living. They themselves do not believe in the religion they pretend to teach. Would these men lay down their lives for their Faith? Ask a Christian of this kind to deny Christ in order to save his life, and he will do it . . .
>
> A Bahá'í denies no religion; he accepts the Truth in all, and would die to uphold it. He loves all men as his brothers, of whatever class, of whatever race or nationality, of whatever creed or colour, whether good or bad, rich or poor, beautiful or hideous. He commits no violence; if struck he does not return the blow . . . As a safeguard against intemperance he does not drink wine or spirits. Bahá'u'lláh has said it is not good for a sane man to take that which will destroy his health and sense.
>
> The religion of God has two aspects in this world. The spiritual (the real) and the formal (the outward). The formal side changes, as man changes from age to age. The spiritual side which is the Truth, never changes. The Prophets and Manifestations of God bring always the same teaching; at first men cling to the Truth but after a time they disfigure it. The Truth is distorted by man-made outward forms and material laws. The veil of substance and worldliness is drawn across the reality of Truth . . .
>
> The Truth is easy to understand although the outward forms in which it is expressed bewilder the intelligence. As men grow they see the futility of man-made forms and despise them. Therefore, many leave the churches, because the latter often emphasize the external only.[29]

Shortly after His arrival, 'Abdu'l-Bahá met the Reverend R. J. Campbell of the City Temple, together with the editor of *The Christian*

*Commonwealth* newspaper. The editor noted that when Rev. Campbell entered the room, 'Abdu'l-Bahá

> rose from his chair and advanced to meet him with smiling face and arms extended. The elder man grasped both the hands of the younger and, retaining them, warmly greeted him . . . Standing face to face, linked hand in hand, in the centre of the room, these two spiritual leaders of world-wide fame – Eastern and Western, but essentially one in their outlook on life – formed an impressive picture . . .'

During the conversation, Rev. Campbell said, 'I should like you to visit the City Temple,' to which 'Abdu'l-Bahá responded saying, 'I should like to come. I know that the City Temple is a centre of progress in the religious world, and seeks to promote a universal understanding.'[30]

Just a few days later, on Sunday, 10 September, 'Abdu'l-Bahá arrived at the City Temple during the evening service to give His first public address in the Western world. 'The visit was kept secret,' wrote Wellesley Tudor-Pole, 'but the congregation was as usual very large, probably well over 2,000.'[31] The entrance of the unannounced group of Persians caused excited speculation. *The Christian Commonwealth* described what happened next:

> The service proceeded as usual until the hymn immediately preceding the sermon. Whilst this was being sung a venerable figure, clad in Persian robes, was seen slowly ascending the stairs of the pulpit. When the hymn was finished Mr Campbell placed the distinguished visitor in his own chair and . . . said:
> 
> '. . . This evening we have in the pulpit of the City Temple the leader of one of the most remarkable religious movements of this or any age . . . The Bahai movement . . . rose on that soil [Persia] just as spontaneously as Christianity rose in the middle territories adjoining, and that faith – which, by the way, is very closely akin to, I think I might say identical with, the spiritual purpose of Christianity – that movement stands for the spiritual unity of mankind; it stands for universal peace among the nations . . . Abdul-Baha is on a visit to this country – a private visit – but he wished to see the City Temple; and I think I am right in saying for the first time in his life he has consented to lift up his voice in public . . . We, as followers

of the Lord Jesus Christ, who is to us and always will be the Light of the World, view with sympathy and respect every movement of the Spirit of God . . . and therefore we give greeting to 'Abdu'l-Bahá.'[32]

'Abdu'l-Bahá then spoke animatedly for about nine minutes, 'in Persian, in full vibrant tones', wrote Tudor-Pole, 'and the whole congregation was held spellbound . . . those of us who were privileged to attend can never forget the wonderful impression produced. It seemed to us as if a new page in history was being turned over and as if a new religious and spiritual epoch was being outwardly launched upon an expectant world before our very eyes.'[33]

After the Master had finished speaking, Wellesley Tudor-Pole read the English translation of His speech:

O Noble Friends; seekers after God! Praise be to God! Today the light of Truth is shining upon the world in its abundance; the breezes of the heavenly garden are blowing throughout all regions; the call of the Kingdom is heard in all lands, and the breath of the Holy Spirit is felt in all hearts that are faithful. The Spirit of God is giving eternal life. In this wonderful age the East is enlightened, the West is fragrant, and everywhere the soul inhales the holy perfume. The sea of the unity of mankind is lifting up its waves with joy, for there is real communication between the hearts and minds of men. The banner of the Holy Spirit is uplifted, and men see it, and are assured with the knowledge that this is a new day.

This is a new cycle of human power. All the horizons of the world are luminous, and the world will become indeed as a garden and a paradise. It is the hour of unity of the sons of men and of the drawing together of all races and all classes. You are loosed from ancient superstitions which have kept men ignorant, destroying the foundation of true humanity.

The gift of God to this enlightened age is the knowledge of the oneness of mankind and of the fundamental oneness of religion. War shall cease between nations, and by the will of God the Most Great Peace shall come; the world will be seen as a new world, and all men will live as brothers.

In the days of old an instinct for warfare was developed in the struggle with wild animals; this is no longer necessary; nay, rather, co-operation and mutual understanding are seen to produce the greatest welfare of mankind. Enmity is now the result of prejudice only.

In the *Hidden Words* Bahá'u'lláh says, 'Justice is to be loved above all.' Praise be to God, in this country the standard of justice has been raised; a great effort is being made to give all souls an equal and a true place. This is the desire of all noble natures; this is today the teaching for the East and for the West; therefore the East and the West will understand each other and reverence each other, and embrace like long-parted lovers who have found each other.

There is one God; mankind is one; the foundations of religion are one. Let us worship Him, and give praise for all His great Prophets and Messengers who have manifested His brightness and glory.

The blessing of the Eternal One be with you in all its richness, that each soul according to his measure may take freely of Him. Amen.[34]

After the service, 'Abdu'l-Bahá wrote the following in the pulpit Bible:

This book is the Holy Book of God, of celestial Inspiration. It is the Bible of Salvation, the Noble Gospel. It is the mystery of the Kingdom and its light. It is the Divine Bounty, the sign of the guidance of God. 'Abdu'l-Bahá 'Abbás[35]

Another among 'Abdu'l-Bahá's first visitors was Archdeacon Wilberforce, in what Lady Blomfield described as 'a remarkable interview':

Our dear friend, the Archdeacon, sat on a low chair by the Master. 'Abdu'l-Bahá spoke to him in His beautiful Persian. He placed His hand on the head of the Archdeacon, talked long to him, and answered many questions. Evidently His words penetrated further than the outer ears, for both were deeply moved.[36]

A week later, 'Abdu'l-Bahá addressed the congregation of St John the Divine, Westminster at the invitation of Archdeacon Wilberforce. 'Abdu'l-Bahá sat in the Bishop's chair on the chancel steps with the Archdeacon beside Him. The 20 September edition of *The Christian Commonwealth* reported that:

Eighteen months ago Archdeacon Wilberforce, who had been watching the Bahai movement for some time with interest, sent a message to Abdul Baha. 'We are all one,' he said, 'there, behind the veil.' And Abdul-Baha replied from his home in Akka, 'Tell him the veil is very thin, and it will vanish quite.'

All who were present in St John's, Westminster, last Sunday evening, could not fail to realise that the veil was vanishing. Archdeacon Wilberforce's beautiful intercessory service was a means to that end . . . Then Dr Wilberforce told of the teacher – 'Master' he called him – who had come to London to emphasise unity and who was present that evening at St John's to proclaim the meaning of it. 'Whatever our views,' the Archdeacon said, 'we shall, I am sure, unite in welcoming a man who has been for forty years a prisoner for the cause of brotherhood and love' . . . Full of expectation, the congregation waited when the Archdeacon for a brief moment left the church. Divested of his surplice, he returned with Abdul-Baha. all eyes were fixed on the leader of the Bahai movement. In his customary Eastern robe and headdress, walking hand in hand with a leader of the West, it did indeed seem that the veil was vanishing.[37]

Throughout His journey through the West, 'Abdu'l-Bahá steadfastly refused to accept money or expensive gifts from anyone, though He greatly enjoyed small gifts such as a box of bon-bons, fruit or flowers. In a scene re-enacted time after time on His travels, Lady Blomfield writes of one attempt to give money to 'Abdu'l-Bahá:

> One day in my presence a lady said to Him: 'I have here a cheque from a friend, who begs its acceptance to buy a good motor car for your work in England and Europe.'
>
> The Master replied: 'I accept with grateful thanks the gift of your friend.' He took the cheque into both His hands, as though blessing it, and said 'I return it to be used for gifts to the poor.'[38]

The Master was very conscious of people's feelings. Many times, visitors would find it very difficult to leave His presence so, when it was time for lunch or dinner, He would simply 'hold out His hand to the humblest or most diffident, lead them into the dining-room, seat him or her at His right hand and talk until all embarrassment had passed away, and the guest felt as though all uneasiness had been changed into the atmosphere of a calm and happy home... We grew to expect that there would be nineteen guests at table,' writes Lady Blomfield, 'so often did this number recur.'[39]

The demands on 'Abdu'l-Bahá's time were constant. The English Bahá'ís tried to organize the flow of those seeking interviews and instituted a system of official appointments. One day, a woman appeared at the door and asked if she could see 'Abdu'l-Bahá. When asked if she had an appointment, she admitted that she hadn't and was promptly told, 'I am sorry, but He is occupied now with most important people, and cannot be disturbed.' Sadly, the woman slowly turned away, but before she could reach the bottom of the steps, a messenger from 'Abdu'l-Bahá rushed out and breathlessly said, 'He wishes to see you, come back!' From the house came the powerful voice of the Master: 'A heart has been hurt. Hasten, hasten, bring her to me!'[40]

'Abdu'l-Bahá seemed to enjoy London. One afternoon Maryam Thornburgh-Cropper drove 'Abdu'l-Bahá through Richmond Park. At one point, 'Abdu'l-Bahá stopped for a few minutes and watched a plane pass by in the distance. During the ride, 'Abdu'l-Bahá spoke highly of English women and mentioned 'that a few days before he had seen a man and a woman racing on bicycles and that the woman had kept ahead of the man. His pleasure and amusement at this outcome was very evident.'[41]

## Bristol, England

On 23 September, 'Abdu'l-Bahá went to Bristol where He stayed at the Clifton Guest House, owned by Wellesley Tudor-Pole. Arriving at midday, the group climbed aboard carriages and toured the 'renowned beauty spots' around Bristol. That evening, the Master had dinner with nineteen of the friends and 'told us that this supper was a great and holy occasion and would be recorded in history. The meal itself, partaken of in love and harmony, was indeed a sacrament and a mark of unity and fellowship...'[42]

After dinner the Master addressed a gathering of 80 people in the salon of the Guest House. A reporter for Bristol's *Daily Chronicle* who attended introduced his article by saying 'East and West came together in a Clifton drawing-room on Saturday night, and once again a new religious message was unfolded – or, rather, not a message so much as a point of view.' The gathering, he noted inaccurately, was a 'drawing room gathering, for Bahaism seeks no proselytes, aiming at the deeper spiritualisation of the existing creeds in the interests of the common task of the regeneration and uplifting of the world.' When 'Abdu'l-Bahá entered the room, He gave them a 'hearty welcome' then spoke in 'a voice of singular sweetness'. The reporter obviously had his own particular understanding of what he heard. What 'Abdu'l-Bahá said, he wrote, was 'not altogether a new idea, it may be objected, but as viewed in the light of the thousand jangling creeds that go to make up our national theology, sufficiently so as to arrest the attention of thoughtful men . . .' When the meeting closed, the reporter was impressed that 'Abdu'l-Bahá prayed 'not folding his hands in the conventional manner, but holding them extended and slightly bent, with concaved palms, towards his breast, as though already gathering in the blessing for which he prayed.'[43]

The next day, He arose at His usual 5 a.m. to dictate letters before breakfasting with the friends. After another tour around the area, the Master gave private interviews before, again, dining with nineteen of the friends. He remarked on 'the pure Clifton air . . . after the smoke and noise of London'. The following day, 'Abdu'l-Bahá returned to London 'after expressing the intention of returning again some day'.[44]

## BYFLEET, SURREY

The only other place in England visited by the Master during his stay in 1911 was Byfleet, in Surrey, to an ancient farmhouse called Vanners, the residence of Alice Buckton. He visited it twice. On 9 September a number of working women from the Passmore Edwards' Settlement were staying for their holidays. They wrote:

> We gathered round him in a circle and he made us sit beside him in the window seat . . . 'Abdu'l-Bahá began by saying . . . 'Are you happy?' and our faces must have shown him that we were. He then said: 'I love you all, you are the children of the Kingdom, and you are accepted by God. Although you may be poor here, you are rich in the treasures of the Kingdom. I am the servant of the poor . . . If all the queens of the earth were gathered here, I could not be more glad!'

'Abdu'l-Bahá knew that we had a treasury box from which we try to help people less fortunate than ourselves. Presently he rose, and said: 'You are dear to me. I want to do something for you! I cannot cook for you (he had previously seen us busy in the kitchen) but here is something for your fund' . . .

Later on he walked in the village, and many poor children came to him, and mothers with sick babies and men out of work. He spoke to them all . . . At tea-time other friends joined us. 'Abdu'l-Bahá liked the cottage garden at Vanners, the little orchard and the roses . . .[45]

'Abdu'l-Bahá's second visit to Vanners took place on 28 September, and this time he stayed overnight. He was 'much struck during the drive by two detachments of Boy Scouts tramping down the road', and when told 'that an act of kindness each day is one of their laws and that some of these boys had put out a fire and assisted at a recent railway accident, he said, "This makes me very happy."' When they arrived they found 'a strangely mixed crowd, assembled at the gate to welcome him . . . as many as could do so pressed into the garden and sat down around him. The silence was most impressive.'

Speaking to the gathering about the 'elaborate civilization of the West', the Master said: 'Luxuries cut off the freedom of communication. One who is imprisoned by desires is always unhappy.' He also spoke about the need for God's messengers, about education, about work and art as forms of worship, about healing, death, and the best way to spread the Bahá'í teachings – to this He answered, 'By deeds. This way is open to all . . .'[46]

He spoke particularly about the poor and the great economic disparities in England: 'I find England awake; there is spiritual life here. But your poor are so *very* poor! This should not be. On the one hand you have wealth, and great luxury; on the other hand men and women are living in the extremities of hunger and want. This great contrast of life is one of the blots of the civilization of this enlightened age.'

There was ample opportunity for 'Abdu'l-Bahá to observe this, both in London and in this Surrey village:

> Those who have been with 'Abdu'l-Bahá notice how, often after speaking earnestly with people, he will suddenly turn and walk away to be alone. At such time no one follows him. On this occasion,

when he finished speaking and went out through the orchard gate into the village, all were struck by his free and wonderful walk . . .

As he passed along the ragged children clustered about him by dozens, the boys saluting him as they had been taught in school, showing how instinctively they felt the greatness of his presence. Most noticeable was the silence of even the roughest men when 'Abdu'l-Bahá appeared. One poor tramp exclaimed, 'He is a good man,' and added, 'Ay, he's suffered!'

He took particular interest in the sick, crippled and poorly nourished children. Mothers carrying their little ones followed him . . .

All day long people of every condition gathered about the gate for a chance of seeing him . . . He will long be remembered as he sat in the bow window in the afternoon sunshine, his arm round a very ragged but very happy little boy . . .

. . . When asked if he did not find the manners of the English rude and awkward, compared with those of the East, 'Abdu'l-Bahá said he had not felt this. As a nation increases in spirituality, the manners become different.[47]

On the morning of the second day, 'Abdu'l-Bahá visited the nearby aviation field at Brooklands.

Though it was windy, an aviator was on the track, when he heard who the visitor was offered to fly for him. 'Abdu'l-Bahá left his friends and walked out into the middle of the course, where he stood alone watching the biplane making wide circles above him.

A Hindu who was learning to fly at the school . . . asked: 'Who is the man in Eastern dress?'

When told, he exclaimed, 'Oh I know him very well through his teachings, which I have studied,' and immediately he went to meet 'Abdu'l-Bahá.

They talked together for some time in Arabic, the young man showing great joy at being in his presence. He afterwards said that for many years he had longed for this moment.

While having tea outdoors . . . 'Abdu'l-Bahá noticed two of the airmen who were wrestling . . . and when they stopped, he went to them clapping his hands and crying in English, 'Bravo! Bravo! that is good exercise.'[48]

## LONDON, ENGLAND

On 1 October, shortly before 'Abdu'l-Bahá departed from London, Regina Núr Mahal <u>Kh</u>ánum and Mírzá Yu'hanna Dávúd came before Him. Regina had come from Baghdad, where her family were followers of Bahá'u'lláh, to marry Mírzá Yu'hanna Dávúd in what was probably the first Bahá'í wedding in the British Isles. 'Abdu'l-Bahá told them, 'Never have I united anyone in marriage before, except my own daughters, but as I love you much, and you have rendered great service to the Kingdom of Abhá . . . I will perform your marriage ceremony today.'[49]

The following day was 'Abdu'l-Bahá's last in London. First, He breakfasted with the Lord Mayor of London at the Mansion House. 'The Lord Mayor said to him that he considered London to be greatly honoured by having such a guest,' wrote Arthur Cuthbert.[50] During the interview 'many subjects were discussed; the freedom and happiness of the people; the efforts made to improve social conditions; prisons and prisoners.' The Master was pleased to hear this, and said: 'It is well with a country when the magistrates are as fathers to the people.'[51]

That afternoon, a reporter asked 'Abdu'l-Bahá about His future plans. To his amazement, 'Abdu'l-Bahá answered him in perfect English, saying that He was going to Paris and then on to Alexandria. When the reporter expressed surprise at His perfect pronunciation, 'Abdu'l-Bahá rose and marched up and down the drawing room, and to the amusement of all those present, began uttering a string of long English words such as 'hippopotamus', laughingly ending by saying 'Very difficult English words I speak.'[52]

'Abdu'l-Bahá's last public meeting in London was at the Passmore Edward's Settlement in Tavistock Place, before 200 people invited by Mrs Thornburgh-Cropper. 'A beautiful spirit prevailed . . . The atmosphere was very different from that of an ordinary meeting or religious gathering.' Professor Michael Sadler officially said goodbye to the Master: 'We have met together to bid farewell to Abdul Baha, and to thank God for his example and teaching, and for the power of his prayers to bring Light into confused thought, Hope into the place of dread, Faith where doubt was, and into troubled hearts the Love which overmasters self-seeking and fear.' 'Abdu'l-Bahá then said:

> O noble friends and seekers for the kingdom of God! . . . Praise be

to God! the signs of friendship are appearing, and a proof of this is that today I – an Easterner – in the London of the West have received extreme kindness, regard, and love, and I am deeply thankful and happy. I shall never forget this time I have spent with you. I leave you with extreme regret, and with prayers for you, that all the beauty of the Kingdom may be yours.[53]

'Abdu'l-Bahá left for Paris on 3 October 1911.

## Paris, France

'Abdu'l-Bahá had rented an apartment at No. 4 Avenue de Camoëns, near the Trocadero and the Eiffel Tower. He had a 'little fair-haired, pleasant-faced French maid [who] presided over its domestic functions and answered the bell'. Mary Hanford Ford remembers Him saying:

> 'This is my home and the home of my friends' . . . and every one was admitted here without question, no matter to what cult or nationality he belonged, no matter how shabby were his clothes. A background of Persian men was always present, for all the Persians in Paris apparently camped in the home of Abdul-Baha during His stay there, but besides the Persians there were French, Germans, English, Hindus, and a large sprinkling of Americans, among whom the tall figures of Mr [Percy] Woodcock and Mr [Mountfort] Mills were always noticeable . . .
> 
> 'Abdul-Bahá speaks only the Oriental tongues, but he understands all that is said in any language, and in Paris his wonderful words were translated by M. Dreyfus into especially perfect French. The little company assembled at No 4 Avenue de Camoens never knew exactly at what time the eagerly expected one would appear. Sometimes he came joyfully, waving a good morning to all, or best of all, greeting each one with a warm hand clasp. At other times, when there had been bad news . . . he would enter with sadness written upon his eloquent countenance.[54]

A flight of steps led from the Avenue de Camoëns into the Trocadero gardens. Lady Blomfield wrote pen-pictures of the Master as he took his daily walk:

Who is this, with branch of roses in hand, coming down the steps? A picturesque group . . . following him, little children coming up to him. They hold on to his cloak, confiding and fearless. He gives the roses to them, caressingly lifting one after another into his arms, smiling the while that glorious smile which wins all hearts.

Again, we saw a cabman stop his fiacre, take off his cap and hold it in his hands, gazing amazed, with an air of reverence, whilst the majestic figure, courteously acknowledging his salutation, passed by with that walk which a friend had described as 'that of a king or a shepherd'.[55]

Lady Blomfield tried to describe 'Abdu'l-Bahá as He spoke. It was, as she noted, an impossible task:

The words of 'Abdu'l-Bahá can be put on to paper, but how to describe the smile, the earnest pleading, the loving kindness, the radiant vitality, and at times the awe-inspiring authority of His spoken words? The vibrations of His voice seemed to penetrate to the very core of being. We were experiencing the transforming radiance of the Sun of Truth; henceforth, material aims and unworthy ambitions shrank away into their trivial, obscure retreats.[56]

Interviews with 'Abdu'l-Bahá could last anywhere from three minutes to an half hour and many requested the privilege. But the length of the interview didn't seem to make much difference in the reactions of those who received the bounty. Mary Hanford Ford had a friend who was a cashier at a large store. The woman was a pure spirit and she spent only three minutes with 'Abdu'l-Bahá. When she entered, 'Abdu'l-Bahá met her with outstretched arms and proclaimed, 'Ah, you are aflame! You are alive! How happy I am when people come to me who are alive not dead!' He took her hands and simply assured her that God would guide her. When she left His room, her face glowed with her happiness.[57]

But one day the Master spoke with infinite sadness following the tragedy of the battle at Benghazi:

I am not happy this morning. I am full of sadness. The news which the paper brought us was such as must fill one with anguish. Animals fight, and when they fight, it is for a cause, an end to be gained.

Men are fighting now, for what? For the ground, our sepulchre, our tomb, our cemetery!

The earth is the first and lowest of terrestrial things created by the Divine Will – and it is our tomb, our sepulchre, our cemetery; our death, not our life – and these men are fighting not for liberty or an ideal, but for ground, for the place of death not life, for a sepulchre, a tomb, a cemetery! . . .

You are a people banded together to increase friendship among nations and races and brotherhood among men. So now, while these men are creating death, you think life, while they are guilty of cruelty, you think tenderness, while they make destruction, you think construction, while they create war, you think peace.[58]

On 15 October, 'Abdu'l-Bahá met a prominent Iranian, Mírzá Muḥammad Khán-i-Qazvíní, a noted scholar of Persian literature, history and culture and a close friend of Edward Granville Browne, the Orientalist. Mírzá Muḥammad had written an introduction to and edited the *Nuqtatu'l-Káf*, a book purporting to be an early history of the Bábí Faith but which was nothing of the kind. Unfortunately, the book had been lent legitimacy in the West through its publication the year before in the prestigious E. J. W. Gibb Memorial Series, in Browne's translation, and 'Abdu'l-Bahá had Mírzá Abu'l-Faḍl write a rebuttal.[59] Mírzá Muḥammad was in Paris when 'Abdu'l-Bahá arrived, and requested to see Him. Forty years later, he wrote about the meeting:

> I entered the room and my eyes fell upon 'Abdu'l-Bahá whom I immediately recognized as I had seen Him picture [sic] many times in various journals, newspapers and certain books . . . He wore a small head-dress which simply was a white piece of cloth wrapped around a small white Fez, and a large brownish labbadih with wide sleeves. His beard and eye brows were white as cotton, and He possessed brilliant, sharp eyes with strong features which from the profile resembled that of Tolstoy. He was sitting on a velvet-covered chair at the head of the room . . . and all around the room . . . were sitting in absolute silence and motionless men and women from Iran, Egypt, America, England, France, etc. . . .
> 
> Quietly, I entered the room, offered my greetings and wanted to sit by the entrance when 'Abbas Effendi raised from His seat, warmly

greeted me, bidding me to move up by saying 'Higher please, higher please.' I went a bit further in the room and was about to sit when again He said: 'Higher please. Come sit here.' And pointed to a chair on His own right hand side, and since I did not wish Him to remain standing, quickly took my seat next to Him on the chair that He had appointed. For the next two or three minutes He continued to greet me and inquired of my well-being . . . He further added: 'I have asked of you and was told that you are not in Paris.' I was a bit bewildered as to how it was that He knew me which had prompted Him to inquire of me. The thought then came to my mind that perhaps this is a ploy to add me to the rank of His well-wishers . . .

'Abdu'l-Bahá quickly turned to [Dreyfus] and it was evident that He was engaged in presenting a talk . . . after concluding His talk, He took my hand and led me to the smaller room situated next to this larger one and we conversed on a variety of topics not related to religion . . . After discussing various matters, He kept me for lunch which among other things included a very delicious broth that contained excellent garbanzo beans – a very rare item in Paris.

On several more occasions, either in His residence or in the house of Dreyfus and his wife, Mrs Barney-Dreyfus, I had lunch or dinner with 'Abbas Effendi until I left Paris.[60]

Later that day, 'Abdu'l-Bahá went into a very poor quarter of Paris to visit Mr and Mrs Ponsonaille. The Ponsonailles were very poor, but when they accepted Bahá'u'lláh, they felt that their work should be among the orphans of the city. Initially, they stopped eating their midday meal in order to give it to the children, and met in an old car until the local clergy tried to take over their work. When the clergy were unsuccessful, they managed to have the car removed. The Parisian Bahá'ís provided Mr Ponsonaille with materials and he built a small cabin with his own hands, in which to continue his work with the orphan children.

'Abdu'l-Bahá arrived with Alice R. Beede, Hippolyte Dreyfus-Barney and Tamaddunu'l-Mulk. Alice Beede wrote:

> I had never seen such a dirty miserable quarter . . . we walked down to the end of a narrow lane or street without sidewalks, on which doors opened to places where soldiers and women were drinking and screaming, while from the small windows bedclothes were hanging

out . . . to the small gate through which we passed and by the discarded car into a small board cabin about 20x25 feet. At one end was a raised platform and desk of rough boards. I can only say as my eyes fell first upon The Greatest Name hanging in a frame from this desk and I saw the crowd of miserably poor, dear little ones gathered there, and as my ears caught the music of their voices (for they were singing), tears filled my eyes and a great lump choked me . . .

Alice Beede described Madame Ponsonaille as 'a woman with a strong, kind and most intelligent face', and her husband as having 'a delicate, most refined face – that of a gentleman in its fullest sense'. After the song Monsieur Ponsonaille read a Tablet sent by the Master. With Mr Dreyfus-Barney translating, the Master said:

I am very glad to be here with you. I am very glad to see you all here. I love you very much. I have been in many beautiful houses, but this is more beautiful to me than any of the others, for the spirit of the love of Baha'o'llah is here. You are all receiving the teachings of God and learning how to act and live and some day you will be great and wise for having learned the truth. I have seen many beautiful rich children, but to me you are more beautiful.

'Abdu'l-Bahá greatly praised the Ponsonailles for their efforts, saying 'This is a great work you are doing for the love of God in this great day, through the power of Baha'o'llah. Your station is great. Your names will go through all ages. Kings and Queens have never been talked of and remembered as you will be. You are workers in the Kingdom of Abha and I am very happy and love you very much.'

He then chanted a prayer and a blessing and, 'coming to where the children were, all crowded close around him, and laying his hands caressingly upon some of their heads and taking the hands of others with a loving smile to all, with difficulty he passed down the aisle to the door.'

Alice Beede wrote that she had to quiet a few of the rough boys before the Master arrived, but after He came, 'they never moved nor spoke and when he passed out they fell over each other in their great desire to have him take their hands'. When 'Abdu'l-Bahá and His companions left, people watched out of every window and doorway.[61]

Another prominent Iranian, Siyyid Ḥasan-i-Taqizadeh, former

Ambassador from Iran to Britain, also came to visit 'Abdu'l-Bahá. The Master spoke with him for a time, then went to address a meeting. Like Mírzá Muḥammad Khán-i-Qazvíní, this man had 'exerted important efforts against the Faith of Bahá'u'lláh . . . the Centre of the Covenant [now] received them with his customary love, affection, and sin-covering eye – never mentioning the past deeds of these individuals – and immersing them in the ocean of His compassion.'[62]

A few days later, 'Abdu'l-Bahá invited the Siyyid to dinner:

> The night that I went to 'Abdu'l-Bahá's house for dinner was rainy and when I left my residence at about 8 p.m. it was difficult to locate transportation, and as such I was a little tardy to arrive . . . and found 'Abdu'l-Bahá and His companions waiting for me. In that gathering, in addition to Mírzá Asadu'lláh Khan, Tamaddunu'l-Mulk was present as well, but the thing that caused my astonishment was that there was no news of dinner! For a while we continued conversing. I had imagined that dinner would be served at eight o'clock (according to the European customs). I was hungry and perplexed. I waited longer, but still no news of dinner. I thought I had come late and they have already had dinner. For a while, 'Abdu'l-Bahá, 'Azízu'lláh Khan and I continued with our conversation, and occasionally because of my hunger and not wishing to overstay my welcome, I wanted to leave, but being reserved I did not say anything. Eventually after a while, perhaps closer to eleven o'clock, one by one the honoured companions begin to arrive, and it was nearly mid-night when they informed us that dinner is served. An extensive table filled with delicious food was spread, including a rice dish that is mixed with Ghaymih stew.[63]

At some point, Siyyid Ḥasan was alone with 'Abdu'l-Bahá when the telephone rang and:

> the French maid came in and informed Him (in French) that He had a telephone call. He asked me: 'What is she saying?' I translated. He said: 'Find 'Azízu'lláh Khán and tell him to take the call.' I translated that too. The maid said that he is not here. He then said: 'Tamaddun should take the call.' The maid responded that he is not there either. Finally, 'Abdu'l-Bahá had to take the call Himself, and went by the phone, which apparently was from an American Baha'i

woman who spoke Persian. When He returned back He said to me: 'That was the first time in My life that I spoke on telephone.'[64]

On 25 October, 'Abdu'l-Bahá was in the home of Laura and Hippolyte Dreyfus-Barney. He told them:

> Last night, when I returned home, I did not sleep. I lay awake thinking and I said to myself: 'Here am I in Paris. O my God! what is Paris and who am I?' I never thought from the darkness of my prison I should come here and be among you, for I was condemned to perpetual imprisonment. When I read the document which told me of my sentence, I said to the officials: 'It is impossible!' And they were astonished. Then I said to them: 'If Abdul-Hamid were immortal and I myself were immortal, then would it be possible for him to condemn me to be in prison forever, but as we are not immortal, then it is impossible. My spirit is free and that can no man imprison.'[65]

A few days later, on 29 October, a dinner followed by a meeting took place at the home of Madame Gabriel Sacy. 'It was distinctly a French reunion', wrote Madame d'Ange d'Astre, 'and Abdul-Baha seemed pleased of the fact.'[66] Although the first Bahá'í community in Europe had been established in Paris, not many French people had yet become Bahá'ís.

'Abdu'l-Bahá gave His first public talk in Paris as a guest of the Alliance Spiritualiste on 9 November. The group's primary focus was the encouragement and development of spirituality, so it was an ideal place for the Master to speak. He started by explaining the Bahá'í Revelation, using language 'coloured and imaginative and touchingly human. He spoke at length and with impressive clearness and repeated several times His contentment at finding Himself in the midst of so large a gathering, whose unity of sentiment and spirituality were forcibly apparent.'[67]

One Sunday morning, 'Abdu'l-Bahá walked into a poor quarter in Paris where groups of men and women tended to be rowdy. One man in particular, a big man with a long loaf of bread, stood in the crowd waving it, shouting and dancing. When 'Abdu'l-Bahá returned from visiting a mission hall, 'The boisterous man with the loaf, suddenly seeing Him, stood still. He then proceeded to lay about him lustily with his staff of life, crying, "Make way, make way! He is my Father, make way!" the Master passed through the midst of the crowd, now become silent and respectfully saluting Him. "Thank you, my dear friends, thank you," He said, smiling round upon them.'[68]

At one point, the Japanese Ambassador to Spain, Viscount Arawaka, was in Paris. His wife had heard about 'Abdu'l-Bahá and greatly wanted to meet Him, but since she had a severe cold, was not able to go out. When 'Abdu'l-Bahá heard of her desire, He immediately went to see her at her hotel. The Master talked to both the Ambassador and his wife about many topics, one of which was the necessity of science and religion to be as the two wings of a bird. He told the Japanese Ambassador:

> There is in existence a stupendous force, as yet, happily, undiscovered by man. Let us supplicate God, the Beloved, that this force be not discovered by science until spiritual civilization shall dominate the human mind. In the hands of men of lower material nature, this power would be able to destroy the whole earth.[69]

This was 34 years before the atomic bombs were dropped on Japan in the Second World War.

Two days before 'Abdu'l-Bahá left Paris, a woman came anxiously into a gathering at the Avenue de Camöens. Breathlessly, the woman said:

> Oh, how glad I am to be in time! I must tell you the amazing reason of my hurried journey from America. One day, my little girl astonished me by saying: 'Mummy, if dear Lord Jesus was in the world now, what would you do?' 'Darling baby, I would feel like getting on to the first train and going to Him as fast as I could.' 'Well, Mummy, He *is* in the world.' I felt a sudden great awe come over me as my tiny one spoke. 'What do you mean, my precious? How do you know,' I said. 'He told me Himself, so of course He *is* in the world.' Full of wonder, I thought: Is this a sacred message which is being given to me out of the mouth of my babe? And I prayed that it might be made clear to me.
>
> The next day she said, insistently and as though she could not understand: 'Mummy darlin', why isn't you gone to see Lord Jesus? He's told me two times that He is really here, in the world.' 'Tiny love, Mummy doesn't know where He is, how could she find Him?'

'We see, Mummy, we see.'

I was naturally perturbed. The same afternoon, being out for a walk with my child, she suddenly stood still and cried out, 'There He is! There He is!' She was trembling with excitement and pointed at the window of a magazine store where there was a picture of 'Abdu'l-Bahá. I bought the paper, found this address, caught a boat the same night, and here I am.[70]

On 1 December, 'Abdu'l-Bahá said goodbye to Europe:

I bid a loving farewell to the people of France and England. I am very much pleased with them. I counsel them that they may day by day strengthen the bond of love and amity to this end – that they may become the sympathetic embodiment of one nation – that they may extend themselves to a universal Brotherhood to guard and protect the interests of all the nations of the East – that they may unfurl the Divine Banner of justice – that they may realize and treat each nation as a family composed of the individual children of God and may know that before the sight of God the rights of all are equal . . .

Beware! Beware! Lest ye offend any heart.
Beware! Beware! Lest ye hurt any soul.
Beware! Beware! Lest ye deal unkindly toward any person.
Beware! Beware! Lest ye be the cause of hopelessness to any creature.[71]

The next day He left Paris for Marseilles and Alexandria.

# 5

# EGYPT AND AN ATLANTIC CROSSING
## *December 1911–March 1912*

### ALEXANDRIA

'Abdu'l-Bahá spent the next few months back in Alexandria. When Juliet Thompson left Him at Thonon, He had charged her with uniting the American Bahá'í community, to fulfil their part of His pact so that He could visit America. She and others succeeded, because on 25 March 1912, He boarded the steamship *Cedric* and began His journey.

Ali Yazdi remembered the Master's departure from Alexandria:

> Again 'Abdu'l-Bahá left us, this time for America. I will never forget the scene of His departure, as He came out of the house and turned to wave His last farewell to His disconsolate family looking down from the veranda above. They were greatly concerned about His safety and well-being. He was sixty-eight years old. He had suffered many hardships and gone through severe trials. He had been in prison for forty years of His life. And now He was undertaking this journey to a far-off country utterly different from any to which He was accustomed.
>
> But 'Abdu'l-Bahá had made up His mind. And when He made up His mind, nothing could change Him. He strode out of the garden gate without looking back. He walked for several blocks near the shore to take the electric train to Alexandria, where He would board the ship that was to take Him to New York. He was followed by about thirty believers who walked silently behind Him. I was one of them.[1] For this journey, the Master brought along His fifteen-year-old grandson, Shoghi Effendi. 'Abdu'l-Bahá had purchased Shoghi Effendi 'long robes, and two turbans, one green and one white like His own, for Shoghi Effendi to wear in the West; when

these were delivered and Shoghi Effendi dressed himself in them to show 'Abdu'l-Bahá, he said the Master's eyes shone with pride and pleasure.'² Ali Yazdi wrote that his good friend 'was in seventh heaven. He had heard so much about America, and he longed to be with the Master as he traveled throughout North America and gave the Message. He looked forward with great anticipation to the experience.'

The day before 'Abdu'l-Bahá departed for America, Shoghi Effendi asked Ali, 'Do you want to go to the ship with me and see my cabin?' The two boys, with some other Bahá'ís, took the electric tram to Alexandria and then to the harbour.

> Before us was the Cedric, a White Star Liner. It was a beautiful ship, one of two that plied regularly between Alexandria and New York, and stopped only at Naples. Shoghi Effendi and I went on the boat, and he took me upstairs and showed me his stateroom, the dining room, and everything on the ship. He was extremely happy, and so was I very happy for him. I made him promise to write to me when he got to America, and he said he would.³

After sailing on 27 March, 'Abdu'l-Bahá gave a talk after dinner to an audience of over 500 passengers and crew, describing the potential of the human race and the high station and virtues of the human kingdom.

But when the ship reached Naples, there was a serious problem which sprang from the actions of Dr Amin Fareed, the nephew of 'Abdu'l-Bahá's wife. Ostensibly one of the Master's secretaries on the journey and a long-time teacher of the Faith in America who had travelled extensively with Lua Getsinger, Fareed was beginning a career that would lead him to become a Covenant-breaker.

When the Italian health inspectors examined the members of 'Abdu'l-Bahá's group, they declared that the eyes of three of the party, a secretary, a cook and Shoghi Effendi, were diseased with trachoma and that those three could not continue. They were ordered to return. 'Abdu'l-Bahá spent a full day trying to change the decision, but He was finally forced to sail for America without Shoghi Effendi. 'Abdu'l-Bahá always believed that Fareed was the root of the problem, having suggested to the Italian authorities that the party were Turks, with whom the Italians were at war. In her book *The Priceless Pearl*, Rúḥíyyih Khánum writes that Shoghi Effendi said that Fareed had insisted to 'Abdu'l-Bahá that Shoghi Effendi be sent home, inventing many arguments in support of the Italian doctors. She writes, 'One can well imagine what heart-break this brought to a boy of fifteen, setting out on the first great adventure of his life, how much more to Shoghi Effendi, so attached to his grandfather, so excited over the trip on a big boat, the great journey to the West in a day when such long voyages were relatively rare and eventful!'[4]

Ali Yazdi remembered that Shoghi Effendi was heartbroken. When Shoghi Effendi returned to Ramleh, doctors there confirmed that he did not suffer from trachoma. Ali said that Shoghi Effendi grew despondent and lost weight, taking a long time before he regained his normal happy outlook on life.[5]

And so, on the afternoon of 30 March 'Abdu'l-Bahá sailed away from Naples on board the White Star liner *S.S. Cedric*, leaving Shoghi Effendi disconsolate on the shore. Travelling with the Master were Siyyid Asadu'lláh-i-Qumí, Dr Fareed, Mírzá Mahmúd-i-Zarqání (the author of *Mahmúd's Diary*), and Mírzá Munír-i-Zayn.

A number of people had suggested that 'Abdu'l-Bahá sail to England and cross the Atlantic to America aboard the brand new ship *Titanic* instead of the much older, slower *Cedric*. Later in America, when He was asked why He didn't, 'Abdu'l-Bahá said, after a long pause during which He looked reflectively out of the window, 'I was asked to sail upon the *Titanic*, but my heart did not prompt me to do so.'[6] When asked the same question at a later date, He responded with, 'God sends a feeling of misgiving into man's heart.'[7]

On board the *Cedric* as it departed from Naples were, in addition to the Master's party, Percy Woodcock and his wife and daughter from Canada, Mr and Mrs Austin from Denver, Colorado and Louisa Mathew from London. The next morning, 'Abdu'l-Bahá visited the others in their cabins, then asked them to attend the ship's prayer service. Afterwards, He mentioned that Phoebe Hearst had sent £500 to repair the road up to the Shrine of the Báb. In recompense, the Master had sent her a valuable ring. This brought up the subject of the Covenant-breakers, who thought that Mrs Hearst was supporting the Faith, even though the ring she had received was worth much more than her donation. Later, He again brought up the activities of the Covenant-breakers and how they had convinced Edward G. Browne to publish a history of the Faith (the *Nuqtatu'l-Kaf*) which they had altered to their own benefit.⁸

Over the next several days, 'Abdu'l-Bahá spoke with many people on a variety of topics, including religious prejudice, the Hands of the Cause of God and transportation. Of ships, trains and carriages, He said that they were 'good for long and tedious journeys; but for recreation and holiday trips, horseback riding in the spring season in the country, which is full of flowers and green foliage and sparkling waters, is the best of all, and gives a unique pleasure'.⁹ When His companions brought up the subject of dirigibles and planes, He said: 'Those who have provided the means for transporting arms and ammunition and the instruments of wars and massacres on earth will do so in the air. There will come to exist such instruments as to cause all the means of destruction in the past to be looked upon as children's playthings.' He also explained the relationship between the soul and the spirit. 'The soul', He said, 'is a link between the body and the spirit. It receives bounties and virtues from the spirit and gives them to the body just as the outward senses carry to the inward senses what they receive from the outer world . . .'¹⁰

On 3 April the ship passed the famous Gibraltar. 'Abdu'l-Bahá examined it through field glasses and noted all the tremendous victories gained by the early, sincere Muslims, saying, 'What a magnificent honor God bestowed on the Muslims in the beginning, and what a disgrace they accepted for themselves in the end.' Evidently, some of the Americans were bothered that the Persians wore their normal clothing and requested that they change into 'attire to suit the circumstances of the time and place'. 'Abdu'l-Bahá responded by asking them 'What harm is there in it? I do not care much about what is unimportant and what is not harmful to the Cause. They are trifles.'¹¹

'Abdu'l-Bahá enjoyed the good weather on 5 April, walking about the deck and looking at a group of islands, probably the Azores, through the field glasses. Later in the salon he told a group, including a newspaper publisher, why He was going to America:

> I am going to America at the invitation of peace congresses, as the fundamental principles of this Cause are universal peace, the oneness of the world of humanity and the equality of the rights of men. As this is the age of lights and the century of mysteries, this

lofty purpose is sure to be universally acknowledged and this Most Mighty Cause is certain to embrace the East and the West.[12]

On Easter Saturday, the evening of 6 April, as the *Cedric* slowly crossed the Atlantic some clergymen announced a meeting to observe the commemoration of the crucifixion of Christ. The Master remarked:

> 'Their speeches . . . will be to the effect that Christ sacrificed Himself in order to redeem us from our sins. But they do not understand the inner meaning.' After the meeting, He spoke extensively on the subject. 'The redemption of sins', He said, 'depends on our acting upon the admonitions of Christ, and the martyrdom of Christ was to cause us to attain praiseworthy morals and supreme station.'[13]

Wireless telegrams began arriving from the Americans on the ship for 'Abdu'l-Bahá on 8 April expressing their joy at His imminent arrival. At 9 p.m. on 9 April, the lights of New York appeared in the distance.[14]

6

# GREETING THE STATUE OF LIBERTY
## 10–20 April 1912

### NEW YORK, NEW YORK

The *Cedric* arrived in New York on the night of Wednesday, 10 April 1912, but the passengers were not allowed to leave the ship until later the next morning because one person was ill with smallpox and several people were sick with typhoid. The sick people had to be taken to Hoffman Island and be quarantined, after which the ship had to be fumigated.[1] The next day, 11 April, when reporters were finally able to board the ship, they found 'Abdu'l-Bahá on the upper deck. Wendell Phillips Dodge, a New York Bahá'í and a journalist, wrote a pen portrait:

> As he paced the deck, talking with the reporters, he appeared alert and active in every movement, his head thrown back and splendidly poised upon his broad, square shoulders . . . A profusion of iron grey hair bursting out of the sides of the turban and hanging long upon the neck; a large, massive head, full-domed and remarkably wide across the forehead and temples, the forehead rising like a great palisade above the eyes, which were very wide apart, their orbits large and deep, looking out from under massive overhanging brows; strong Roman nose, generous ears, decisive yet kindly mouth and chin, a creamy white complexion, beard same colour as his hair, worn full over the face and carefully trimmed at almost full length.[2]

'Abdu'l-Bahá wasted no time in establishing how reporting should be done:

> The pages of swiftly appearing newspapers are indeed the mirror of the world . . . But it behooveth the editors of the newspaper to

be sanctified from the prejudice of egotism and desire, and to be adorned with the ornament of equity and justice.

There are good and bad newspapers. Those which strive to speak only that which is truth, which hold the mirror up to truth, are like the sun . . . Those who play for their own little selfish ends give no true light to the world and perish of their own futility.[3]

As the ship passed by the Statue of Liberty, 'Abdu'l-Bahá stood and threw his arms wide open in greeting, saying: 'There is the new world's symbol of liberty and freedom. After being forty years a prisoner I can tell you that freedom is not a matter of place. It is a condition. Unless one accept dire vicissitudes he will not attain. When one is released from the prison of self, that is indeed a release.'[4]

Women's suffrage was a big issue of the day in America and one of the reporters asked: 'What is your attitude toward woman suffrage?' The Master responded by stating: 'The modern suffragette is fighting for what must be, and many of these are willing martyrs to imprisonment for their cause . . . If women were given the same advantages as men, their capacity being the same, the result would be the same. In fact, women have a superior disposition to men; they are more receptive, more sensitive, and their intuition is more intense.'[5]

'Abdu'l-Bahá told them of a pilgrim going to Jerusalem. The Master had told the pilgrim that 'love for God should be to him as a telegraph wire, one end in the heavenly kingdom, the other in his heart. The pilgrim answered that his telegraph wire had broken down. The Master had replied, "Then you will have to use wireless telegraphy." '[6]

Stanwood Cobb noted that when 'Abdu'l-Bahá came ashore, He was immediately surrounded by 'alert and inquisitive reporters'. But the Master was perfectly at home with them. Most of the reporters, Cobb recalled, were quickly entranced by the majestic figure. One reporter asked, 'What do you think of America?' 'I like it,' replied the Master. 'Americans are optimistic. If you ask them how they are they say "All right!" If you ask them how things are going, they say, "All right!" This cheerful attitude is good.' The reporters were captivated.[7]

Immigration officials recorded the arrival of 'Abdu'l-Bahá and His party. The Master was listed as being 69 years of age (he was actually 67), 5 feet and 5 inches tall with grey hair and blue eyes. The manifest also listed His profession as an author and that He had paid His own passage.

## GREETING THE STATUE OF LIBERTY

Several hundred Bahá'ís had gathered at the pier to meet 'Abdu'l-Bahá as His ship docked at noon. 'Abdu'l-Bahá sent word that the friends should leave and meet Him that afternoon at the home of Edward and Carrie Kinney. Many did not wish to leave, but 'Abdu'l-Bahá remained aboard the ship until His followers finally dispersed. Not all left, however. Juliet Thompson described what happened:

> Marjorie [Morten] and I had suggested to them that the Master might not want this public demonstration, but their eagerness was too great to be influenced by just two, and so we had gone along with them – only too glad to do so, to tell the truth.
>
> During the morning the harbour misted over. At last, in the mist we saw: a phantom ship! And at that very moment some newsboys ran through the crowd, waving Extras. 'The Pope is dead! The Pope is dead!' they shouted. The Pope was *not* dead. The Extras had been printed only on a rumour; but what a symbol, and how exactly timed!
>
> Closer and closer, ever more substantial, came that historic ship, that epoch-making ship, till at last it swam out solid into the light, one of the Persians sitting in the bow in his long robes, 'abá, and turban. This was Siyyid Asadu'lláh, a marvellous, witty old man, who had come with the Master to prepare His meals.
>
> He told us later that when the ship was approaching the harbour and the Master saw, as His first view of America, the Wall Street skyscrapers, He had laughed and said: 'Those are the minarets of the West.' What divine irony!
>
> The ship docked, but the Master did not appear. Suddenly I had a great glimpse. In the dim hall beyond the deck, striding to and fro near the door, was One with a step that shook you! Just that one stride, charged with power, the sweep of a robe, a majestic head, turban crowned – that was all I saw, but my heart stopped.
>
> Marjorie's instinct and mine had been true. Mr Kinney was called for to come on board the ship. He returned with a disappointing message. The Master sent us His love but wanted us to disperse now. He would meet us all at the Kinneys' house at four.
>
> Everyone obeyed at once except Marjorie, Rhoda [Nichols], and myself! Marjorie, who loves the Teachings but has never wholly accepted them, said: 'I can't leave till I've seen Him. I *can't*.

I WON'T!' So, though we followed the crowd to the street, we slipped away there and looked around for some place to hide. Quite a distance below the big entrance to the pier we saw a fairly deep embrasure into which a window was set, with the stone wall jutting out from it. Here we flattened ourselves against the window, Rhoda (who is conspicuously tall) clasping a long white box of lilies which she had brought for the Master. Just in front of the entrance stood Mr Mills' car, his chauffeur in it. Suddenly it rolled forward and, to our utter dismay, parked directly in front of us. Now we were caught: certain to be discovered. But there was no help for it, for Marjorie still refused to budge till she had seen the Master.

Then, He *came* – through the entrance with Mr MacNutt and Mr Mills, and turned and walked swiftly toward the car. In a panic we waited.

A few nights ago Marjorie and I had a double dream. In her dream, I was out in space with her. In mine, we were in a room together and the Master had just entered it. He walked straight up to Marjorie, put His two hands on her shoulders and pressed and pressed till she sank to her knees. And while she was sinking, she lifted her face to His and everything in her seemed to be dying except her soul, which looked out through her raised eyes in a sort of agony of recognition.

Today, after one glance at the Master, this was just the way she looked.

'Now,' she said, 'I *know*.'

As the Master was stepping into the car, He turned and – *smiled* at us.[8]

Almost all the major newspapers in New York carried headlined stories about 'Abdu'l-Bahá during the next several days:

PROPHET OF BAHAIS HERE – *New York City Sun*

BANISHED FIFTY YEARS, LEADER OF BAHAI HERE: PERSIAN PHILOSOPHER FAVORS WOMAN SUFFRAGE AND WILL TALK PEACE – *New York City Evening Mail*

ABDUL BAHA ABBAS IS HERE TO PREACH BROTHERLY LOVE – *New York Evening World*

PERSIAN TEACHER OF WORLD-PEACE IS HERE – *New York City Evening World*

ABDUL BAHA HERE TO CONVERT AMERICA TO HIS PEACE DOCTRINE – *New York Herald*

ABDUL BAHA ABBAS, HEAD OF NEWEST RELIGION, BELIEVES IN WOMAN SUFFRAGE AND DIVORCE – *New York City Evening World*

ABDUL BAHA, DAZED BY CITY'S RUSH, CALLS NEW YORK A BEEHIVE – *New York Herald*⁹

'Abdu'l-Bahá's words about truth and accuracy weren't always heeded. The *New York City Evening Mail* reported that 'Abdu'l-Bahá was met by 'fully a thousand of his followers', while the *New York City Evening World* said that He was met by a 'party of about forty prosperous looking persons'. The *New York Sun* stated that He was welcomed by 'more than three hundred of his American disciples'. The *Sun* also quoted Arthur Dodge as saying that there 'were probably 20,000,000 Bahais in the world'. The *New York Herald* reported that 'Abdu'l-Bahá 'had his cloak lined with sable fur'.¹⁰

Some of the newspapers made a few rather strange remarks. "Abdul is sixty-eight, but looks ninety . . . His voice is strong,' reported the *New York City World*, while the *Evening World* stated that 'members of the sect were known originally as Babists, after The Bab, but they are now called Bahais, after the Bahas, father and son . . . Of course nobody could be named Baha without having a beard . . . Abdul Baha is a really delightful prophet. He says he isn't a prophet, by the way . . .'

"Abdul Baha's philosophy is of a sort which the Occidental mind does not grasp in the first sentence . . .' reported the *New York Herald*.¹¹

The *New York City Evening Mail* wrote in an editorial:

> Don't laugh at Abdul Abbas. He has an idea . . . people with ideas generally are laughed at. But after the world has laughed long enough, it turns around and eats the idea very solemnly and very greedily, and digests it, and makes it part of its bone and fiber . . .
>
> We are not personally acquainted with Abdul Abbas, and we

cannot tell how much of charlatanry may be mixed up with his doctrine. But the idea in itself is good stuff . . . he is the strange anomaly of an oriental mystic who believes in woman suffrage and in Broadway. He is worth his picture in the papers.[12]

One reporter from the *New York Times* wrote that after she had finished her interview with 'Abdu'l-Bahá, she sat and talked with His interpreter. In her article, she wrote:

A faith that is lived must grow, and Bahaism spreads in India, in Africa, in Persia, in England and France, and in the United States. It is not easy to give up prejudices, but Bahais who have done so find that they are considerably happier without them. 'I used to wash my hands after shaking hands with a Christian,' said a Mohammedan Bahai. 'Now I want to shake hands with all the world.'[13]

One reporter from Pittsburgh was especially interested in 'Abdu'l-Bahá's arrival. That was Martha Root, who had become a Bahá'í three years previously.

## Martha Root

Martha Root worked for the *Pittsburgh Post* newspaper as its Society and Religious Editor. She first learned about the Bahá'í Faith in Pittsburgh's Child's Restaurant in 1908 from Roy Wilhelm. On 19 September 1909, Martha wrote to Helen Goodall stating bluntly, 'I am a Bahai.' One week later, she published an extensive article in her paper about the history and ideals of the Faith.

When 'Abdu'l-Bahá arrived in America, Martha met Him as both a reporter and a Bahá'í. She attended every possible meeting at which He spoke in New York and Washington, then followed Him to Chicago. Martha was intensely affected by the Master and she arranged a meeting in her home town of Pittsburgh on 7 May. She had two private interviews with 'Abdu'l-Bahá. At one she told Him of the lumps in her breast, for which He prescribed alum. In spite of her not using the alum correctly, it appeared to check the cancer she had, the cancer that would ultimately cause her to ascend to the Abhá Kingdom in 1939.

Martha attended the Unity Feast in West Englewood, New Jersey, and it proved to be a high point in her life. Roy Wilhelm had invited her and she thanked him for years afterward.

Martha had first tried to begin her travel-teaching career in 1911, but 'Abdu'l-Bahá had dissuaded her. When He was in America, she submitted a plan for a world teaching trip, but the Master only reluctantly agreed and then with certain conditions. In January 1915, however, she could no longer be restrained and began the first of her world-encircling journeys. During the following 24 years, Martha circled the globe four times and, according to Shoghi Effendi,

> travelled four times to China and Japan and three times to India, visited every important city in South America, transmitted the message of the New Day to kings, queens, princes and princesses, presidents of republics, ministers and statesmen . . . as well as a vast number of people in various walks of life . . . established a record that constitutes the nearest approach to the example set by 'Abdu'l-Bahá Himself.[14]

Among her many important contacts were her eight meetings with Queen Marie of Romania. Shoghi Effendi appointed Martha Root as a Hand of the Cause of God shortly after her passing.[15]

\* \* \*

During His first day in New York, 'Abdu'l-Bahá met the Bahá'ís at the home of Edward and Carrie Kinney. Instead of the Bahá'ís welcoming Him, 'Abdu'l-Bahá welcomed them: 'How are you? Welcome! Welcome! After arriving today, although weary with travel, I had the utmost longing and yearning to see you and could not resist this meeting.' He went on to say, 'I was in Egypt and was not feeling well; but I wished to come to you in America. My friends said: "This is a long journey; the sea is wide; you should remain here." But the more they advised and insisted, the greater My longing to take this trip and now I have come to America to meet the friends of God.'[16]

## Edward and Carrie Kinney

Edward and Carrie Kinney were both born in New York and married there in 1895. Soon afterward, Howard MacNutt invited them to his house to introduce them to 'a prophet like Jesus'. Before going, Carrie told her husband:

> 'Your friend must be crazy to write you this. Why don't you go without me?' He said 'No, I am sure that Howard wants to meet you'. . . 'I am taking you there tonight,' He said firmly.
>
> We drove to the MacNutts' house in a horsecab that took us an hour and a half . . . I became very much frightened to hear that Bahá'u'lláh claimed to be the Spirit of Truth, whose coming Jesus had promised . . .
>
> On the way home in the carriage, I said to Ned, 'The MacNutts are very nice, but I don't want to go back there to see them again.' Ned replied, 'I believe that what we heard is true.' I was very much disturbed . . .
>
> Ned stayed up very late. He wrote a letter to 'Abdu'l-Bahá asking for confirmation of His Father's station. I did not think that Ned would ever hear from Him Whom he now called the Master . . . In a month's time, Ned received a Tablet from the Master written in red ink. It included the words, 'You have been chosen.'
>
> The first time that the Bahá'ís came to the house they looked very strange to me. I tried to be polite, but I couldn't. They frightened me. Instead I ran upstairs to the bathroom and locked the door . . .
>
> Gradually I was moved to come downstairs and meet them. Soon I started to listen. One night after everyone had left, Ned and I sat down in the living-room and talked together . . . Suddenly I realized that I believed what Ned was saying.[17]

In 1907, the Kinneys went on pilgrimage. While in Haifa, Carrie fell very ill and Edward was told she would die. Edward went to 'Abdu'l-Bahá, Who told him that Carrie would wake up and ask for soup, which He gave Edward instructions on how to make. Carrie soon recovered and the Kinneys spent the next year working with Dr Zia Bagdadi to establish a tuberculosis hospital in Alexandria, Egypt.

After that year, the Kinneys returned to New York, then went back to Haifa in 1909, where 'Abdu'l-Bahá told them about Bahá'u'lláh losing His wealth and said to the Kinneys, 'May God give you the treasure of the Kingdom, the breath of the Holy Spirit. If, perchance, you are overtaken by poverty, let it not make you sad.' A few years after 'Abdu'l-Bahá's visit to America, the Kinneys, once wealthy, had to struggle financially, but they were happy.[18]

When 'Abdu'l-Bahá gave His first talk in America, it was in the Kinneys' home. Juliet Thompson wrote, 'When I arrived . . . He was sitting in the center of the dining room, near a table strewn with flowers . . . At His knees stood the Kinney children, Sanford and Howard, and His arms were around them . . . No words could describe His ineffable peace. The people stood about in rows and circles: several hundred in the rooms, which all open into each other. In the dining room many sat on the floor.'[19]

'Abdu'l-Bahá gave Edward the name 'Saffa', meaning serenity, while calling Carrie 'Vaffa', which meant certitude and fidelity. With 'Abdu'l-Bahá's departure and their increasing poverty, the Kinneys moved to a small cabin near Green Acre. Later they moved to an area near Boston, then back to New York.

'Abdu'l-Bahá designated Edward and Carrie Kinney as 'Pillars of the Faith in the City of the Covenant'. Edward passed away in 1950 and Carrie followed nine years later.[20]

\* \* \*

Howard Colby Ives attended that first meeting and his life was changed forever.

### Howard Colby Ives

Howard Colby Ives was a seeker who had not been happy with the conventional definitions of words such as God, faith, heaven, hell and the like, but who became a Unitarian minister in New York. One day in October of 1911, he picked up a copy of *Everybody's Magazine* and found an article about 'Abdu'l-Bahá's projected visit to America. Soon thereafter, a friend asked him to review some notes taken at a Bahá'í meeting. He wasn't very interested in 'Oriental cults' so when he received an invitation a few days later to a Bahá'í meeting, he was more upset than happy. He went only out of a sense of obligation to his friend.

At the meeting, he met Mountfort Mills, who was the chairman. The subject was 'The Divine Springtime', and in the weeks following he was baffled why Mr Mills devoted so much time to him. But by February, all discussion was about 'Abdu'l-Bahá and His impending arrival. Then one cold February night, Ives suddenly said: 'I would very much like to have a talk with him alone, without even an interpreter.' Mills replied that without any interpreter he wouldn't learn much. But the thought remained. Then 'Abdu'l-Bahá arrived and Ives wrote:

Finally the day [11 April] arrived . . . I did make an effort to get at least a glimpse of Him . . . A glimpse was all I succeeded in getting. The press of eager friends and curious ones was so great that it was difficult even to get inside the doors . . . I strove to get where I could at least see Him. All but impossible. At last I managed to press forward where I could peep over a shoulder and so got my first glimpse of 'Abdu'l-Bahá . . .

. . . the very next morning, early, I was at the Hotel Ansonia . . . before nine o'clock in the morning I was there . . . Already the large reception room was well filled. Evidently others also were conscious of a similar urge . . . I did not want to talk to anyone . . . I withdrew to the window overlooking Broadway and turned my back upon them all. Below me stretched the great city but I saw it not. What was it all about? Why was I there? What did I expect . . . ? I had no appointment. Plainly all these other folk had come expecting to see and talk with Him. Why should I expect any attention . . . ?

So I was somewhat withdrawn from the others when my attention was attracted by a rustling throughout the room. A door was opening far across from me and a group was emerging and 'Abdu'l-Bahá appeared saying farewell . . . His fez was slightly tilted and as I gazed, His hand, with a gesture evidently characteristic, raised and, touching, restored it to its proper place. His eyes met mine as my fascinated glance was on Him. He smiled and, with a gesture which no word but 'lordly' can describe, He beckoned me. Startled gives no hint of my sensations. Something incredible had happened. Why to me, a stranger unknown, unheard of, should He raise that friendly hand? I glanced around. Surely it was to someone else that gesture was addressed, those eyes were smiling! But there was no one near and again I looked and again He beckoned and such understanding love enveloped me that even at that distance and with a heart still cold a thrill ran through me as if a breeze from a divine morning had touched my brow!

Slowly I obeyed that imperative command and, as I approached the door where still He stood, He motioned others away and stretched His hand to me as if He had always known me. And, as our right hands met, with His left He indicated that all should leave the room, and He drew me in and closed the door. I remember how surprised the interpreter looked when he too was included in this general dismissal. But I had little thought then for anything but this incredible happening. I was absolutely alone with 'Abdu'l-Bahá. The halting desire expressed weeks ago was fulfilled the very moment that our eyes first met.

Still holding my hand 'Abdu'l-Bahá walked across the room towards where, in the window, two chairs were waiting. Even then the majesty of His tread impressed me and I felt like a child led by His father, a more than earthly father, to a comforting conference. His hand still held mine and frequently His grasp tightened and held more closely. And then, for the first time, He spoke, and in my own tongue: Softly came the assurance that I was His very dear son.

What there was in these simple words that carried such conviction to my heart I cannot say. Or was it the tone of voice and the atmosphere pervading the room, filled with spiritual vibrations beyond anything I had ever known, that melted my heart almost to tears? I only know that a sense of *verity* invaded me. Here at last *was* my Father . . . My throat swelled. My eyes filled. I could not have spoken had life depended on a word. I followed those masterly feet like a little child.

Then we sat in the two chairs by the window . . . At last He looked right into me. It was the first time since our eyes had met with His first beckoning gesture that this had happened. And now nothing intervened between us and He looked at me. *He looked at me!* It seemed as though never before had anyone really seen *me*. I felt a sense of gladness that I at last was at home, and that one who knew me utterly, my Father, in truth, was alone with me.

As He looked such play of thought found reflection in His face

> . . . it was as if His very being opened to receive me. With that the heart within me melted and the tears flowed. I did not weep, in any ordinary sense . . . It was as if a long-pent stream was at last undammed . . .
>
> He put His two thumbs to my eyes while He wiped the tears from my face, admonishing me not to cry, that one must always be happy. And He laughed. Such a ringing, boyish laugh . . .
>
> I could not speak. We both sat perfectly silent for what seemed a long while, and gradually a great peace came to me. Then 'Abdu'l-Bahá placed His hand upon my breast saying that it was the heart that speaks. Again silence . . . No further word was spoken, and all the time I was with Him not one single sound came from me. But no word was necessary . . .
>
> Suddenly He leaped from His chair with another laugh as though consumed with a heavenly joy. Turning, He took me under the elbows and lifted me to my feet and swept me into His arms. Such a hug! No mere embrace! My very ribs cracked. He kissed me on both cheeks, laid His arm across my shoulders and led me to the door.
>
> That is all. But life has never been quite the same since.[21]

Ives began to almost inhabit 'Abdu'l-Bahá's house, he was so attracted. One day, the Master was talking about His interpretation of a Christian doctrine, one that was very different to what Ives had been taught. Puzzled as to how 'Abdu'l-Bahá could be so certain, Ives abruptly asked:

> 'How is it possible to be so sure? . . . No one can say with certainty what Jesus meant after all these centuries of misinterpretation and strife.'
>
> He intimated that it was quite possible.
>
> It is indicative of my spiritual turmoil and my blindness to His station, that instead of His serenity and authority impressing me . . . it drove me to actual impatience. 'That I cannot believe.' . . .
>
> I shall never forget the glance of outraged dignity the interpreter cast upon me. It was as though he would say: 'Who are you to contradict or even to question 'Abdu'l-Bahá!'
>
> But not so did 'Abdu'l-Bahá look at me. How I thank God that it was not! He looked at me a long moment before He spoke. His calm, beautiful eyes searched my soul with such love and understanding

that all my momentary heat evaporated. He smiled as winningly as
a lover smiles upon his beloved, and the arms of His spirit seemed
to embrace me as He said softly that I should try my way and He
would try His.[22]

Ives struggled for several months to understand the reality of 'Abdu'l-Bahá's message. He was the pastor of the Brotherhood Unitarian Church in Jersey City. He had organized the church in mid-1911, but by late 1912 the church was in financial trouble and he was forced to close it. Ives wrote to 'Abdu'l-Bahá about this and about his growing interest in the Faith. The Master turned Ives's anxiousness about the failure of his church into opportunity:

> In brief: be thou not unhappy. This event has happened so that thou mayest become freed from all other occupations, day and night thou mayest call the people to the Kingdom; spread the teachings of Bahá'u'lláh; inaugurate the Era of the New Life; promulgate the Reality, and be sanctified and purified from all save God. It is my hope that thou mayest become as such.
>
> Crown thy head with this diadem of the Kingdom whose brilliant jewels have such illuminating power that they shall shine upon centuries and cycles.[23]

\* \* \*

From the moment He arrived, 'Abdu'l-Bahá was in constant demand, but He found time to write to Munírih Khánum saying, 'O Amata'l-Bahá! With utmost ease I arrived in New York. However, I was not for a moment free of My thoughts for all of you, especially Rúhá Khánum and Shoghi Effendi.' Rúhá Khánum had been in France with the Master, but was very ill when He arrived in New York.[24]

There was a seemingly endless flow of people who wanted to see Him and there were many invitations to visit churches and private homes. Reverend J. T. Bixby, an elderly Unitarian minister who was writing an article on the Bahá'í Faith for the *North American Review*, came on 12 April. 'It was incredible to me', wrote Howard Colby Ives, 'that any soul could be so impervious to the influence emanating from 'Abdu'l-Bahá.' Question after long hypothetical question ensued, and

Ives became impatient. But 'Abdu'l-Bahá did not. 'He never flagged in interest but it seemed to be more an interest in the questioner than in his questions. He sat perfectly relaxed, His hands in His lap with palms upward, as was characteristic of him. He looked at the interviewer with that indescribable expression of understanding love which never failed.' At last, 'Abdu'l-Bahá led his visitor to the door and laughing, took a large bunch of roses and laid them in the Reverend's arms. The visitor, now humbly bowing, looked 'so surprised, so radiant, so humble, so transformed.'[25] 'Abdu'l-Bahá said, 'These beautiful roses will express to you the love and fragrance of the Bahai Spirit.'[26]

Bixby had asked the Master if *A Traveller's Narrative* was 'substantially correct', not knowing that 'Abdu'l-Bahá had written it. 'Abdu'l-Bahá answered, 'It is an authority.' When Bixby asked about some of E. G. Browne's writings, which included statements by Bahá'u'lláh's Covenant-breaking half-brother Mírzá Yaḥyá, 'Abdu'l-Bahá said Browne 'interviewed various people and automatically wrote down all he heard. Naturally when he met the enemies of Baha'o'llah he heard nothing favourable. Would you go to the Vatican to hear praises of the Protestants? Would you consult Jewish rabbis as to the reality of Christ?'[27] Nevertheless, Bixby went on to write a negative article about 'Abdu'l-Bahá.

The flow of visitors on 12 April included two with opposing views: Mr W. H. Short of the New York Peace Society, and Hudson Maxim, an inventor of weaponry. Mr Short noted that 'All the members of the New York Peace Society feel the truth and inspiration of what you have said.' Mr Maxim had different ideas:

> H. M. 'I understand that you are a messenger of peace to this country. What is your opinion about modern war? . . .'
>
> 'Abdu'l-Bahá. 'Everything that prevents war is good.'
>
> H. M. 'Christ said He came to make war . . .'
>
> 'Abdu'l-Bahá. 'We have the history of the world for nearly six thousand years . . . Let us now try peace for awhile. If good results follow, let us adhere to it. If not let us throw it away and fight again. Nothing will be lost by the experiment.'
>
> H. M. 'Evolution has now reached a period in the life of nations where commerce takes the place of warfare. Business is war, cruel, merciless.'

'Abdu'l-Bahá. True! War is not limited to one cause. There are many kinds of war and conflict going on, political war, commercial war, patriotic and racial war; this is the very civilization of war . . .

Maxim. 'Less men are killed in war in a year now than are killed by our industries through preventable accidents.'

'Abdu'l-Bahá: 'War is the most preventable accident.'[28]

The same day, Ella Quant and Margaret La Grange attended a gathering after which they had a private interview with 'Abdu'l-Bahá. Ella later wrote that when they entered the room with 'Abdu'l-Bahá, He was sitting on a couch with a Persian man seated on each side of Him. Then one of the men rose and gave his seat to a lady. This greatly bothered Ella, who could only think, 'Who is worthy to sit beside 'Abdu'l-Bahá?' She wondered if 'Abdu'l-Bahá could read the question in her mind. Later, the two women were invited to meet the Master. First, He seated Margaret in a chair positioned exactly so that she could look into His eyes – which fulfilled Margaret's secret desire. Then 'Abdu'l-Bahá brought Ella over and seated her on the couch beside Him. 'Thus did He teach us, the friends, everywhere, not by rebuke, but with touching example, that the Sun of God's bounty shines upon all and only the veils of self hide us from an ever-increasing realization of its effulgence.'[29]

'Abdu'l-Bahá was at a meeting on 13 April at the home of Marjorie Morten. He had already seen 140 people during the morning and scores more kept coming, but His sense of humour never flagged:

> With His celestial eloquence the Master had described the spiritual springtime.
> '*Va tábistán*,' He began and paused for Ahmad to translate.
> Dead silence. Poor Ahmad had lost the English word. But while he stood helpless, the Master supplied it Himself.
> 'Summer!' He laughed. Whereupon a little ripple of delight ran through the audience. His charm had captured them all.[30]

On 14 April, three days after 'Abdu'l-Bahá arrived in New York, the *Titanic*, which He had been encouraged to sail aboard, was sunk with the loss of 1,500 lives. The Master was driving through New York with Mr MacNutt the day the newspapers all ran the story. He asked,

Shall any of these things you are now looking upon remain or endure? If you possessed all you could wish for, – these great buildings, wealth, luxury, the pleasures of life in this world, would any of these things increase your eternal happiness or insure you everlasting existence? I am summoning you to the world of the Kingdom.[31]

Nine days later, when giving a talk at the home of Agnes and Arthur Parsons in Washington, 'Abdu'l-Bahá returned to the theme of disasters and death:

Within the last few days a terrible event has happened in the world, an event saddening to every heart and grieving every spirit. I refer to the *Titanic* disaster, in which many of our fellow human beings were drowned, a number of beautiful souls passed beyond this earthly life. Although such an event is indeed regrettable, we must realize that everything which happens is due to some wisdom and that nothing happens without a reason. Therein is a mystery; but whatever the reason and mystery, it was a very sad occurrence, one which brought tears to many eyes and distress to many souls. I was greatly affected by this disaster. Some of those who were lost voyaged on the *Cedric* with us as far as Naples and afterward sailed upon the other ship. When I think of them, I am very sad indeed. But when I consider this calamity in another aspect, I am consoled by the realization that the worlds of God are infinite; that though they were deprived of this existence, they have other opportunities in the life beyond, even as Christ has said, 'In my Father's house are many mansions.' They were called away from the temporary and transferred to the eternal; they abandoned this material existence and entered the portals of the spiritual world. Forgoing the pleasures and comforts of the earthly, they now partake of a joy and happiness far more abiding and real, for they have hastened to the Kingdom of God. The mercy of God is infinite, and it is our duty to remember these departed souls in our prayers and supplications that they may draw nearer and nearer to the Source itself.

These human conditions may be likened to the matrix of the mother from which a child is to be born into the spacious outer world. At first the infant finds it very difficult to reconcile itself to its new existence. It cries as if not wishing to be separated from its narrow abode and imagining that life is restricted to that limited space. It is reluctant to leave its home, but nature forces it into this world. Having come into its new conditions, it finds that it has passed from darkness into a sphere of radiance; from gloomy and restricted surroundings it has been transferred to a spacious and delightful environment. Its nourishment was the blood of the mother; now it finds delicious food to enjoy. Its new life is filled with brightness and beauty; it looks with wonder and delight upon the mountains, meadows and fields of green, the rivers and fountains, the wonderful stars; it breathes the life-quickening atmosphere; and then it praises God for its release from the confinement of its former condition and attainment to the freedom of a new realm. This analogy expresses the relation of the temporal world to the life hereafter – the transition of the soul of man from darkness and uncertainty to the light and reality of the eternal Kingdom. At first it is very difficult to welcome death, but after attaining its new condition the soul is grateful, for it has been released from the bondage of the limited to enjoy the liberties of the unlimited. It has been freed from a world of sorrow, grief and trials to live in a world of unending bliss and joy. The phenomenal and physical have been abandoned in order that it may attain the opportunities of the ideal and spiritual. Therefore, the souls of those who have passed away from earth and completed their span of mortal pilgrimage in the *Titanic* disaster have hastened to a world superior to this. They have soared away from these conditions of darkness and dim vision into the realm of light. These are the only considerations which can comfort and console those whom they have left behind.

Furthermore, these events have deeper reasons. Their object and purpose is to teach man certain lessons. We are living in a day of reliance upon material conditions. Men imagine that the great size and strength of a ship, the perfection of machinery or the skill of a navigator will ensure safety, but these disasters sometimes take place that men may know that God is the real Protector. If it be the will of God to protect man, a little ship may escape destruction, whereas the greatest and most perfectly constructed vessel with the best and most skilful navigator may not survive a danger such as was present on the ocean. The purpose is that the people of the world may turn to God, the One Protector; that human souls may rely upon His preservation and know that He is the real safety. These events happen in order that man's faith may be increased and strengthened. Therefore, although we feel sad and disheartened, we must supplicate God to turn our hearts to the Kingdom and pray for these departed souls with faith in His infinite mercy so that, although they have been deprived of this earthly life, they may enjoy a new existence in the supreme mansions of the Heavenly Father.[32]

'Abdu'l-Bahá made His first public talk in America on the same day as the *Titanic* disaster, 14 April, at the Church of the Ascension. Juliet Thompson had been instrumental in setting up this talk because she and the rector, Percy Grant, had an unusual relationship. Grant was a charismatic man who, according to Juliet, in the very pulpit he was offering to 'Abdu'l-Bahá, had

> . . . with all his great force, his disturbing magnetism and the fire of his eloquence . . . opposed my unshakeable belief, thundering denunciations of 'the subtle', 'the Machiavellian Oriental' of the slumbering and superstitious Orient – the Orient that brought to the West 'nothing but disease and death' . . . He had even gone so far as to openly name 'the Bahá'í sect' in his pulpit and to warn his flock against it.
> And *now*, framing that matchless head of the Master, who sat there so still in His Glory, hung the victor's wreath! Oh for words vivid and sublime enough to make you *see* Him sitting there, in the very spot where He had been so violently denied![33]

But 'Abdu'l-Bahá's transformative powers were in evidence. When He entered the church,

> . . . the altar and the whole chancel were banked with calla lilies. On the back of the Bishop's chair hung *a victor's wreath*, an exact reproduction of the Greek victor's wreath, classically simple: a small oval of laurel with its leaves free at the top . . .
> Dr Grant read first a prophecy from the Old Testament pointing directly to this Day, to Bahá'u'lláh; then the thirteenth Chapter of Corinthians. These were not the lessons for the day but specially chosen.

At the end of the Second Lesson, just as the choir began to sing in a great triumphant outburst 'Jesus Lives!' 'Abdu'l-Bahá with that step of His, which has been described as the walk of either a shepherd or a king, entered the chancel, 'suddenly come to His Temple!' Percy Grant had quietly left his seat and gone into the vestry-room and had returned with the Master, holding His hand. For a moment they stood at the altar beneath that fine mural, *The Resurrection* by John La Farge; then with beautiful deference Percy led the Master to the Bishop's chair. (This broke the nineteenth canon of the Episcopal Church, which forbids the unbaptized to sit behind the altar rail!)

The prayers over, Dr Grant made a short introductory address, speaking not from the pulpit but the chancel steps. Never shall I forget what I saw then. Percy, strong and erect, with his magnificently set head ('like the head of some Viking' as Howard MacNutt says), giving, with a fire even greater than usual – with a strange, sparkling magnetism – the Bahá'í Message to his congregation; and behind him: a flashing Face, unlike the face of any mortal, haloed by the victor's wreath, visibly inspiring him. For with every flash from those eyes, which were fixed on Dr Grant, would appear a fresh charge of energy in him. There was something wonderfully rhythmic in this transmission of fire to the words and the delivery of the man speaking. Was it the sign of some susceptibility in this hitherto unyielding man to the power of 'Abdu'l-Bahá? Or was it just that Power: transcendent, irresistible, quickening whom it chose?

. . . Against His high background of lilies He stood, His face uplifted in prayer, His eyes closed, the palms of His hands uplifted. I seemed to feel streams of Life descending, filling those cupped hands. On either side of Him knelt the clergymen, facing the altar. Percy Grant's head was bowed low. It was a breathless moment. Then the Master raised His resonant voice and chanted.

The recessional hymn was 'Christ our Lord has risen again.'[34]

Stanwood Cobb wrote that 'Abdu'l-Bahá almost never stood still when He spoke. He paced back and forth and His words were 'enhanced rather than diminished by the presence of a translator'. 'Abdu'l-Bahá would make a statement which the translator would then translate. While the translator put the words into English, 'Abdu'l-Bahá would stand and smile, occasionally nodding to affirm important points or as if to approve of the translation. 'He constantly illumined this translation with the dynamic power of His own spiritual personality.' When He spoke:

> the Persian words . . . boomed forth almost as musically as in operatic recitatives. While He spoke He was in constant and majestic motion. To hear Him was an experience unequalled in any other kind of platform delivery. It was a work of art, as well as a spiritual service. First would come this spiritual flow of thought musically expressed in a foreign tongue. Then, as the translator set forth its meaning to us, we had the added pleasure of watching 'Abdu'l-Bahá's response to the art of the translator. It was, all in all, a highly colourful and dramatic procedure.[35]

The next day, 15 April, Edward Getsinger wrote to Agnes Parsons:

> New York has given 'Abdu'l-Bahá a most *dignified and* praiseful reception. Sunday morning service in Church of Ascension . . . He was given the Bishop's chair to sit in and the church was crowded to standing room. Next day 7 of the greatest dailies reported His words in most elegant terms. Ella Wheeler Wilcox today in NY Journal gives a great laudation to Him in a three column article. The great men of the city are beseeching for interviews. The bishop of the Episcopal Diocese of NY comes at 5 today. Mr Carnegie asks for him at his home . . .[36]

But the Master's visit to the Church of the Ascension created a controversy, because the Master had been seated in the Bishop's Chair and had addressed the congregation from the chancel, thus breaking an Episcopalian canon, as described above by Juliet Thompson. It became a great debate as newspapers took sides, and did not quiet down until the Bishop himself went to 'Abdu'l-Bahá at the Hotel Ansonia and thanked Him for honouring the Church with His visit.[37]

* * *

'Abdu'l-Bahá met many famous people while travelling in the West. One of them was Kahlil Gibran.

## Kahlil Gibran

Kahlil Gibran was a celebrated Lebanese poet and painter who happened to live across the street from Juliet Thompson, who knew him quite well. He worked on an Arab newspaper which left him free to paint and write. He showed Juliet almost all his books while they were still in manuscript. Gibran told her that he was thinking of 'Abdu'l-Bahá when he wrote *The Son of Man* and that he was going to write another book with 'Abdu'l-Bahá as the centre. Gibran learned about the Faith when someone gave him some Writings of Bahá'u'lláh in Arabic.

When Juliet told him that the Master was coming, he asked if she would ask the Master if he would allow him to sketch Him. The Master gave him one hour, starting at 6.30 in the morning. Juliet said: 'He made an outstanding head. It doesn't look like the Master – very faint likeness. Great power through the shoulders. A great radiance in the face.'

Gibran adored the Master and would go to Juliet's flat often to see Him. After the Master left, he spent his time writing books. He talked about the Master often, but he couldn't accept 'Abdu'l-Bahá's station. Years later, Gibran went to a Bahá'í Centre when the Master's motion picture was going to be shown. When he saw the Master on the screen, he began to cry. Juliet wrote that he had been asked to speak and when his turn came, he jumped onto the platform with his face covered in tears and said: 'I declare that 'Abdu'l-Bahá is the Manifestation of God for this day!' He was strongly affected by 'Abdu'l-Bahá even though he didn't understand the Master's station.[38]

* * *

While 'Abdu'l-Bahá was in New York, Bahá'ís in other cities were constantly asking for the Master to visit them. Agnes Parsons, in Washington, DC, was one. On 15 April, Edward Getsinger wrote to her: 'We have tried to have 'Abdu'l-Bahá say that he would for certain be your guest, but without avail. He said "I cannot be bound to any place or arrangement before the day arrives. The spirit arranges to set the contingencies."'[39]

## Lua and Edward Getsinger

Louisa (Lua) Moore accepted the Faith of Bahá'u'lláh on 21 May 1897. A year later, she married Edward Getsinger, a professional lecturer with a degree in homeopathic medicine. Within a few months, Edward had also become a Bahá'í. In the spring of 1898, the Getsingers went to California to teach, where they introduced Phoebe Hearst to the Faith. When Mrs Hearst decided to visit 'Abdu'l-Bahá in 1898, she invited the Getsingers to travel with her. This first pilgrimage by American Bahá'ís completely transformed the Getsingers and pushed them to the forefront of the Faith in America.[40]

Both Edward and Lua were deeply involved in the project to build the Temple in Chicago and in the efforts to save the American Bahá'í community from the Covenant-breaking activities of Ibrahim Kheiralla, despite the fact that Kheiralla had originally been their teacher. The Getsingers travelled extensively across America at the behest of the Master, teaching in small towns and areas that rarely received Bahá'í teachers. Lua also travelled to Paris and Haifa, where she stayed for a year, in 1902.

When 'Abdu'l-Bahá arrived in America, Lua had been in California, at the request of the Master, for over a year and was a bit disheartened, writing that 'I have no permission to leave Cal. as yet . . .'[41] But she was soon allowed to travel east. While Lua awaited permission to travel, Edward was busily occupied with the Master's arrangements, working from seven in the morning until eleven at night. Since 'Abdu'l-Bahá moved only as directed by the spirit, Edward's job was doubly difficult.[42]

In 1913 Lua and Edward visited 'Abdu'l-Bahá in Egypt, then travelled at His request to India.[43] Edward returned to America in July 1914, but Lua carried on until November, when she sailed to Haifa and stayed in 'Abdu'l-Bahá's household for seven months. He finally told her to return to America and teach, so in September 1915 she left Haifa with war refugees on the American navy ship *Des Moines*. When she reached Egypt, she was too ill to continue, so she stayed, continuing to teach in spite of her illness until her heart failed on 1 May 1916.[44]

\* \* \*

Bishop Birch of New York came to visit 'Abdu'l-Bahá on 16 April. The Master talked about material and spiritual civilization:

> Praise be to God that stupendous material developments are obtained in this country; but material civilization alone does not safeguard the progress of a nation; because through material civilization, dynamite, Krupp guns, projectiles and Mauser's rifles are invented: thus the infernal instruments of human fratricide are multiplied and constantly perfected. Therefore, natural civilization fosters both good and evil. All this warfare, and bloodshed, and all this feverish multiplication of military armaments are the results of material civilization. When material civilization joins hands with spiritual civilization, then it will be perfect . . . Consequently just as 'good' is advanced through material civilization, 'evil' has taken the same pace. Earthly civilization must become the handmaid of heavenly civilization. Natural civilization is like unto the body of man. If the body is animated by the spirit, it is alive, otherwise it is a corpse which in time will become decomposed.

When the Bishop expressed his pleasure at 'Abdu'l-Bahá's words, the Master replied:

> I am likewise very grateful to you. Praise be to God that your churches are free from prejudice. They are not so creed-bound as to be unable to breathe. Many Christian Churches in Europe are as yet extremely dogmatic, but I have already spoken in churches belonging to your denomination. The congregations consisted of most delightful and intelligent people. This is a great distinction. [45]

May Maxwell and Juliet Thompson spent as much time as possible with the Master. On the same day as the Bishop's visit, 16 April, Juliet wrote that 'May Maxwell and I were together in the Master's room. He was lying back on His pillow, May's baby [Mary – later to become Amatu'l-Bahá Rúḥíyyih Khánum] crawling over Him, feeding first the baby, then May and me with chocolates.'[46] Later that day, someone asked 'Abdu'l-Bahá: 'Those who assume the direction of Bahá'í affairs are often criticized. If a man has a superior intellect, should he come down to the station of those who are less capable?' 'Abdu'l-Bahá replied:

> Capacity and privilege in this Cause are intrinsic. Whosoever has a great power of speech, whosoever has a greater power of attraction,

whosoever has a greater sincerity, will advance, no matter what happens. In other movements, positions are like public offices; but in this Cause the people advance because of their innate qualities, – because their works echo in the hearts of men.[47]

In *Arches of the Years*, Marzieh Gail writes about Dr Florian and Grace Krug: how she became a Bahá'í and he halted his opposition to her Faith. It began when 'Abdu'l-Bahá placed the hand of Grace into the hand of Florence Khan, Marzieh's mother. Grace was Dr Krug's second wife and stepmother to his children, Charles and Louise. Gail writes about the surprising conversion of Dr Krug:

> A distinguished family . . . patriarch, a leading New York surgeon, Dr Florian Krug, was brought into the Faith by the Master . . .
> Florian Krug, you might say, was an unlikely Bahá'í . . . He was born in Germany in 1859, he attended Freiburg University and was a member of the Hasso-Borusso Studenten Korps. This means his face bore scars. He had fought forty-seven duels. Once the tip of his nose was cut off but the thoroughgoing Germans sewed it back on again. He was especially proud of a deep scar running almost the length of his jawbone on his left cheek . . .
> There were historic family quarrels after Grace . . . became a Bahá'í. The siblings cowered, watched and trembled on their perch at the head of the stairs, as their father below them would scream at his wife and hurl down Bahá'í books.
> In spite of everything, Grace Krug invited the Master to speak at their home, and the young people heard their father shouting, 'If that old man comes into this house I'll have the doorman throw him out!' Both Charles and Louise described the fateful day of the visit. Charles said his father's attitude was: 'Now I can get my hands on the *ringleader* of this bunch!'
> Louise said, 'We were terrified. Charlie and I were standing there by the door as 'Abdu'l-Bahá came in. He put His arms out with that wonderful gesture – you could feel the love pouring out. He walked right up to my father and looked him straight in the face. And he said: "Dr Krug, are you happy?". . . my father just *wilted*. He was like a bird letting its wings down, to enjoy the sun. From that time on, never a word against the Master . . .'

Charles said that after 'Abdu'l-Bahá had finished His lecture, and all the ladies rushed toward Him, 'Pa came out of his corner like a traffic cop, all but knocking the women down. He shouted, "Can't you see, 'Abdu'l-Bahá is *tired*?" Then he took the Master's arm and led Him to a chair.'[48]

'Abdu'l-Bahá later spoke of the station of Grace Krug, saying that:

> The time will come when her whole family will be proud of Mrs Krug and her faith. Her husband is still distant and heedless; the time will come when he will feel himself exalted on account of Mrs Krug's faith. I see what they do not see. Ere long the whole of her family will consider the faith of that lady as the crown of honour on their heads.[49]

Grace and Florian Krug were in Haifa when 'Abdu'l-Bahá ascended to the Abhá Kingdom. Dr Krug's fingers closed the Master's earthly eyes for the final time.[50]

While 'Abdu'l-Bahá was in New York, He met many people and taught them many things. One well-known story involves teaching 'Mr M' (Mountfort Mills) how to pray:

> When 'Abdu'l-Bahá was in New York, He called to Him an ardent Bahá'í and said, 'If you will come to Me at dawn tomorrow, I will teach you to pray.'
>
> Delighted, Mr M arose at four and crossed the city, arriving for his lesson at six. With what exultant expectation he must have greeted this opportunity! He found 'Abdu'l-Bahá already at prayer, kneeling by the side of the bed. Mr M followed suit, taking care to place himself directly across.
>
> Seeing that 'Abdu'l-Bahá was quite lost in His own reverie, Mr M began to pray silently for his friends, his family and finally for the crowned heads of Europe. No word was uttered by the quiet Man before him. He went over all the prayers he knew then, and repeated them twice, three times – still no sound broke the expectant hush.
>
> Mr M surreptitiously rubbed one knee and wondered vaguely about his back. He began again, hearing as he did so, the birds heralding the dawn outside the window. An hour passed, and finally

two. Mr M was quite numb now. His eyes roving along the wall, caught sight of a large crack. He dallied with a touch of indignation but let his gaze pass again to the still figure across the bed.

The ecstasy that he saw arrested him and he drank deeply of the sight. Suddenly he wanted to pray like that. Selfish desires were forgotten. Sorrow, conflict and even his immediate surroundings were as if they had never been. He was conscious of only one thing, a passionate desire to draw near to God.

Closing his eyes again he set the world firmly aside, and amazingly his heart teemed with prayer, eager, joyous, tumultuous prayer. He felt cleansed by humility and lifted by a new peace. 'Abdu'l-Bahá had taught him to pray!

The 'Master of 'Akká' immediately arose and came to him. His eyes rested smilingly upon the newly humbled Mr M. 'When you pray,' he said, 'You must not think of your aching body, nor of the birds outside the window nor of the cracks in the wall!' He became very serious then, and added 'When you wish to pray you must first know that you are standing in the presence of the Almighty!'[51]

Racial segregation in the United States and particularly among the Bahá'ís was a frequent subject for 'Abdu'l-Bahá. He constantly urged the friends to associate with each other in the utmost joy and happiness. On Wednesday 17 April He hosted such a gathering at the home of Saffa and Vaffa Kinney. Bahá'ís and their friends, both black and white, attended and He prepared and served the meal Himself. The Master told his audience that 'although we are of different individualities, different in ideas and of various fragrances, let us strive like flowers of the same divine garden to live together in harmony'. When concluding, He added that 'I am joyful, for I perceive the evidences of great love among you.'[52]

With the Master on his journey through New York that day to the Kinney home was a Swiss Bahá'í who had travelled from the other side of the continent to see Him.

## John Bosch

John Bosch had emigrated to California and was in the wine business, though that soon changed. He first learned about the Faith on a train when he happened to meet a friend, Mrs Beckwith, who happened to be reading a book about 'Abdu'l-Bahá. John told her, however, that if he sat by her, they were going to talk and he wasn't going to let her read. When she put the book down and John saw the cover, he picked it up and began reading, forgetting to talk with his friend. After glancing at a few pages, he asked where he could buy it and was directed to Helen Goodall. One day, John simply showed up at Mrs Goodall's home and told her about meeting Mrs Beckwith and reading the book. Mrs Goodall invited him in and she, along with Kathryn Frankland, talked with him about the Faith. John left with an armload of things to read. John began attending meetings about the Faith at Mrs Goodall's home, sometimes being the only man with 25 to 45 women. John wrote that 'I was the only man and never said a word. I let them all talk by themselves.' He wrote to 'Abdu'l-Bahá accepting the Faith in 1905.[53]

When John heard that 'Abdu'l-Bahá was arriving in America, he was so eager to see Him, and thinking that the Master might not go west, he was on a train from San Francisco to Washington the day after the Master arrived in New York:

> John took the first train East, fretting because it didn't go fast enough. In Washington he phoned one of the believers and learned that the Master was still in New York. John left on the night train. At five-thirty the next morning he was at the Hotel Ansonia, and he went upstairs to see the door of the Master's room. Dr Getsinger (Lua's husband) was there and recognized John from a photograph. John asked for an appointment and 'Abdu'l-Bahá sent word, 'In a few minutes.' Then Dr Getsinger called John in.
>
> 'I went as a business man. I had some questions to ask. When I saw Him I forgot everything. I was empty.' Then, in the conversation that followed, 'Abdu'l-Bahá told John all the things he had wanted to know.
>
> Foolishly I said, 'Oh, 'Abdu'l-Bahá, I came three thousand miles to see you.' He gave a good hearty laugh – you know what a wonderful laugh He had . . . And He said, 'I came eight thousand miles to see *you*.' 'I told Him I was in the wine business and grossed fifteen thousand tons of grapes in one season, which makes over two million gallons of wine. 'Oh, 'Abdu'l-Bahá,' I said, 'I am a foreigner, born in Switzerland, and have not the command of the English language. I

would love to be a speaker. All I am doing is to give away pamphlets and as many books as are printed.'

He looked serious. He said, 'You are doing well. I am satisfied with you. With you it is not the movements of the lips, nor the tongue. With you it is the heart that speaks. With you it is silence that speaks and radiates.'

We had tea together. I was there about half an hour. He said, 'You are one of the family; you come in and out anytime you want to.'

It was a cold, snowy day. In the forenoon John was in and out of the room, watched people coming by the dozens to see 'Abdu'l-Bahá, listened to 'Abdu'l-Bahá's words to them. Around noon . . . he saw many people rising in the lobby: 'When His majesty came – how straight He walked! – they all rose.'

'Abdu'l-Bahá walked to the first of three waiting automobiles. The other two were already filled with Bahá'ís and their friends . . .

'Abdu'l-Bahá grabbed my hand and pulled me into the rear seat; Mountfort [Mills] closed the door and I was alone with 'Abdu'l-Bahá.

. . . Just as I stepped into the machine and was seated, 'Abdu'l-Bahá looked at me. He just looked at me, and all at once with an *immense* sigh – or what you call it better than a sigh – like the whole world would be lifted from Him so He could have a rest, He put His head on my left shoulder, clear down as close as He could, like a child, and went to sleep.

I was still as a mouse; I didn't want to move – I didn't want to wake Him up. The trip was nearly a half hour and often I wondered what the others thought – that 'Abdu'l-Bahá was looking out of the window all the time. He woke up just as we stopped at the Kinneys' home.[54]

For the next five days, John attended every meeting with 'Abdu'l-Bahá that he could. He was then booked in the same train car as the Master for the trip to Washington, during which he was given the name of 'Núráni', meaning filled with light. John then rode with 'Abdu'l-Bahá on the train to Chicago and was present at the dedication ceremony for the temple. When a person from Switzerland was called for to shovel a spade-full of dirt for the corner stone, John passed the bounty to an elderly Swiss woman.

John was ready to return to California on 2 May, but 'Abdu'l-Bahá took his hand and led him into an elevator and up to His room. John was alone with the Master and Dr Bagdadi. 'Abdu'l-Bahá lay on His bed and talked of the meeting He had just completed with 400 women. 'Abdu'l-Bahá found their attire amusing (Marzieh Gail describes their stiff skirts, jutting bosoms, hair pads and hats that looked like wedding cakes or birds' nests). Finally, the Master told John it was time to go. Before leaving the room, however, the Master filled his arms with a cake and so many apples and bananas that someone had to push the elevator button for him.[55]

John spent as much time as possible with 'Abdu'l-Bahá when He finally arrived in California. In 1914, he married Louise Stapfer. The couple, fluent in French, pioneered to Tahiti and were present in Haifa when the Master passed away and John was one of those who carried the Master's casket. Shoghi Effendi gave John the first copy of 'Abdu'l-Bahá's Will and Testament to take back to the Bahá'í Convention in Chicago in 1922.[56]

* * *

Kate Carew, a reporter from the *New York Tribune*, published an article about 'Abdu'l-Bahá that filled one full page and spilled over onto another. Kate Carew, whose real name was Mary Williams, was the first woman to become famous for her interviews and was also called the first woman caricaturist. Sketching her subjects, who included Mark Twain, Sarah Bernhardt, Lillian Gish, Jack London, J. P. Morgan, Pablo Picasso, Winston Churchill, Theodore Roosevelt and the Wright brothers, put them at ease, allowing them to open up to her. Her article about 'Abdu'l-Bahá included illustrations she drew herself. It is full of the excitement of discovery and wonder at the man she came to interview on 18 April:

> I stopped for a moment [outside the Hotel Ansonia] to watch the well dressed, well fed looking crowd pass to and fro . . . I said to myself: 'Well, of all the places to find the Master!'. . .
>
> On my way to the more rarefied atmosphere of the upper floors I found myself hoping that the Baha would tell me I had a lovely soul. They say he finds out the strangest things about you . . . I felt all sorts of mystic possibilities awaited me the other side of the door. I stripped my mind of all its worldly debris . . .
>
> At my finger's pressure on the bell the door flew open with a

most unholy speed. No fumes of incense, no tinkling bells, no prostrate figures and whispered benedictions . . . Slipping into a ready chair, I looked about to find myself one of a concourse of people all actuated by the same interest.

My editor had given me the information that there were five thousand Bahaites in America and about twenty million in the world, so why I should have expected to have the Baha all to myself I do not know, but I did.

I solaced my disappointment by studying the visitors, curious to learn what sort of people the faith drew to itself. An enthusiastic, plump, middle-aged little person, gowned in a very worldly manner . . . My glance then caromed with a man who had sped down the corridor ahead of me. He had flying coattails and a black sombrero, so I classified him as from the Middle West . . .

After, several groups of foreigners, alert, silent, expectant, drew my regard. Many prosperous-looking businessmen and many interesting women. There was a pretty girl on a narrow seat . . . A stout man, baldish, with a fringe of long hair on his neck, had the remaining two-thirds of the seat.

Suddenly there was a stir, murmurs of 'The Master!' Many stood up, a few rushed from the room . . . 'Abdu'l-Bahá entered.

He is scarcely above medium height, but so extraordinary is the dignity of his majestic carriage that he seemed more than the average stature . . . While slowly making the round of the room his soft, penetrating, faded eyes studied us all, without seeming to do so.

One and another he termed 'My child!' – and they were not all young who responded to this greeting. He stopped longest before the young girls and boys, those 'blossoms on life's branch,' as he speaks of them in Oriental imagery.

A blushing young woman introduced her escort – 'Master, we have just been married.' Such a look of joy illumined the face that in repose looks like a sheet of parchment on which Fate has scored deep, cabalistic lines. He did not want to leave them. He held their hands a long time, then turned and blessed the young man. My dears, if that young man ever thinks of straying from the path of loyalty, methinks the pressure of that hand will weigh heavy on his soul. He patted several people on the cheek, an old man, an apple-cheeked youth and myself . . .

We seat ourselves about him. A good-looking young Turk understudying Dr Fareed explained modestly: 'You know it is very difficult to translate the Master literally. I can tell you the words, but no one could possibly interpret the beautiful soul that informs them.'

Rather nice, that, I thought!

The Baha repeated a statement he had made that day to the students of Columbia University . . .

After a few more questions and answers the meeting is declared adjourned. Abdul-Baha arises and passes into the inner room, where he gives some private hearings. No one starts to go. He has actually made New York people forget the dinner hour. That in itself is a victory, I think. Don't you?

From my corner I wait my turn, again absorbed watching the human current. Bride and groom pass with ecstatic faces. Middle West smooths his dominant coattails . . . Newspaper people go in and out, Turks, Syrians, business men, domestic and society women. Children . . .

As I respond to Dr Fareed's signal and pass into the inner room I notice everywhere symptoms of departure. I get the impression of a large, masculine family migrating from one part of the world to another, bringing messages of good cheer and brotherly feeling. It is very inspiring.

I find the Baha seated in a comfortable easy chair at the bay window. Dr Fareed sits near him as soon as I have taken my place. His beautiful voice, like a golden echo, follows close the termination of each sentence. The master looks very spirituelle. He is in a relaxed attitude . . . So much more akin to the spirit world than this does he seem that I find myself often addressing Dr Fareed personally, referring to him in the third person.

'Do you think our luxury degenerate,' I ask, 'as in this great hotel?'

Abdul-Baha strokes his long white beard. 'Luxury has a limit. Beyond that limit it is not commendable. There is such a thing as moderation. Men must be temperate in all things.'

'Does the attention paid at present in this country to material things sadden you?' . . .

'Your material civilization is very wonderful. If only you will allow divine idealism to keep pace with it there is great hope for general progress.'

'Is there any way of making this life in a commercial city less crude for the young boy and girl?'

'It would be well to get them together and say, "Young ladies, God has created you all human; isn't it a pity that you should pass your energy along animalistic lines? God has created you men and women in order that you may acquire his virtues, that you may progress in all the degrees, that you may be veritable angels, holy and sanctified."'

'There are so many temptations put in their way,' I murmur.

The Abdul Baha looks very sympathetic, but his singsong tones are relentlessly firm. 'Let them try a little of the delicacy of the spiritual world, the sweetness of its perfection and see which life is preferable . . . '

I noticed a trembling of the eyelids and that the gestures of arranging his turban and stroking his beard were more nervously frequent. Dr Fareed answered to my inquiry, 'Shall I go now?' 'He has been giving of himself to every one since 7 o'clock this morning. I am a perfect physical wreck, but he is willing to go on indefinitely.'

Abdul Baha opened the half-closed eyelids to say: 'I am going to the poor in the Bowery now. I love them.'

I was invited to accompany them. The Baha met my assent with a most Chesterfieldian expression of pleasure. Mr Mills, president of the Bahaite Society in New York, had placed his car at the disposal of Abdul Baha. Can you picture your Aunt Kate and Abdul Baha going to it, hand in hand, through the Ansonia corridors? Perhaps the guests didn't gurgle and gasp! Perhaps! I did feel rather conspicuous, but I braced myself with the thought of the universal brotherhood and really got along fairly well.

When we were seated in the machine, every inch of space taken by some member of the suite, I caught myself thinking what an amusing little anecdote I might make of this happening. Just then the Master said to me in a gentle but firm voice: 'Remember, you press people are the servants of the pubic. You interpret our words and acts to them. With you is a great responsibility. Please remember and please treat us seriously.'

Often during the interview I had felt like saying: 'You dear old man! You fine old gentleman!' I felt more than ever like it now. As if anyone could hold up that pure white soul to ridicule.

There was another gasp of surprise at the Bowery Mission as, still hand in hand – he just wouldn't let me go – the Baha and I trotted through a lane composed of several score of society's members. A few of the young ladies had their arms filled with flowers, which afterward filled the automobile. Some four hundred men were present, belonging to the mission.

Just before the services were concluded I saw the courier stealthily approach the platform and hand the Baha a green baize bag. Of course, I wasn't going to let that go on without finding out all about it, and to my whispered inquiry the Baha said, smilingly: 'Some little lucky bits I am going to distribute to the men.'

What you don't expect! I had the surprise of my life! For what do you suppose those lucky bits were? Silver quarters, two hundred dollars worth of them! There! Guess you didn't expect it, either.

Think of it! Some one actually coming to America and distributing money. Not here with the avowed or unavowed intention of taking it away. It seems incredible.

Possibly I may be a little tired of mere words, dealing in them the way I do, but that demonstration of Abdul Baha's creed did more to convince me of the absolute sincerity of the man than anything else that had happened . . .

The Master stood, his eyes always turned away from the man facing him, far down the line, four or five beyond his vis-à-vis, so that when a particularly desperate looking specimen came along he was all ready for him, and, instead of one quarter, two were quietly pressed into the calloused palm . . .

I had said good night on the platform, so my last view of Abdul Baha was as he stood at the head of the Bowery Mission line, a dozen or more derelicts before him, giving to each a bit of silver and a word of blessing.

And as I went out into the starlight night I murmured the phrase of an Oriental admirer who had described him as: *The Breeze of God.*[57]

Kate Carew missed the final part of this amazing evening. When 'Abdu'l-Bahá returned to the hotel, He encountered the chambermaid, to whom He had given flowers earlier. Ella Quant had witnessed this earlier event when the maid, who cleaned 'Abdu'l-Bahá's apartment, emerged from His room with her arms filled with roses. She showed the flowers to Ella and said in amazement, 'See what He gave me! See what He gave me!'[58] On this occasion, the Master stopped her and asked her to hold out her apron, whereupon He filled it with all the quarters that had not been passed out at the Bowery, about $20 worth. When one of 'Abdu'l-Bahá's retinue told the startled young woman what He had been doing, she immediately replied that, 'I will do the same with this money. I will give away every cent of it.'

When Kate Carew and 'Abdu'l-Bahá went to the Bowery Mission, a group of boys had made fun of the 'Orientals in flowing robes and strange head-gear'. They began to get rather loud and a few sticks were thrown before Carrie Kinney, part of the Master's party, dropped back to talk with them. She told the boys that 'Abdu'l-Bahá was a very holy man who had spent much of His life in prison because of His love for truth and that He was going to talk with the men at the Bowery Mission. With that explanation, one of the boys asked if they could go. Mrs Kinney said no, but if they came to her house, she would arrange for them to meet the Master. Howard Colby Ives tells the rest of the story when about thirty of the boys arrived for their meeting:

> We followed them up the stairs and into 'Abdu'l-Bahá's own room . . . 'Abdu'l-Bahá was standing at the door and He greeted each boy as he came in; sometimes with a handclasp, sometimes with an arm around a shoulder, but always with such smiles and laughter it almost seemed that He was a boy with them. Certainly there was no suggestion of stiffness on their part, or awkwardness in their unaccustomed surroundings. Among the last to enter the room was a colored lad of about thirteen years. He was quite dark and, being the only boy of his race among them, he evidently feared that he might not be welcome. When 'Abdu'l-Bahá saw him His face lighted up with a heavenly smile. He raised His hand and exclaimed in a loud voice so that none could fail to hear; that here was a black rose.
>
> The room fell into instant silence. The black face became illumined with a happiness and love hardly of this world. The other boys looked at him with new eyes. I venture to say that he had been called a black – many things, but never before a black rose.[59]

# 7

# 'WHITE AND BLACK SITTING TOGETHER'

*20–28 April*

## Washington, DC

'Abdu'l-Bahá arrived almost unannounced in Washington, DC on 20 April. At noon that day, Mason Remey frantically telephoned Florence and Ali-Kuli Khan:

> 'Hurry! The Master is arriving at the station in half an hour!' They dropped forks and knives, collected Rahim and Marzieh, and ran out into the street, breathless, trying to catch a public victoria – their chance of reaching the station on time. With fervent prayers, and urging short cuts on the driver, they made it five minutes before the train pulled in. Florence rushed to the florist's in the station and bought two bouquets for the children to present . . . Three autos drew up outside the station to receive the party, one bringing Hippolyte Dreyfus-Barney.[1]

Agnes Parsons added:

> 'Abdu'l-Bahá, Dr Fareed, Dr Getsinger and two Persians arrived in Washington about one o'clock on Saturday . . . Mrs [Alice Barney] Hemmick sent her motor and I, my [horse-drawn] carriage to meet the party. 'Abdu'l-Bahá had asked that the time of this arrival be kept quiet as He was anxious that no demonstration be made. He was met by Mirza Sohrab, Florence Khan and her children . . .[2]

According to Joseph Hannen,

> The train was just on time. Among the usual crowd of travellers there was a quaint note lent by the party of Orientals, in the midst of whom, cool, collected and ever the Master of the situation, 'Abdu'l-Bahá was seen. Quietly he passed through the gates, stopping at the threshold to greet the children of Mirza Ali Kuli Khan. The admonition of the guard to 'pass along – don't block the passage,' disturbed the Servant of God not at all . . .[3]

Marzieh Gail continued, partially with her own remembrance and partially her mother's:

> As 'Abdu'l-Bahá paced along the walk beside the tracks and was about to enter the vaulted station, Marzieh looked above her at His left shoulder . . . and saw on that shoulder a silver, almost fully opened curl . . . The welcomers were distributed among the three autos, and Florence found herself in M. Dreyfus's car . . . Marzieh had disappeared. Florence jumped out and ran up to look in 'Abdu'l-Bahá's car ahead. Marzieh was on His lap and He pointed to the child and smiled.[4]

'Abdu'l-Bahá had requested that a house be rented for Him during His stay in Washington, but Agnes Parsons invited Him to stay at her house. At first, He refused, but when He was told how the house had already been prepared for Him and that Mrs Parsons would be heartbroken, He relented.

\* \* \*

## Ali-Kuli Khan and Florence Khan

Ali-Kuli Khan, a Persian Bahá'í, had been one of the Master's secretaries in 'Akká and came to Washington, DC in 1901 where he quickly found work as the secretary to the Persian Minister. He translated the *Kitáb-i-Íqán*, the *Seven Valleys* (with his daughter Marzieh) and the *Glad-Tidings* into English and translated 'Abdu'l-Bahá's correspondence with American Bahá'ís.

In 1904, he married Florence Breed and the couple had three children, Rahim, Marzieh and Hamideh. Khan became the Persian Chargé d'Affaires in Washington in 1910 and later served on the National Spiritual Assembly of the United States.[5] 'Abdu'l-Bahá said that the marriage was the first between the East and the West and a symbol of the unity of the Bahá'í Faith.

While 'Abdu'l-Bahá was in America, Ali-Kuli Khan was instrumental in bringing many important people into His presence and the Khans frequently hosted the Master for meals when He was in Washington.

## Agnes Parsons

Agnes Parsons was a wealthy socialite who first heard about the Bahá'í Faith in 1908 and became a Bahá'í when she went on pilgrimage in 1910. While there, she asked 'Abdu'l-Bahá if He would stay in her house in Washington, DC if He came to America; He responded in the affirmative. He not only stayed with her in Washington, He also stayed at her summer home in Dublin, New Hampshire. 'Abdu'l-Bahá remarked repeatedly on her spirituality. Agnes Parsons became a fine speaker about the Faith and always had an invitation for travelling teachers to give talks in her home.

During her second pilgrimage in 1920, 'Abdu'l-Bahá told her that she should organize a convention for the unity of the 'coloured and white races'. For a woman of her social standing to promote the unity of the black and the white was tradition-breaking.

## Joseph and Pauline Hannen

Joseph and Pauline Hannen were married in 1893. Pauline became a Bahá'í through the efforts of Mírzá Abu'l-Faḍl in 1902 and was able, over a few years, to bring her mother, Amalie Knobloch, her sisters, Fanny and Alma Knobloch, her husband and his mother, Mrs M. V. Alexander, into the Faith. Alma went to Germany and raised up a Bahá'í community there (see pp. 312-13 in this book) while Fanny went to South Africa.[6]

Pauline and Joseph were the prime movers of racial integration in Washington in the early years of the Faith there. Initially, Pauline feared black people, but her study of Bahá'u'lláh's Writings forced her to change her attitude. Pauline taught the Faith to her black washerwoman, then she and Joseph began inviting blacks to meetings in their home – a rather daring thing to do at that time. Pauline also initiated a children's Sunday school in Washington.[7]

Joseph became an able administrator, replacing Mason Remey on the Bahá'í Temple Unity Executive Board in 1910. During 'Abdu'l-Bahá's visits to Washington, DC and Chicago, Joseph took the notes from which about thirty of the Master's talks were transcribed for publication in *Star of the West* and *The Promulgation of Universal Peace*. In 1916, 'Abdu'l-Bahá sent the first of the *Tablets of the Divine Plan* to the southern states in care of Joseph.

Louis Gregory, in his 'In Memoriam' for Pauline Hannen, wrote that 'her activities were inseparable from those of her husband':

> These two rare souls were united in service, teaching every rank, color, class and creed, amid rural scenes and in many cities, in Washington, where they resided, from the lowly prisoners in jail to the social leaders. How healing to the sick; how consoling to the distressed; how enlightening to children and to those of mature years; how harmonizing in influence; how self-sacrificing; how ceaselessly active! Their southern origin, freedom from prejudice, warmth of heart and knowledge of the Word of God, admirably fitted them for the stupendous and glorious task of harmonizing the races, assigned them by the Master.[8]

Joseph died in 1920, hit by a car. 'The sudden passing of "Brother Joseph", as he was lovingly called by his many Bahá'í friends, was accepted by his widow with sweet resignation that could be born only of the Spirit. She bravely set out to earn her own living, holding one place and then another . . .'[9] Shoghi Effendi named Joseph Hannen as a Disciple of 'Abdu'l-Bahá.[10] Pauline died in 1939.

\* \* \*

Before 'Abdu'l-Bahá arrived, Ali-Kuli Khan considered what questions he would ask upon His arrival:

> Dr Khan realized that the one thing he wanted most to know was some prayer he might utter quickly and from deep within his heart, when the moment came when, as the representative of his country

(then Persia) in Washington he must make some instant diplomatic decision. When these moments came, as they did frequently – Dr Khan felt that while he always sincerely did his best, his wisdom was very limited and finite. If only he might have a prayer that would draw to him a greater wisdom. Ah, if he only might have such a prayer.

So the day came when 'Abdu'l-Bahá was to arrive and Dr Khan, accompanied by the Washington believers, drove to the station to meet Him. The greeting was warm and deeply moving, and Khan's heart was still filled with this one question he wanted most to ask the Master. And they were perhaps halfway back, driving up Pennsylvania Avenue, when 'Abdu'l-Bahá suddenly told Khan this story:

It had happened when Bahá'u'lláh had been gone from Baghdad for some two years. At that time no one knew where He was and all hearts were sick with the fear that they never would see Him again. At this time 'Abdu'l-Bahá was a small boy, and the continued absence of His Beloved Father had become unendurable. So, one night, all night long, the little boy (whom, even then, Bahá'u'lláh referred to as The Master) paced restlessly up and down saying, shouting, beseeching, Ya Allah el Mustaghas! Ya Allah el Mustaghas! all night long. And in the morning, when dawn was breaking, a messenger came to the door to say that a stranger was at the city gate and had sent word to the Family that He wished them to bring to Him fresh raiment and water to bathe in . . . So 'Abdu'l-Bahá knew His beloved Father had returned.

And Dr Khan knew the cry that he, too, might utter in his moments of need Ya Allah el Mustaghas (which . . . means Oh, Thou, help me in my extremity!).[11]

That same evening, 20 April, when speaking at the Orient-Occident-Unity Conference in Washington's Public Library, 'Abdu'l-Bahá said:

> May this American democracy be the first nation to establish the foundation of international agreement. May it be the first nation to proclaim the universality of mankind. May it be the first to upraise the standard of the Most Great Peace, and through this nation of democracy may these philanthropic intentions and institutions be spread broadcast throughout the world. Truly, this is a great and revered nation. Here liberty has reached its highest degree. The

intentions of its people are most praiseworthy. They are, indeed, worthy of being the first to build the Tabernacle of the Most Great Peace and proclaim the oneness of mankind. I will supplicate God for assistance and confirmation in your behalf.[12]

Less than a decade after 'Abdu'l-Bahá spoke these words, President Woodrow Wilson took the first step toward establishing the 'foundation of international agreement' with the League of Nations, flawed though it was. And it was in San Francisco that the next step was taken with the creation of the United Nations in 1946.

'Abdu'l-Bahá's first morning in Washington was filled with many interviews, but He spent a half hour with Agnes Parsons' young son, Jeffrey. They looked at Jeffrey's toys, books and pictures, then went to the roof to see the view. Mrs Parsons noted that 'Abdu'l-Bahá 'never required an interpreter when with a child'.[13]

Washington journalists recorded 'Abdu'l-Bahá's activities, writing that when He 'swept through the Capitol, even the Supreme Court of the United States saw fit to adjourn . . .' Receptions organized for 'Abdu'l-Bahá included the elite of government, diplomatic and academic circles.[14]

One night during dinner Mr Parsons suggested to 'Abdu'l-Bahá that they might visit the Library of Congress some evening to see it lit up. 'Abdu'l-Bahá immediately said, 'Let us go tonight.' So, even though it was already 7.30 p.m., the party went to the Library. They rode the elevator to the rotunda so they could look down on the reading room. 'Abdu'l-Bahá was beginning to examine some bronze busts around the rotunda when Mr Parsons tried to direct the group to another part of the library. 'Abdu'l-Bahá replied, 'When one undertakes to see a thing one should see it.' He continued around the rotunda until He had examined each bronze figure, asking who each represented. The Master then went with Mr Parsons to the area where he worked and 'Abdu'l-Bahá began to examine it as thoroughly as He had examined the rotunda.

Mr Parsons turned to his wife and said: 'If we go over this Division so thoroughly the lights will be turned off before we shall have finished.' This was no sooner said than the Library Superintendent, Bernard R. Greene, appeared and was introduced to 'Abdu'l-Bahá. The Superintendent quickly gave the order that the lights were to be left on until 'Abdu'l-Bahá had finished His tour.[15]

Years later, Dr Herbert Putnam, the Librarian of the Library of Congress during 'Abdu'l-Bahá's visit, sent Mrs Parsons his impressions of 'Abdu'l-Bahá:

> It is of an EXTRAORDINARY NOBILITY: physically, in the head so massive yet so finely poised, and the modeling of the features; but spiritually, in the serenity of expression, and the suggestion of grave and responsible meditation in the deeper lines of the face. But there was also in his complexion, carriage, and expression, an assurance of the complete health which is a requisite of a sane judgment. And when, as in a lighter mood, his features relaxed into the playful, the assurance was added of a sense of humor without which there is no true sense of proportion. I have never met anyone concerned with the philosophies of life whose judgement might seem so reliable in matters of practical conduct.[16]

The Master spoke at the Universalist Church on 21 April, and on 23 April spoke at three meetings. The first was at Howard University, an all-black institution. He arrived at noon and was welcomed by music from a band, and then spoke to more than 1,000 members of the faculty and student body. Joseph Hannen wrote, 'This was a most notable occasion, and here, as everywhere when both white and colored people were present, 'Abdu'l-Bahá seemed happiest.'[17]

'Abdu'l-Bahá spoke on the subject of racial harmony and the unity of humankind, noting that colour is unimportant except as an adornment and a source of charm:

> Today I am most happy, for I see here a gathering of the servants of God. I see white and black sitting together. There are no whites and blacks before God. All colours are one, and that is the colour of servitude to God. Scent and colour are not important. The heart is important. If the heart is pure, white or black or any colour makes no difference. God does not look at colours; He looks at the hearts. He whose heart is pure is better. He whose character is better is more pleasing. He who turns more to the Abhá Kingdom is more advanced.[18]

In teaching the American believers about racial unity, 'Abdu'l-Bahá did not command. His appeal rather was to reason, to logic, to faith and to facts. He exposed the false hopes of the arrogant white race, not by disproof but by drawing in a quite natural manner a picture of the true antecedents of the Kingdom, showing it to be involved in the original creation of man.[19]

After Howard University, the Master had lunch with the Khans. Seated around the table were some of the most active Bahá'ís in America including Ali-Kuli Khan, his wife Florence and her mother Alice Breed, Agnes Parsons, Helen Goodall and Ella Cooper from California, Edward Getsinger, Juliet Thompson, Mason Remey and a few others, including the Turkish Ambassador, Ḍíyá Páshá. They were also part of the white social elite and 'Abdu'l-Bahá used the event to demonstrate the Bahá'í teachings and challenge the practice of social segregation:

> About nineteen guests were present at the luncheon. Some were 'very prominent in the social and political life of Washington' . . .
>
> About an hour before the luncheon 'Abdu'l-Bahá had sent word to Louis Gregory to come to the Khans' for an interview. 'Louis arrived at the appointed time, and the conference went on and on,' a good friend, Harlan Ober, has recounted. ' 'Abdu'l-Bahá seemed to want to prolong it.' Finally luncheon was announced, and, as 'Abdu'l-Bahá led the invited guests to the dining room, Mr Gregory waited for the chance to leave the house unobtrusively. 'All were seated when suddenly . . . 'Abdu'l-Bahá stood up, looked all around, and then said to Mírzá Khan, Where is Mr Gregory? Bring Mr Gregory! There was nothing for Mírzá Khan to do but find Mr Gregory . . . Finally Mr Gregory came into the room with Mírzá Khan. 'Abdu'l-Bahá, Who was really the Host . . . had by this time rearranged the place setting and made room for Mr Gregory, giving him the seat of honor at His right. He stated He was very pleased to have Mr Gregory there, and then, in the most natural way as if nothing had happened, proceeded to give a talk on the oneness of mankind.'[20]
>
> Gently yet unmistakably, 'Abdu'l-Bahá had assaulted the customs of a city that had been scandalized only a decade earlier by President Roosevelt's dinner invitation to Booker T. Washington [an eminent black scientist]. Moreover . . . the place setting that 'Abdu'l-Bahá

had rearranged so casually had been made according to the strict demands of Washington protocol.²¹

Interestingly, Agnes Parsons describes the scene above more briefly: 'There was some delay in the luncheon, as 'Abdu'l-Bahá saw fit to arrange the places of some of the guests.'²²

Before Agnes Parsons became a Bahá'í she had been a Christian Scientist and she asked 'Abdu'l-Bahá about mental suggestion as a cure for physical disease. The Master said that 'some illnesses, such as consumption and insanity, developed from spiritual causes – grief, for example – and that these could be healed by the spirit'. Mrs Parsons then asked if it might be possible that broken bones could also be healed by the spirit. On the table in front of them was a large bowl of salad. The Master indicated the salad and laughed: 'If all the spirits in the air were to congregate together, they could not create a salad! Nevertheless, the spirit of man is powerful. For the spirit of man can soar in the firmament of knowledge, can discover realities, can confer life, can receive the Divine Glad-Tidings. Is not this greater than making a salad?'²³

After the luncheon, Florence and Khan hosted a reception. In addition to the Turkish Ambassador and his family, Duke Lita and his wife, Admiral Robert Peary and Alexander Graham Bell were present. 'Abdu'l-Bahá gave a short talk and His words 'were simple and of captivating sweetness, a startling clarity'. Ḍíyá Páshá, a 'fierce Muhammadan', was riveted on the Master as He spoke. Afterwards he turned to Juliet Thompson and said: 'This is irrefutable. This is pure logic.'²⁴

Juliet Thompson was also there when 'Abdu'l-Bahá was introduced to Admiral Peary, who had 'just succeeded in publicly disgracing Captain Cook and proving himself, and not Captain Cook, the discoverer of the North Pole'. Juliet said that:

> . . . at that moment . . . he looked like a blown-up balloon.
>
> I was standing beside the Master when Khan brought the Admiral over and introduced him.
>
> The Master spoke charmingly to him and congratulated him on his discovery. Then, with the utmost sweetness, added these surprising words: For a very long time the world had been much concerned about the North Pole, where it was and what was to be found there. Now *he*, Admiral Peary, had discovered it and that *nothing* was to

be found there; and so, in forever relieving the public mind, he had rendered a great service.

I shall never forget Peary's nonplussed face. The balloon collapsed!²⁵

'Abdu'l-Bahá also suggested that the Admiral should 'explore the invisibilities of the Kingdom'.²⁶

Following the reception at the Persian Embassy, there was another at Mrs Parsons' house. But the long day was not yet over. Although very tired, the Master addressed a third meeting that evening to the Bethel Literary and Historical Society at the Metropolitan African Methodist Episcopal Church. 'I am reminded curiously of a beautiful bouquet of violets gathered together in varying colors, dark and light,' He began, before giving a profound talk on science and the benefits of research. 'All blessings are divine in origin, but none can be compared with this power of intellectual investigation and research, which is an eternal gift producing fruits of unending delight,' He said.²⁷

At that time, Washington was the most racially and socially mixed Bahá'í community in America, but it had deep racial unity problems. The upper classes, including people like Mr and Mrs Parsons, still upheld the long-standing social conventions of racial segregation that were not easily overcome. Many whites were afraid to host multiracial gatherings in their homes for fear of what others would say. Many blacks were also reluctant to attend meetings because of their fear of insults and discriminatory treatment. An example: once 'Abdu'l-Bahá said He wanted to host a unity Feast. A committee organized for the event selected one of the city's most exclusive hotels – one that was known for its refusal to admit black people. The black Bahá'ís thought it might be better if they did not attend and so avoid the problem of the colour bar. 'Abdu'l-Bahá, however, insisted they attend and in the end, all the Bahá'ís, both black and white, sat side by side in the previously segregated hotel.²⁸

Arthur Parsons once commented to 'Abdu'l-Bahá

> that he wished all the blacks would return to Africa, to which the Master wryly replied that such an exodus would have to begin with Wilber, the trusted butler of the Parsons household . . . It is remarkable, then, that 'Abdu'l-Bahá subsequently chose Agnes Parsons to

spearhead the Racial Amity campaign initiated by the Bahá'í community and just as remarkable that she transcended her social milieu in order to carry out this mandate.[29]

Nine-year-old Rene Hopper, her mother, Marie, and their cook, Eurithra, were staying with friends in Washington. The Hoppers took Eurithra to one of the meetings and the cook immediately recognized Who 'Abdu'l-Bahá was. Both Marie and Eurithra wished to serve the Master with their own hands so they invited Him to tea. 'Abdu'l-Bahá accepted, but attached the condition that they invited some black people. Since they were just visiting and the only black person they knew was Louis Gregory, they invited him. 'Abdu'l-Bahá came and Rene sat at His feet. Later, Rene and her mother had a private interview with the Master. Rene made a special basket filled with flowers to give to 'Abdu'l-Bahá. When He appeared at the door for their interview, Rene ran down the hall and into His outstretched arms. Rene learned a lesson about true giving that day when she saw another young girl leaving 'Abdu'l-Bahá's room with her special basket. At first, Rene was upset because of all the love she had put into making the basket, but when she thought about it, she realized what the true meaning of giving was.[30]

* * *

**Louisa Mathew and Louis Gregory**

The amazing story of the marriage of Louisa (Louise) Mathew, an Englishwoman, and Louis Gregory, a black American, actually began on 11 April 1911 in Alexandria, Egypt. Both Louisa and Louis were visiting 'Abdu'l-Bahá and were among the listeners that day when He said: 'Intermarriage is a good way to efface racial differences. It produces strong, beautiful offspring, clever and resourceful.'[31] Louis later wrote to Pauline Hannen, 'Last year we visited Abdul Baha at Ramleh and the Holy Tomb at Akka and although greatly attracted to each other not even dimly realized its future bearing . . .'[32]

'Abdu'l-Bahá invited Louisa to return to the United States with Him on the *Cedric*. When she joined Him in Naples, He asked her to go with Him for a walk on deck.

Then He turned round and said, 'I said what I did because I saw a seed in your heart.' Then almost immediately added, 'Now is the watering time.' I could not understand what He meant – I only thought it must be something of a spiritual nature. A moment later He turned round again and said, 'I saw one seed in your heart, I wish it to produce many seeds.'

In this country [United States] 'Abdu'l-Bahá first revealed to me symbolically, through a white flower which He told me to give to Mr Gregory and by looking at me in a peculiar way conveyed his meaning to me, that He wished me to marry Mr Gregory. Curiously enough after this love began to grow in my heart and the desire for the marriage whereas before I only liked Mr Gregory as a friend. Later 'Abdu'l-Bahá said before Dr Getsinger, Fareed and others in the train to Chicago to me, 'How are you and Mr Gregory getting along?' Startled I answered 'What do you mean, we are good friends?' To which He replied emphatically and with His face wreathed in mischievous smiles, 'You must become *very* good friends.'

Before He left Chicago I asked 'Abdu'l-Bahá plainly one morning early if I had understood aright that He wished Mr Gregory and myself to marry. He said 'yes'. He did wish it. 'I wish the white and the colored people to marry' He added.

Then on my intimating that as a woman I could do nothing to bring it about He asked, 'Do you love him, would you marry him if he asked you?' and I replied 'yes'. Then He said 'if he loves you he will ask you.' Later in the morning as I learnt some time afterwards, He told Louis it would give Him much pleasure if he and I would marry, which came as an utter surprise to Louis who had no thoughts of marriage. 'Abdu'l-Bahá said 'What is the matter? Don't you love her?' 'Yes, as a friend' Louis said. 'Well think of it' said 'Abdu'l-Bahá, 'and let me know; . . . marriage is not an ordinance and need not be obeyed, but it would give me much pleasure if you and Miss Mathew were to marry.'[33]

'Abdu'l-Bahá announced the marriage to the Bahá'í community while He was in Dublin, New Hampshire and the wedding was planned for 27 September in New York City. The Master was in Denver, Colorado, on His way to California on that day, but the union was His work and the ceremony was performed in the City of the Covenant, as He had expressly wished. The ceremony took place at a Church of England (Episcopal Church) with nine witnesses present, including the minister and his wife, and representatives of the Bahá'í Spiritual Assemblies of New York, Philadelphia and Washington.

The American Bahá'í communities had long misunderstood racial unity and interracial marriage and when 'Abdu'l-Bahá had invited the unsuspecting Miss Mathew to travel with Him on the *Cedric* to America, He had gradually prepared her to understand His wishes. They completely understood that 'Abdu'l-Bahá was using their union as an example. Their love for the Master gave them the courage to confront the social prejudices prevalent at the time and their marriage was long and happy. 'Abdu'l-Bahá wrote to them, 'I beg of God that through you good fellowship may be obtained between the white and the black for you are an introduction to the accomplishment.'[34]

Louis Gregory passed from this earthly plane in 1951. Six days after his passing, Shoghi Effendi appointed him a Hand of the Cause of God.

* * *

On 24 April Ali-Kuli Khan was driving 'Abdu'l-Bahá to the third meeting of the day, at the home of Alexander Graham Bell. 'Abdu'l-Bahá was in very good form and His voice rose loud enough to be heard over the noise of the car. People on the street could hear him saying: 'O Bahá'u'lláh! What hast Thou done?' Mr Bell had been present at the Khan's reception the day before and had been completely captivated. This man, who had invented the telephone in hopes of helping his deaf wife hear, was the president of a scientific society, which he had invited Master to address:

> After the Master was seated, discussion of scientific issues continued. Each spoke of his experiences and discussed his discoveries. After several people had spoken, Mr Bell asked Ali Kuli Khan . . . to relate the history of the Faith. Then Mr Bell thanked the Master for coming to his home and asked Him to address the guests.
>
> The Master began his talk by praising their good manners and praiseworthy qualities. He then spoke of the importance and the results of science, the greatness of this age and the interdependence

of society, and paid a glorious tribute to the new Dispensation. Mr Bell was extremely delighted and rose to thank the Master for His talk. The hearts of those present were so moved that when the next member arose to give his talk, he could only say, 'The talk of the Master from the East was so wonderful that I find myself inadequate to say anything' and sat down.[35]

During this first visit to Washington, Florence Khan had requested a photo of 'Abdu'l-Bahá with her children. 'Abdu'l-Bahá agreed, but it wasn't that simple with three lively children:

> Florence worried, thinking that if the photographer did not come upstairs at once, the three active children would play about and crush their well-ironed clothes. Everyone's garments were complicated then . . . and a maid could spend half an hour ironing an infant's lacy, layered dress.
> The youngest began running back and forth, to the Master, then away from Him.
> 'Come here!' He said to the tiny girl. 'Give me a kiss!'
> Hamideh leaned toward Him then coquettishly withdrew her face . . .
> 'Very well,' He said, 'if you will not kiss me, I will kiss you.'
> . . . The photographers came in and requested 'Abdu'l-Bahá to sit in a large chair while the children grouped about Him . . . The children were told to hold very still because there was going to be a flash and a loud noise.[36]

Charles and Mariam Haney took their young child Paul (the future Hand of the Cause of God) to a children's meeting on 25 April. At the meeting, the two-year-old infant screamed when he saw 'Abdu'l-Bahá and Agnes Parsons recalled:

> I thought at the time, that the child had probably been overwhelmed by seeing a greater spirituality in 'Abdu'l-Bahá than many saw. I spoke of this to Mr and Mrs Haney, for the latter had shown such distress when it occurred. I believe Mr Haney agreed with me. He said: "Three months before the child was born we were in Acca . . . I told ['Abdu'l-Bahá] I thought the baby had been conscious of

more than we were, and 'Abdu'l-Bahá's answer was, "You have much insight".³⁷

(When Paul was born, his mother had written to 'Abdu'l-Bahá and the Master had bestowed His own name, 'Abdu'l-Bahá, on the child. Paul became a very active Bahá'í and served on the National Spiritual Assembly of the United States and Canada and on its southern successor, the National Spiritual Assembly of the United States. Shoghi Effendi appointed him a Hand of the Cause of God in 1954 immediately after the death of Hand of the Cause Dorothy Baker.)

That evening, 25 April, the Turkish Ambassador, Ḍíyá Páshá, hosted a dinner for 'Abdu'l-Bahá. The Ambassador asked the Khans for a guest list of Bahá'ís. On the night, Florence Khan was seated on 'Abdu'l-Bahá's right with the Ambassador directly across from the Master. Roses filled the tables and were piled up in the centre of the table where 'Abdu'l-Bahá and Ḍíyá Páshá were seated. The Ambassador beamed his happiness. 'Abdu'l-Bahá gave a short talk which Ali-Kuli Khan translated. He mentioned Rudyard Kipling's famous line, 'East is East, and West is West and never the twain shall meet.' Then He pointed to the Khans and to the Ambassador's beautiful American daughter-in-law and said, 'The East and West have already met, apparently with happy results, and in future these unions will increase.'³⁸ Afterwards, the Ambassador walked the Master to his carriage.

One of the guests was the Ambassador's nephew, Mírzá Zia. Mrs Parsons met the young man a few years later at Green Acre and asked when he had become a Bahá'í. Mírzá Zia answered that he had become a Bahá'í the night of his uncle's dinner party.³⁹ Ḍíyá Páshá became enamoured with 'Abdu'l-Bahá and in the following days called on him almost daily. The Master reciprocated and commonly invited the Ambassador to go with Him as He drove around the city.

While in Washington, Juliet Thompson had a lesson in obedience. She recorded the event:

> I was so thankful to be in Washington. At those daily meetings in Mrs Parsons' house I would see many of my old friends, friends of my childhood. Mrs Elkins went with me every day to the meetings: sometimes, when all the chairs were taken, standing the whole afternoon, although she was far from well.

One day, however, she was not with me. That night she was giving a small dinner and an opera party and she had to rest for this. So, being free for an hour or so, I decided to stay at Mrs Parsons' and have a little visit with Edna.

While Edna and I were talking, the Master suddenly entered the room. 'I am going out for a drive,' He said, 'but wait till I return, Edna, and you too, Juliet, wait. I will see you in a short time.'

So I waited – waited and waited. Half-past six came. Seven. We were to dine at half-past seven and the Elkinses' house was a long way off, rather indirect on the car-line.

'Go, Juliet,' urged Edna. 'I will explain.'

But how could I? My Lord had told me to stay.

And now I shall have to digress and tell what may seem, just at first, another story: When I was ten years old, (and I remember the time because that year we were living with my grandmother) a very presumptuous idea took possession of me. I began to dream of some day painting the Christ. I even prayed that I might. 'O God,' I would pray, 'You know Christ didn't look like a woman, the way all the pictures of Him look. *Please* let me paint Him when I grow up as the King of Men.' And I never lost hope of this till I saw the Master. Then I knew that no one could paint the Christ. Could the sun with the whole universe full of its radiations, or endless flashes of lightning be captured in paint?

Imagine my surprise and dismay, fear, joy and gratitude all mixed together, at the news given me by Mrs Gibbons when the Master first came to New York. The night before He landed she had received a Tablet in which He said: 'On My arrival in America Miss Juliet Thompson shall paint a wonderful portrait of Me.' This was in response to a supplication from Mrs Gibbons asking that her daughter might paint Him, which she never did, though the Master graciously gave her permission, even more graciously adding those words about me.

It was a little after seven when the Master came back from His drive. Entering the room in which He had left me and where of course I was still waiting, He said: 'Ah, Juliet! For your sake I returned. Mrs Hemmick wanted to keep Me, but I had asked you to wait; therefore I returned.' After a pause He added: 'Would you like to come up and paint Me tomorrow?'

So I learned the reward of obedience. *Such* a reward for so small an act of obedience! Once in Haifa He said to me: 'Keep My words, obey My commands and you will marvel at the results.'[40]

One day 'Abdu'l-Bahá was with Juliet and told her that 'she teaches well'. He then went on to say:

> I have met many people who have been affected by you, Juliet. You are not eloquent, you are not fluent, but your *heart* teaches. You speak with a feeling, an emotion which makes people ask: 'What is this she has?' Then they inquire; they seek and find. It is so too with Lua [Getsinger]. You never find Lua speaking with dry eyes! You will be confirmed. A great bounty will descend upon you. You will become eloquent. Your tongue will be loosed. Teach, always teach. The confirmations of the Holy Spirit descend upon those who teach constantly. Never feel fear. The Holy Spirit will give you the words to say. *Never fear.* You will grow stronger and stronger.[41]

In His last few days in Washington, 'Abdu'l-Bahá met many important people. On the evening of the Turkish Ambassador's dinner party, after 'Abdu'l-Bahá had returned to the Parsons' home, former President Theodore Roosevelt came to see him. Others who met 'Abdu'l-Bahá in Washington included Mabel Boardman, National Secretary of the American Red Cross; Mrs Colonel House, the wife of a confidant of Woodrow Wilson; and the Honourable William Sulzer, who later became the Governor of New York. After a half hour with the Master, Sulzer said, 'I feel as though I have met Elijah. As though I have talked with Moses.'[42]

A few newspapers had written that 'The enemy of Christ has arrived' and one night, after 'Abdu'l-Bahá had given a talk to a very large group of people in a Washington church, someone threw a bundle of pamphlets into His carriage. The pamphlet declared that 'These Bahá'ís are the enemies of Christ and they are destroying his edifice. Is it permissible that we leave Christ, who has given his life for us for this person?' 'Abdu'l-Bahá said, however, that no one paid any attention to the pamphlets and everyone showed their joy and appreciation at the message the He had delivered.[43]

On 27 April Mrs Parsons hosted a reception, with refreshments, for 'Abdu'l-Bahá. Three hundred people, all in formal dress, attended and each reverently paid their respects to the Master. 'Abdu'l-Bahá then went to a private room where He met many of the guests individually. When He met Admiral Wainwright, the Master told him that he was a good admiral because he stood for peace. The Admiral replied that was because 'My wife makes me do so!'[44]

One of 'Abdu'l-Bahá's visitors was the US Secretary of the Treasury, Lee McClung, with whom He breakfasted the following day. McClung's comment after meeting 'Abdu'l-Bahá was: 'I felt as if I were in the presence of a great Prophet – Isaiah – Elijah – no, that is not it. The presence of Christ – no. I felt as if I were in the presence of my Divine Father.'[45] 'Abdu'l-Bahá was introduced to a member of the US Supreme Court to whom He said, 'It is possible to establish such unity among the powers of the whole world as is found in the United States of America.'[46]

Mrs Parsons saw a young woman at the meeting, Mrs Niles, with whom she'd had a bond since the younger woman was a child. When Mrs Parsons found out that Mrs Niles had yet to meet 'Abdu'l-Bahá, she brought her to the Master and introduced her. She records that 'Abdu'l-Bahá, looking from one to the other and immediately understanding their bond, said: '"Mother; daughter." I replied: "She has a very lovely mother of her own." Then He turned to her and said: "You are very fortunate to have two mothers."'[47]

'Abdu'l-Bahá left Washington for Chicago at 5.30 p.m. on 28 April. While he was preparing to leave, the British Ambassador very humbly and reverently paid Him a final visit. To see Him off were the Turkish Ambassador and his son, the Khans, Mason Remey and a few others. The train crossed the Potomac River and into Virginia, where 'Abdu'l-Bahá praised the green scenery. The greenery, however, then made Him sad: 'Whenever I see such scenes, I feel great sorrow, for the Blessed Beauty liked verdure and greenery very much. God shall never pardon those who imprisoned Him in that place.'[48] Maḥmúd-i-Zarqání noted that the Master praised the sleeping cars and their cleanliness and the electric lights, but because of the train's speed, He was unable to sleep.

# 8

# THE MOTHER TEMPLE OF THE WEST
## *29 April–11 May*

### CHICAGO, ILLINOIS

'Abdu'l-Bahá and His group travelled on the train all the next day, not reaching Chicago until the night of 29 April. Because of some misunderstanding about His schedule, 170 delegates to a Bahá'í convention waited in vain for His appearance. This prompted the *Chicago Daily News* to headline: 'BAHAIST CHIEF MISSING'. It went on to ask, 'Where is Abdul-Baha, son of Baha'o'llah . . . who was coming to Chicago to-day to preach the universal brotherhood of man? Chicago Bahaists – there are said to be 40,000,000 followers in the world – asked each other this question and failed to find an answer.'[1]

Then after 'Abdu'l-Bahá did arrive, the Chicago newspapers covered the story:

PROPHET ABDUL BAHA HERE – *Chicago Examiner* which also reported that the Faith had 15,000,000 followers.

WORLD HARMONY IS AIM OF ABDUL-BAHA – *Chicago Inter-Ocean* which reported that there were 40,000,000 Bahá'ís.

BELIEVE ABDUL BAHA MAY BE SECOND DOWIE . . . SEE POSSIBLE FULFILLMENT OF PROPHECY – *Chicago Examiner* reporting that the leader of the Dowie Church in Zion City had prophesied that a new prophet would appear in Zion in 1912.

The *Chicago Advance* was quite caustic, stating that 'Bahaism may be summed up in the word that "nothing matters". All religions are equally true or equally false, as you may choose to put it. It seems to have but one article in its creed and that is "universal tolerance". As a civil creed that is sound. As an ethical creed that is rotten.'² The *Chicago Daily News* wrote that 'Abdu'l-Bahá was not happy with some of the coverage. It reported that 'Abdu'l-Bahá said:

> 'A reporter must be a purveyor of truth . . . The newspapers are leaders of the people and the people must be able to rely on what they read. Now, some reporter on a Chicago morning newspaper said that I wore a gown and turban with red and white stripes. I never wore such colours. He said my beard reached to my waist. Look at it.' The beard, in truth, came scarcely to the chest.³

'Abdu'l-Bahá immediately brought up the subject of unity and the oneness of humanity in relation to racial unity at His first meeting at Hull House. One example of this disunity was given by Maḥmúd-i-Zarqání:

> One day, Dr Zia Bagdadi invited Mr [Louis] Gregory, a black Bahá'í, to his home. When his landlord heard about this, he gave notice to Dr Bagdadi to vacate his residence because he had had a black man in his home.⁴

On one of the first days the Master was in Chicago, Maria Ioas took her son Monroe and went to see Him. One of her greatest desires was to be given a flower that 'Abdu'l-Bahá had held in His hand. She had thought about asking pilgrims who were going to 'Akká to bring her one, but had decided that it would be presumptuous on her part. Maria and Monroe had to wait at the Plaza Hotel the entire afternoon until He finally returned from His engagements. When He arrived at the hotel and saw them, He greeted them lovingly and told them to come to His room. Maria hesitated, knowing how tired He must be, but He again beckoned her to follow. One of His interpreters then quietly said: 'When 'Abdu'l-Bahá says come, you must come.' So she and Monroe followed the Master into His reception room. Moments later, He emerged from His private room with roses and smilingly handed one to her.⁵

## Leroy Ioas

Maria's son, 17-year-old Leroy Ioas, also went to see the Master when He was staying at the Plaza Hotel. Leroy had a great interest in Bahá'u'lláh and 'Abdu'l-Bahá, and was very eager to meet the Master. As the group of Bahá'ís hurried towards the hotel Leroy suddenly said that they must hurry because the Master was leaving by the far side of the building. When his father asked how he knew, Leroy said that he could see the light radiating from Him. So they ran around to the other door and found 'Abdu'l-Bahá leaving, just as Leroy had stated. Leroy and his father paused, not wanting to delay the Master, but He motioned them to come. When they hesitated, He motioned again. When Leroy took the Master's outstretched hand, he used both of his hands because he wanted to see if 'Abdu'l-Bahá had hands like ordinary people. Leroy later said, 'As I looked at the Master, I saw His physical form, but shining through it were flashes of light, flashes of light, bright and shining. The spiritual power simply flooded through Him and I was overcome.'[6]

Leroy loved to watch 'Abdu'l-Bahá's eyes. He said that they were 'ever-changing, now stern, now loving, filled with all the pathos of the world and then again, all its joy. Everything was revealed in His eyes, what one saw depended entirely upon what the Master was thinking.' While listening to the Master, Leroy once wished that He would look into his eyes – which the Master did almost immediately. Leroy said that 'It was as if He looked through you, as if He saw your soul, before your beginning and beyond your ending.'[7]

On another day, Leroy went to see 'Abdu'l-Bahá and on the way he bought a large bunch of white carnations to give to the Master. By the time he arrived at the hotel, however, Leroy had decided not to give the Master the flowers. When his father asked him why, Leroy said 'I'm not going to take them. I come to the Master offering Him my heart and I do not want Him to think I am currying favor.' So, Leroy's father then presented the flowers to 'Abdu'l-Bahá who was delighted with their fragrance. After the Master finished His talk, He shook the hand of every visitor and gave each person one of Leroy's carnations. Then Leroy began to hope that he would be able to shake hands with 'Abdu'l-Bahá before all the carnations were gone. Just as he had that thought, 'Abdu'l-Bahá turned to him, took a red rose from His coat, pricking His finger in the process, and gave the rose with the drop of His blood to Leroy. Leroy then knew that the Master knew who had given Him the carnations.⁸

Leroy Ioas was elected to the National Spiritual Assembly in 1932 and served as its chairman for fourteen years. He was named a Hand of the Cause of God in 1951; he was called to serve the Guardian in Haifa in 1953 and did so until his passing in 1965, notably as Secretary-General of the first International Bahá'í Council and in the construction of the superstructure of the Shrine of the Báb. One of the doors of the Shrine bears his name in honour of his services.

**Corinne True**

When Corinne True was on pilgrimage in 1907, she brought with her a petition from the Chicago House of Spirituality (an early form of what would become a Bahá'í Spiritual Assembly), with a list of signatures of those who wished to build a Bahá'í House of Worship, a Mashriqu'l-Adhkár. It was a rather audacious proposal from such a small group who really had no idea how audacious the idea actually was. In 'Akká, Mrs True was presenting 'Abdu'l-Bahá with various pieces of correspondence when the Master suddenly indicated the as yet unmentioned roll wrapped in brown paper, stating that it was about the Mashriqu'l-Adhkár, the American Temple.

After Mrs True described the countryside around Chicago, 'Abdu'l-Bahá told her that the Temple should be located away from the busy centre of the city, but close to the shore of Lake Michigan because of the beauty of a lakeside location. He told her, 'First the building, with nine sides, in the middle; then a circular court about that; leading from this circle were to be nine avenues; between each a garden, and in the middle of each garden a fountain of water.' 'Abdu'l-Bahá also told her that the project would cause her to suffer and be misunderstood and that she would have to pray for strength.⁹

When she asked 'Abdu'l-Bahá what He wanted her to do upon her return. He replied, 'I wish you to live in Chicago. I wish you to work for the Mashriqu'l-Adhkár.' The Master then took her hand and she felt as though 'a great power was pulsing through her'.

Thornton Chase, named by the Master as the first American Bahá'í, along with Carl Scheffler and Arthur Agnew, members of Chicago's

House of Spirituality, arrived in the Holy Land right after Corinne True had departed and 'Abdu'l-Bahá surprised them all when, responding to a question by Mr Chase about the Temple, He said, 'When you return consult with Mrs True – I have given her complete instructions.' These directions baffled the three men because, up to that point, only men had served on the House of Spirituality and were involved in decision-making.

Being given the responsibility for the Temple was extremely challenging, particularly as a woman in a country where women did not yet have the opportunity to vote. Because of the marked individualism of those days in the Bahá'í community, there were many 'philosophical' differences. The Bahá'ís of that time were immature in the ways of the Faith and 'Abdu'l-Bahá used Corinne True to begin a transformation of the Bahá'í community. 'Abdu'l-Bahá encouraged her to consult with the House of Spirituality, but disunity grew. Based on her talks with 'Abdu'l-Bahá, she searched for a suitable temple site north of Chicago while the House of Spirituality looked to the south. Finally, a site to the north, where the temple now stands, was selected, though unity was far from complete.

Corinne True wanted a nation-wide committee to develop the Temple plans so that it would not be just Chicago's Temple, but America's (which at that time also included Canadian believers). When 'Abdu'l-Bahá enthusiastically approved of this plan, things moved forward. The next thing 'Abdu'l-Bahá did was send the Americans a Tablet in which He stated that women should be on the new national committee. With this directive, the Bahá'í Temple Unity was created and three women, including Corinne True, were elected to the Executive.

Corinne had desperately wished to meet 'Abdu'l-Bahá when He landed in New York, but her son Davis was critically ill. When 'Abdu'l-Bahá finally arrived in Chicago, one of the first things He did on the morning of 30 April was to go to the True home to see Davis. After the visit, He told Corinne that Davis was better than expected, which she took to mean that he would recover. All that afternoon, Corinne was busy with 'Abdu'l-Bahá. The final meeting was the Bahá'í Temple Unity Convention where 1,000 people heard the Master speak on the significance of the Temple. From His talk, Corinne realized that the Temple wasn't simply something to unite the American Bahá'ís, but an instrument to unite all humankind.

While the Master kept Corinne busy, her son Davis passed away and she later realized that when He had said that Davis was better than expected, He really meant spiritually. In spite of her son's death, she was at the Temple site the next day. The day after the Temple dedication, the True family held a Bahá'í funeral for their son. Later 'Abdu'l-Bahá went to the cemetery and prayed not only for her son, but for other children buried there. Davis was the fourth son she had lost. Nathanael had died in 1899 and Kenneth in 1900, both due to heart failure caused by a new drug. Laurence drowned in 1906 and her husband, Moses, died in 1909. No men of her family were left.

Corinne True was raised by Shoghi Effendi to the rank of Hand of the Cause of God in 1952.[10]

\* \* \*

On 30 April, 'Abdu'l-Bahá told the more than 1,000 people gathered at the closing session of the Bahá'í Temple Unity Convention that:

> Among the institutes of the Holy Books is that of the foundation of places of worship. That is to say, an edifice or temple is to be built in order that humanity might find a place of meeting, and this is to be conducive to unity and fellowship among them. The real temple is the very Word of God; for to it all humanity must turn, and it is the centre of unity for all mankind. It is the collective centre, the cause of accord and communion of hearts, the sign of the solidarity of the human race, the source of eternal life. Temples are the symbols of the divine uniting force so that when the people gather there in the House of God they may recall the fact that the law has been revealed for them and that the law is to unite them. They will realize that just as this temple was founded for the unification of mankind, the law preceding and creating it came forth in the manifest Word.[11]

1 May was an extremely important day for the Chicago Bahá'í community – 'Abdu'l-Bahá was going to dedicate the site of the Mashriqu'l-Adhkár. Before the dedication, the Master had a special early morning meeting with the Bahá'ís who had come from California for the Convention and the Temple dedication, joined by Elizabeth Muther from Honolulu. When Dr Frederick D'Evelyn said that California was the Golden State,

'Abdu'l-Bahá replied that He hoped it would become the Diamond State and that He expected great things from its Bahá'ís.[12]

At the Temple dedication, a marquee large enough to hold 300 people had been set up. A special entrance had been made on the eastern side so that 'Abdu'l-Bahá's carriage could enter easily. 'Abdu'l-Bahá, however, arrived later than expected by taxi and, instead of using the special entrance, called for Mrs True to enter the taxi, then continued around the property, ending up on the northern side.[13] When He finally dismounted from the taxi, 'the majesty and simplicity of his mien as he briskly advanced on foot toward the tent – a far spread line of the friends forming an escort just behind him – constitute a scene which will be remembered by those who witnessed it as one of the most impressive experiences of their lives.' Inside the tent, the 300 seats were arranged in three concentric circles, with nine aisles separating blocks of seats and an open space in the centre.[14]

A committee had spent several sessions trying to put together a programme, but 'in the event itself, it was joyfully realized by the committee . . . that 'Abdu'l-Bahá needed no guidance other than that of the Holy Spirit.'[15] As the tent filled, young Leroy Ioas scrambled inside and 'squeezed up in front and sat on the ground to be right next to what was going on' and to be close to 'Abdu'l-Bahá.[16] When the 300 seats were filled and with 200 more people standing around the outside edge of the tent, 'Abdu'l-Bahá began His talk on the power of the Cause of Bahá'u'lláh and about the importance of the Houses of Worship in America and 'Ishqábád, saying:

> The power which has gathered you here today notwithstanding the cold and windy weather is, indeed, mighty and wonderful. It is the power of God, the divine favor of Baha'u'llah which has drawn you together. We praise God that through His constraining love human souls are assembled and associated in this way.
>
> Thousands of Mashriqu'l-Adhkárs, dawning points of praise and mention of God for all religionists will be built in the East and in the West, but this, being the first one erected in the Occident, has great importance. In the future there will be many here and elsewhere – in Asia, Europe, even in Africa, New Zealand and Australia – but this edifice in Chicago is of especial significance.[17]

During his talk, 'Abdu'l-Bahá noticed someone in the crowd shivering. He paused His oration to say 'I'm afraid you are cold.' 'We're not!' came back the reply. 'Then you are denizens of Chicago,' 'Abdu'l-Bahá said.[18]

After the talk, 'Abdu'l-Bahá led the crowd to the nearby ceremonial site 'where in the great amphitheatre afforded by the panorama of woods, fields and the expanse of water', ground was to be broken.[19] The Master asked where the centre of the temple site was located and prepared to begin the hole for the cornerstone.

But all didn't go according to plan. Irene Holmes, from New York, handed 'Abdu'l-Bahá a golden trowel to dig the hole for the dedication stone. But it wasn't strong enough to break through the ground. 'Abdu'l-Bahá called for stronger tools, and

> an ax, borrowed from someone across the street, was handed to 'Abdu'l-Bahá, who swung it powerfully, again and again, until He broke into the earth below. Finally, a shovel was produced by a young man who had borrowed it from a work crew . . . When the shovel was handed to the Master, Corinne True reportedly suggested to Him to have women participate in the ceremony. 'Abdu'l-Bahá called on Lua Getsinger to come forward . . . Corinne was the second one to dig up a shovelful of earth. Following her, representatives from different races and nationalities took their turn with the shovel. After placing the stone in the hole, the Master pushed the earth around it and declared that 'The Temple is already built.'[20]

As everyone else began to leave, Leroy Ioas and Charlie Greenleaf 'rushed to get some of the soil 'Abdu'l-Bahá had dug from the ground' as a remembrance of the day. Greenleaf asked 'Abdu'l-Bahá to bless his handful of earth.[21]

The story of the dedication stone is interesting in its own right. When the Temple had been first proposed in 1903, a Persian Bahá'í had sent a letter to the American Bahá'ís saying that 'the glory and honour of the first stone is equivalent to all the stones and implements which will later be used there'. This excited Nettie (Esther) Tobin, 'a loving, humble woman who earned a meagre living as a seamstress'. Praying that God would send her something she could offer as a gift, she went to a nearby construction site, told the foreman about the Temple, and asked if she could have an inexpensive building stone. The foreman liked her story and showed her a pile of broken limestone blocks that were no good for building and said she could take one. With the help of a neighbour, she wrapped her stone in a piece of carpet, tied on a clothesline and dragged it home.

To get the stone to the Temple site, it was carried by hand on two different streetcars, dragged on the ground, and carried in a wheelbarrow. One of the streetcar conductors was not thrilled to have a rock on board, but finally allowed them to put it on the back platform. The last six blocks from the closest streetcar station were the most difficult. At first, Nettie, her brother Leo Leadroot, and Mírzá Mazlúm, an elderly Persian Bahá'í neighbour, tried to carry the stone, but after three blocks they were exhausted. Corinne True and Cecilia Harrison had been waiting at the Temple site for them and finally went to look for them. Mírzá Mazlúm had the three women put the stone on his back and he managed to stagger another half block before coming to the end of his endurance. The stone was left there overnight. Nettie came back the next morning with a homemade cart. Trying to load the stone into the cart by herself, she managed to break the handle of the cart and injure her wrist. A helpful fellow repaired her cart and helped her load the stone into it. With two blocks to go, Nettie managed to persuade a newsboy to help her get the cart to the western corner of the Temple land and onto the site, where the cart abruptly collapsed in pieces. There, the stone stayed. People in other parts of the world, including 'Abdu'l-Bahá, sent stones for the Temple, but none ever arrived. So, on the day He broke the ground, only Nettie Tobin's contribution of "the stone which the builders refused" would be available to serve as the marker dedicated by 'Abdu'l-Bahá'.[22]

Mary Revell of Philadelphia attended the dedication meeting and secretly hoped to kiss the hem of 'Abdu'l-Bahá's robe, something a Bahá'í in Iran had written and asked her to do. Unfortunately, the Master was on the far side of the crowd until, suddenly, He walked directly over to Mary and stood in front of her just long enough for her to accomplish her great desire.[23]

One California Bahá'í, Georgiana Dean, had moved from the west coast at the request of 'Abdu'l-Bahá to care for Mrs Dealy, who was going blind. Miss Dean had abandoned a good job and a love for California to fulfil the Master's request. When Miss Dean met the other California Bahá'ís, she was overwhelmed by homesickness. Harriet Cline suggested she take her problem to 'Abdu'l-Bahá, which she did. When Miss Dean returned from her interview, 'tears were streaming down her face, but it shone with a radiance I have seldom seen. "He told me to stay with Mrs Dealy as long as she needed me, and I am going to obey with all my heart and soul."' Through her sincerity, however, her prayers were answered. Within a few days, Mrs Dealy no longer needed her and she was able to return to California.[24]

On 30 April Mrs Dealy attended a meeting when 'Abdu'l-Bahá spoke at the Masonic Temple in Chicago. There were more than 1,000 people at the meeting, but Mrs Dealy hoped to see the Master. She sent her son, Paul, to request that 'Abdu'l-Bahá talk with her. One of the Master's interpreters told her to sit on the aisle where 'Abdu'l-Bahá would leave. Leroy Ioas remembered that:

> As the Master went up the aisle He stopped and greeted her lovingly. She reached for His hand and said, "Abdu'l-Bahá, please put your hand on my forehead, and I *know* that I will see.' 'Yes, my daughter,' He answered, 'you will see. But you will have to choose. You may have your spiritual sight or your physical sight – which do you desire?' She said with emotion: 'Abdu'l-Bahá, that is no choice! I would be blind a thousand years before I would give up my spiritual sight!' 'Well said, my daughter, well said,' replied the Master as He touched her shoulder and continued on His way out. Sitting next to her on that bench, Leroy realized with a chill how in that moment she had decided on her destiny. She was steadfast.[25]

Mrs Dealy said that 'Abdu'l-Bahá told her that, though her physical sight was lost, 'she would see visions of the Kingdom and live ever in the unseen light. And she says it was true' and that she had many visions of the Master.[26]

Ella Bailey, one of the Californians who had come to see Him, had her private interview one day. She later said that He had repeated her name several times:

> 'Oh, Ella Bailey, Ella Bailey! Oh, Ella Bailey, Ella Bailey! Oh Ella Bailey!' . . . He kept repeating my name as He looked off into space. But He put into my name every possible emotion. That was the wonder of it.

> ... In those few words he gave me all the emotions of a lifetime. He gave suffering but with it He gave me faith and strength. This made me feel His spiritual power and His truth.[27]

'Abdu'l-Bahá expressed a desire to go to the Chicago zoo. He had never seen a large zoo, so on 3 May He was very happy as they made ready to go. Someone told Him that, since this was spring, most of the animals would have new babies and they would keep in hiding. 'Abdu'l-Bahá went in any case with a group of five or six. As they approached the animals, He motioned to the others to stay behind and He went forward on His own. 'As He approached each cage, the small animal-mother brought out all her babies to show Him, then hurried them back to safety and protection from the following friends.'[28]

One day, 'Abdu'l-Bahá and a group of friends were under a grove of trees near Lake Michigan and He said: 'Some of you may have observed that I have not called attention to any of your individual shortcomings. I would suggest to you, that if you shall be similarly considerate in your treatment of each other, it will be greatly conducive to the harmony of your association with each other.'[29]

On 5 May, 'Abdu'l-Bahá met with a group of 35 children in the hotel's salon. After listening to them sing the song *Softly His Voice is Calling Now*, the Master called each child to Him individually. Some He took on His lap, others He kissed or stroked their hair:

> ... all with such infinite love and tenderness shining in His eyes and thrilling in the tones of His voice, that when He whispered in English in their ears to tell Him their names, they answered as joyfully and freely as they would a beloved father ... The children's joy and His own happiness seemed to culminate when one dear little tot ran to Him and fairly threw herself into His arms.[30]

Afterwards, 'Abdu'l-Bahá gave each child an envelope full of rose petals, then invited them all to Lincoln Park across the road from the hotel for a photograph. He then asked for time alone and walked over to a statue of Abraham Lincoln, at which He gazed for a while. One photograph was taken of 'Abdu'l-Bahá with Musette Jones and Joseph Ioas. When a copy of the photo was later shown to the Master, He wrote over the little girl's heart, *'Rouhieh'*, which meant 'spiritual'.[31]

'Abdu'l-Bahá greatly enjoyed the children. Years later He said, 'I had them gathered. It was very good. They were very spiritual children. There was a little girl there. Jokingly I said to her: "I want you to marry this boy." She said: "I want an Eastern husband."'[32]

Two days earlier, 'Abdu'l-Bahá had granted a final interview to Harriet Cline and Henrietta Wagner, who were to leave for California the following day. They waited for their interview with many others until someone announced, 'There will be no more interviews this morning.' The two women were crushed and sat there in shock at the thought of going home without seeing the Master one last time. But then came the Master's melodious voice calling, 'Mrs Cline and Mrs Wagner'. When Mrs Cline entered 'Abdu'l-Bahá's presence, He put an arm around her and said, 'You are my daughter, you are my daughter, I have prayed for you many, many times.' Her tears poured out uncontrollably until she looked up into 'Abdu'l-Bahá's eyes. His smile and happiness suddenly filled her and, she said, a 'sense of great inner calmness took possession of my soul'. Mrs Cline was then able to give Him a message from the Bahá'ís of Tropico, a suburb of Los Angeles, 'and told him how they were praying that he would come to California.'[33] But for long weeks and months, it was not clear whether he would go to California or not.

## WILL 'ABDU'L-BAHÁ GO TO CALIFORNIA?

In April, Bahá'ís on the West Coast feared that 'Abdu'l-Bahá would not be visiting them, so they went to visit Him. Just as John Bosch had done, Helen Goodall, Ella Cooper and Ella Bailey travelled across the country to meet him. Arriving in Washington, they followed him when he went to Chicago, where they were joined by the other Californian Bahá'ís who had come as delegates to the Convention, and were able to stay in 'Abdu'l-Bahá's hotel. One day, 'Abdu'l-Bahá sent for Mrs Goodall, Mrs Cooper and Miss Bailey.

> Earlier in the day they had put flowers in His room for which He now thanked them . . . saying: 'You are more to me than the flowers for you are my living flowers. These flowers have only colour, but you have life . . .'
>
> Another day He said: 'Mrs Goodall's value is not known now; it will be in the future. She has no other thought than to serve the

Cause. God has certain treasuries hidden in the world which he reveals when the time comes. She is like one of these treasuries.'[34]

Filled with humility and thankfulness, most of the California party returned home to find a telegram from 'Abdu'l-Bahá in Chicago which read 'will be here one week after which I go to Boston and Montreal then come to California. Will see you there in June God willing.'[35]

'Abdu'l-Bahá had asked Lua Getsinger to travel to California in advance of his visit, as she wrote to a friend on 25 May, although, she wrote, 'it is not definitely decided'.[36] But about a month later, Helen Goodall and Ella Cooper were surprised to receive a telegram from the Master summoning them to New York. At that point, 'Abdu'l-Bahá planned to leave for the Orient after New York and He wished to see them before he left. The Bahá'ís in California had almost given up all hope of seeing 'Abdu'l-Bahá in the west and were sending a stream of letters expressing their disappointment.[37]

Harriet Wise had a message from 'Abdu'l-Bahá to the California Bahá'ís that read:

> Convey to them my greetings and love. It has become necessary to depart for the Orient. Certain obligations have come up, so I must depart for the Orient. I move according to Divine Wisdom. I have infinite longing to meet you, but what happens now is according to Divine Wisdom, that is, I must depart for the East. Altho I leave, yet my heart is with you. There is no separation between us and I am never free from mentioning your names.[38]

The West Coast Bahá'ís desperately wanted 'Abdu'l-Bahá to visit, but it remained just a hope for many months. On 24 June John Bosch and Luther Burbank received a Tablet from 'Abdu'l-Bahá which read, 'As to my coming to California it is a little doubtful, for the trip is far and the weather hot and from the labours of the journey the body of 'Abdu'l-Bahá hath not much endurance. Nevertheless we shall see what God hath decreed.'[39]

On 3 July Lua Getsinger wrote to Agnes Parsons saying 'His going to Cal. at all is doubtful.' Lua herself, though, was still to go to California: 'I am commanded to return there and teach the Cause! It is very difficult to leave the Beloved – Yet, I do gladly and willingly . . .'[40] But according to Juliet Thompson, Lua was so traumatized by the idea of leaving Him that in an attempt to delay, she deliberately went into the woods and walked through poison ivy. Later, in bed with her feet terribly swollen:

> '*Look* at me, Julie,' she said. '*Look* at my feet. Oh, please go right back to the Master and tell Him about them and say: 'How can Lua travel now?'
>
> I did it, returned to the Master's house, found Him in His room and put Lua's question to Him. He laughed, then crossed the room to a table on which stood a bowl of fruit, and, selecting an apple and a pomegranate, gave them to me.
>
> 'Take these to Lua,' He said. 'Tell her to eat them and she will be cured. Spend the day with her, Juliet.'
>
> Oh precious Lua – strange mixture of disobedience and obedience – and all from love! I shall never forget her, seizing first the apple, then the pomegranate and gravely chewing them all the way through till not even a pomegranate seed was left: thoroughly eating her cure, which was certain to send her to California.
>
> In the late afternoon we were happily surprised by a visit from the Master Himself. He drew back the sheet and looked at Lua's feet, which by that time were beautifully slim. Then He burst out laughing.
>
> 'See,' He said, 'I have cured Lua with an apple and a pomegranate.'
>
> But Lua revolted again. There was one more thing she could try, and she tried it. The Master had asked me to paint her portrait and I had already had one sitting. The following day, at the Master's house, she drew me aside.
>
> 'Please, Julie, do something else for me. Go to the Master, now, and say: 'If Lua is in California, how can I paint her?'
>
> I went straight to His room with Valíyu'lláh Khán to translate. 'My Lord,' I said, 'You have commanded me to paint Lua. If she is in California and I here, how can I do it? The portrait is begun; how can I finish it?'
>
> Again the Master burst out laughing, for this of course was too transparent.
>
> 'In a year,' He said, 'Lua will join Me in Egypt. She will stay in New York a few days on her way to Me and you can paint her then, Juliet.'

So poor Lua had to go to California. There was no way out for her. ⁴¹

Lua probably left for California about 11 July; three weeks later she again wrote to Agnes Parsons from San Francisco revealing the despair of the Californians:

> The Doctor says I am on the verge of collapse . . . But I am trusting in the Words of 'Abdu'l-Bahá to make me strong and well – hoping the confirmations of the Holy Spirit through the Center of the Covenant will enable me to arise and serve in the Cause better then I have ever done. It was very difficult for me to leave 'Abdu'l-Bahá – for His Face spells <u>home</u> and all that is worth while in this <u>material</u> world for me.
>
> I am poor comfort to the people here who were expecting to see Him waiting anxiously and longing for His coming . . . A week ago Friday I got out of bed to go to the meeting – and that day His Message came that He was called to the Orient and could not come to the Coast. Never, so long as I live – shall I forget their faces, their bowed heads and the silence – broken by one bitter stifled sob of a poor woman who was there on crutches. Two days afterwards in meekness and submission they as an assembly wrote a short little letter to 'Abdu'l-Bahá acknowledging His decree in loving acceptation. A day or so later I rec'd a letter from one who was present saying – 'The Friday afternoon meeting is a thing of the past and now we all know that what we had hoped for, longed for and lived for will not be – and that only the people with money to pay their way to Him – will be able to see or experience the Light of God, which you taught us, attends 'Abdu'l-Bahá – and we must go on in the same old weary human way! The divine Presence that can obliterate and destroy the human way – will not shine upon us! We must still remain in this "far country" of human darkness unable to see or reach our Home . . .' – It is all very heart breaking! ⁴²

On 1 August 'Abdu'l-Bahá wrote to John Bosch, saying:

> O thou who art longing for the visit of 'Abdu'l-Bahá! Thy yearning letter was wonderfully eloquent and its effect on 'Abdu'l-Bahá was

inexpressible. I greatly long to fulfil the request of the friends, but am as yet in these parts, until later the requirement of wisdom will be revealed. If the western cities demonstrate their infinite firmness in the Covenant, this will act as a magnet to draw 'Abdu'l-Bahá . . . [43]

And on 5 August Lua received an optimistic message from 'Abdu'l-Bahá 'saying if all the assemblies unite in Cal. it may be the means of attracting Him here after all.'[44]

'Abdu'l-Bahá's strength was heavily taxed by the work He was doing in the east and the journey west would be long and tiring. But when they knew that 'Abdu'l-Bahá would be attracted by the love and unity of the friends, Hyde Dunn, Willard Hatch and another believer stayed up all night, praying that the Master would make the journey. And on 13 August 'Abdu'l-Bahá sent a wire to John Bosch that actually suggested that He might go to California: 'Your telegram was the cause of much happiness. God willing I will depart for the western part. Give these glad tidings to each and all.' John told Marzieh Gail that this was the first telegram announcing the Master's journey West. [45]

When 'Abdu'l-Bahá finally arrived in California, He told the friends, 'Your love drew Me to you.'[46] But before that happened, the Master would have much to do back East.

## Cleveland, Ohio and Pittsburgh, Pennsylvania

On 6 May 'Abdu'l-Bahá left Chicago for Cleveland, Ohio. When He arrived that afternoon, He was met by many of the friends and a lot of newspaper reporters:

GIVES NEW CREED TALK – *Cleveland Plain Dealer*
'Abdu'l-Bahá was expected to set up a branch of the Faith in Cleveland.

BAHAISTS TO HEAR VENERABLE LEADER – *Cleveland Plain Dealer*

WED RACES? SURE . . . – *Cleveland News*
'Perfect results follow the marriage of black and white races. All men are the progeny of one . . . They are of different colors, but the color is nothing . . . I believe Abdul Bahá is absolutely right. It is inevitable

that all races will unite . . . It is the only logical conclusion.'

## BAHAIST APPROVES UNIONS OF RACES – *Cleveland Plain Dealer*[47]

'Abdu'l-Bahá, however, told them, 'My message is the oneness of humanity and universal peace . .' and that evening gave a talk in the auditorium of His hotel to over 500 people. There was standing room only and the audience was 'enchanted by His charm and speech'.[48]

The newspapers did bring one soul, at least, into the Faith in Cleveland. A city dignitary read about 'Abdu'l-Bahá's arrival and His comments at meetings. After reflecting on what the Master had said, he felt convinced of the truth and greatness of the Bahá'í teachings and wrote to 'Abdu'l-Bahá wishing to 'submit . . . a statement of his conviction and recognition'.[49]

Leaving Cleveland early the following morning, 'Abdu'l-Bahá and His party stayed that night in Pittsburgh. After a meeting with the Bahá'ís, 'Abdu'l-Bahá met with a group of philosophers, doctors and journalists, with whom He spoke about the diagnosis of disease:

> If one is fully cognizant of the reason for the incursion of disease and can determine the balance of elements, he can cure diseases by administering the food that can restore the normal level of the deficient element. In this way there will be no need for medicines and other difficulties will not arise.[50]

Next morning, He departed from Pittsburgh at 9 a.m. for the 12-hour train journey back to Washington.

## WASHINGTON, DC

'Abdu'l-Bahá arrived back in Washington on 8 May and stayed in an apartment at 14 Harvard Street. Agnes Parsons stopped off at the house on her way to the train station to leave flowers and the kind of chocolate nougats He particularly liked.

The next day, 'Abdu'l-Bahá was very tired and Agnes Parsons suggested He take a rest and not worry about the constant stream of visitors. Saying 'God bless you for that suggestion, I am very tired', He 'rested splendidly' until nearly four o'clock.[51]

On 10 May 'Abdu'l-Bahá, Dr Bagdadi, Dr Fareed and Agnes Parsons drove to the Capitol. "Abdu'l-Bahá expressed a wish to go inside, where he examined the statuary and paintings, then we walked the grounds and sat for a short time near a large tree. We also drove to the [Washington Monument] and went up to the top in the elevator. 'Abdu'l-Bahá looked with great interest out of each window.'[52]

'Abdu'l-Bahá only stayed three days in Washington, but that was enough to provoke the opposition of a few 'narrow-minded' ministers. At the end of an evening meeting, the Master said:

> Although I pay great respect to the feelings of people in order that they may not run away or make the least objection, yet the religious ministers of Washington have denounced us . . . The denunciation by the leaders of religion is a proof of the greatness and influence of the Cause because no one pays any attention to something insignificant.[53]

# 9

# THE CITY OF THE COVENANT
## *11 May–19 June*

### NEW YORK, NEW YORK

The newspapers again noted 'Abdu'l-Bahá's arrival in New York, but not all were complimentary. The New York *Churchman* objected to the Bahá'í Faith, saying:

> Its purpose is, no doubt, laudable; and it excites the sympathy of those who see in all the great ethnic religions glimpses of that Light which lighteth every man that cometh into the world. But Bahaism is not Christianity; and Abdul Baha does not profess to be a Christian. What right, then, has he to preach in a Christian church?[1]

On the morning of 12 May 'Abdu'l-Bahá and His companions took a ferry to New Jersey and then a train to Montclair, New Jersey, to speak at the Unity Church. The rector, Dr Edgar S. Wiers, introduced Him, saying, 'Today we shall read from the New Gospel, that is, from the teachings of Bahá'u'lláh instead of the Bible.'[2] After lunch at the home of Charles Edsall, He returned to New York.

That evening, 'Abdu'l-Bahá gave a powerful talk at a public meeting of the Peace Forum at the Grace Methodist Episcopal Church:

> When we review history from the beginning down to the present day, we find that strife and warfare have prevailed throughout the human world. Wars – religious, racial or political – have arisen from human ignorance, misunderstanding and lack of education. We will first consider religious strife and conflict.
>   It is evident that the divine Prophets have appeared in the world to establish love and agreement among mankind. They have been

the Shepherds and not the wolves. The Shepherd comes forth to gather and lead his flock and not to disperse them by creating strife. Every divine Shepherd has assembled a flock which had formerly been scattered. Among the Shepherds was Moses. At a time when the tribes of Israel were wandering and dispersed, He assembled, united and educated them to higher degrees of capacity and progress until they passed out of the wilderness of discipline into the holy land of possession. He transformed their degradation into glory, changed their poverty into wealth and replaced their vices by virtues until they rose to such a zenith that the splendour of the sovereignty of Solomon was made possible, and the fame of their civilization extended to the East and the West. It is evident, therefore, that Moses was a divine Shepherd, for He gathered the tribes of Israel together and united them in the power and strength of a great nationhood.

When the Messianic star of Jesus Christ dawned, He declared He had come to gather together the lost tribes or scattered sheep of Moses. He not only shepherded the flock of Israel but brought together people of Chaldea, Egypt, Syria, ancient Assyria and Phoenicia. These people were in a state of utmost hostility, thirsting for the blood of each other with the ferocity of animals; but Jesus Christ brought them together, cemented and united them in His Cause and established such a bond of love among them that enmity and warfare were abandoned. It is evident, therefore, that the divine teachings are intended to create a bond of unity in the human world and establish the foundations of love and fellowship among mankind. Divine religion is not a cause for discord and disagreement. If religion becomes the source of antagonism and strife, the absence of religion is to be preferred. Religion is meant to be the quickening life of the body politic; if it be the cause of death to humanity, its nonexistence would be a blessing and benefit to man. Therefore, in this day the divine teachings must be sought, for they are the remedies for the present conditions of the world of humanity. The purpose of a remedy is to heal and cure. If it be productive of worse symptoms, its absence or discontinuance is preferable.

At a time when the Arabian tribes and nomadic peoples were widely separated, living in the deserts under lawless conditions, strife and bloodshed continual among them, no tribe free from the menace of attack and destruction by another – at such a critical time Muhammad appeared. He gathered these wild tribes of the desert together, reconciled, united and caused them to agree so that enmity and warfare ceased. The Arabian nation immediately advanced until its dominion extended westward to Spain and Andalusia.

From these facts and premises we may conclude that the establishing of the divine religions is for peace, not for war and the shedding of blood. Inasmuch as all are founded upon one reality which is love and unity, the wars and dissensions which have characterized the history of religion have been due to imitations and superstitions which arise afterward. Religion is reality, and reality is one. The fundamentals of the religion of God are, therefore, one in reality. There is neither difference nor change in the fundamentals. Variance is caused by blind imitations, prejudices and adherence to forms which appear later; and inasmuch as these differ, discord and strife result. If the religions of the world would forsake these causes of difficulty and seek the fundamentals, all would agree, and strife and dissension would pass away; for religion and reality are one and not multiple.

Other wars are caused by purely imaginary racial differences; for humanity is one kind, one race and progeny, inhabiting the same globe. In the creative plan there is no racial distinction and separation such as Frenchman, Englishman, American, German, Italian or Spaniard; all belong to one household. These boundaries and distinctions are human and artificial, not natural and original. All mankind are the fruits of one tree, flowers of the same garden, waves of one sea . . . Shall racial ideas prevail and obscure the creative purpose of unity in his kingdom? Shall he say, 'I am a German,' 'I am a Frenchman' or an 'Englishman' and declare war because of this imaginary and human distinction? God forbid! This earth is one household and the native land of all humanity; therefore, the human race should ignore distinctions and boundaries which are artificial and conducive to disagreement and hostility. We have come from the East. Praise be to God! We find this continent prosperous, the climate salubrious and delightful, the inhabitants genial and courteous, the government equitable and just. Shall we entertain any other thought and feeling than that of love for you? Shall we say, 'This is not our native land; therefore, everything is objectionable'? This would be gross ignorance to which man must not subject himself. Man is endowed with powers to investigate reality, and the reality is that humanity is one in kind and equal in the creative plan. Therefore, false distinctions of race and native land, which are factors and causes of warfare, must be abandoned.

. . . Wolves, lions, tigers are ferocious because it is their natural and necessary means for obtaining food. Man has no need of such ferocity; his food is provided in other ways. Therefore, it is evident that warfare, cruelty and bloodshed in the kingdom of man are caused by human greed, hatred and selfishness. The kings and rulers of nations enjoy luxury and ease in their palaces and send the common people to the battlefield – offer them as the food and targets of cannon. Each day they invent new instruments for the more complete destruction of the foundations of the human race . . .

What ignorance and degradation, yea even greater than the ferocious beasts themselves! For a wolf will carry away and devour one sheep at a time, whereas an ambitious tyrant may cause the death of one hundred thousand men in a battle and glory in his military prowess, saying, 'I am commander in chief; I have won this mighty victory.' Consider the ignorance and inconsistency of the human race. If a man kills another, no matter what the cause may be, he is pronounced a murderer, imprisoned or executed; but the brutal oppressor who has slain one hundred thousand is idolized as a hero, conqueror or military genius . . .

In Persia previous to the middle of the nineteenth century among the various tribes and peoples, sects and denominations there existed the greatest animosity, strife and hatred. At that time, too, all the other nations of the East were in the same condition. Religionists were hostile and bigoted, sects were at enmity, races hated each other, tribes were constantly at war; everywhere antagonism and conflict prevailed. Men shunned and were suspicious of each other. The man who could kill a number of his fellow creatures was glorified for his heroism and strength. Among religionists it was esteemed a praiseworthy deed to take the life of one who held an opposite belief. At this time Bahá'u'lláh arose and declared His mission. He founded the oneness of the world of humanity, proclaimed that all are servants of the loving and merciful God Who has created, nourished and provided for all; therefore, why should men be unjust and unkind to each other, showing forth that which is contrary to God? ...

... Therefore, it is evident that the essential foundations of the divine religions are unity and love. If religion be productive of discord among mankind, it is a destroyer and not divine, for religion implies unity and binding together and not separation. Mere knowledge of principles is not sufficient. We all know and admit that justice is good, but there is need of volition and action to carry out and manifest it. For example, we might think it good to build a church, but simply thinking of it as a good thing will not help its erection. The ways and means must be provided; we must will to build it and then proceed with the construction. All of us know that international peace is good, that it is conducive to human welfare and the glory of man, but volition and action are necessary before it can be established. Action is essential ...

The foundations of all the divine religions are peace and agreement, but misunderstandings and ignorance have developed. If these are caused to disappear, you will see that all the religious agencies will work for peace and promulgate the oneness of humankind. For the foundation of all is reality, and reality is not multiple or divisible. Moses founded it, Jesus raised its tent, and its brilliant light has shone forth in all the religions. Bahá'u'lláh proclaimed this one reality and spread the message of the Most Great Peace. Even in prison He rested not until He lighted this lamp in the East. Praise be to God! All who have accepted His teachings are lovers of peace, peacemakers ready to sacrifice their lives and expend their possessions for it. Now let this standard be upraised in the West, and many will respond to the call. America has become renowned for her discoveries, inventions and artistic skill, famous for equity of government and stupendous undertakings; now may she also become noted and celebrated as the herald and messenger of universal peace. Let this be her mission and undertaking, and may its blessed impetus spread to all countries. I pray for all of you that you may render this service to the world of humanity.[3]

On 13 May 'Abdu'l-Bahá appeared as the guest of honour at a meeting of the New York Peace Society held at the Hotel Astor. Before the meeting, The Master had a high fever and was in bed. Juliet Thompson tried to get him to stay and rest but He laughed, 'I work by the confirmations of the Holy Spirit. I do not work by hygienic laws. If I did, I would get nothing done.'[4]

There were 2,000 people at the Peace Society meeting, including some well-known personalities such as Rabbi Stephen Wise, Mr Short (a friend of Andrew Carnegie), Anna Spencer of the Ethical Society, Dr Percy Grant, Professor William Jackson of Columbia University and Mr Topakyan, the Persian Consul General. When 'Abdu'l-Bahá entered the hall, the cheers shook the building. Anna Spencer introduced 'Abdu'l-Bahá to the gathering, describing Him as the Prophet of the East, after which Dr Grant spoke of the imprisonment He had suffered for promoting peace and unity. Mr Topakyan said of the Master, 'Our guest of honor has stood as a Prophet of enlightenment and peace for the Persian Empire, and a well wisher of Persia may well honor Him . . . In closing, I am happy to say that 'Abdu'l-Bahá is the Glory of Persia today.'[5] It was an amazing introduction from a man representing the country that had so persecuted the Faith preached by the Master. Then Professor Jackson, who had been to Persia, said that world peace would only come about through this 'blessed Cause'.[6] When 'Abdu'l-Bahá spoke, He was 'visibly tired and His voice was hoarse', but 'He delivered a unique speech on the Teachings of Bahá'u'lláh for the age and on the establishment of peace'.[7]

Mary Revell and her daughter, Rebecca, had been in New York that weekend to listen to 'Abdu'l-Bahá. They were departing for the train to return home to Philadelphia when Rebecca suddenly realized that she had left her luggage where she had stayed. Collecting the luggage forced a delay in their departure and allowed them to go to 'Abdu'l-Bahá's talk to the friends at His residence that evening, which was on the top floor of the Hudson Apartment House. When Mary and Rebecca arrived, they found the room filled with people. 'Abdu'l-Bahá sat on a divan with an empty seat on either side of Him. Some of those present had wondered who the Master was saving the seats for, but Mary and Rebecca's entrance resolved the question. 'Abdu'l-Bahá motioned the mother and daughter to sit beside Him.[8]

The next day, 14 May, 'Abdu'l-Bahá went to Lake Mohonk, a four-hour train ride north of New York, for the main meeting of the International Peace Society. During the lectures earlier in the day, most of the delegates talked about materialistic matters such as the internal unity of countries. When 'Abdu'l-Bahá began to speak about the unity of all the peoples of the world, the reformation of the whole world, and how the Manifestation of the Most Great Name would bring about the complete unity of the world, the audience was amazed, so much so that at the end of the Master's twenty minutes, they requested that He continue. Being very tired, He apologized and prepared to leave. Before He could do so, all of the dignitaries and delegates came by to shake His hand and some embraced Him.[9]

Later, 'Abdu'l-Bahá encountered a group of young people to whom He told this story in relation to the effects of the peace conference:

> Once the rats and mice held an important conference the subject of which was how to make peace with the cat. After a long and heated discussion it was decided that the best thing to do would be to tie a bell around the neck of the cat so that the rats and mice would be warned of his movements and have time to get out of his way.
>
> This seemed an excellent plan until the question arose as to who should undertake the dangerous job of belling the cat. None of the rats liked the idea and the mice thought they were altogether too weak. So the conference broke up in confusion.
>
> Everyone laughed, 'Abdu'l-Bahá with them. After a short pause He added that that is much like these Peace Conferences. Many words, but no one is likely to approach the question of who will bell the Czar of Russia, the Emperor of Germany, the President of France and the Emperor of Japan.
>
> Faces were now more grave. 'Abdu'l-Bahá laughed again: There is a Divine Club, He said, which shall break their power in pieces.[10]

'Abdu'l-Bahá returned to the same theme the next day when speaking about the peace conference:

> Once I wrote to the Persian friends that if the workers of peace conferences do not apply in their own lives what they advocate, they are like those wine sellers who convene and make emphatic speeches regarding the harmfulness of wine and proposing its prohibition. But when they go out of the meeting, they begin again to sell wine and to do what they were doing in the past. Therefore it is necessary for the power of execution and effect to spiritually penetrate the body of the world.[11]

Later that evening, 'Abdu'l-Bahá called Dr Zia Bagdadi and sent him on a wild adventure beginning at 9 o'clock at night:

> 'Abdu'l-Bahá gave [Dr Zia Bagdadi] the key to His New York apartment and asked him to get a Persian rug to give to Mr Smiley, the president of the International Peace Society. Even though others said no one could make the journey and return before the scheduled departure at 10:00 AM the next morning, Dr Bagdadi said, 'I am not afraid to try anything for you, my Lord.'
>
> Since there were no passenger trains at that time of the night, Dr Bagdadi jumped on the caboose of an already moving freight train. The trainman protested until he saw 'Dr' written on the professional card and agreed to let the passenger remain on the train, not knowing his 'urgent mission' concerned a rug. About 2:00 AM Dr Bagdadi awakened Mrs Grace Ober [Grace Robarts] and her sister Ella Robarts, who were staying in 'Abdu'l-Bahá's apartment, selected a rug, dashed back to the station, caught a train, and arrived back at Lake Mohonk station with an hour left before 10:00 AM although an hour's drive lay ahead of him. The only vehicle in sight was the wagon of the mail carrier, who agreed to take him. Dr Bagdadi arrived just as 'Abdu'l-Bahá was shaking hands with Mr [Albert] Smiley and preparing to leave. Mr Smiley, on receiving the rug, said, 'Why this is just what I have been seeking for many years! You see, we had a Persian rug just like this one, but it was burned in a fire and ever since my wife has been broken-hearted over it. This will surely make her very happy.'[12]

## Grace Robarts Ober and Harlan Ober

Grace Robarts and Harlan Ober were dedicated Bahá'ís who had the bounty of marrying in the presence of 'Abdu'l-Bahá. Grace is described by her long-time friend Muriel Ives, the wife of Howard Ives, as having the

> habit, so extraordinarily a part of her throughout her whole life, of considering the welfare of everyone but herself; of continually giving, from morning till night, of friendship, service, inspiration . . . she was, to an amazing degree, a friend to all the world . . . During

the months of 'Abdu'l-Bahá's stay in America in 1912 Grace had the honour of being indeed the 'servant' in His home in whatever city He was staying. He chose her to go ahead and secure an apartment for Him and have it in readiness upon His arrival. Then she would care for His home as a housekeeper and hostess while he and His secretaries and those Persians who had the privilege of serving Him in various capacities, remained there. She kept the home immaculate, and always ready for the constant stream of guests from morning to might, Bahá'ís and inquirers and souls in difficulty . . .[13]

How this came about is recounted in Muriel's memoirs as told to her by Grace herself:

So she went to 'Abdu'l-Bahá and begged that, when he returned to New York, she might help with that household . . . 'Abdu'l-Bahá looked at her very searchingly and said, 'Greece (His loving nickname for Grace) Greece, are you SURE you wish to serve ME?' Grace said, 'Oh, YES! More than anything else in the world!' 'Abdu'l-Bahá made no answer but walked away. The next morning this scene was repeated. On the third morning, Grace . . . went to Him a third time – and this time He became very stern. Are you VERY SURE you wish to SERVE ME? Grace was startled at the sternness but she didn't waver. 'YES I am VERY SURE.'

So then he nodded. 'Very well go, settle up your affairs, and we will meet in New York.' Jubilant and radiant, Grace settled up her 'affairs'. Then, with wings on her feet, she went to New York. Lua was already there and together they prepared for 'Abdu'l-Bahá's arrival.

The day came. . . He came in. He welcomed Lua warmly, glanced at Grace as at a complete stranger, and turned away. Grace was appalled, shocked. Hadn't He recognized her? Had He forgotten her? Had she misunderstood the permission to come to New York? Or had she displeased Him and was this punishment?

Whatever it was, it continued with no let-up . . . She worked in that household until long after midnight – cleaning, cooking, scrubbing, and then she would rise at five in the morning to begin all over again. She worked as she had never worked before in all her life and Abdu'l-Bahá ignored her completely.

[One day, when 'Abdu'l-Bahá had gone out], she thought of the white roses that had been delivered that morning, as they were daily, for 'Abdu'l-Bahá's room. The one bright spot in these dreadful days for Grace had been that she was the one to arrange these roses each morning. So, with the long florists' box in her arms, she climbed up to 'Abdu'l-Bahá's room at the top of the house, where He had wished to be. She reached the top of the third flight – and found the door not only closed, but locked against her. And always before it had stood wide open! This, for Grace, was the last straw . . . she sank down on the floor and wept with the fallen roses scattered around her. At last, the sobs faded, her tears spent themselves, and, exhausted, she gathered up the roses and went back downstairs.

. . . Grace – it was now past noon – was hungry. So, she went down to the kitchen to get something to eat. And in that house that fed, each day, so many dozens of people, there was nothing to eat but one egg and a small piece of leftover bread in 'Abdu'l-Bahá's breadbox . . . So Grace boiled her one egg and put her small portion of bread on a plate. Putting the egg in an egg cup, she chipped the shell – and the egg, as bad as an egg can get, exploded in her face. She cleaned up the mess and returned to her bit of leftover bread. And, as she crumbled the bread, eating it crumb by crumb she realized, suddenly, exactly what she was doing – she was, blessedly, eating the crumbs of the bread of life from 'Abdu'l-Bahá's table. She began to eat even more slowly as the spirit of prayer came to possess her.

Not long after this the household returned . . . and that evening Lua came to Grace and said, 'The Master has asked me to tell you that He knows you wept.' And this was the first time it had occurred to Grace that all this dreadful experience might have a reason, a pattern. And – if this were true she must find out what the reason could be. So she went up to her room to pray about it. To pray for illumination and wisdom and the selflessness to understand. And as she prayed she heard a small voice saying 'Are you as happy scrubbing the garbage pails as you are arranging the roses?' And she suddenly realized what the spirit of true service was. It was to rise to selfless joy in offering the service, no matter what form that service might take. And as this truth swept over her, suffusing her, illuminating her, the door opened, and 'Abdu'l-Bahá walked into the room. His arms were outstretched; His dear face was glorified.

'Welcome!' He cried to Grace, 'Welcome to the Kingdom!' And he held her close, embracing her deeply. And never did He withdraw Himself from her again.[14]

Harlan Ober became a Bahá'í in 1906 and was privileged to be on a very early teaching trip to India at the behest of 'Abdu'l-Bahá. On 17 July 1912, Grace and Harlan were married at the instigation of 'Abdu'l-Bahá:

> Lua came to Grace and told her that it was the wish of 'Abdu'l-Bahá that she marry Harlan Ober. Grace was shocked . . . 'How could I think of marrying Harlan Ober?' Lua smiled, 'I'm only repeating 'Abdu'l-Baha's request,' she said gently. So Grace quickly put the idea out of her mind. The next morning Lua came the second time to deliver the same message. Again Grace dismissed it all as being utterly fantastic. The third morning when Lua came she added her own remarks to the message. 'You'd better really consider this, Grace, 'Abdu'l-Bahá does not make suggestions lightly.' Grace, this time, realized how serious this was. 'But what does He want me to do? Write to Harlan Ober, whom I scarcely know – and propose to him? How could I? Oh, Lua I do want to be obedient but how on earth can I?' Lua hugged her and patted her consolingly. 'I'll do it,' she said. 'I know Harlan very well – it was through me he came into the Faith. I can do this easily.' So Lua wrote to Harlan – and Harlan, radiant at the thought that he was obeying a suggestion of his beloved Master, took the next train to New York from Boston where he lived. He came at once to see Grace and together they went walking through Central Park where he proposed and Grace, still dazed and uncertain, accepted – because it was the will of 'Abdu'l-Bahá.[15]

On 17 July the friends gathered at 'Abdu'l-Bahá's house at 309 West 78th St for the usual meeting. Instead of the meeting, however, Edward Getsinger announced that there would be a surprise. A few minutes later, Harlan and Grace came down, Grace dressed in a white dress and carrying a large bouquet of white roses. Juliet Thompson was present as well and recorded her impressions: 'Grace and Harlan stood together, transfigured; they seemed to be bathed in white light. Mr Ives, standing opposite, married them. Back in the shadow sat the Master . . . At the end of the wedding He blessed the marriage.'[16]

Howard Colby Ives remembered:

> 'Abdu'l-Bahá rose . . . He swept the room with a glance at once enfolding and abstracted. He raised his hands, palm upwards, level with his waist, His eyes closed and He chanted a prayer . . . in tones to me unequalled in all experience, mellifluous (honey-like), is the nearest descriptive word, but how inadequate . . . my heart was certainly moved far more by the chanting Voice and the flowing, musical periods, than by the interpreter's version of the wedding prayer, beautiful as it is. [17]

\* \* \*

On Sunday 19 May 'Abdu'l-Bahá spoke at the Church of the Divine Paternity on Central Park West. 'Abdu'l-Bahá's talk on progressive revelation and the teachings of Bahá'u'lláh captivated the audience. Juliet Thompson said that the Byzantine architecture of the church made her 'think of the worship of the early Christians'. She was greatly surprised to see a man there she knew. He had been a 'hopelessly unconvertible atheist', but was as captivated as the rest of the audience.[18]

Howard Colby Ives introduced 'Abdu'l-Bahá at the Unitarian Brotherhood Church in New York later that day, saying among other things:

> I hope I may be allowed to make one personal allusion . . . There have come to this country vast numbers of socalled prophets, – people who . . . line their pockets with our money and go away . . . Lest you may think it is possible to believe such a thing of 'Abdu'l-Bahá, let me tell you that his friends here provided a beautiful apartment for him in the Ansonia . . . He accepted it with thanks, but paid for it all himself. Never since in this country has he accepted one cent from anybody. [19]

On the following two days the Master spoke to 'an enthusiastic gathering of women suffragists' about the equality of men and women, and also about the education of children.

## Boston, Massachusetts

On 22 May 'Abdu'l-Bahá travelled to Boston, where His first public talk was to 800 Unitarian ministers at their American Unitarian Association Conference. In addition to the ministers, over 2,000 other people were there and the presiding officer was the Lieutenant-Governor of Massachusetts.[20] But even though this was supposed to be an 'intellectual group holding, probably, the most "advanced" opinions in religious thought,' 'Abdu'l-Bahá was speaking to those who could not hear. 'A very interesting old gentleman, but he told us nothing new' was the comment of many.[21]

The next day the Master met many people, but one journalist stood out. After listening to 'Abdu'l-Bahá for only five minutes, he accepted the Cause 'and decided to write and publish articles on the Faith'.[22]

On 'Abdu'l-Bahá's birthday, 23 May, over a hundred guests were at Francis Breed's home in Cambridge to celebrate the event. Alice Breed, the mother-in-law of Ali-Kuli Khan:

> . . . had baked Him a birthday cake with sixty-eight candles, and to symbolize universality and the love many bore Him . . . had decorated it with tiny flags of the United States, Persia and England. Her first cake fell and she had to bake another . . . Significantly, He did not stay for the festivities. He forgave this time, but had forbidden the celebration of His birthday.[23]

Stanwood Cobb took his 75-year-old father to see 'Abdu'l-Bahá in Boston. His father was sympathetic to Stanwood's attraction to the Bahá'í Faith, but claimed that he himself was too old to change. When his father met the Master, Stanwood was bewildered to see his father dominate the conversation. His father proceeded to 'enlighten' 'Abdu'l-Bahá about spiritual themes. Stanwood was shocked. 'Abdu'l-Bahá, though, simply smiled and listened, covering them both with His love. Stanwood's father left feeling that he'd had a wonderful interview with the Master and Stanwood learned a lesson in humility and the power of being a good listener.[24]

'Abdu'l-Bahá returned to New York on 26 May, arriving at 6 p.m.

## New York, New York

A few days before 'Abdu'l-Bahá's journey to Boston, the landlord of the Hudson Apartment House 'had complained about the excessive comings and goings of the visitors'.[25] The Master had therefore decided that large meetings would take place at the Kinney home. Now, back in New York, 'Abdu'l-Bahá moved completely out of the apartment hotel, since the landlord felt that 'the comings and goings of so many diverse people', the 'additional work and difficulty' put upon the staff, and the 'incessant inquiries' to the hotel's management were more than they wished to cope with. 'Abdu'l-Bahá didn't argue; He simply left. But as usual, He showered them with His love as He departed, making them feel quite ashamed of their behaviour. The staff begged Him to stay, but He did not, moving into the Kinney home at 789 West End Street for a few days until a house could be rented for him elsewhere.[26] He told Carrie Kinney, '. . . while I am in your home I will be the host and you will be the guests'.[27]

On 1 June Juliet Thompson went to the Master to begin painting His portrait. When she arrived, He asked, 'Can you paint Me in a half hour?'

> 'A half hour, my Lord?' I stammered, appalled. I can never finish a head in less than two weeks.
>
> 'Well, I will give you three half hours. You mustn't waste My time, Juliet.'
>
> He told me to come to Him Saturday morning, June 1, at seven-thirty.
>
> I went in a panic. He was waiting for me in the entrance hall, a small space in the English basement where the light – not much of it – comes from the south. In fact I found myself faced with every kind of handicap. I always paint standing, but now I was obliged to sit, jammed so close to the window (because of the lack of distance between the Master and me) that I couldn't even lean back. No light. No room. And I had brought a canvas for a life-size head.
>
> The Master was seated in a dark corner, His black 'abá melting into the background; and again I saw Him as the *Face of God*, and quailed. How could I paint the Face of God?
>
> 'I want you,' He said, 'to paint My *Servitude* to God.'

'Oh my Lord,' I cried, 'only the Holy Spirit could paint *Your* Servitude to God. No human hand could do it. Pray for me, or I am lost. I implore You, inspire me.'

'I will pray,' He answered, 'and as you are doing this only for the sake of God, you will be inspired.'

And then an amazing thing happened. All fear fell away from me and it was as though Someone Else saw through my eyes, worked through my hand.

All the points, all the planes in that matchless Face were so clear to me that my hand couldn't put them down quickly enough, couldn't keep pace with the clarity of my vision. I painted in ecstasy, free as I had never been before.

At the end of the half hour the foundation of the head was perfect. [28]

In early June a magazine, the *American Review of Reviews*, summarized several stories from other publications, including this one from the *Fortnightly Review* of England:

Surely the dawn of a new day was heralded on the Sunday evening when the Archdeacon of Westminster walked hand in hand with the venerable Abdul Baha up the nave of St. John's Church, and invited him not only to address the congregation but to offer for them his prayers and blessings.

Considering the dignity and conservatism of the Established Church of England, and the fact that this little-known Persian prophet has come to the western world to proclaim the dawn of the millennium, to announce that the Messiah awaited by all the nations has actually lived, taught and died upon this earth within the past century, and to preach what he and his followers believe to be the new world religion, designed to include and supersede all others and to unite all nations under the banner of a common faith, this would hardly seem an extravagant statement. When we add to it the assertion of the *Contemporary Review* that, within a week after his arrival in England, where he was almost unknown, Abdul Baha delivered an address from the pulpit of the City Temple in London, being introduced by its rector as the leader of one of the most remarkable religious movements of this or any other age, it seems evident that at least a part of the Episcopal Church is inclined to accord the courtesy of a respectful hearing. [29]

The *Fortnightly Review* then noted that:

> A few weeks ago Abdul Baha and his little group of disciples landed in New York, quietly and almost unheralded by the newspapers. Courtesies similar to those he had received in London were at once extended to him by the Rev. Percy Stickney Grant and others of the clergy . . . he has been speaking constantly to those who cared to seek him out . . .
>
> Abdul Baha . . . makes no claim that he is himself the Messiah. He says plainly that he is not even a prophet, only Abdul Baha, the servant of God.[30]

Dr Percy Grant, at whose church in New York 'Abdu'l-Bahá had given His first public talk in America, invited the Master to be a guest speaker at a People's Forum at the Church of the Ascension on 2 June. The format of this meeting was more open than others and people were allowed to ask questions. The Master gave a powerful talk in response to the question: 'What can the Orient bring to the Occident?' This was an intriguing topic, since only a year before, Dr Grant had vehemently proclaimed from the same pulpit at which the Master now stood that the Orient had brought to the West nothing but disease and death. The Master, from the Orient, praised Christ and the Law of God and called the church a collective centre for humanity. He also stated that this same collective centre was now the revelation of Bahá'u'lláh and it would assure a civilization of peace.

The Master's talk left Dr Grant visibly shaken and he could only praise the Master as He took questions from the audience. 'Abdu'l-Bahá, sitting at the centre of the chancel, responded warmly and enjoyed the exchange. 'He pushed back His turban and smiled as He answered, often very wittily.'[31]

Later that day, 'Abdu'l-Bahá visited Mr Penshoe, a US Cabinet member, at his summer home where He spent the night. Mr Penshoe had invited notables and national statesmen to meet 'Abdu'l-Bahá the following day and they all listened respectfully as He spoke. One person asked about the possibility of international war, to which 'Abdu'l-Bahá said, 'Tremendous changes will take place in Europe. The great centralized powers will break up into smaller independent states.'³²

## Philadelphia

On Saturday 8 June 'Abdu'l-Bahá went to Philadelphia. Ethel and Jessie Revell, daughters of Mary Revell, decided to board the train at the North Philadelphia station in order to see Him early. Ethel was extremely excited: 'I could scarcely keep myself together – I felt my body would fly to pieces with joy, as I awaited the hour.' As they boarded the train, they saw the Master sitting by the window with Lua Getsinger and Annie Boylan. Ethel managed to sit behind Him until they arrived at the main station. Being very tired, 'Abdu'l-Bahá went directly to the Rittenhouse Hotel for the night.³³

The following day, 'Abdu'l-Bahá spoke both at the Unitarian Church and at the Baptist Temple. The pastor of the latter, Dr Russell H. Conwell, had visited 'Abdu'l-Bahá in 'Akká in 1909 and at that time had invited Him to speak in his church if He ever came to America. The Master had accepted the invitation and now, three years later, was fulfilling His promise. He spoke to about 3,000 people in the church.

At 9 o'clock the next morning, 'Abdu'l-Bahá visited the Revell home at 1429 Mayfield Street and spoke about the life of Bahá'u'lláh. Mary had already travelled to New York in April to see Him. On that occasion he had said to her: 'This is a firm believer. Her spirit is bigger than her body.'³⁴

When 'Abdu'l-Bahá arrived at the Revell home, He called the house 'The Bahá'í Home'. The house was filled to overflowing with about fifty people sitting on chairs, the floor, the stairs and standing in the upstairs hall. Jessie and Ethel missed His talk because they were bringing a nearly-blind lady to the house. During His stay, the Master gave Mary's grandson, Ellwood, the name of 'Hossein' as well as two silver quarters.³⁵ Jessie had a private meeting with 'Abdu'l-Bahá before He left and said that she wanted to be of service to the Faith. He responded by telling her, 'You are a smiling angel and you will always be of service in the Kingdom.'³⁶ In 1950 the Guardian called Ethel and Jessie Revell to Haifa to serve there, and in 1952 appointed both of them to the Bahá'í International Council, the predecessor to the Universal House of Justice.

After 'Abdu'l-Bahá and all the visitors had departed, Mary Revell discovered that all the sandwiches and refreshments she had prepared remained, completely forgotten.

## NEW YORK, NEW YORK

On his return to New York 'Abdu'l-Bahá spoke with the Bahá'ís about the differences that are created after the Manifestation of God leaves the earthly plane. These differences and splits would not happen this time, He proclaimed, because of Bahá'u'lláh's Covenant. He also clearly stated that He was the Centre of that Covenant:

> But the Blessed Beauty has shut the door on such differences and has referred all affairs to the House of Justice so that whatever the House of Justice commands, all must obey and submit to it. He said that if the Bahá'ís should become divided into two branches, each establishing a House of Justice of its own in opposition to the other, both would be false. Bahá'u'lláh wrote His Covenant with His own pen and, prior to the establishment of the House of Justice, He appointed and confirmed the Centre of the Covenant, 'Abdu'l-Bahá, directing that 'whatever He does is correct'. 37

By 12 June 'Abdu'l-Bahá was extremely exhausted. Juliet Thompson wrote that 'He talked for a long while to the people. But this I could see was pure sacrifice. His vitality seemed gone. At times He could scarcely bring forth the words, yet He gave and gave.'38

Nevertheless, He continued to go out and speak at public meetings, and at gatherings at His house. At one of these He said, 'What I have spoken is according to the capacity of the people and the exigency of the time. "The father makes gurgling sounds for the new-born infant, although his wisdom can measure the universe" [Rumi].'39

Shortly after 'Abdu'l-Bahá arrived in New York in April, a movie company had asked if they could film Him. The idea horrified some of the Bahá'ís, but He replied at once:

> 'Khaili Khub'('Very good') . . . The result was that he appeared before the camera at the entrance of the Hotel Ansonia . . . It was a wonderfully impressive sight, for 'Abdu'l-Bahá as he approached the

camera, was exhorting Bahá'u'lláh to bless this means for the spreading of the Heavenly Cause throughout the world.

Early in June we conceived the idea of an extended motion picture in which 'Abdu'l-Bahá would appear in various scenes. He consented at once . . . Furthermore, it is our intention – 'Abdu'l-Bahá's consent having already been willingly given – to take a record of his voice on the Edison talking machine.[40]

On 18 June several scenes were filmed at the home of Howard MacNutt. Film-making was fairly new technology and, though the final result was good, there were a few problems during filming. In the first scene, 'Abdu'l-Bahá is shown driving in a car and meeting with the friends – and then hurrying to the house faster then the cameraman could focus, resulting in a blurred sequence.[41] The second scene shows the Master walking and talking with His attendants, while the next has 'Abdu'l-Bahá speaking and walking up to the house, again walking faster than the cameraman's ability to focus. The following scene showed 'Abdu'l-Bahá with a group of children, both black and white, and was followed by a scene of the Master at a public meeting. The final part of the movie showed 'Abdu'l-Bahá shaking hands with people as they depart.[42]

On 19 June, 'a historic day for the Bahá'ís of New York', 'Abdu'l-Bahá publicly clarified His station as Centre of the Covenant to about 125 people who had gathered at His house on West 78th Street. He spoke of Bahá'u'lláh's Tablet of the Branch and forcefully explained the meaning of the Covenant and of His own station as the Centre of the Covenant.[43]

Later that day, Juliet Thompson was working on 'Abdu'l-Bahá's portrait while Lua Getsinger watched. Juliet recorded what happened next:

> I had just begun to work, Lua in the room sitting on a couch nearby, when the Master smiled at me; then turning to Lua said in Persian: 'This makes me sleepy. What shall I do?'
>
> 'Tell the Master, Lua, that if He would like to take a nap, I can work while He sleeps.'
>
> But I found that I could not. What I saw then was too sacred, too formidable. He sat still as a statue, His eyes closed, infinite peace on that chiseled face, a God-like calm and grandeur in His erect head.
>
> Suddenly, with a great flash like lightning He opened His eyes

and the room seemed to rock like a ship in a storm with the Power released. The Master was blazing. 'The veils of glory', 'the thousand veils', had shrivelled away in that Flame and we were exposed to the Glory itself.

Lua and I sat shaking and sobbing.

Then He spoke to Lua. I caught the words, '*Munádíy-i 'Ahd.*' (Herald of the Covenant.)

Lua started forward, her hand to her breast.

'*Man?*' (I?) she exclaimed.

'Call one of the Persians. You must understand this.'

Never shall I forget that moment, the flashing eyes of 'Abdu'l-Bahá, the reverberations of His Voice, the Power that still rocked the room. God of lightning and thunder! I thought.

'I appoint you, Lua, the Herald of the Covenant. And I AM THE COVENANT, appointed by Bahá'u'lláh. And no one can refute His Word. This is the Testament of Bahá'u'lláh. You will find it in the Holy Book of Aqdas. Go forth and proclaim, 'This is THE COVENANT OF GOD in your midst."

A great joy had lifted Lua up. Her eyes were full of light. She looked like a winged angel. 'Oh recreate me,' she cried, 'that I may do this work for Thee!'[44]

It was because 'Abdu'l-Bahá had that morning made 'this emphatic, authoritative statement in public' that New York was 'invested with that distinction' of being named the 'City of the Covenant'.[45]

## 10

# SUMMER TRAVELS
## *21 June–30 August*

### MONTCLAIR AND WEST ENGLEWOOD, NEW JERSEY

Midsummer had come to New York, and with it, the summer heat. New York was hot and humid, and the friends in Montclair, New Jersey had begged the Master to visit. Leaving New York on 21 June, He stayed at a rented house in Montclair, often 'going to the market ... and preparing the meals Himself, for invited friends and visitors. In general, during His travels, He would always supervise kitchen matters. For Himself, He required the least possible amount of food, but for His guests He provided lavishly.'[1]

Newspapers commonly put their own, not always accurate, understandings of the Master's words in their columns. The *New York Times* wrote that "Abdul Baha ... head of the Bahaists, who number 14,000,000 ... will make his home in Montclair ... Abdul Baha recently spoke in Unity Church here, and was so impressed by the reception he received and by the physical aspects of the town that he expressed his desire to take up his abode in the town ..."[2]

'Abdu'l-Bahá hosted a Unity Feast on 29 June at the home of Roy Wilhelm in Englewood. About 200 friends came from New York and the neighbouring area. Mr Wilhelm lived on a large site with a pine grove surrounded by lawns and flowers of every hue. Tables had been set up under the trees and 'Abdu'l-Bahá was given an armchair in the shade.

'Abdu'l-Bahá looked rested and loving, 'smiling joyously and radiating the spirit of good will'.[3] As the friends surrounded Him on the lawn, He warmly welcomed them all, Christians, Jews and Muslims, white and black. He called two ladies to sit on either side of Him – 'Mrs Krug in her very elegant clothes, the other a poor and shabby old woman. But both faces, the wrinkled one and the smooth, pretty one, were beautiful with the same radiance.'[4]

'Abdu'l-Bahá spoke about the significance of the Feast:

> This is a delightful gathering; you have come here with sincere intentions, and the purpose of all present is the attainment of the virtues of God. The motive is attraction to the divine Kingdom. Since the desire of all is unity and agreement, it is certain that this meeting will be productive of great results. It will be the cause of attracting a new bounty, for we are turning to the Kingdom of Abhá, seeking the infinite bestowals of the Lord . . .
>
> True Bahá'í meetings are the mirrors of the Kingdom wherein images of the Supreme Concourse are reflected. In them the lights of the most great guidance are visible. They voice the summons of the heavenly Kingdom and echo the call of the angelic hosts to every listening ear. The efficacy of such meetings as these is permanent throughout the ages. This assembly has a name and significance which will last forever. Hundreds of thousands of meetings shall be held to commemorate this occasion, and the very words I speak to you today shall be repeated in them for ages to come. Therefore, be ye rejoiced, for ye are sheltered beneath the providence of God. Be happy and joyous because the bestowals of God are intended for you and the life of the Holy Spirit is breathing upon you . . .
>
> How many blessed souls have longed for this radiant century, their utmost hopes and desires centred upon the happiness and joy of one such day as this. Many the nights they passed sleepless and lamenting until the very morn in longing anticipation of this age, yearning to realize even an hour of this time. God has favoured you in this century and has specialized you for the realization of its blessings. Therefore, you must praise and thank God with heart and soul in appreciation of this great opportunity and the attainment of this infinite bestowal – that such doors have been opened before your faces, that such abundance is pouring down from the cloud of mercy and that these refreshing breezes from the paradise of Abha are resuscitating you. You must become of one heart, one spirit and one susceptibility. May you become as the waves of one sea, stars of the same heaven, fruits adorning the same tree, roses of one garden in order that through you the oneness of humanity may establish its

temple in the world of mankind, for you are the ones who are called to uplift the cause of unity among the nations of the earth.

First, you must become united and agreed among yourselves. You must be exceedingly kind and loving toward each other, willing to forfeit life in the pathway of another's happiness. You must be ready to sacrifice your possessions in another's behalf.[5]

'Abdu'l-Bahá's words and presence thrilled His audience. After His talk, a huge Persian feast, prepared by the Persians in His entourage, was offered to everyone. As people began to eat, Juliet Thompson wrote that

> . . . a storm blew up – a strange, sudden storm, without warning. There was a tremendous crash of thunder; through the treetops we could see black clouds boiling up, and big drops of rain splashed on the tables.
>
> The Master rose calmly and, followed by the Persians, walked out to the road, then to the end of it where there is a crossroad. A single chair had been left there and, as I watched from a distance, I saw the Master take it and sit down, while the Persians ranged themselves behind Him. I saw Him lift His face to the sky. He had gone a long way from the house; thunder still crashed and the clouds rolled frighteningly low, but He continued to sit perfectly motionless, that sacred, powerful face upturned to the sky. Then came a strong, rushing wind; the clouds began to race away; blue patches appeared above and the sun shone out. And then the Master rose and walked back into the grove.[6]

As the guests were served, 'Abdu'l-Bahá went from one to another with a vial of attar of rose, anointing each one of the friends.

There were still sixty people there after dark, lingering and unable to leave the love, unity and beauty. The Master talked to them by the light of candles held by the ladies seated on the lawn with 'a resounding call to arise from the tomb of self in this Day of the Great Resurrection and to unite around Him to vivify the world'. He left them, disappearing into the night: 'Peace be with you. I will pray for you.' His melodious voice chanted the last words echoing forever in their hearts.[7]

## New York, New York

Upon returning to New York at the end of the month, 'Abdu'l-Bahá continued to meet the people and answer their questions. One person asked how He liked all the tall buildings in America. He responded, 'I have not come to see very tall buildings or places of interest in America. I look always for the foundation of the love of God in the realm of the hearts. I have no inclination to see other sights.'[8] In a similar vein, the manager of the luxurious Plaza Hotel in New York once offered to give 'Abdu'l-Bahá a tour of the elegant building. The Master declined and later told the friends, 'When I see magnificent buildings and beautiful scenery, I contrast them with the memories of the prison and of the persecutions suffered by the Blessed Beauty and my heart is moved and I seek to avoid such sightseeing excursions.'[9]

On 4 July Juliet Thompson took her mother – whose birthday it was – to visit 'Abdu'l-Bahá. At one point, the Master brought Juliet's mother to sit next to Him on the sofa. As Juliet, Carrie Kinney and Georgie Ralston solemnly looked on, Juliet's mother laughed, 'Look at them! They are jealous of me!' 'Then', replied 'Abdu'l-Bahá, 'we will make them more jealous!' and he seized her hand and drew her still closer. After dinner, 'Abdu'l-Bahá spoke of tests:

> 'Even the sword,' He said, 'is no test to the Persian believers. They are given a chance to recant; they cry out instead: "*Yá Bahá'u'l-Abhá!*" Then the sword is raised,' – He shot up His arm as though brandishing a sword – they cry out all the more "*Yá Bahá'u'l-Abhá!*" But some of the people here are tested if I don't say "How do you do?"'[10]

On 9 July 'Abdu'l-Bahá invited Juliet Thompson to go with Him to the Natural History Museum. It was a very hot afternoon and soon 'Abdu'l-Bahá sat down on a ledge to rest. Since it was still a long way to the Museum entrance, Juliet went off looking for a closer entrance. She found an employee's entrance, which was locked. Just beyond, she found a way with a sign saying 'No Thoroughfare'. Ignoring the sign, she rushed by, only to be stopped by the shrill whistle of a watchman. She explained about 'Abdu'l-Bahá whereupon the watchman turned and looked at Him. 'Is he a Jew?' he asked. 'A descendant of Abraham,' Juliet replied. The watchman escorted 'Abdu'l-Bahá into the Museum.

In the Museum, the group went through a room which had a huge whale hanging from the ceiling. The Master laughed and said, '*He* could hold seventy Jonahs!' 'Abdu'l-Bahá took them directly to the Mexican exhibit where He noted traces of Persian art in the elaborately carved glyphs and said that the glyphs were better than those from Egypt and that before 'a great catastrophe' in history there had been a connection between Asia and America.[11]

Later that day, a group of Californians, including Helen Goodall, Ella Cooper and Harriet Wise, arrived in New York to see 'Abdu'l-Bahá. After a bath and dinner, the women took a taxi to the house where He was staying. Arriving, they stepped out of the cab to find 'Abdu'l-Bahá sitting on the steps of the house awaiting them. 'Very welcome! Very welcome! It is good that you have come,' He said. He called Mrs Goodall to sit beside Him and tell Him of the California Bahá'ís. She told Him that they were in great unity, but wished that she could have brought all of them to see Him. 'They are here. You did bring them . . . I am made happy by your coming.'[12]

At one meeting, Ella was very taken with Ruth White. Seeing this, 'Abdu'l-Bahá called Ella over and asked what her new friend was saying, then strongly cautioned, saying 'Be very careful.' Though Ella did not understand, she heeded the warning – Ruth White later attacked the Faith and became a Covenant-Breaker.[13]

Alice Buckton, who had come from England to be with the Master, asked Him about psychic forces. He told her 'not to tamper with the psychic forces in this world. It hampers and retards the condition of the soul both in this world and especially the world to come. These forces are real, but not to be active on this plane.' The Master said that the human soul was like a child in the womb: the child had eyes, ears, hands and feet, but they were not to be used in the world of the matrix. He said that the whole purpose of that world was to prepare us for this world. Similarly, the purpose of this world is to prepare us for the next, where 'all these forces will then be in their proper sphere for activity'.[14]

'Abdu'l-Bahá one day went to Schenectady, New York where He visited the General Electrics Works along with Stanwood Cobb and Rev. Moore. His guide was Charles Steinmetz, known as the 'wizard of electricity' because of his development of alternating current. Cobb noticed that the 'wizard of electricity' was 'eagerly absorbing 'Abdu'l-Bahá's elucidation of electricity'. Rev. Moore said that 'Steinmetz's jaw seemed to drop open as he drank in 'Abdu'l-Bahá's talk.'[15]

Stanwood Cobb reported that Edward (Saffa) Kinney once asked 'Abdu'l-Bahá if He knew everything. The Master responded by saying, 'No, I do not know everything. But when I need to know something, it is pictured before Me.' Cobb wrote that Shoghi Effendi said that 'Abdu'l-Bahá had the power of intuition, a power of the soul, 'available in its totality'. 'Abdu'l-Bahá would commonly end a conversation by saying that there wasn't time for a fuller answer, but if the listener would meditate, the truth would come.[16]

At a meeting at the Master's home in mid-July, an eminent woman doctor asked Him what caused all the calamities and troubles in the world of creation? 'Abdu'l-Bahá replied:

> Calamities are of two kinds. One kind results from bad morals and misconduct such as falsehood, dishonesty, treachery, cruelty and the like. Surely, misdeeds bring forth evil consequences. The other kind is the result of the exigencies of the contingent world, of consummate divine law, and of universal relationships, and is that which is bound to happen, as, for instance, changes, alterations, life and death. It is impossible that a tree should not wither or that life should not end in death.[17]

At another meeting later in the month, someone asked about the long lives of some people in the Bible. 'Abdu'l-Bahá explained that

> the long lives mentioned in certain books and narratives have a different basis. For instance, it was a custom in former times to mention a dynasty or family by the name of one person only. However, the people in the following ages thought that the length of time that a family survived was the length of the life of the family's founder.[18]

Martha Root attended a talk by 'Abdu'l-Bahá on 19 July when He told the story of 'Alí-Muḥammad Varqá and his 12-year-old son Rúḥu'lláh, both of whom were martyred in Iran for refusing to recant their faith. Martha was so affected by the story that twenty years later she wrote a moving account of the Varqá family, 'White Roses of Persia'.[19]

On 20 July *Harper's Weekly* magazine carried an article about 'Abdu'l-Bahá written by Charles Johnston. In it he noted that:

During the past few months there has appeared at peace conferences, in fashionable pulpits, and at select meetings of devotees, a venerable Oriental with benign eyes and a patriarchal beard who is heralded as head of a new world-religion . . . It is a great and compelling thing to find a deeply religious man not of one's own faith and civilization. Such a one cannot fail to deepen our sense of religion. And these men ['Abdu'l-Bahá and Bahá'u'lláh] have this in addition, that, holding the universal truths, they have honestly and in the face of dire persecution striven to carry them out. They live their religion, as well as teach it. This is their power.[20]

## Dorothy Beecher Baker

At some time during the summer, Ellen Beecher took her granddaughter Dorothy to meet 'Abdu'l-Bahá. At only 14 years of age, Dorothy was extremely shy and was very tense when she entered the room where 'Abdu'l-Bahá was speaking, fearing that He would speak to her. But the Master simply smiled at her and motioned for her to sit on a foot-stool next to Him. Initially, Dorothy was still terrified that He might speak to her, but as He seemed to pay no further attention to her, she relaxed.[21]

Somehow unknown to herself, when 'Abdu'l-Bahá finished speaking, Dorothy 'found herself facing Him, elbows on her knees, chin in hands, unwilling and unable to remove her gaze from His face'.[22] What He talked about, Dorothy could never remember but it was from that time that she considered herself be a Bahá'í. She didn't speak to Him at all, but she could not think of anything else for a long time. One day, she wrote Him a letter saying that she wished to serve the Faith. He replied in His own Hand, 'Dearest child, Your goal is great and God is All-Bountiful. My hope is this: that you succeed in your desire.'[23]

Before He left New York, 'Abdu'l-Bahá requested Dorothy's grandmother come to see Him. He was busy talking with others when she arrived, but He immediately turned to her and said, 'I called you to say that your granddaughter is My own daughter. You must train her for Me.'[24]

Dorothy became an extremely effective speaker. She was elected to the National Spiritual Assembly of the United States and Canada in 1937 and was appointed a Hand of the Cause of God in 1951.

\* \* \*

## BOSTON, MASSACHUSETTS

'Abdu'l-Bahá was 'very tired and weak', and when Agnes Parsons wrote to him from her summer home in Dublin, New Hampshire, 'begging Him to go there to meet some seekers after truth as well as for a change of surroundings and climate', He accepted.[25] Leaving New York at 8 o'clock on the morning of 23 July, He passed through Boston, staying two days at the Victoria Hotel. Juliet Thompson had hoped to see Him before He left, to say goodbye. She got up early and went to His house, only to find a teary woman who said He'd left:

> 'When?'
> 'Twenty minutes ago.'
> 'I will go to the station.'
> I jumped on a subway train and reached the station in a few minutes. But nowhere did I see the Master and the Persians. I stopped a porter.
> 'Did a party of foreigners pass through here just now?'
> 'Egyptians?'
> 'Yes!' There wasn't a minute to explain.
> 'Yes. Go to track 19.'
> But track 19 was deserted except for the gateman.
> 'Has a party of foreigners passed this way?' I asked him.
> 'Turks?'
> 'Yes.'
> 'They are on the train.'
> 'I suppose I couldn't go through?'
> 'Yes, go through but come right back.'
> Smiling my thanks, I dashed down the platform. At one of the windows on the train I saw *a white turban*.
> '*Could* I get on the car?' I asked the conductor.
> 'Yes, get on. It's all right.'[26]

That evening he spoke at a public meeting, dined with the Breeds (where the celebration of His birthday described earlier had taken place), returned late to His hotel, and on the morning of the 24th met friends and seekers in Boston for four hours, beginning at 8 o'clock. He then gave three public addresses, one at the Golden Circle Club where He was asked whether Arabic might become the universal language. He said that it would not. Despite His tiredness he then spoke at the Boston Theosophical Society, and the following morning again met visitors and paid a short visit to Green Acre before leaving Boston for Dublin.[27]

## Dublin, New Hampshire

'Abdu'l-Bahá arrived in Dublin in the evening and spent just over three weeks there. Dublin, in 1912, was an artist's colony and a fashionable summer resort. Many famous, rich and well-known people had summer houses in the area, including George DeForest Brush, a painter, the McVeagh family, which included not only the US Secretary of the Treasury but also a future Ambassador to Japan, and the Cabot family, one of the richest families in the United States. Mark Twain, the writer, also visited the town.[28]

Agnes Parsons had a summer house in Dublin to which she invited 'Abdu'l-Bahá and which He used as his home. Though He only accepted one invitation to speak publicly while in Dublin, every day He gave several informal talks to those who gathered around Him.

The local people weren't sure what to think of 'Abdu'l-Bahá at first, but He quickly calmed their fears. The local newspaper, *The Keene Sentinel*, wrote: 'Abdul Baha, a Persian, who is the expounder of Baha Philosophy first promulgated by his father, Baha Ullah, is to speak at the Unitarian Church at Dublin Sunday. Abdul Baha has been spending two or three weeks in Dublin with friends. He is an eminent philosopher and for forty years was held in prison by the Mohammedans . . .' The *Peterborough Transcript* reported, 'The venerable Persian, Abdul Baha, bears so much resemblance to Santa Claus that two little tots begged to take out their go-cart and get it filled with presents from him. They had espied the supposed Santa Claus sitting on the piazza of the Wilcox Inn and felt that the opportunity was too good not to be improved.'[29]

The way 'Abdu'l-Bahá allayed the suspicions of the people of Dublin was to, first, exemplify the social, moral and spiritual ideals of the Bahá'í Faith. 'People learned that He was not a religious fanatic, but was a person who put His religious principles to work in His own life.'[30]

'Abdu'l-Bahá met with some of the most important intellectual and cultural figures of the day in Dublin. Since the town was a retreat for many rich people, the Master cautioned the Bahá'ís that must be careful not to give the impression that they were there to catch the rich and prominent. He told them to only teach people if they asked about the Cause. However, when Mrs Parsons suggested that His arrival not be announced for a few days so that He might get some rest, 'Abdu'l-Bahá responded, 'We have come for work and service and not for leisure.'[31]

Mrs Parsons had arranged for 'Abdu'l-Bahá to stay in her house, which was called Day-Spring. The room they gave to the Master was on the second storey and had a veranda with a view out over the countryside with its green plains and mountains. Another room was set up as an office with three desks and two tables.

Mrs Parsons had a red shawl and one day she asked the Master the significance of the colour. He replied that red expressed activity, but if taken to extremes could stimulate war. Of the other colours, 'Abdu'l-Bahá said that green expressed joy, yellow was indicative of love, blue promoted thought and black expressed sorrow. He added that 'one should wear black only as a convenience, because it does not soil easily'.[32]

Nancy Bowditch, George DeForest Brush's daughter who later became a Bahá'í, remembered that 'Abdu'l-Bahá told Mrs Parsons to give the Bahá'í message to Mrs Bowditch's father. The Master warned her, however, that Mr Brush would only laugh at her when she did so. Mrs Parsons' approach resulted in what the Master had predicted, but shortly before he died, Mr Brush expressed his desire to become a Bahá'í.[33]

On 27 July the Parsons took the Master for a drive through the McVeagh woods, drove around a lake and paused at a boathouse to enjoy the view. As they arrived back in Dublin village, 'Abdu'l-Bahá insisted that all bills associated with His stay there should be sent to Him. Everywhere He went on His travels, He always paid the cost in spite of many offers of financial help from others.[34]

Mr Harmon, a prominent Boston Theosophist, visited the Master on the 28th. He had written a book on Theosophy and the Buddhist teachings and spent considerable time reading passages for 'Abdu'l-Bahá and showing Him the illustrations he had drawn. The Master listened with great love and patience, but also made many comments that removed Harmon's superstitions. The next day, 'Abdu'l-Bahá commented on people like Mr Harmon, saying:

What captives of superstitions people are! What troubles they endure for the sake of name and fame! What fruit will these superstitions bear? All are transitory and perishable and no trace of them will remain. It will be as though they had never existed. They are sowing seeds in barren land. Man ought to sow pure seeds in a fertile soil.[35]

From about this time, Mrs Parsons asked permission of the Master 'to ask people to come Monday, Wednesday and Friday afternoons of the coming week at five to hear 'Abdu'l-Bahá and it was granted'. Later, he spoke every day at her house.[36]

George Latimer, a young and enthusiastic Bahá'í from Portland, Oregon, arrived in Dublin on 29 July. 'Abdu'l-Bahá greeted him with 'You are welcome, welcome. You have taken trouble and travelled a long distance. I met your mother and father in Chicago. When a person has a great longing, the distance will seem to him very short.' The Master then asked about the Bahá'ís in Portland; were they united and did they meet. When Siyyid Asadu'lláh arrived with tea, 'Abdu'l-Bahá told George in English, 'Persian tea! You drink Persian tea.'

A little later, George was talking with Ahmad Sohrab and mentioned that Dublin, being in the mountains, was a good place for 'Abdu'l-Bahá to rest. Though He was beyond what George thought was hearing range, 'Abdu'l-Bahá answered him, saying, 'Our aim is not to rest, but to become assisted to serve the Cause no matter where we are. Our purpose is to become enabled to render a service at the Holy Threshold. If this be realized, it will be very good. Otherwise life itself is meaningless.'[37]

'Abdu'l-Bahá then asked George what the friends were doing in Portland:

> G.L.: They are all working in different professions. The members of our assembly are workers. They are all poor people.
>
> 'Abdu'l-Bahá: Always the poor ones advance toward the Kingdom of God. The poor are very near to the Divine Kingdom, they are very favored before God, for their hearts are tender . . . Are the souls progressing in Portland? Are they becoming more spiritual day by day? Are they becoming more illumined, more enlightened? Are they advancing or stationary?
>
> G.L.: This year is much better. Last year little was accomplished through misunderstandings of the friends.

'Abdu'l-Bahá: Stagnation is the cause of retrogression. Man must always advance. As soon as man remains stationary in a certain cause he will go backward. Therefore strive that men may advance day by day, that he may progress in all the worlds . . . If the faith of man does not progress day by day, he is retrogressing.[38]

On 30 July, at Mrs Parsons' house, 'Abdu'l-Bahá explained that:

Confirmation is not dependent on talent, knowledge or wisdom. Many unimportant persons have made significant discoveries . . . The disciples of Christ were apparently abased, yet they achieved something which Napoleon never did: they changed the whole aspect of the world. So it is evident that everything comes about through the assistance of God.[39]

That evening, 'Abdu'l-Bahá went with Mrs Parsons to the station to meet the Hannens and Mrs Hannen's sister, Fanny Knobloch. While waiting for the train, 'Abdu'l-Bahá 'suddenly left the little group and strode over to a ragged and bare-foot country boy who was standing between two carriages', and said to him in English, 'How are you?' The boy, unperturbed by his unusual conversant, replied, 'Alright.' At this, the Master laughed with great appreciation and promptly gave the boy a quarter. Suddenly, there were several other boys before the Master, all proclaiming that they were 'Alright' and each being rewarded with a quarter.[40]

As soon as the Hannens were comfortably lodged at the Dublin Inn, the Master, of course, asked if they were happy. When they asked what His plans were after America, 'Abdu'l-Bahá said that He would certainly return to Europe. Miss Knobloch asked 'Stuttgart?' to which the Master replied laughingly, 'Perhaps' (He did go). Mrs Hannen then said, 'They are supplicating for it.' 'Abdu'l-Bahá more seriously said:

See how much we have moved from one place to another. How far New York is from here: Washington, Chicago, Philadelphia, the many places we have visited. And now these ladies have come to invite me to come to California. They are supplicating that I should come to California. Now these two have come to insist that we shall go; and letters are coming about it. A letter came yesterday from the

Spiritual Assembly, asking how it came that we went to other places and not there. Now Mrs Hoagg is going to build an aeroplane and take me there. What do you advise? Shall I ride on it? [41]

'These two' referred to above were Emogene Hoagg and Harriet Cline, who had come specifically to plead for 'Abdu'l-Bahá to visit California. Mrs Hannen suggested that a plane wouldn't be very safe, but 'Abdu'l-Bahá smilingly said, 'When I ride on it, it is the Ark of Noah.'

The following day Joseph Hannen had to leave because of a promise he'd made. The Master agreed, saying:

> The Bahá'ís must be prompt in the fulfilment of their promises, and perform whatever promise they have given. In reality, the length or shortness of the meeting has no influence whatever. It depends on capacity. A piece of dry wood, as soon as it comes in contact with fire, receives the ignition; but a piece of wet wood, even if it stays in the fire a long time, is not ignited . . . Although the length of time of the meeting with Mr Hannen is short, yet it is my hope that its results will become manifold.[42]

One person asked if, because of their abundance in Dublin, there was any good in flies or mosquitoes. 'Abdu'l-Bahá answered, saying:

> What is the use of your creation? What benefit have you given the world? The same benefit that you have given to the world, the mosquito has. You say the mosquito harms and sucks in the human blood; but you kill animals and eat them. Therefore, you are more harmful than the mosquito . . . the reality of the matter is this: The world of life, the world of existence is connected, each with the other. All the created beings are the members of this stupendous body. Each one is a member and that member should not remain imperfect.[43]

George Latimer asked 'Abdu'l-Bahá what should be done for people who were initially interested in the Faith but who have lost that interest. 'Abdu'l-Bahá responded:

> It is because you do not finish with them. They have their old superstitions and their hearts are attached to them; after a while

they become cool again. They must have a new birth as His Holiness Christ said. They must become Bahais. That only their idea that Bahais are good is not enough. People are ignorant, they must become wise; they are blind, they must have sight . . . they must become heavenly, – then they will become Bahais.[44]

Another questioner asked about helping the poor. 'Abdu'l-Bahá said that the friends should try to assist those who needed help:

> Whosoever is a believer and assured, firm in the Cause, there is no doubt that he will contribute towards the assistance of the poor. This is an evidence of the faith. But if a person comes in contact with another who is in the utmost need, and he sees that he can help, and if he fails, this is an evidence of the weakness of his faith . . . Continue according to your ability, not beyond your power, and tell him to content himself with it . . . He is not able to work, that is why he needs your assistance; if he were able to work it is not allowable to assist him. Lazy people should not be assisted; otherwise everybody would leave his work and expect others to support him. There would be no end to it.[45]

A day or two later, 'Abdu'l-Bahá talked about charitable works:

> As charitable works become praiseworthy, people often perform them merely for the sake of fame and to gain benefit for themselves, as well as to attract people's admiration. But this does not render needless the teachings of the Prophets because it is spiritual morals that are the cause of training one's innate nature and of personal progress. Thus will people offer service to one another with all their hearts for the sake of God and in order to fulfil the duties of devotion to Him and service to humanity and not for the purpose of acquiring praise and fame. [46]

George Latimer left on 1 August, but not before hearing one last talk of 'Abdu'l-Bahá:

> All the people of the world are sowing in barren ground and they ride on the surface of the water. Therefore you consider that all their

efforts are fruitless; they strive, work, endure troubles, but in the end they come empty-handed into this world and they leave empty-handed. But the friends of God are under the shade and protection of the Blessed Perfection. They sow in pure soil, they ride on the surface of iron and steel. That is why they gather many harvests and their writings bestow Eternal Significances. Therefore they must be in the utmost happiness and rejoicing that God has chosen them from among the people and distinguished them with this most Eminent Bounty.[47]

'Abdu'l-Bahá also visited the Marienfield Summer School in Chesham, New Hampshire, on 1 August. This camp was run by Dr Charles Henderson for boys between the ages of 12 and 18. When 'Abdu'l-Bahá arrived, He was immediately surrounded by the boys. After giving them a short talk and praising their good manners, the boys showed the Master the tents they lived in and some of their gymnastic exercises.

The following day, 'Abdu'l-Bahá was sitting with Mrs Burton of Pasadena, California, Cordie Cline and Emogene Hoagg on Mrs Parsons' porch watching Mrs Parsons and some of her friends practising golf on the lawn. He remarked:

> It is customary in Persia to say of one who is successful in a certain undertaking, 'He carried the ball out of the field.' . . . If many people attempt something, and one is successful, it will be said 'He carried the ball.'
>
> Today all of the women of the world are striving to raise the banner of equality and establish the fact that woman is the equal of man. But, God willing, the American woman will "carry this ball," and thus demonstrate that God has created all humanity equal.[48]

Mrs Tatum now entered; her automobile had been at the disposal of 'Abdu'l-Bahá while he was in Dublin. After greetings, 'Abdu'l-Bahá said:

> I am thinking of making a heavenly automobile. His Holiness Bahá'u'lláh has constructed for you the Auto of the Kingdom. Have you read that Elias went up in a chariot of fire? This was not outwardly a chariot of fire, but a chariot of the Fire of the Love of God on which he rode and ascended. Now Bahá'u'lláh has constructed a

heavenly automobile out of the Fire of His Love. The motor force of that machine is the Fire of His Love.

Mrs Tatum then remarked 'that 'Abdu'l-Bahá always seemed to think of automobiles when he saw her, and she wished she might inspire a more spiritual thought. 'Abdu'l-Bahá answered: "One must often bring serious discussions through jokes, and then they will give happiness and rejoicing. Some people have frowns and are always serious. This is because of the narrowness of their thoughts. All should be openhearted and smiling." '49

Later in the month, Mrs Tatum was talking with 'Abdu'l-Bahá and said, 'I feel so dejected today. I am unhappy with myself.' The Master replied:

> This is a sign of progress. The person who is satisfied with himself is the manifestation of Satan and the one who is not satisfied is the manifestation of the Merciful One. An egotist does not progress but the one who thinks himself imperfect will seek perfection for himself and will progress . . . the attainment of absolute perfection for a human being is impossible; thus, however much he may progress he is still imperfect and has above him a point higher than himself.50

On one occasion, Mrs Parsons had invited a group of twenty prominent people. Culture, science, art, wealth, politics and achievement were all represented. Mrs Parsons was eager that the Master tell them about Bahá'u'lláh, and the guests apparently expected just such a lecture, but instead He told them stories that made them all laugh. Then He encouraged his guests to tell stories and everyone had a great time, though they learned little about Bahá'u'lláh.51

On 3 August 'Abdu'l-Bahá talked about simplicity and teaching:

> The explanations must be adapted to the capacity of the hearers and suited to the exigency of the time. Beauty of style, moderation in delivery and suitability of words and meanings are necessary. It is not only a matter of uttering words. In 'Akká, Mírzá Muḥammad-'Alí would hear me speak and would repeat my words exactly on other occasions but he did not understand that a thousand wisdoms

and ingredients other than speech are necessary. In the days of Baghdád and Sulaymáníyyih, Shaykh 'Abdu'l-Husayn was told that the Blessed Beauty was attracting the Kurds to Himself by quoting Ṣúfí and gnostic terms. This poor Shaykh obtained a copy of the [Conquests of Mecca] and committed its passages to memory. But wherever he quoted them, he saw that none lent an ear to him. He was greatly puzzled as to why people did not listen to him. The Blessed Beauty said, 'Tell the Shaykh that We are not in the habit of reading the Conquests of Mecca but We impart to them the verses of True Civilization.'[52]

Though most of 'Abdu'l-Bahá's time was spent with the rich, famous and white people, He gave special attention to their black servants, treating them no differently than their employers. On 4 August 'Abdu'l-Bahá addressed a group of 28 black people and spoke of the importance of unity and amity between black and white people. He told them of the upcoming marriage of Louisa Mathew, a white woman, and Louis Gregory, a black man. The white people in the audience were amazed at the influence the Cause of Bahá'u'lláh had on everyone, while the black people were very pleased to hear about such integration. Some Americans considered the creation of unity between blacks and whites to be nearly miraculous and as difficult to accomplish as 'splitting the moon in half', but here was 'Abdu'l-Bahá showing that it could happen.[53]

By now, 'Abdu'l-Bahá was speaking to visitors every afternoon at the Parsons home. Alice Breed, however, was not impressed by some of the people at these meetings. Writing to Thornton Chase on 6 August, she commented on 'the cold blooded, unresponsive, unspiritual persons'. One day she thought 'Abdu'l-Bahá looked very tired, but then Charles McVeagh, the brother of the US Secretary of the Treasury, asked a question. 'Abdu'l-Bahá sat forward on the edge of the couch and 'sent thundering forth with this mighty Spirit which seems to come at His bidding, and told of how people throughout the ages have worshipped the Dawning Points instead of the Sun which rises in different places and which is the Reality.' 'Abdu'l-Bahá spoke about the Manifestations of God with 'the most intensely dramatic expression I have yet seen from Him. Such gradation of voice until He spoke of the Jews even crucifying Jesus, in a whispered awesome breath. He would laugh His little triumphant laugh when He made an indisputable point, and His eyebrows would suddenly project from His brow in the most astonishing and effective manner.'[54]

Mrs Breed had no idea of the effect the talk had on the Master's audience, but years later, Agnes Alexander met Charles McVeagh in Japan, where he had just been appointed as the US Ambassador. When Agnes Alexander offered the new ambassador a Bahá'í booklet, he amazed her by saying that he already knew about the Bahá'í Faith. He invited her to tea to meet his wife and offered to help her in any way he could.[55]

Mrs Breed and her husband had a good talk with the Master one day and she wrote to Thornton Chase, 'What particularly delights me is that I <u>always</u> find him so <u>sane and normal</u>, and his answers <u>satisfy</u> me.'[56] As Phillip E. Tussing comments,

> In the case of Mrs Parsons, 'Abdu'l-Bahá taught her through His interactions with her friends and family. Howard Colby Ives was taught on a high spiritual plane and through prayer. On a more down-to-earth level, Alice Ives Breed was most able to receive the Bahá'í Message as a deflator of the balloons of people's pretensions, and as a very sensible approach to spiritual matters.[57]

On 5 August, a devoted woman told 'Abdu'l-Bahá that a friend had warned her not to go to His talk that day 'lest she fall in a trap'. The Master responded that 'It has always been the practice of the heedless to hold back the sincere ones from the Cause of God. As for a trap, praise be to God that we have been trapped happily for sixty years and we have no desire to escape.' At the meeting, 'Abdu'l-Bahá 'spoke humorously' about philosophers, saying,

> They say that had there been a spiritual world they would have sensed it. But . . . inability to sense a thing is not a proof of the nonexistence of that thing. If inability to sense constitutes proof of perfection, the cow must be the greatest philosopher, for she does not realize anything beyond the animal world.

Everyone had a good laugh at this. Later, a group of men and women from the meeting were driving with the Master when they passed a herd of cows who, spooked by the cars, ran off in panic. One of the ladies cried out, 'Oh Master; see the crowd of philosophers. How frightened they are running away from us.' Maḥmúd-i- Zarqání wrote that 'Abdu'l-Bahá laughed so heartily that He tired Himself.[58]

The following day, 'Abdu'l-Bahá talked about why the Manifestations had to suffer and undergo such hardships:

> Whatever occurs is the cause of the elevation of the Word of God and the victory of the divine Cause, even though outwardly it may appear to be a great affliction and hardship. What hardship, grief or affliction could be greater than that which occurred at the time when the Blessed Beauty was exiled from Ṭihrán? . . . All were in utter despair. But that exile became the cause of the raising of the Call and exalting the Word of God, of fulfilling the prophecies of the Prophets and of guiding the people of the world. Had it not been for this exile, these things would not have appeared and these great events would not have occurred.
>
> Consider the case of Abraham. Had He not been exiled, He would not have received that greatest blessing; neither a Jacob nor an Isaac would have risen; the fame of the beauty of Joseph would not have been spread throughout the world. He would not have become the ruler of Egypt; no Moses would have appeared; no Muhammad, the divine Messenger, would have come. All these are a result of the blessings of that exile. It is the same now.[59]

A few days later, 'Abdu'l-Bahá met a young man who asked Him where He had learned His philosophy. The Master replied that He had learned it 'In the same school where Christ studied.' He then proceeded to explain why Plato's concept of God, that the Supreme Being was dispersed into infinite forms, was wrong and that God is the Reality through Whom all things exist.[60]

The next day, someone asked the Master whether the existence of evil comes from God. 'Abdu'l-Bahá replied:

> There is no evil in existence. Evil is non-existence. All that is created is good. Ignorance is evil and it is the non-existence of knowledge; it has no existence of its own. Hence, evil is the non-existence of good. Want of wealth is poverty; absence of justice is oppression; want of perfection is deficiency. All of these opposites imply non-existence and not existence.[61]

Very early one morning when the main street of Dublin was almost devoid of people, one of the guests at the hotel glanced out her window and saw 'Abdu'l-Bahá walking and dictating to His secretary. As they walked, an old man dressed in ragged and very dirty clothes passed by. 'Abdu'l-Bahá sent His secretary to fetch the poor fellow. 'Abdu'l-Bahá appeared to try to cheer up the man and was finally able to coax a wan smile. The old man's trousers were particularly holey. Abruptly, 'Abdu'l-Bahá laughed and said the man's trousers were not very serviceable. 'Abdu'l-Bahá quickly stepped into the shadows of the porch and fumbled under His clothes. Moments later, He emerged carrying His trousers which He handed to the unfortunate fellow, saying, 'God go with you.' Then, as though nothing unusual had occurred, He turned to His secretary and continued His morning's work.[62]

As his time in Dublin drew to a close, 'Abdu'l-Bahá attended a performance by John Linden Smith at the outdoor Teatro Bambino on 14 August. Agnes Parsons described the play as an 'extravaganza'.[63] Initially, 'Abdu'l-Bahá took a seat, but after a short while, saying that it was hot, moved to sit in the shade of a tree. Nancy Bowditch played the part of a maid and told her daughter about seeing 'Abdu'l-Bahá arrive and then meeting Him afterwards:

> My mother, acting as the maid, appeared in an upstairs window and proceeded to shake a dusty mop out of the window . . . While she was at the window, playing her part with gusto, she looked across the audience to the green lawn behind them. There she saw, coming across the lawn, a man robed in a long, light-colored coat, with white hair and beard, and a white turban. His feet were not visible because of the long coat, and He appeared to be floating across the lawn. She felt as if He had walked out of the pages of the Bible! As He neared the audience, He turned and sat down under a tree until the play was ended. After this . . . people began to form a line to shake hands with Him. Mother got in line behind her sister Mary. When He shook Mary's hand, He noted that she was a fine horseback rider and said that He would give her a fine horse to ride if she would come to His country. When mother's turn came, he shook hands and said very little, but turned and spoke in Persian to a man behind Him. Shortly, another man, a tall American with reddish hair and mustache came forward and walked with mother into the garden. This man was

Harlan Ober. He told mother something about the visitor, 'Abdu'l-Bahá, and about His Father, Bahá'u'lláh. He also spoke of some of the principles of the Faith. When mother heard these principles she said she believed in them. Then Harlan exclaimed, 'Then you must be one of us!' This rather frightened mother and she did not ask any more, but she never forgot that afternoon.

Nancy later left Dublin only to return a few years later as a Bahá'í to establish a Bahá'í community in nearby Peterborough, New Hampshire.[64]

On the evening of 15 August, 'Abdu'l-Bahá went to the home of Raphael and Mrs Pumpelly to meet some of Dublin's elite. Mr Pumpelly had been a well-known geologist and professor of mining at Harvard University. When someone asked 'Abdu'l-Bahá for a story, Mrs Parsons quickly suggested 'the story of Ios, a pretty Persian tale with a moral'. 'Abdu'l-Bahá told the story to mild applause. 'Then, alert and with eyes flashing, He turned to the host saying: "NOW I will tell you a story and it isn't going to be a sermon!"' The Master, dressed in His usual flowing robe and white turban and standing amidst the formally dressed Americans, proceeded to tell a riotous Arabian story that had His listeners

> shouting and swaying from side to side with amusement. In the midst of the applause He arose, bade goodbye to the assemblage, and left the room with the children of the family grasping His hands and coat as they followed Him to the car. While we were driving home, speechless with happiness, He said with the simplicity of a child: 'Now are you pleased with me?'[65]

Two of the Pumpelly children, Raphael Jr and Daisy, as well as a granddaughter, Amélie, later became Bahá'ís. Daisy married a black boxer named John Bates.[66]

On 'Abdu'l-Bahá's last day in Dublin, Elise Pumpelly Cabot, a photographer and artist, photographed the Master. These are the well-known 'smiling' pictures of 'Abdu'l-Bahá.

Of all the rich and famous in Dublin, only George DeForest Brush ultimately became a Bahá'í. Though none of the rest joined the Faith 'Abdu'l-Bahá espoused, they did give it their respect. Several of them were later able to open doors for Bahá'ís elsewhere that otherwise would have remained closed.[67]

## Green Acre, Maine

'Abdu'l-Bahá travelled to Green Acre on 16 August in a car specially brought up by Alfred Lunt. When the Master arrived at Green Acre, over 500 people welcomed Him. To reach the hotel from the gate, about a mile away, He passed a road lined with a thousand Japanese lanterns, contributed and hung by the people of Green Acre.[68] 'Abdu'l-Bahá said that they were very beautiful.

### Sarah Farmer and Green Acre

Sarah Farmer had a vision of Green Acre as a peaceful and beautiful place where people could study all the various religions in order to create a more spiritual world. In 1894, she dedicated Green Acre to the ideals of peace and religious unity, invited speakers of various persuasions and encouraged her guests to listen without prejudice. Financial difficulties almost brought her dream to collapse, and because her health was failing, she went on a cruise in January 1900. While on the ship, she met two friends who were on their way to visit 'Abdu'l-Bahá. Sarah cabled ahead and asked 'Abdu'l-Bahá if she could join her friends. 'Abdu'l-Bahá said yes.[69]

Sarah's time with the Master created a powerful bond that would affect the futures of both her and Green Acre. When she returned, the courses took on a much more Bahá'í-like flavour and some felt that this was a betrayal of the original ideal. This and her worsening financial burdens caused her health to deteriorate even more.

But the coming of 'Abdu'l-Bahá quickly changed things. While He was there, He said, 'This is hallowed ground made so by your vision and sacrifice. Always remember this is hallowed ground which I am pointing out to you.'[70]

On 21 August, Julia Culver, Margaret Klebs, Sarah Farmer, Fannie Morse, Ivy Drew Edwards, Celia Richmond, Alfred Lunt and Harry Randall accompanied 'Abdu'l-Bahá on a carriage ride to the top of Monsalvat, a part of the Green Acre property. After walking around and talking alone with Sarah Farmer, 'Abdu'l-Bahá returned to the others and, waving His arms, announced, 'This is where the first Bahá'í University will be built.' Then He pointed to the centre of the area and He told those around Him that the second American House of Worship, 'a great Mashreq'ul-Azkar [sic] would be built and that the whole hill would be covered with institutions of learning, science, and religion, and to impress us with the importance of this Center, He said already it had been created and was not a prophecy alone and the Mashreq'ul-Azkar hung low over that place.'[71]

\* \* \*

With the coming of 'Abdu'l-Bahá, the atmosphere of Green Acre became more divine and spiritual. He majestically occupied Green Acre, greeting everyone in English with 'Good morning? How are you? Are you well? Are you happy? Very happy?' Upon receiving His answer, He would say, also in English, 'Very well? Very happy? *All right!*'[72]

Because of Sarah Farmer's attempts at building open-mindedness, many people with extremely diverse ideas, such as spiritualists, philosophers, artists, fortune-tellers, ascetics and educators, were seen on its grounds. Many sought only to push their own superstitious views. During his week-long stay at Green Acre, 'Abdu'l-Bahá 'completely swept away the cobwebs of their superstitions'.[73] On 17 August He spoke of true knowledge:

> In cities like New York the people are submerged in the sea of materialism. Their sensibilities are attuned to material forces, their perceptions purely physical. The animal energies predominate in their activities; all their thoughts are directed to material things; day and night they are devoted to the attractions of this world, without aspiration beyond the life that is vanishing and mortal. In schools and temples of learning knowledge of the sciences acquired is based upon material observations only; there is no realization of Divinity in their methods and conclusions – all have reference to the world of matter. They are not interested in attaining knowledge of the mysteries of God or understanding the secrets of the heavenly Kingdom; what they acquire is based altogether upon visible and tangible evidences. Beyond these evidences they are without susceptibilities; they have no idea of the world of inner significances and are utterly out of touch with God, considering this an indication of reasonable attitude and philosophical judgement whereof they are self-sufficient and proud.

As a matter of fact, this supposed excellence is possessed in its superlative degree by the animals. The animals are without knowledge of God; so to speak, they are deniers of Divinity and understand nothing of the Kingdom and its heavenly mysteries. As deniers of the Kingdom, they are utterly ignorant of spiritual things and uninformed of the supernatural world. Therefore, if it be a perfection and virtue to be without knowledge of God and His Kingdom, the animals have attained the highest degree of excellence and proficiency. Then the donkey is the greatest scientist and the cow an accomplished naturalist, for they have obtained what they know without schooling and years of laborious study in colleges, trusting implicitly to the evidence of the senses and relying solely upon intuitive virtues. The cow, for instance, is a lover of the visible and a believer in the tangible, contented and happy when pasture is plenty, perfectly serene, a blissful exponent of the transcendental school of philosophy. Such is the status of the material philosophers, who glory in sharing the condition of the cow, imagining themselves in a lofty station. Reflect upon their ignorance and blindness.

Nay, rather, the virtue of man is this: that he can investigate the ideals of the Kingdom and attain knowledge which is denied the animal in its limitation. The station of man is this: that he has the power to attain those ideals and thereby differentiate and consciously distinguish himself an infinite degree above the kingdoms of existence below him. [74]

## Fred Mortensen

On the night of 20 August, 'a horrifying young man came to a meeting at the Kinneys' house. From head to foot he was covered with soot. His blue eyes stared out from a dark gray face.'[75] This was Fred Mortensen, a reformed criminal. When he was young Fred had got into all kinds of trouble, determined 'to be as tough as any'. One day, Fred and his gang saw some bananas in a shop window and thought that they looked really good. Fred later wrote, 'About this time I heard a dog barking inside the store and looking in, I saw a large bulldog. That seemed to aggravate me and, to show my contempt for the watch-dog . . . I broke the window, took the bananas and passed them around . . . it cost me sixteen dollars to pay for broken windows, to keep out of jail.'[76]

But in 1904, Fred's brothers and gang decided to rob a train. Fred's younger brother stole a big bag of mail. Then Fred spotted the police racing up, so the gang split in all directions. Fred didn't think his younger brother could outrun the police while carrying the bag of mail so he took it and ran. His brother escaped, but that left the police to chase him. 'In my haste to get away from them, I leaped over a thirty-five foot wall, breaking my leg, to escape the bullets whizzing around about – and wound up in the "garden at the feet of the Beloved".'[77]

At Fred's trial he was defended by Albert Hall who introduced him to the Faith:

> It was he who brought me from out the dark prison house; it was he who told me, hour after hour, about the great love of 'Abdu'l-Bahá for all His children and that He was here to help us show that love for our fellowmen. Honestly, I often wondered then what Mr Hall meant when he talked so much about love, God's love, Bahá'u'lláh's love, Abdu'l-Bahá's love, love for the Covenant, love for us, from us to God, to His Prophets, etc. I was bewildered.[78]

Fred's great-grandson, Justin Penoyer, writes:

> Because Fred could not read at this time, Hall gave him a dictionary to use in order to read a Bahá'í book also provided by Hall. With the aid of these new books, Fred taught himself how to read. For reasons even he did not completely understand at the time, Fred's experience in jail had a profound impact. However, as soon as he was able to walk, Fred decided it was time to leave. While in jail, he lured a guard close enough to his cell to take him by the neck, strangle him to unconsciousness, and take the keys.
>
> Fred spent the next four years as a fugitive. He fled first to California, where he worked for the Oakland paper. After experiencing the great earthquake of 1906 . . . Fred decided the Midwest was a far safer region. He then toured the Dakotas, moving from town to town, occasionally finding employment with local papers. It was during this time that Fred rediscovered the book given to him by Albert Hall. Yet unlike four years prior . . . his mind became fixated upon the words of 'Abdu'l-Bahá. Though faced with possible arrest, in 1910 he returned to Minneapolis to visit Hall . . . to learn more

about the Bahá'í Faith: 'I returned to become more bewildered, so I thought; and I wondered why.'

Fred was in regular communication with Albert Hall who, despite his status as an attorney, did not turn him in to the police. This, combined with Fred's surprise at a complete lack of attention given by the authorities, gave the impression that he need no longer fear prosecution for his jailbreak. No longer a fugitive, Fred moved to Minneapolis.[79]

When he heard that 'Abdu'l-Bahá was at Green Acre, and 'that he might go back to his home (Palestine) and not come west, I immediately determined to go and see him. I wasn't going to miss meeting 'Abdu'l-Bahá after waiting so long to see him . . . So I left home, going to Cleveland.'[80]

Despite his enthusiasm, Fred was anxious about meeting 'Abdu'l-Bahá. After all, who was he, a poor man with dubious history, to meet one such as 'Abdu'l-Bahá? Yet the night before he left Cleveland, Fred had a dream: 'I was 'Abdu'l-Bahá's guest; that I sat at a long table, and many others were there, too, and of how He walked up and down telling stories, emphasizing with his hand. This, later, was fulfilled and He looked just as I saw Him in Cleveland.'

Because his funds were low, Fred had to 'hobo' his way to Green Acre. Trains ran, at this time, on coal power; coated with soot and grime, they were filthy outside the travelers' compartments. This was not only most unpleasant, but also dangerous and exhausting. 'Riding the rods', as it was known, Fred hopped a coal train on the Nickel Plate Railway from Cleveland to Buffalo, New York. He arrived around midnight, where he then jumped a train headed for Boston, arriving around nine the next morning.[81]

Fred continues the story:

The Boston and Maine Railway was the last link between 'Abdu'l-Bahá and the outside world so it seemed to me, and when I crawled off from the top of one of its passenger trains at Portsmouth, New Hampshire, I was exceedingly happy. A boat ride, a street car ride, and there I was, at the gate of Paradise. My heart beating double time . . .

I had a letter of introduction from Mr. Hall to Mr. Lunt,

and in searching for him, I met Mrs. Edward Kinney, who, dear soul, was kind enough to offer me a bed. She awakened me next morning about six o'clock, saying I'd have to hurry if I wished to see 'Abdu'l-Bahá.

Arriving at the hotel, I found quite a number of people . . . on the same mission, to see 'Abdu'l-Bahá. Being one of the last arrivals, I was looking around . . . when someone exclaimed, 'Here He comes, now.' . . . When Ahmad [Sohrab] introduced me to him, to my astonishment he looked at me and only said, 'Ugh! Ugh!' not offering to shake hands with me. Coming as I had, and feeling as I did, I was very much embarrassed. After greeting several others and was about to go to His room, he suddenly turned to me and said in a gruff voice . . . 'Sit down,' and pointed to a chair . . . I meekly obeyed, feeling rebellious over what had happened. Such a welcome, after making that difficult trip! My mind was in a whirl.

. . . It seemed but a minute until Ahmad came down and said; "Abdu'l-Bahá wishes to see Mr. Mortensen.' Why, I nearly wilted. I wasn't ready. I hadn't expected to be called until the very last thing . . . He welcomed me with a smile and a warm hand-clasp . . . His first words were 'Welcome! Welcome! You are very welcome,' – then, 'Are you happy?' – which was repeated three times. I thought, why do you ask me that so many times? Of course I am happy . . .

Then, 'Where did you come from?'
Answer: 'From Minneapolis.'
Question: 'Do you know Mr. Hall?'
Answer: 'Yes. He told me about the Cause.'
Question: 'Did you have a pleasant journey?'
Of all the questions I wished to avoid this was the one! I dropped my gaze to the floor – and again he put the question. I lifted my eyes to his and his were as two black, sparkling jewels, which seemed to look into my very depths. I knew he knew and I must tell . . .
Answer: 'Riding under and on top of railway cars.'
Question: 'Explain how.'
Now as I looked into the eyes of 'Abdu'l-Bahá I saw they had changed and a wondrous light seemed to pour out. It was the light of love and I felt relieved and very much happier. I explained to him how I rode on the trains, after which he kissed both my cheeks, gave me much fruit, and kissed the dirty hat I wore . . .

> When he was ready to leave Green Acre I stood nearby to say goodbye, and to my astonishment he ordered me to get into the automobile with him. After a week with him at Malden, Massachusetts, I left for home with never-to-be-forgotten memories of a wonderful event – the meeting of God's Covenant . . . [82]

Fred's story was far from over, for he became a very different person after his time with 'Abdu'l-Bahá. Fred later recollected his experience:

> These events are engraved upon the tablet of my heart and I love every moment of them. The words of Bahá'u'lláh are my food, my drink, and my life. I have no other aim than to be of service in his pathway and to be obedient to His Covenant.[83]

'Abdu'l-Bahá referred to Fred as 'My son.'[84] Yet because of his appearance and the attention 'Abdu'l-Bahá had shown him, certain Bahá'ís became jealous and this 'resulted in Fred's near-expulsion from the early Bahá'í community'.[85] But just a year later Fred received a Tablet from 'Abdu'l-Bahá:

> That trip of thine from Minneapolis to Green Acre will never be forgotten. Its mention will be recorded eternally in books and works of history. Therefore, be thou happy that, praise be to God, thou hast an illumined heart, a living spirit, and art vivified with merciful breath.[86]

As Fred's great-grandson writes, 'thirty-two years later . . . the Guardian of the Bahá'í Faith included Fred's story in *God Passes By*,' and on his passing in 1946, cabled his family: 'Grieve passing beloved Fred. Welcome assured in Abhá Kingdom by Master . . . His name is forever inscribed Bahá'í history.'[87]

Hand of the Cause Louis Gregory called him 'Frederick the Great'.[88]

\* \* \*

During 'Abdu'l-Bahá's last days at Green Acre he met many people, including one girl who said, 'I have come to ask for your assistance. Please tell me what I am fitted to do so that I may occupy myself with it.'

The Master asked, 'Do you have trust in me?' She replied, 'Yes.' He then said to her, 'Be a perfect Bahá'í. Associate with Bahá'ís. Study the teachings of Bahá'u'lláh. Then you will be assisted in whatever you undertake to do.' She then said, 'I am a good Jewess.' The Master then said: 'A good Jew can also become a Bahá'í. The truth of the religion of Moses and Bahá'u'lláh is one. Turn toward Bahá'u'lláh and you will acquire peace and tranquillity, you will hear the melody of the Kingdom, you will stir people's souls and you will attain the highest degree of perfection. Be assured of this.' When she heard the Master's words she was so impressed that she threw herself at His feet and wept. [89]

## Malden, Massachusetts

It was mid-August. 'Abdu'l-Bahá was extremely tired and asked if one of the believers might have a 'house on a hill' in which He could rest for a couple of weeks. Though many were offered, 'Abdu'l-Bahá chose the home of Maria Wilson in Malden, Massachusetts. The Master stayed in the house for ten days, but several in His party stayed there for several weeks while He went to California.[90]

'Abdu'l-Bahá left Green Acre on 23 August for Malden, where He spent six days. Malden is near Boston, and on the 27th the Master gave a talk to the Theosophical Society there. The chairman of the meeting introduced Him as follows:

> Several months ago I attended a convention on the emancipation of religions in this city. Many people of different religions and sects spoke, each one praising the beliefs of his own sect. But a very august personage then stood. By His bearing and by the first few words of His address, everyone felt that this person was spiritual and divinely inspired; that His explanations were heavenly; that He was speaking from God; that He could transform the souls; that He was with God and was the herald of peace and love; that what He said was first practiced by Himself; and that He was a flame from the Kingdom which brightened and illuminated the minds and hearts of all. That august person was 'Abdu'l-Bahá. I am not worthy to introduce His Holiness to you. You will yourselves know Him better than I.[91]

One Boston resident who was investigating the Faith at that time and who would later be named by the Guardian as a Disciple of 'Abdu'l-Bahá was William Henry Randall, known as Harry.

## William Henry Randall

Harry Randall had a great interest in all religions and had studied many of them. His introduction to the Bahá'í Faith had begun in February 1911 when one of his neighbours called to invite him to a talk by a woman from London about a new religion. He didn't really want to go, but he hated to disappoint a friend so he accepted. The woman was Alice Buckton and Harry found her talk moderately interesting, but no more. He courteously thanked her as he left and was baffled when Miss Buckton said, 'You are the only one in the room who has seen the light. I will send someone to tell you more about this Faith.'[92]

A week later, Harlan Ober appeared at Harry's desk, saying that Miss Buckton had sent him. It just happened to be lunchtime, so the two sat down at Harry's club for lunch and talk. After asking many searching questions, Harry invited Harlan to his home to meet his family, which Harlan did two weeks later. Their discussions of the Faith continued into 1912.

When 'Abdu'l-Bahá came to Boston in May, many people invited Harry to meet Him, but invariably he said, 'No. I do not care to meet Him. I know He is a wonderful man, but I do not care to meet Him.' Finally, someone asked if Harry would at least go and listen to 'Abdu'l-Bahá, which he agreed to do. Harry did go and listen to 'Abdu'l-Bahá's talk and afterwards, one of the friends asked if he would run to the grocery, buy some grape juice and take it to the Master at the Victoria Hotel. Harry did so, purchasing six bottles of grape juice, and took them to the hotel. He gave them to a Persian man who soon returned with a glass of juice on a tray and asked, 'You have been so kind as to get this grape juice for 'Abdu'l-Bahá, Mr Randall, would you take it to Him yourself?' This was the last thing Harry wanted to do because he had an 'inner warning' not to, but he thought that would be discourteous so accepted the tray.

When he arrived at 'Abdu'l-Bahá's room, he hoped to just put the tray on a table and escape. At first, it looked as though he might be able to do just that since 'Abdu'l-Bahá was sitting in the centre of a large room with His eyes closed. Harry didn't want to disturb the Master, but finally said, 'Here is the glass of grape juice.' 'Abdu'l-Bahá opened His eyes and told Harry to put it on a table and that He would have it with His dinner. Harry turned and walked to the door, thinking that he was going to escape when 'Abdu'l-Bahá suddenly said, 'Sit down.'

Harry later wrote:

It was said in a most commanding manner which invited no argument, although His eyes were closed again. I sat. I waited. And I waited. I was not used to being kept waiting and I was getting angry clear through. I felt I had almost been trapped, so to speak.

Pretty soon it seemed to me that every part of my body had gone to sleep. I had that same prickling all over my body. I had it in my arms and legs and I was feeling very uncomfortable and getting angrier and angrier all the time. The clock ticked the minutes away and I looked over at 'Abdu'l-Bahá and said to myself: 'He has gone sound asleep and I have to wait here!'

I did not know then that 'Abdu'l-Bahá was wide awake and I was sound asleep. The minutes ticked away and finally I said to myself: 'I have got to sit here. I do not dare to go now. I have practically consented by sitting down to stay.' Suddenly I thought, 'Here I am in the presence of a tired old man and I cannot remain reposeful for ten minutes. What good has my study of all the religions of the world done for me?'

When I thought this I became quiet and the prickly sensation left me and I was at peace. Well, in about twenty minutes 'Abdu'l-Bahá said to me: 'You have just been wasting your time listening to the murmur of the leaves that have fallen off the tree of life. If you want life you must become a leaf upon the tree of life . . . Great is the power of the intellect but until it becomes the servant of the heart it is of little avail.'

He arose and held my hands and looked into my face and stroked me, all in silence for some time. Then He spoke softly in Persian and my mind heard this in English: 'Great is the power of the intellect but it is dead without love. It needs the vivifying fragrance of love to make it the servant of God.' He then blessed me and said, 'Be happy.'[93]

Harry Randall's wife, Ruth, had tuberculosis in both lungs and, having been intensely affected by his first meeting with 'Abdu'l-Bahá, Harry decided to ask 'Abdu'l-Bahá for help. On Sunday, 28 August, Harry went to the home of Maria Wilson, where 'Abdu'l-Bahá was staying in Malden. Harry thought that if 'Abdu'l-Bahá was all that the Bahá'ís were saying He was, then surely He could cure Ruth's illness.

When Harry arrived at the Wilson home, it was packed with people. He managed to get into the house and explained his request to one of the Master's secretaries. The secretary said that 'Abdu'l-Bahá was reading His mail from Persia and that if He wished to see Harry, He would call for him. The secretary informed Harry that over a hundred others had also either asked to see the Master or wanted to invite Him somewhere and that He never accepted any until the Spirit moved Him to do so.

With so many people ahead of him, Harry was pessimistic of seeing 'Abdu'l-Bahá, particularly since the Master didn't even know he was there. He turned glumly, noticed Harlan Ober, so went over to talk with him. Suddenly, a voice called, "Abdu'l-Bahá will see Mr Randall.' Shocked, Harry went to the porch where he found 'Abdu'l-Bahá still reading His mail. When the Master finally looked up, Harry started to say, 'I wanted to know if You . . .', but 'Abdu'l-Bahá simply said, 'Yes, I will come and see your wife this afternoon.'[94]

At 4 o'clock that afternoon, Harry returned to the Wilson home with a car and a chauffeur to take 'Abdu'l-Bahá to see Ruth. Standing there ready to go was 'Abdu'l-Bahá – together with His complete set of Persian attendants and Harlan and Grace Ober. Ruth described what happened next:

> 'Abdu'l-Bahá clapped His hands and the Persians got into the car, Grace and Harlan and my husband were standing on the sidewalk. The Master pointed to the Obers and said: 'You wait here' – and motioned Harry to sit on the floor of the car. This did not please Harry but he did it. 'Abdu'l-Bahá laughed and joked and seemed very happy. Several times He looked at Harry and laughed heartily. Harry knew later in life that he was being taught a lesson in humility.
>
> When they came to . . . the driveway He ordered the chauffeur to stop and wait. They all got out and walked up the driveway, upon reaching the porch 'Abdu'l-Bahá changed to a white 'abá and a white turban. My mother opened the door and 'Abdu'l-Bahá walked right through the house to the porch where I was lying . . . When He

opened the screen door . . . He looked directly at me and at that moment I was aware of the fact that I had known Him always.

We had invited a number of people to meet Him and mother introduced them to Him and when she came to me He pushed His hand towards me and said: 'I know her well!' He . . . took Margaret [Ruth's 5-year-old daughter, later named Bahíyyih by the Master] in His arms and asked her if she was happy. She was a little frightened because she had never seen such a long beard and such a wrinkled countenance . . . Then He asked me why I thought I was sick and I made some senseless reply. He asked Dr Fareed to take my pulse. Then 'Abdu'l-Bahá came and leaned over me and placed His hand on my forehead. He looked deep into my eyes. At that moment I knew that my life was a book which He could read at will. He then told me to do the same things that my physician had told me, besides telling me to eat my noonday meal in the sun . . . He arose after a few minutes and went into the house. When He came to the library door He looked in and raised His eyes heavenward saying: 'This is a beautiful house, someday it will become a beautiful home' . . . Good-byes were said and they walked down the driveway to the waiting car. Again He placed my husband on the floor of the car. [95]

As they departed, 'Abdu'l-Bahá, through one of His interpreters, told Harry 'not to mind if your wife does not like sweet things, that she will when she is better'. Then 'Abdu'l-Bahá told Harry that he should always keep her in the light. Baffled by these comments, when he returned home later, Harry asked Ruth what 'Abdu'l-Bahá meant. Each Sunday, Harry had brought home a box of fancy chocolates as a special treat for her and at that moment, she tearfully told him that she always struggled to eat even one of them to please him. Then she told him 'about the light': that because, as a child, she had had to walk down a dark street each week to get baked beans for dinner, she had been afraid of shadows ever since. After hearing these admissions, Harry was amazed at 'Abdu'l-Bahá's depth of understanding.

Ruth wrote that within hours, she was feeling better. Two weeks later, she visited her regular doctor. He examined her and exclaimed, 'What have you been doing? You are so well!' Soon Ruth was completely cured of tuberculosis.[96] This was Harry's second big step toward becoming a Bahá'í. Later, Green Acre completed his journey.

'Abdu'l-Bahá later wrote of Harry, 'He is the essence of the love of God, he has eliminated his self in His Holiness, Bahá'u'lláh, and has arisen in service to the Kingdom of God.'[97]

11

# NORTH TO CANADA
## *30 August–9 September*

Some time that summer 'at the pressing invitation of the friends in California', 'Abdu'l-Bahá decided that he would, after all, visit the Western part of America. But there was somewhere he wanted to go first. May Maxwell, 'Abdu'l-Bahá's 'beloved handmaid, distinguished disciple'[1] had established the first permanent Bahá'í community in Canada, after having established the first Bahá'í community in France a decade earlier. On the occasion of her move from Paris to Montreal as the bride of the talented young architect Sutherland Maxwell, 'Abdu'l-Bahá had written to her, 'Thou wert as pure gold and didst enter the fire of tests . . . Gird up then thy loins, strengthen thy resolve, and arise with a mighty heart to promote the Word of God . . . in that remote region.'[2] Now, there was a small but thriving Bahá'í community in Montreal.

### May and Sutherland Maxwell

When still a young girl, May Bolles dreamed that 'Abdu'l-Bahá beckoned her from across the sea. She hadn't known it was 'Abdu'l-Bahá at the time, but she knew when she met Him in 1898 when she visited 'Abdu'l-Bahá in 'Akká and Haifa during the historic first pilgrimage by Westerners, organized by Phoebe Hearst. She was deepened in the Faith by Mírzá 'Abu'l-Faḍl in Paris in 1901. William Sutherland Maxwell met May in Paris that same year and decided that he wanted to marry her. She felt likewise, but refused to leave Paris because of her efforts at teaching the Faith and establishing the Bahá'í community there. It wasn't until 'Abdu'l-Bahá gave her permission to leave Paris in 1902 that she and Sutherland did marry. Their only child, Mary Maxwell, just two years old at the time of 'Abdu'l-Bahá's visit to Montreal, later became Amatu'l-Bahá Rúḥíyyih Khánum through her marriage to Shoghi Effendi, Guardian of the Bahá'í Faith.

Sutherland Maxwell became a distinguished architect in Canada, responsible for many important government buildings as well as private homes. Later, he was the architect of the Shrine of the Báb on Mount Carmel. He was appointed to the rank of Hand of the Cause of God three months before his passing on 25 March 1952. May died in Buenos Aires in 1940 during a teaching trip and was given the 'priceless honour of a martyr's death' in addition to the 'sacred tie [with 'Abdu'l-Bahá] her signal services had forged . . . a double crown deservedly won'.[3]

## Montreal, Canada

Some years after His visit to Montreal, 'Abdu'l-Bahá wrote to the believers in Canada:

> . . . many souls warned Me not to travel to Montreal, saying, the majority of the inhabitants are Catholics, and are in the utmost fanaticism, that they are submerged in the sea of imitations, that they have not the capability to hearken to the call of the Kingdom of God, that the veil of bigotry has so covered the eyes that they have deprived themselves from beholding the signs of the most great guidance . . . But these stories did not have any effect on the resolution of 'Abdu'l-Bahá. He, trusting in God, turned his face toward Montreal. When He entered that city He observed all the doors open, He found the hearts in the utmost receptivity and the ideal power of the Kingdom of God removing every obstacle . . .[4]

'Abdu'l-Bahá took with Him only Mírzá Mahmúd and Ahmad Sohrab. His other attendants were to prepare for the westward journey, which would start directly from Montreal via Toronto. 'Abdu'l-Bahá said, 'We have a long distance to go and must therefore leave as soon as possible.'[5] 'Abdu'l-Bahá arrived in Montreal on 30 August 'on a bright moonlit evening' and stayed with May and Sutherland Maxwell at their home on Pine Avenue. When He entered the house, He said, 'This is my home, all that is in it is mine.' Turning to May, He continued 'You are mine – your husband and child. This is my home.'[6]

Sutherland, although greatly involved in the Maxwell brothers' architectural firm, a good sportsman and a member of many clubs in Montreal, particularly those connected with the arts, was a reserved person who did not enjoy a lot of attention. 'All his sensitive Scots reticence shrank from the publicity and limelight that would be thrown upon him as the host of such an attention-attracting guest as the Persian Prophet and His entourage.' He explained to May that although he wanted 'Abdu'l-Bahá to be their guest, he really didn't want the Master to stay in the house and would book a suite for him at the Windsor Hotel. The day before 'Abdu'l-Bahá's arrival, however, Sutherland rushed into the bedroom and 'looking critically at [the] furniture declared: "This is not good enough for 'Abdu'l-Bahá, I'm going right down to Morgans to buy a new set",' then rushed downtown and bought a whole new suite just for the Master. Sutherland met the Master at the railway station and humbly begged Him to stay in the Maxwell home. The Master accepted.[7]

By the time 'Abdu'l-Bahá arrived in Montreal, Sutherland was devoted to Him, but he hadn't always been so. May said that her husband used to say to her, 'You have become a Bahá'í. Very well, you are responsible for this yourself. I have no hand in it. You must not speak to me about it any more.'[8] But those days had long gone. Sutherland had become a Bahá'í and had gone on pilgrimage with May in early 1909. May is reported to have said that 'he was so proud of the Master's visit that if kings had come to their home he would not have felt so exalted. The room in which the Master stayed was considered by him to be holy and he would not allow anyone to enter it.'[9]

The morning after His arrival, 'Abdu'l-Bahá visited the home of Henry Birks, directly across the street from the Maxwells. Geraldine Birks was a very sickly child of about twelve. Because she was not allowed out of the house due to her health, May would send two-year-old Mary over to play with her, almost like a live doll. On this day, Mrs Birks asked if 'Abdu'l-Bahá could visit their home and even 'sent her carriage from that side of the street to this side of the street out of courtesy to 'Abdu'l-Bahá'. The Master, however, walked across the street, but so as not to offend Mrs Birks, had May ride across in the carriage. Once inside, He spoke with Geraldine and embraced her, then told her parents that she must be allowed to go out into the sunlight and walk or she would only get worse. When her parents began to follow the Master's instructions, Geraldine rapidly improved until she was completely healthy.[10]

Later, 'Abdu'l-Bahá visited Henry Birks' jewellery shop, where He bought small gifts to give to people as He travelled. He always gave small gifts to porters, waiters, chambermaids, and others.

In the meantime, Sutherland Maxwell went to the customs house to collect the Master's luggage. He said that 'when the inspector opened the first suitcase and saw a picture of the Master, he asked, "Is this the picture of the prophet from Persia?"' When he received an affirmative reply, the inspector said, 'There is no need to inspect these goods,' and released all the luggage. The same thing happened when they left Montreal and re-entered the United States.[11]

In the afternoon of that first day, the Master went for a ride through Montreal at Sutherland's invitation. When they reached the Roman Catholic Cathedral of Notre Dame (Marie-Reine-du-Monde) 'Abdu'l-Bahá said He would like to see it. 'Everything was quiet and no one was in sight. The Master alighted and went in to see the huge building. With rapt attention, He gazed . . .'[12] After wandering through the church, He noted that the church was present in Canada, so far away from where Christianity had started in Galilee and Calvary, because of the sacrifice of the early Christians who had travelled the world to spread their faith.[13]

That day, as His carriage passed the Unitarian Church of the Messiah, 'Abdu'l-Bahá said, 'Tomorrow we will raise the Call of God in this place.'[14] And indeed, on 1 September, 'the Master's address on the unity of humanity and the oneness of the Manifestations of God . . . was so enthusiastically received by the audience that it is difficult to describe adequately, especially the effect of the prayer he chanted . . . A wonderful change came over the hearts of the people of the city . . .'[15]

As elsewhere, newspaper reporters were eager to report the Master's visit. Newspaper headlines in Montreal were similar to elsewhere, with one exception:

RACIALISM WRONG SAYS EASTERN SAGE – *The Gazette*

MATERIALISM NO PHILOSOPHY, SAYS ORIENTAL SEER – *Montreal Daily Star*

APOSTLE OF PEACE HERE, PREDICTS AN APPALLING WAR IN THE OLD WORLD – *Montreal Daily Star*[16]

The French-language newspaper *Le Canada* was for the rich and comfortable. Its reporting of 'Abdu'l-Bahá concentrated on the economic well-being of people and described the Master as 'an aged man who has some resemblance to a Muslim priest'. The *Daily Herald* was more interested in His teachings about international peace and amity. Another French-language newspaper, *Le Nationaliste*, carried a story by 'Caliban' that said that 'Abdu'l-Bahá 'stood a good chance of becoming a prophet' because He had travelled so far. 'Caliban' sneeringly wrote that someone needed an unusual name like 'Abdu'l-Bahá before he could call himself a prophet. He called 'Abdu'l-Bahá's teachings 'sentimental communism'.[17]

That, however, was not the majority reaction. Many people came to the Maxwell home to visit 'Abdu'l-Bahá, and he gave four talks there to crowds of people. His last public address at St James Methodist Church on 5 September drew twelve hundred listeners.[18]

One who came to the Maxwell residence was a minister. When he left, the Master gave him an armful of red American Beauty roses, sending him away amazed at the majesty and courtesy of the 'Prisoner from the East'.[19] Montreal was, in a religious sense, a divided city, between English-speaking Protestants and French-speaking Catholics. One day the Master was talking with a group about the early days of Christianity. One of those present, a Protestant, asked a question about Saint Paul. 'Abdu'l-Bahá immediately thundered 'Peter, not Paul!' May said that the house almost shook with the emphasis the Master put on the name Peter. He refused to talk about Paul and would only talk about Peter.[20]

'Abdu'l-Bahá invited a number of people to lunch at the Maxwell home on 2 September. As they ate, He said, 'Come! We are in Montreal, Canada, in this home, eating Persian rice which has been cooked by Mírzá Ahmad. This has a relish all its own; what a tale it makes!' He then said:

> To be grateful for the blessings of God in times of want and trouble is necessary. In the abundance of blessings everyone can be grateful. It is said that Sulṭán Maḥmúd cut a melon and gave a portion of it to Ayáz who ate it cheerfully and expressed his gratitude. When the Sulṭán ate a little of the same melon, he found it bitter. He asked, 'How did you eat such a bitter melon and show no sign of disliking

it?' Ayáz answered, 'I had eaten many sweet and palatable things from the hands of the Sulṭán and I thought it very unworthy of me to express dislike on eating a slightly bitter thing today.' Thus man, who is immersed in the blessings of God, should not be grieved if he experiences a little trouble. He should not forget the manifold divine bounties.[21]

Later that day, he spoke about the amassing of weapons of war, saying 'before international peace is established, a great war will in all certainty take place.'[22]

The Maxwells' daughter Mary was very spirited, which He loved. When interviewed at the Maxwell home in 1975, Amatu'l-Bahá Rúḥíyyih Khánum related that, 'small, strong, chubby and highly independent', she was not fond of being touched at that young age. When 'Abdu'l-Bahá came one day into the drawing room and swooped her up to give her a kiss, two-year-old Mary Maxwell responded with a mighty slap that sent His turban flying off His head! Mother May witnessed this horrible breach of behaviour and said to the Master, 'Oh 'Abdu'l-Bahá, she is very naughty! What shall I do to punish her?' 'Abdu'l-Bahá responded, 'Leave her alone, she is the essence of sweetness.' Rúḥíyyih Khánum said that 'Abdu'l-Bahá then chased her energetically around the room until He caught her. Wrapping little Mary in His arms, He gave her a kiss.[23]

'No good reports have reached me of my conduct during his visit,' said Rúḥíyyih Khánum, many years later.[24] On another occasion, 'Abdu'l-Bahá was resting and May emphatically told Mary, 'Don't you disturb the Master. He is very, very tired, and don't you make any noise.' But the moment her mother's back was turned, she shot into the room.[25] 'Abdu'l-Bahá Himself recounted what happened next:

> Today I was resting on the chaise lounge in my bedroom and the door opened. The little girl (Mary Maxwell) came in to me and pushed up my eyelids with her small fingers and said 'Wake up, 'Abdu'l-Bahá!' I took her in my arms and placed her head on my chest and we both had a good sleep.[26]

Rúḥíyyih Khánum said, 'I was so attracted to Him that it was hard to keep me away from Him at all.'[27] Mary would commonly sit on

'Abdu'l-Bahá's lap while He would stroke her curly hair and say, 'She is precious! She is precious!'

May Maxwell later told her daughter that she had never seen anyone so interested in everything as 'Abdu'l-Bahá. He even watched the milkman arrive in his horse and wagon, depositing bottles of milk:

> As He stood there watching the milkman on his daily round – the man delivering at each door-step the morning paper – early workmen on their way to work – what were His thoughts? What was the penetration of his all-knowing, all-searching spirit in these humble lives in their unconscious journey to Him! They glanced at His mighty prophetic Figure with wonder and traces of unconscious respect, & went their way – never, never to be the same again. The light of his glance had fallen on them – the warmth & power of His Spirit had for a fraction of time surrounded them in their daily rounds, their common destiny.[28]

The Master, as always, had a tremendous effect on people in all walks of life. After staying with the Maxwells for a few days, 'Abdu'l-Bahá decided that He should move into the Windsor Hotel because He would be more accessible to more people. The Maxwell's cook, described as 'a difficult and disagreeable person but a very good cook', had been extremely busy during His stay because of all the lunch and dinner parties arranged for people who wished to meet the Master. When she heard that 'Abdu'l-Bahá was leaving, she went to May and pleaded with her to have the Master stay, saying that she was completely willing to 'work my fingers to the bone if He would only please not go, if He would only stay'. It broke her heart that 'Abdu'l-Bahá was leaving.[29]

One day, 'Abdu'l-Bahá went to the Maxwell brothers' office. There, May introduced Mr Maxwell's secretary, Miss Parent, to the Master. Miss Parent said, 'I could not keep my eyes away from him – it is a face you cannot forget!' 'Abdu'l-Bahá turned to May and said simply, 'You can trust her.'[30]

The day after His move to the Hotel Windsor, 'Abdu'l-Bahá went for a walk and got lost. He had been very tired after His last talk and went out alone to walk and refresh Himself. After a while, He boarded a tram which went out of the city. Finally, when He decided to return to the hotel, He took a taxi. The driver asked 'Abdu'l-Bahá which hotel to go to, but the Master didn't remember. He simply told the driver to go straight ahead and very soon they arrived at the hotel. 'With His hair dishevelled and His smiling face, He told us how He had gotten lost.'[31]

That very evening the Master spoke at the Socialist Club, where the president introduced Him by saying that He 'will teach us the principles of brotherhood, prosperity and the upliftment of the poor'. The audience were so delighted with his talk that they 'broke into spontaneous applause, clapping their hands with joy and excitement . . . the walls of the building seemed to vibrate to their foundations'. Next day, the newspapers published glowing accounts and many newcomers came to visit. 'This is all through the confirmations of the Blessed Beauty,' said 'Abdu'l-Bahá. 'Otherwise, even if the king of Persia had come here he would not have been able to bring about even one such meeting.' When the Bahá'ís expressed their happiness 'to see the extent to which the Cause of God had penetrated the hearts', 'Abdu'l-Bahá replied:

> The greatness of the teachings of Bahá'u'lláh will be known when they are acted upon and practiced. Not one of a hundred has as yet come into force. All of your thoughts should be turned toward bringing these blessed teachings into practice.[32]

Many years later, 'Abdu'l-Bahá's concern for the poor and suffering was described by May Maxwell in a letter describing a conversation that had taken place in their home:

> I remember when the Master was in Montreal and there had been a strike for months in Dublin, women and children starving and a generally desperate condition. It had affected me very painfully; I slept little and could barely eat, and had that terrific helpless feeling, not knowing what to do about it. All this Sutherland told to the Master, begging Him to tell me that my attitude was all wrong; and as he spoke the Master turned very white and great beads of perspiration formed on His brow through His own agony and human sufferings; then He said, 'If more people felt as your wife does the world would not be in this dark and terrible state.' Then He added, 'However, you must strive to overcome these feelings, do everything in your power to help, pray, then leave it with God, because the

world will grow steadily much worse, and if you suffer like this you will not be able to survive.'

Nevertheless His Words opened a door of help to these strike sufferers, and on my return to Montreal I went to a very wealthy and prominent Irishman here, whom I had never even seen, burst into tears in his office, to his astonishment and mine, and asked him what he was going to do about it. Well, to end the story, he headed a committee to raise a fund which we sent to Dublin through private channels and which came just in time to succour thousands of women and children.[33]

At some time during His visit, 'Abdu'l-Bahá advised Sutherland and other friends present, that:

> You must cling to those things which prove to be the cause of happiness for the world of man. You must show kindness to the orphans, give food to the hungry, clothe the naked and offer help to the poor so that you may be accepted in the Court of God.[34]

This Sutherland did, serving as treasurer for several years of the Colborne Street Milk Depot founded by his wife and others in 1911, an organization that provided milk to needy children and helped to decrease the infant mortality rate in Montreal.[35]

On 4 September 'Abdu'l-Bahá visited Mount Royal. To reach its summit, they rode a cable car of which the Master said, 'This cable car is like a balloon flying in the air.' 'Abdu'l-Bahá enjoyed the view with the whole city spread out below.[36]

On 5 September, the Archbishop of Montreal visited 'Abdu'l-Bahá to thank Him for what He was telling the people 'concerning the purpose of the appearance of Christ and the other Manifestations. He was pleased to learn about other meetings and talks. The Master said to him, "Tonight I shall speak at the Methodist church. You may come if you wish."'[37] It is not recorded whether the Archbishop accepted the Master's invitation, but other clergymen at the meeting 'were so deferential in His presence, they could not find words to express their gratitude'.[38]

On 8 September the *Toronto Star Weekly* asked:

> What is it that strikes one most in this remarkable man? Is it his message . . .? Is it his power of thought, his manner of expression, the privations he has endured? No; it is none of these. It is his great sincerity. He is a man with a mission, and he believes in it with all his soul . . . There was a wonderful breadth and depth of feeling in that sermon [at the Unitarian church]. It was not the message of a fanatic or a hermit, or a man unconversant with modern thought and modern life. It was Eastern, yet it was Western.[39]

Unfortunately, after leaving the Methodist church on the evening of the 5th, the Master had caught a cold. His departure from Montreal was therefore delayed for a few days, during which the only place he went was the Maxwell home. On his last day, he told the friends gathered there, 'I have sown the seed. You must water it. You must educate the souls in divine moral, make them spiritual and lead them to the oneness of humanity and to universal peace.'[40]

With these admonitions, the Master left Montreal by train on the morning of 9 September, setting out on the long journey to California. But he kept in touch with the Maxwells as he travelled from city to city. Towards the end of October, he wrote:

> I am very pleased with the glad tidings of the exaltation of the Cause of God in Montreal and the unity of the believers. Convey wondrous Abhá greetings to all.[41]

## 12

# CALIFORNIA BOUND

### *9–30 September*

Just before leaving Montreal the Master revealed a Tablet in which he said:

> It is because the friends of California, and particularly those of San Francisco, have so frequently called and pleaded, expressed despair and wept and sent incessant supplication, that I have determined to go to California.[1]

But He was tired, and had been ill. When the train reached Toronto, he got out and 'walked a little on the platform, saying that He was exhausted'.

> We have not gone far, yet we feel tired. How will the great distance to California be traversed? We have no choice, as in the path of God we must regard troubles as blessings and discomforts as greatest bounties.[2]

### BUFFALO, NEW YORK AND NIAGARA FALLS

The Master stopped in Buffalo, New York on 10 September, and spent two days there. His companions persuaded Him to visit Niagara Falls, so He spent the 50-cent fare and rode the trolley to the famous site. 'Abdu'l-Bahá walked to the overlook and gazed out over the immense cascade. The sight brought His Father to mind, 'There were small waterfalls in Mázindarán which Bahá'u'lláh liked so much that He used to camp near them for several days . . . So much electricity can be generated from this water that it will suffice the whole town . . .'[3]

'Abdu'l-Bahá ate some fruit and walked in the park for a while. Some of His companions suggested that He stay a few days in Buffalo to rest, but He said he could not waste even a half day. After returning to Buffalo, the Master walked through its streets. When He encountered several poor people, He gave a little money. The Master was quickly flanked by a large but very courteous crowd; people noted that this was the man they were reading about in the newspapers.

The next day, 'Abdu'l-Bahá met many visitors, including a man from Ottawa who declared that there were 2,000 people there who believed in the golden age and wanted the Master to visit, but He could not. He did, however, write a special Tablet that He entrusted to the man, who departed like a 'ball of fire'.[4]

In the evening of 11 September, 'Abdu'l-Bahá went to the Church of the Messiah to give a talk. When He arrived, the minister gratefully welcomed Him and gave Him a copy of the official church newsletter which contained a long article about the history and teachings of the Faith. After one of the Master's secretaries translated the article, He told the minister that he had published everything in the newsletter and left Him nothing to say. 'Abdu'l-Bahá spoke anyway. Interestingly, after 'Abdu'l-Bahá's talk, the minister encouraged his congregation to go to Bahá'í meetings and learn the truth for themselves. The Master stayed to talk about the importance of His journey until 2 o'clock in the morning.

## CHICAGO, ILLINOIS

'Abdu'l-Bahá was up and packed before dawn and calling for the rest of His party to get up. As He left, He gave the hotel manager a $1 tip for the chambermaid since she was not there at that time. They took a taxi to the train station, where the taxi driver demanded more than the usual fare. 'Abdu'l-Bahá ignored him, saying, 'A man may give $1,000 without minding it but he should not yield even a dollar to the person who wishes to take it wrongfully, for such wrongful behaviour flouts justice and disrupts the order of the world.'[5]

Leaving Buffalo, the train passed Niagara Falls and went through green fields and forested hills, but by noon the train was becoming crowded and very hot. The heat made 'Abdu'l-Bahá very weary; He said, 'The friends in America expect Me to visit each city. How would this be possible? It is impossible to sit in a train every day from morning until afternoon; the body cannot stand it.'[6]

The train arrived in Chicago in the evening of 12 September and 'Abdu'l-Bahá waited until everyone else had got off before He slowly stepped onto the platform. A huge crowd awaited Him, but they quickly formed into two lines down which He passed with His usual majesty. At the station, He encountered Sachiro Fujita, whom He told to come with Him.

## Sachiro Fujita

Sachiro Fujita first saw 'Abdu'l-Bahá from a lamp post he had climbed in order to see over the crowd. As soon as the Master saw him, He said, 'Come down Zachias, for this day I would sup with thee.'[7] Fujita joined 'Abdu'l-Bahá for the drive to the True home. After He had rested, 'Abdu'l-Bahá again encountered Fujita:

> So, how is our Japanese Effendi? Recently the government of Japan has undergone a change. A new emperor has come to the throne. The sovereignty of the former Mikado has come to an end; all the hue and cry have ceased, a handful of dust was thrown over him and covered all his imperial regalia. Such was the kingdom of the Mikado . . . But as you are a believer in God, you have a kingdom which will never collapse and will be everlasting.[8]

Thus began a spiritual journey for Fujita that resulted in his serving both 'Abdu'l-Bahá and Shoghi Effendi in Haifa for many years. In 1965, on Mount Carmel, Sylvia Ioas interviewed him about his amazing life:

> I left Japan in 1903, and landed in San Francisco November 9th, 1903, and remained in San Francisco about a year. Then I happened to meet Mrs Kathryn Frankland in Oakland. There I received Message, Bahá'í Message [when I was] about 17. [I was] in Oakland about 5 years. I finished my high school in California, then I went from there to Cleveland, Ohio. From there I wish to attend University of Michigan, but [in] 1912, 'Abdu'l-Bahá came to United States. From then I went to Chicago to meet Him. That's when really my Bahá'í life began.
>
> I was in Cleveland, Ohio, there was a Bahá'í, Doctor [Pauline] Barton-Peek[e]. She informed me 'Abdu'l-Bahá in Cleveland, and I

was away. I didn't get the message the next morning. Then, immediately, I went Doctor Barton-Peek[e]'s office. I ask, message just received, I can call or not. She says, 'Well, too bad that 'Abdu'l-Bahá just left.' I says, 'Well, I'm very sorry I was away, I couldn't meet Him. When can I make contact with 'Abdu'l-Bahá?' [She] says, 'The best thing is you can wire to Mr Windust in Chicago, maybe he will tell you just when to come to Chicago.' So immediately, I wired to Mr Windust, he says he's waiting for any time for arrival of 'Abdu'l-Bahá. So, I took opportunity, I went to Chicago.

About 8 o'clock in the evening He arrive in Chicago. He was very nice. At the front of LaSalle Station, embrace me, 'My Japanese.' And then, He says, 'You follow Me.' He is going to Mrs True's home . . . We had a wonderful time . . .

I received Tablet in 1905. I had received message 1904, but actually Bahá'í since I received the Tablet, the first Tablet, of 'Abdu'l-Bahá.

One day 'Abdu'l-Bahá asked me, 'Would you like to go to California?' I said, 'certainly'. Can you leave [your] work? I said, 'yes.' I went back to Cleveland and took leave, went to California with 'Abdu'l-Bahá's party.

On the way we made many stop. First of all St Paul, Minneapolis, Denver, Colorado, Salt Lake City, and San Francisco. Jenabi Al-Akbar and Doctor Farid, Ahmad Sohrab, and Mirza Mahmud, are all together, six in the party.[9]

After the western journey, Fujita returned to Chicago with 'Abdu'l-Bahá. When the Master left America, He was worried about Fujita, but Corinne True offered him a room in her home. Fujita lived there for seven years until 'Abdu'l-Bahá called him to the Holy Land, where he served for the rest of his long life. He is buried on Mount Carmel.

\* \* \*

During this second stay in Chicago, 'Abdu'l-Bahá chose to stay in Corinne True's home for a day or two before moving to a hotel. When He arrived with his secretaries, Corinne served them all tea. Unfortunately, it was a type of tea that Persians don't like, and some of them remarked that 'there was better tea'. But the Master drank it anyway, saying, 'This tea is very good because it has been prepared with love.'[10]

The Trues' downstairs rooms were constantly filled with people for meetings or those just wishing to meet 'Abdu'l-Bahá. Large as they were, they still weren't large enough for the crowds. People lined the hallways and were stacked up on the stairs. When the Master became tired, He had to leave the house and go for a walk to find space to unburden Himself of the constant demand for His attention.

One lady, Ida Slater, had known the Bahá'ís for about ten years, but had never joined the Faith. One day she and her husband arrived and went upstairs to meet the Master. Only five minutes later, they emerged, strongly moved and with Ida in tears. The Master had told her, 'You have sought the kingdom of God in many ways and have journeyed far and it was good; but now, you have come home.' 'I knew', she told Albert Windust, 'I had come home when I entered the presence of 'Abdu'l-Bahá. Those were not tears of sorrow; they were tears of spiritual joy.'[11]

Corinne's daughter Arna had a fever and cough and was afraid she had tuberculosis, a disease which had been in the True family and from which two of her brothers had been diagnosed as having died. She was understandably worried that she, too, had the disease. She had planned to marry Leo Perron, but felt it very unfair to do so if she actually had the fatal ailment. As she worried about what to do, 'Abdu'l-Bahá kept touching her shoulder. One day, when Arna had just taken her temperature and was still holding the thermometer, 'Abdu'l-Bahá took it from her and broke it in two, telling her that she would be well and could marry. Arna soon recovered and married Leo.[12]

## Kenosha, Wisconsin

On 15 September 'Abdu'l-Bahá, Corinne and several other Bahá'ís were scheduled to go to Kenosha, Wisconsin, where He was to give a talk. As the time approached for their departure from the True home, the Master was speaking to a group of believers. When one of His secretaries tried to remind Him about the train schedule, 'Abdu'l-Bahá ignored him and kept speaking until it was too late to catch the train. Everyone was disappointed when they arrived at the railroad station to find that their train had left – except the Master. Only 'Abdu'l-Bahá seemed unbothered. The party boarded the next train to Kenosha and were travelling when they noticed the train slow down. They stared in amazement as they passed the wreckage of the earlier train, which had collided with another train.¹³

The Covenant-breakers had been busy in Kenosha trying to take advantage of 'Abdu'l-Bahá's visit. The previous May, Shuʻáʻuʼlláh, the son of the Arch-breaker of the Covenant, Mírzá Muḥammad-ʻAlí, had written a letter to the *Kenosha Evening News*. Published on the front page, the letter attacked 'Abdu'l-Bahá, accusing Him of trying to substitute His own writings for Bahá'u'lláh's. 'Abdu'l-Bahá ignored the attack. In July, Ibrahim Kheiralla wrote to the same paper supporting the claims of Mírzá Muḥammad-ʻAlí. These activities worried the Bahá'ís in Kenosha, but 'Abdu'l-Bahá had told them that nothing would come of them:

> The bats fly away from the rays of the sun and hiding themselves in dark and narrow nitches they blame the sun saying 'Why do not the rays of the sun reach our dark corners and crannies? And why does it not associate and affiliate with us?' What relationship is there between the all glorious sun and the weak-eyed bats! What friendship exists between the nightingale of the rose garden of significances and the gloomy crows! The sun travels in its own sphere and is entirely above the fluttering blindness of the bats.¹⁴

A number of the American Bahá'ís had yet to terminate their association with the Covenant-breakers and this was a danger 'Abdu'l-Bahá was pointing out. One of these was Frederick Nutt. The Master took Mr Nutt with Him to Kenosha so that he might see the Covenant in action. He also went to lift the spirits of the faithful Kenosha Bahá'ís. When He arrived in Kenosha, 'Abdu'l-Bahá was taken to the Bahá'í Hall to meet them. He sat in a ceremonial chair that had previously been left empty during gatherings to symbolize His presence. Following the meeting, which was, 'a divine and joyous festival, the people like heavenly angels of the utmost spirituality, prayerfulness and gratitude',¹⁵ the Master gave a public address at the Congregational Church and then stayed overnight with the Henry Goodall family before returning to Chicago the following day.¹⁶

Despite the success of the visit, 'Abdu'l-Bahá 'seemed to be depressed', and spoke to the members of his entourage about how disunity had begun in the Islamic cycle. He also said:

I am bearing the discomforts of this journey with stopovers so that the Cause of God may be protected from any breach. For I am still not sure about what is going to happen after me. If I could be sure, then I would sit comfortably in some corner, I would not leave the Holy Land and travel far away from the Most Holy Tomb. Once, after the martyrdom of the Báb, the Cause of God was dealt a hard blow through Yaḥyá. Again, after the ascension of the Blessed Beauty, it received another blow. And I fear that self-seeking persons may again disrupt the love and unity of the friends. If the time were right and the House of Justice were established, the House of Justice would protect the friends. [17]

## Chicago, Illinois

'Abdu'l-Bahá tested both the faith and courage of many of the Bahá'ís He met and Corinne True was one He really challenged. First, He had put her in charge of the Temple project, a woman dealing with many men. Then, as they stood at the train station before He left for Minneapolis, 'Abdu'l-Bahá told her, 'Mrs True, I want you to speak in public. I want you to tell the people about the Faith.' This completely floored Corinne and she objected, saying, 'But Master, I can't do it; I have no training, no experience . . . I'm too frank.' The Faith, she thought, had many gifted speakers, but she didn't consider herself to be one of them. Knowing what she was frantically thinking, 'Abdu'l-Bahá told her how to do it: 'Forget what you can't do. Stand up and turn your heart wholly toward me. Look over the heads of the audience and I'll never fail you.'[18]

Then the Master beckoned Albert Windust, who was a young printer and the editor of *Star of the West*. Albert hurried over and no sooner had he seated himself than the Master slapped his leg hard, three times, saying at each blow, 'There are many wolves in Chicago!' The meaning was clear – some Bahá'ís lusted for power and prestige. 'Abdu'l-Bahá did not name names, but was telling the young editor to be cautious and vigilant. The Master made similar warnings to others, not to promote paranoia, but so that they would be vigilant about people who could take advantage of the young Bahá'í community.[19] He particularly warned against some of the Persians in America. Three of his entourage, Dr Amin Fareed, Ahmad Sohrab and Tamaddunu'l-Mulk all later broke the Covenant.

Covenant-breaking was also the topic of 'Abdu'l-Bahá's final talk in Chicago. He began by talking about the various types of bonds that connect people, including family bonds, patriotism and political association. The bond that was stronger than them all, He said, was the bond and oneness of reality, or a spiritual bond. This bond was the bond of the Holy Spirit and it was to create this bond that Bahá'u'lláh suffered. He went on to say:

> Inasmuch as great differences and divergences of denominational belief had arisen throughout the past, every man with a new idea attributing it to God, Bahá'u'lláh desired that there should not be any ground or reason for disagreement among the Bahá'ís. Therefore, with His own pen He wrote the Book of His Covenant, addressing His relations and all people of the world, saying, 'Verily, I have appointed One Who is the Centre of My Covenant. All must obey Him; all must turn to Him; He is the Expounder of My Book, and He is informed of My purpose. All must turn to Him. Whatsoever He says is correct, for, verily, He knoweth the texts of My Book. Other than He, no one doth know My Book . . .
> Beware! Beware! lest anyone should speak from the authority of his own thoughts or create a new thing out of himself.
> Beware! Beware! According to the explicit Covenant of Bahá'u'lláh you should care nothing at all for such a person. Bahá'u'lláh shuns such souls.[20]

In part, this warning was given because Ibrahim Kheiralla, who had caused such havoc in the early Bahá'í community, still lived in Chicago. Kheiralla expected 'Abdu'l-Bahá to send for him and possibly ask for favours, but the Master, though He left His door open if Kheiralla came in sincerity and humility, refused to have anything to do with him.

Corinne True told the story of a cleaning woman who greatly wished to meet 'Abdu'l-Bahá, but was too embarrassed by her rough, workworn hands to do so in the public reception line. Mrs True urged her to go to 'Abdu'l-Bahá and finally, hoping to simply touch His robe and dash away before He saw her hands, she approached the Master. As she bent over to touch His robe, He took one of her hands and raised her up. 'Abdu'l-Bahá carefully examined the captive hand and 'with deep love and understanding gazed into her eyes. "Sacrifice!" He uttered simply.'[21]

Before He left, He spent some time with Corinne True. At one point, she tearfully told Him that she had had a very sad life with sad things to bear. 'Abdu'l-Bahá replied, 'I know, I know, Mrs True, because I have sent them to you.' His answer, instead of causing consternation, brought peace to her heart because now she knew why these things had happened. They were to make her strong. Later she became a great support for anyone who had lost a loved one.[22]

The next day, He was up early to say goodbye to the friends. 'Wherever I go, you will be in my thoughts,' He said. He also told the reporter from the *Police Journal* that 'A newspaper must in the first instance be the means of harmony among the people. This is the prime duty of the proprietors of newspapers, to eradicate misunderstandings between religions and races and nationalities and promote the oneness of mankind.'[23]

## Minneapolis/St Paul, Minnesota

'Abdu'l-Bahá left for Minneapolis at 10 a.m. on 17 September with Mírzá Mahmúd, Ahmad Sohrab, Dr Fareed, Siyyid Asadu'lláh-i-Qumí, Mírzá 'Alí-Akbar Nakhjavání and Fujita. On the train, 'Abdu'l-Bahá appeared tired, sad and uneasy. He noted that He 'did not sleep at all last night. The ark of the Cause is beset by tempests and storms on all sides. But the confirmations of the Ancient Beauty are with us.'[24]

Shortly before the train arrived in Minneapolis, Albert Hall and some friends boarded to ride in with Him. In the city, the party stayed at the Plaza Hotel that night. To the reporters gathered at the hotel to hear Him, He said that He was tired and would see them in the morning. Many invitations were extended to Him, but He replied:

> We cannot stay more than two days. We come and in each city we create a stir, scatter some seeds, awaken the people, inform them of the Most Great Call and then leave. In this short space of time our work is to proclaim the Cause of God and, praise be to God, the results are evident day by day and accompanied by great confirmations.[25]

On the morning of the 18th, 'Abdu'l-Bahá met with many people in the assembly hall of the hotel. A Jewish rabbi met the Master and invited

Him to speak in his synagogue. 'Abdu'l-Bahá accepted this invitation and spoke with the rabbi:

> 'I have come from your original homeland, Jerusalem. I passed forty-five years in Palestine, but I was in prison.' The rabbi said, 'We are all prisoners in this world.' The Master added, 'But I was imprisoned in two prisons. Even then I was contented and was completely happy and grateful.' The rabbi then said, 'The Prophets of God have always been imprisoned and now His Holiness 'Abdu'l-Bahá, the chosen one of God, is imprisoned.' The Master stated: 'I am but the servant of God; but the practice of the people has always been to persecute all the Prophets and the holy ones and then later to prostrate themselves at the mention of their names.'[26]

Later that morning, 'Abdu'l-Bahá gave a talk at the Commercial Club. In the evening, He addressed the congregation at the rabbi's synagogue, proving the station of both Christ and Muhammad. So persuasive was His oration that afterwards many approached the Master with 'utmost humility and admiration. One of them said openly that he would no longer be a Jew.'[27]

On the 19th, the city's newspapers reported on their unusual guest. The *Minneapolis Journal* wrote:

> Long before the other guests at the Plaza Hotel were astir today, Abdul Baha Abbas, head of the Bahaists of the world, who believes and teaches the eventual harmony and unity of religious mankind... was up and about in parlor 603, pacing quietly across the room... At 7 a.m. the five members of his party called at his parlor to pay their respects... He smiled faintly, and two beautiful, large hazel eyes looked about the room. He rose from the divan on which he had been sitting and walked toward the window. Except that his complexion is dark and he is short of stature, he looked not unlike the portraits of General Robert E. Lee, the contour nose being particularly striking.
>
> ... he shook hands with several visitors, and his hand felt like a silken glove. H. S. Fugeta, a Japanese from Cleveland, who had joined the party at Chicago, came in and knelt beside a window chair, where Abdul Baha had seated himself, and the leader placed

his hands on the head of the kneeling man and uttered prayer in Persian. The syllable were strangely effective and rhythmetrical.[28]

The next day, the *Tribune* newspaper wrote:

> PROPHET OF GLORY VISITS MINNEAPOLIS. Groups of curious people watched the progress through Loring park yesterday of an aged man with white turban and a flowing white beard, who walked with his hands behind his back, and was followed by a group of fez-crowned men, who spoke in a low voice and paid the aged man great deference . . . The aged man was Abdul Baha, from the Far East, 'Prophet of Glory'. . . . Abdul Baha is one of the most picturesque religious figures in the Orient. He is 68 years old and was imprisoned for 50 years for his beliefs.[29]

With a group of friends, 'Abdu'l-Bahá visited the Walker Art Gallery on the morning of 19 September. After looking at the ancient artefacts, the Master noted that rich people in the West collected antique objects 'in order to render a service to the world of art', while wealthy Persians collected horses, all for the purpose of satisfying their whims and promoting their status. He concluded by saying that 'in comparison to service to the Cause, both attitudes are barren, producing no result. For example, if the effort these people put into gathering these objects and the millions of dollars spent acquiring them, were employed for the Cause of God, their stars of happiness and prosperity would shine evermore from the horizon of both worlds.'[30]

In the afternoon, 'Abdu'l-Bahá met with a diverse group in the home of Albert Hall. Later, Dr Clement Woolson collected the Master and drove Him the fifteen miles from Minneapolis to St Paul, crossing the Mississippi River on the way. When they arrived at Dr Woolson's home, the Master spoke to the gathered friends. Afterwards, He took a walk in the garden where several children approached and asked about His own country and why He was in St Paul. After listening respectfully to His answers, they followed the Master to the house and asked if they could enter. 'Abdu'l-Bahá gave each of them some coins, and wrapped them in His love. One very small child leaped from his father's lap, ran to 'Abdul-Bahá and said, 'I love you first and then my father.'[31]

When the time came to return to Minneapolis, 'Abdu'l-Bahá left the house to find two cars available to Him, one belonging to some enthusiastic women who were new Bahá'ís and the other to Dr Woolson. Initially, 'Abdu'l-Bahá sat in the car with the women, but when Dr Woolson indicated that it was his car that was to carry Him to his next meeting, the Master changed vehicles. Dr Woolson had to drive at full speed to get 'Abdu'l-Bahá to the meeting on time. He would have been late had He driven with the women – their car broke down and they arrived very late. In recompense, however, their late arrival resulted in their having dinner with the Master.[32]

Before His departure from Minneapolis on the morning of 20 September, 'Abdu'l-Bahá told His followers, 'You must have deep love for one another. Go to see each other and be consoling friends to all. If a friend lives a little distance from the town, go to see him.'[33]

'Abdu'l-Bahá's train passed through the small town of Aitkin, Minnesota, pausing briefly to let off and board passengers. On the platform were a small boy, aged one-and-a-half, and a man, waiting for the boy's aunt to disembark. Suddenly, the young lad's attention was grabbed by a very unusual man standing in one of the train exits. The stranger was dressed in a white, full-length robe, wore a turban and had a white beard. The stranger was, of course, 'Abdu'l-Bahá, but the boy wouldn't know this for 28 years. The little boy was William Sears (Bill), who would be appointed a Hand of the Cause of God 45 years later. That night, Bill had the first of a long-running series of dreams about 'Abdu'l-Bahá, but not until 1940 when his new wife, Marguerite, showed him a picture of the Master would Bill know Who it was he had seen.[34]

## Omaha and Lincoln, Nebraska

'Abdu'l-Bahá arrived in Omaha late on the 20th and went directly to His hotel. The next morning, one of His secretaries read the news about war in the Balkans. His response was:

> Our own 'war' is good because it conquers all. When a crown of thorns was placed on the head of Christ, He saw with His own eyes the crowns of kings under His feet. Now, when I look, I see all the powers and nations defeated, scattered and lost in the wilderness while the Cause of God is victorious over all and subdues all. All future events are evident and visible to the eyes of the holy Manifestations.[35]

'Abdu'l-Bahá's purpose in stopping in Nebraska was to visit William Jennings Bryan, the future US Secretary of State. Bryan had visited 'Abdu'l-Bahá in 'Akká in 1906. He had tried to make a second visit, getting as far as Haifa, but was unable to see Him due to the activities of the Master's enemies. Now, 'Abdu'l-Bahá was attempting to return his visit.

'Abdu'l-Bahá arrived at the station just as the train for Lincoln was departing, so they had to wait for the next. Suddenly, seeing their Persian robes, a man ran up and said that the Bahá'ís in Omaha had received a telegram from Minneapolis and had been looking for the Master. He quickly went to bring the other Omaha Bahá'ís and 'Abdu'l-Bahá spoke with them about the calamities that had afflicted the Cause, saying, 'Up to now, whatever has occurred has had the effect of spreading the Cause of God.'[36] Because 'Abdu'l-Bahá had missed the train, the local Bahá'ís had the bounty of His company all evening until midnight when the next train left.

'Abdu'l-Bahá arrived in Lincoln at 3 o'clock in the morning. At a more appropriate hour, the party telephoned the Bryan home but found that Mr Bryan was off electioneering for Woodrow Wilson. Mary Bryan and her daughter, Ruth, invited 'Abdu'l-Bahá to visit nevertheless and He did so. The party hired a car and drove many miles to the Bryan estate. Mrs Bryan hurried out to meet the Master and both she and her daughter expressed their great joy at His visit. Mrs Bryan made tea for all and gave them a tour of her home. Over tea, 'Abdu'l-Bahá spoke to Mrs Bryan about her husband and His own work:

> I have come especially to Lincoln to repay the visit you made to me during your trip around the world. At that time I was much grieved because on your second visit to Acca you were prevented from coming to see me by the surveillance of the guards. Those were difficult and troublesome days indeed! As it was impossible then to meet you, I was longing and praying for a greater opportunity and a better chance.
>
> Consider the power of His Holiness Bahá'u'lláh! I was a prisoner, and no one would ever have thought that I would be allowed to leave, for one moment, the fortified town of Acca! But God took the chain from my neck and put it around the neck of Abdul Hamid. He is now surrounded with far worse sufferings than those with which he surrounded me . . .

From the day that I landed in America I have been anticipating meeting Mr Bryan and you. I am very sorry that he is not here, but, praise be to God, you are his noble and worthy representative . . .

I love this country with an exceeding love, for its inhabitants are a noble people and its government is fair and just . . . I hope that this illustrious democracy may become confirmed in the establishment of Universal Peace, and Mr Bryan may become the standard-bearer of the invulnerable army of International Arbitration . . .

. . . convey to your respected husband my love and warm greeting, and say to him on my behalf: '. . . I shall never forget our meeting in Acca, and ever pray that you may become assisted in the accomplishment of such service as to cause you to shine like a brilliant star from the horizon of everlasting glory forever and ever. Your aims and intentions are honourable, and their full realization conducive to the public weal. In all your undertakings you have been aided by God in the past, and will be similarly reinforced in the future. If the wide scope of their results are not quite manifest now, they will become evident afterward. Work for the sake of God and for the improvement of humanity without any expectation of praise and reward . . . The present is always unimportant, but we must make our present so filled with mighty, altruistic deeds as to assume significant weight and momentous importance in the future. A shallow present will surely be followed by a superficial future . . .[37]

Before leaving, 'Abdu'l-Bahá signed a guest book and, in His own hand, wrote a prayer for assistance when Mrs Bryan asked for prayers for her husband.

When the party arrived back at their hotel in Lincoln, they were met by a group of Arabs who had read about His arrival in the newspaper. 'Abdu'l-Bahá expressed happiness that His 12-hour visit had become the cause of spreading the teachings of God. The party boarded the train at 11 o'clock that night. His aides tried to persuade Him to get a sleeping compartment, but He simply replied, 'We must all be together. The only purpose of this journey is to serve the Cause of God. We have no other aim. We will all sleep in our coach seats.'[38]

## Denver, Colorado

'Abdu'l-Bahá and His party arrived in Denver at about two o'clock in the afternoon and were met by Mr and Mrs Ashton and a few other friends. He was taken to the Hotel Shirley where He begged a few hours of sleep. Less than three hours later he was giving newspaper interviews to the waiting reporters. Later He went to the home of Mrs Roberts, which was so filled with people that some were standing in the entrance. He told the crowd:

> God has chosen you for the worthy service of unifying mankind; God has chosen you for the purpose of investigating reality and promulgating international peace . . . God has chosen you to blend together human hearts and give light to the human world. The doors of his generosity are wide, wide open to us but we must be attentive, alert and mindful, occupied with service to all mankind . . .[39]

On 25 September Denver's *Daily News* carried a full-page article that included a photo of the whole travelling party, but with some of them misidentified:

> NEW JOHN THE BAPTIST PREACHING UNIVERSAL BROTHERHOOD . . . Venerable, Impressive and Imposing Figure From Oriental Lands Comes to Give, Asking Nothing But to Be Heard
> . . . For when this aged man – whose presence in the dominant personality defies age – speaks, when the keen dark eyes become afire with words he utters – the first impression of Abdul Ba-ha becomes but a superficial one . . . I was thrilled for an hour by the flow of sonorous words that rolled from the lips of this man of the Orient, who has a message for all the world.[40]

The *Denver Post* of the same day carried this article:

> 'ABDUL BA-HA ABBAS–PERSIAN TEACHER–TO CONVERT DENVER. A Man of God has come to town. With the arrival yesterday of Abdul Ba-ha Abbas, a quicker spirit of tolerance, of brotherly love, of sincerer charity, of all those virtues which lift man

above the beast was given wing and must, before his departure, have its effect upon every man and woman who comes within the radius of this wise man of the East.

Abdul Ba-ha entered the city without any of the glitter or pomp which is the attribute of nobility. He came . . . companioned by five devoted servants of the faith he preaches and by a reputation for sanity and holiness which makes the most hardened cynic a respectful spectator.

It was with a sense of levity that I received the assignment to call on the Ba-ha. 'Another of those Oriental teachers and prophets come to work on the emotions of women and long-haired men,' I thought. 'Another of those cunning gentlemen of Persia, who have deep wisdom concerning the spiritual strivings and material cupidities of this, our native land.'

In such fettle I approached the presence of his apartments at the Shirley. In a far corner of the room, leaning back in his chair as though oppressed by a great weariness, his white beard flowing over his breast, his brown hands, carrying one simple jeweled ring, folded, and his eyes sending a kindly greeting toward the door, sat the Ba-ha . . .

There was nothing theatrical, nothing spectacular in the scene. The atmosphere was vital with that brand of religion which can emanate only from one who is utterly pure in heart; who has found the truth . . . The story of this man is rich in romance. Imprisoned for twenty years, exiled after that because he proclaimed the doctrine of brotherly love, equality of all men and the need of a recognition of the value of a spiritual life . . . he set out to give the message to the world at large . . .

'Why was that man imprisoned?' I asked Dr Fareed. 'Why was Christ crucified?' he answered quickly . . . The Ba-ha talks with a strong voice, sitting moveless as he speaks and waits for Dr Fareed to pass on his message . . . Certainly Denver has not in the past been honoured by the presence of a Godlier man than this simple hearted Persian, whose only weapon, whose only charm is the Word. This he gives unto his hearers in that ornate, courteous form that is like rich embroidery . . .

'If you have a word or an essence which a brother has not, offer it with the tongue of love and kindness. If it is accepted the end is attained. If not with regard to him, deal not harshly, but pray.'

The above is one of those delicate sentiments offered by the Ba-ha in parting, and which it might be well for every man and woman in this city of many strifes to cut out and paste in their hats or on their mirrors.[41]

The *Denver Post* provided a car to take 'Abdu'l-Bahá to the Church of Divine Science. The Master told His companions:

Behold the power and confirmation of the Blessed Beauty: The pastor comes in person with all humility to invite us and the proprietor of a leading journal sends his automobile for our use, so that we may raise the call of God in the church. Truly, such confirmations have never been seen in other dispensations and in no age have the Manifestations of the Cause of God met with such reverence and honor. But . . . we must not consider that they are due to our addresses or our eloquence. These shining lights which you see will instantly darken if the origin of their bounty is severed from them.[42]

'Abdu'l-Bahá spoke with many people in Denver and told each what they needed to hear. To one He said:

I have come to your city and found tall buildings and advancement in material civilization. Now I will lead you to my own city which is the world above. Its administration is the oneness of humanity, its law is international peace, its palaces are ever shining with the lights of the Kingdom, its season is always spring, its trees are ever green, its fruits are fresh and sweet, its sun is ever ascending, its moon is always full, its stars are ever brilliant and its planets are ever circling. That is our city and the Founder is Bahá'u'lláh. We have enjoyed the pleasures of this city and now I invite you to that city. I hope you will accept this invitation.[43]

To another he said: 'Man is like a bird in a cage. A bird cannot attain freedom merely by knowing that in the free world there are pure breezes, spacious skies, beautiful gardens, pleasant parks and fountains; rather, the bird must find a power to break the cage and soar into the wide firmament.'[44]

He then related a story about detachment:

The Persian friends travel mostly on foot. They sleep whenever they get tired. They rest wherever they see a shady tree. Once a person came to an Amír. The Amír wished to present him with a gift and with insistence gave him a robe. Later, when he became tired, he lay down under a tree in the forest with the robe folded under his head. But he could not sleep as he repeatedly imagined that a thief was crouching nearby to take away the robe. At last he rose, threw the robe away and said, 'As long as this robe is with me, I shall not find rest. To find rest, I must give it up.' How long will you desire a robe for your body? Release your body that you may have no need for a robe.[45]

One day 'Abdu'l-Bahá and His attendants went for a walk through Denver. As they passed a statue of an American hero, the Master noted that, 'Their victories are trifling in comparison with the first victories of Islam, yet they are famous and a source of honour to all who know them.' 'Abdu'l-Bahá attracted much attention, partly because of His unusual dress, but also because of His majesty. One of His companions mentioned that some of the people thought them simply a picturesque sight, an amusing comedy. 'Abdu'l-Bahá replied, 'Yes, it is a heavenly act, a performance of the Kingdom, a wonderful pageant.' Later, as they rode the train to a meeting, some of the passengers were seen talking about them. 'Abdu'l-Bahá sent one of His companions to tell them that they were, 'neither Turks nor Arabs, neither of the East nor of the West, rather we are of heaven and of God'.[46]

Shortly before leaving Denver, someone asked Him about eating meat. The Master noted that birds have beaks so they can pick up seeds while goats and cows have teeth for eating grass. Carnivores have claws like forks and sharp teeth for eating meat. Man, however, does not have teeth for eating meat. 'God', He said, 'has given Him beauty of form and has created him blessed and not rapacious and bloodthirsty.'[47]

## GLENWOOD SPRINGS, COLORADO

Abdu'l-Bahá left Denver on the train at nine in the morning of 26 September. They travelled all day, and the speed and jolting motion of the train greatly tired Him, so his attendants begged Him to stop and rest, since California was such a great distance away. So when the train arrived in Glenwood Springs at two o'clock in the morning, the party disembarked and checked into the Hotel Colorado.

The appropriately named *Daily Avalanche* newspaper (the town being surrounded by high mountains) contained a story about the Master headlined, "Abdu'l-Baha Abbas of Persia, lecturer and philosopher, stays in Glenwood Springs a day and enjoys the cave baths."[48]

In the morning after tea, the Master left the hotel for a walk. Glenwood Springs was surrounded by high, forest-mantled mountains with wild flowers in abundance. 'Abdu'l-Bahá wandered through the park-like garden adjacent to the hotel until He reached the river where there were bath houses and hot springs. The whole group went to the baths, which were in a special room into which hot water came from a natural cave. The water was very hot and most people could tolerate it for only 15 minutes or so. Fujita recounted years later to Sylvia Ioas: 'He got so tired. He say He want to go to bath. We had the hot spring there, yeah. And He went and all of us . . . Then He stay in the hot springs longer than anybody else. And when He come out, He call me, "Give me massage." Relaxed. Slept hours!'[49] The Master said, 'Today I am relieved of fatigue. We have been to many lovely places during this journey but because of our work we had no time to look at the scenery. We did not even think of a moment's rest. Today, however, we have had a little respite.'

As the Master viewed the clear, rushing water of the river and the majestic mountains and parks, He said, 'May God not have mercy on the tyrants who kept the Blessed Beauty imprisoned between four walls in 'Akká. How such scenes were loved by Him! Once He said that He had not seen greenery for several years.'[50]

'Abdu'l-Bahá walked back to the hotel and said how nice it would be to eat in the gardens. The hotel manager, who recognized 'Abdu'l-Bahá from the Denver newspapers, immediately brought out a large table and chairs. Fujita remembered that there were only five chairs at the table. When 'Abdu'l-Bahá asked why there was no chair for Fujita, the waiter said, 'Well, he is your servant.' 'Abdu'l-Bahá then said, 'That doesn't matter. Make another place. It doesn't make any difference whether servant, or different colour. We are all one. He would sit there, and Fujita come here.' 'It was so beautiful. And all the Persians, five of 'em, around. And so, then the waiter was very much surprised,' remembered Fujita later.[51] The hotel guests gradually became aware of Who was in their midst and began to come by and hear about the Cause of God.

Later in the afternoon, while 'Abdu'l-Bahá was crossing a bridge, a messenger gave them a telegram which reported that Thornton Chase, America's first Bahá'í, was seriously ill in Los Angeles. The news dampened the Master's spirits.[52]

In the afternoon, Fujita and some of the Persians took a short walk around Glenwood Springs. Fujita recalled that:

> . . . on the way back I saw a little shop, with a great big watermelon, ripe, red. So, I, myself, like watermelon, so I bought it and carried big watermelon like this, and when I brought home to 'Abdu'l-Bahá, sitting He watch me, 'What do you got there?' He says. I said, 'I have watermelon.'
>
> 'All right, come!' Immediately, He put His hand in the centre of the watermelon and started eating. 'Wait, 'Abdu'l-Bahá, I want to bring you a knife and a fork!' 'No, never mind.' I was glad. And then we had to share with all Bahá'ís. And then at midnight we took train.[53]

## Salt Lake City, Utah

'Abdu'l-Bahá and His party arrived in Salt Lake City on the afternoon of 28 September. Bahá'ís travelled from other areas to have the bounty of seeing 'Abdu'l-Bahá, including Feny Paulson, from Missoula, Montana. She had received a telegram stating that 'Abdu'l-Bahá would be in Salt Lake City on a certain date so she arrived a day early. Overnight, she shared a room at the YWCA, with which she was not impressed. Apart from the construction scaffolding in the entry hall and the dim light, the food was disgusting, with a fly in the German fries, a chicken still with many feathers attached and roaches at the soda fountain. Feny spent much of the next day visiting all the various train stations in the city, trying to find the one where 'Abdu'l-Bahá would arrive. Finally, at one station she saw at the far end of the platform 'an oriental picture in an occidental setting' and was soon greeted by the Master's 'powerful greeting: "Alláh'u'Abhá!"' The enlarged group took a motor stage into Salt Lake City to the Salt Lake City Hotel, but it was too expensive, so they walked to the Kenyon Hotel.[54]

There was a large agricultural convention and State Fair in town when they arrived which interested the Master. 'Abdu'l-Bahá visited the agricultural exhibition and spent some time exploring it. He visited a display of agricultural machines, asking about their cost and use, then went to the area where fruits and vegetables were displayed. As He examined the 'grapes, apples, pears, pomegranates, cabbages and very large pumpkins', He praised American agricultural progress. When the section manager saw his exotic visitor he rushed over to be introduced, then accompanied 'Abdu'l-Bahá through the area, offering Him samples of fruit (though sale and consumption were prohibited). Afterwards, 'Abdu'l-Bahá directed His attendants to buy seeds of some of the fruits and flowers to be sent to the Holy Land to be planted at the Shrine of Bahá'u'lláh.[55]

In addition to the agricultural display, the Mormon Convention was being held in the city and there was a parade down one of the main roads. The road was lined with a huge crowd of spectators behind ropes, waiting for the beginning of the parade. Fujita said:

> We walked down to the street. There, the street was lined up with people, and there was gonna be a parade of celebration. We didn't know anything about it. 'Come' [He said and we] walked right in the centre of the street, and on the car line, six of us, He is ahead, like this. All the people lined up and thought, 'Head of the procession is coming down.'[56]

At one point on the parade route, there was a special section roped off. When 'Abdu'l-Bahá, in His flowing robes and majestic bearing, walked up to the roped-off section, a reporter quickly took advantage to get a story, which appeared the next day on the front page of the newspaper.

As 'Abdu'l-Bahá returned to His hotel, He saw an important church leader 'walking proudly' with a group of people. The leader had spoken out calling 'Abdu'l-Bahá a false Christ.[57] The next morning, 'Abdu'l-Bahá and His group went to the Mormon Temple. Fujita reported, 'Can't get in . . . Strange thing, they don't let us in.' 'Abdu'l-Bahá said, 'This Salt Lake City is beautiful, but spiritually dead.'[58]

Later, Feny Paulson received a phone call telling her to come for an interview with 'Abdu'l-Bahá. His first words to her were 'Luxury and comfort are not the all-important things in this life,' recalling to her vividly her mentioning the dirty conditions at the YWCA. He also said that He was her Father, which strongly affected her because she had never known her father. The Master then gave her a locket-sized photo of Himself 'as a father gives a treasure to one of His children'.

After her interview, Feny and Ahmad Sohrab went shopping and bought a leg of lamb for the journey. They all had a long wait at the train station before the departure and 'Abdu'l-Bahá told Feny that where she lived was 'dark, very, very dark', meaning spiritually. He asked her to write, which she did during the following years, receiving a Tablet in return each time.

'Abdu'l-Bahá told Fujita and Feny to stay and see that the luggage was safely loaded aboard the train, after which He left. With 'Abdu'l-Bahá's departure, Feny just couldn't stay with the luggage and also left. She later said that her disobedience brought her 'trouble and weeks and even months of delay with baggage. Life would be easier if we knew the wisdom of obedience.'[59]

# 13

# 'YOUR LOVE DREW ME TO YOU'
## *1–26 October*

## SAN FRANCISCO AND OAKLAND, CALIFORNIA

'Abdu'l-Bahá and His party rode on the train all of Monday, 30 September, crossing Nevada and California. In the afternoon He spoke 'about spiritual education and intellectual training':

> Peter was devoid of all schooling and so untrained that he could not remember the days of the week. He would tie up seven loaves of bread and open one each day. When he opened the seventh parcel he would know that it was the seventh day and that he had to go to the synagogue. However, under Christ his spiritual education was such that he became the cause of the enlightenment of the world.[1]

The train arrived in San Francisco at almost midnight on 1 October, where the Master was met by Dr Frederick D'Evelyn, William and Georgia Ralston, Helen Goodall, Ella Cooper and others. Dr D'Evelyn, as soon as he saw the Master, rushed to Him and threw himself at His feet. The newly arrived group was taken to a house at 1815 California Street which had been rented for the Master by Mrs Goodall and was ideal for meetings. The first floor rooms had large doors connecting them that could be opened, essentially creating one very large room.

### Helen Goodall and Ella Cooper

Helen Goodall's daughter Ella had learned about the Faith in 1898 from her friend Helen (Nell) Hillyer and told her mother about it. Nell was a protégé of Phoebe Hearst and was studying the Faith with Lua Getsinger at a study class in San Francisco arranged by Phoebe. Helen

Goodall and Ella were so interested that they travelled to New York to learn more from Anton Haddad, an early travel teacher to America sent by the Master to counteract the damage done to the early community by Ibrahim Kheiralla,[2] and both Ella and Nell Hillyer were members of the first historic pilgrimage to 'Akká by Westerners arranged by Mrs Hearst. Mother and daughter Helen Goodall and Ella Cooper later went on pilgrimage together in 1908, and their home in Oakland became a centre for teaching the Cause. Shoghi Effendi later named Mrs Goodall a Disciple of 'Abdu'l-Bahá and gave Ella the title of Herald of the Covenant.[3]

When He was in California, 'Abdu'l-Bahá showed Helen Goodall extraordinary kindness. He asked her to come to his house every morning as early as possible and to remain all day. He repeatedly praised her pioneering efforts and called her the spiritual mother of the first Spiritual Assembly in the area. When He left, He told her, 'I leave my sheep in your care.' Back in New York the Master spoke 'of the firmness of the California friends and said to one of the old Bahá'ís there, "I have planted a garden in California and it must not be disturbed."'[4]

* * *

With the arrival of the Master, the longings of the Bahá'ís in California were at last fulfilled. They flocked to see him. 'From early morning the enthusiasm, eagerness, excitement, joy and singing of the believers surrounded 'Abdu'l-Bahá . . . it was the ultimate example of a joyful reunion among the lovers of God.'[5]

Like many people when they first saw Him, Ramona Allen (Brown) tried to describe 'Abdu'l-Bahá. But:

> How can anyone describe Him. Each one of us saw Him with our own spiritual and physical eyes . . . In the Master's presence I felt as though I were in another world . . . Despite His advanced age and the vicissitudes He had endured, His carriage was majestic and His posture remarkable. He seemed to me to be about five feet, nine inches tall, although His long 'abá and His white turban may have caused Him to appear taller . . . He was strong and vibrant. He walked lightly, so that there were moments when He seemed hardly to touch the ground.

'Abdu'l-Bahá enjoyed walking. His secretaries usually accompanied Him. On the street people would turn and glance at Him, and many curious eyes followed Him as He strolled along with great dignity and grace in His Eastern robe and turban. 'Abdu'l-Bahá always wore His native dress, which was a full-length, light-coloured robe, over which He wore an 'abá, or cloak, of beige, tan, brown or cream color. His shoes were of soft brown leather, partly covering the instep and heel. He wore a low turban wound around with folds of soft white material from under which His wispy silver hair fell to His shoulders. Encircling His often-smiling lips was a white mustache and a short, rounded beard. The Master had well-defined, slightly bushy, white eyebrows. To the astonishment of each person who talked with Him, His eyes seemed to change color as He spoke. Sometimes they looked blue or hazel or grey . . . When the Master's face was in repose, deep lines often appeared on His cheeks and between His brows, and His eyes looked sad and showed the suffering He had endured. However, when 'Abdu'l-Bahá smiled, the sadness vanished, and one saw only glorious beauty . . . The Master's complexion was a warm, light tan. His hands were square, strong, yet delicate; when He held your hand, His clasp felt warm and friendly.

As with His eyes so did 'Abdu'l-Bahá's voice change when He spoke . . . At times it was soft and gentle, low and penetrating; or it was loud and firm . . . Despite the Master's fatigue at times . . . He welcomed everyone with a beaming smile, and in His pleasing and vibrant voice would ask 'Are you happy?'

He loved the sound of laughter and often told stories and anecdotes to make us laugh.[6]

On 2 October 'Abdu'l-Bahá met the Bahá'ís in Mrs Goodall's home. He told the gathered friends that 'I have come from the Orient to the Occident – this vast distance have I crossed . . . simply to meet you . . . for the hearts are connected and the spirits are exhilarated . . . Praise be to God! We have assembled here, and the cause of our gathering here is the love of God.'[7]

Seventeen-year-old Juanita Marie Storch was in the audience that day and carefully watched the Master. She noticed the beautiful way He used His hands, never pointing but using His hands like a cup from which He offered His bounties. After the meeting, when 'Abdu'l-Bahá passed down the line of people shaking hands and came to Juanita, He took her hand and 'looked into my eyes. It was only a second but it seemed ten minutes'. A few days later, Juanita attended another meeting and when 'Abdu'l-Bahá took her hand in greeting, He said, 'In Persia it is not the custom to kiss the young ladies. You are My daughter, I am very fond of thee. Rest assured in Me.' Those final words came to her unbidden at various times in the future.

Juanita's other memory of 'Abdu'l-Bahá came at a meeting where everyone hoped to have a private interview – except her. She couldn't think of anything to ask. But then Mírzá Maḥmúd insisted that she go so up she went:

> Dr Fareed was inside and had taken Katheryn Holsti's hand and taken her with me. She had an eye affliction . . . I pushed Katheryn ahead of me as 'Abdu'l-Bahá came to His doorway and said in a low voice, 'This is my sister.' So, 'Abdu'l-Bahá gave a discourse on being sisters. Then all of a sudden I could not see Him. There was just a brilliant warm light. I was not afraid. It was something I could not write about or tell for some time afterwards. Later, downstairs, Katheryn said she was disappointed. She expected a miracle for her eyes. I was the one who experienced the miracle![8]

After starting His visit to California on such a spiritual note, a question from a reporter for *The Examiner* newspaper to 'Abdu'l-Bahá asking, 'What do you think about women's fashions?' must have been disappointing. 'Abdu'l-Bahá replied:

> We do not look upon the dresses of women, whether or not they are of the latest mode. We are not the judge of fashions. We rather judge the wearer of dresses. If she be chaste, if she be cultured, if she be characterized with heavenly morality, and if she be favored at the threshold of God, she is honored and respected by us, no matter what manner of dress she wears.[9]

The newspapers were, once again, full of stories about 'Abdu'l-Bahá's visit. On 7 October the *San Francisco Examiner* headlined,

'ABDUL BAHA BRINGS GOSPEL OF PEACE . . . Abdul Baha,

head of the Bahai religious movement, spoke at the First Unitarian Church . . . the venerable leader of the faith which now numbers more than three million followers looked like a patriarch of old as he stood in the pulpit and addressed the multitude in the church, on peace and love for all mankind.

The *San Francisco Monitor* took a different point of view:

> BAHA . . . If Catholics should find themselves bitten by curiosity to look into these diabolical things, let them make the Sign of the Cross and pray that they may be freed from temptation. They might say a prayer, too, for the silly deluded ones who have been caught in the net, that they be freed from their sins. For there are many of them . . . Keep away from Baha, no matter how beautifully his 'gentle teachings' may be exploited during his stay in San Francisco. Don't go near him. Stay at home and say the Rosary instead . . .[10]

The same day the *Monitor* warned the people to avoid 'Abdu'l-Bahá, the Master went to the public park, which He greatly enjoyed. Walking by a lake, He saw the remains of a few marble pillars left by the 1906 earthquake. Looking at them, He said, 'The world and its condition will change to such a degree and the Bahá'í Cause will prevail to such an extent that nothing but a remnant – like these pillars – will remain of the previous order.'[11]

Earlier that day 'Abdu'l-Bahá talked about the material progress of the world. He said that some countries had reached the 'apex of material progress'. Physically, they were like healthy bodies, but unfortunately they were empty of spirit. He noted that a spiritless body was a dead one until it acquired spiritual capacity. Then He said:

> The people of America have a great capacity for the acquisition of spiritual qualities but they are immersed in material affairs. They are like machines which move uncontrollably; they move but are devoid of spirit. They will attain perfection when the spirit of divine civilization is breathed into them . . . [12]

On 4 October two Japanese Bahá'ís came to see 'Abdu'l-Bahá and He was delighted to see them. He told them, 'This is an historic event. It is out of the ordinary that an Iranian should meet Japanese people in San Francisco with such love and harmony. This is through the power of Bahá'u'lláh . . . I like the Japanese greatly because they are audacious and intelligent. Whatever they turn their attention to, it becomes a success.'[13]

Two Japanese believers were serving the Master at this point – Fujita and the first Japanese Bahá'í, Kanichi Yamamoto, known to his friends as Moto. Moto was Mrs Goodall's butler.

## Kanichi Yamamoto

Kanichi Yamamoto had became a Bahá'í in Hawaii in 1902 and wanted to write 'Abdu'l-Bahá of his acceptance, but with only rudimentary English, he struggled to compose his letter. Finally, at the suggestion of his Bahá'í teacher, Elizabeth Muther, he wrote his letter in Japanese. 'Abdu'l-Bahá's reply answered all his questions.[14]

Moto wrote several letters to 'Abdu'l-Bahá, all in Japanese, and received replies to each. In 1904, one of Moto's letters reached the Master via Helen Goodall and He showed it to Yúnis Khán-i-Afrúkhtih (Youness Afroukhteh), one of His secretaries:

> The Master mused, 'Well now, you do not know Japanese.'
> 'No, Beloved,' I volunteered. 'I hardly know English.'
> 'So, what are we to do with this letter?' He remarked, smiling.
> I bowed, and in my heart proposed, 'The same thing you do with other letters.'
> 'Very well then,' He said, 'We will rely on the Blessed Beauty and will write him a reply.'[15]

'Abdu'l-Bahá's Tablet to Moto began: 'O thou who art the single one of Japan and the unique one of the extreme Orient! . . .'

Moto married in 1908 in an elaborate American-style wedding planned by Helen Goodall. All the local Bahá'ís and the Japanese friends of the couple were present. Afterwards, Moto told his new wife: 'I don't want you to be like a Japanese wife, always bowing. I want you to be like an American wife and boss me!'[16]

When the Master arrived in Oakland, Moto 'had the privilege of living in this home and serving his beloved Master during those glorious days'. Moto was married with three small sons. 'Abdu'l-Bahá 'loved the three little Yamamoto boys, gave them Persian names and held them on His lap'.[17]

* * *

Moto arranged a meeting for 'Abdu'l-Bahá to speak at the Japanese YMCA on 7 October. The president began the meeting by reading a Scripture lesson in Japanese, which was followed by the singing of *Nearer My God to Thee*, also in Japanese. Mr Kanno, a Japanese poet and philosopher, then gave a short talk which he concluded with a poem to 'Abdu'l-Bahá. The Master's talk was in Persian, translated by Dr Fareed into English, which the Rev. Kazahira retranslated into Japanese. As He left, mothers in the audience held out their babies which He blessed saying, 'Good baby; Japanese baby.'[18]

The President of Leland Stanford University, Dr David Starr Jordan, who was very attracted by the Faith, came to visit 'Abdu'l-Bahá and ask Him to speak at the university. So, on 8 October 'Abdu'l-Bahá went to the university. Afterwards, Lua Getsinger wrote to Agnes Parsons:

> We have had a most wonderful day with 'Abdu'l-Bahá here. This morning he spoke to fifteen hundred students – introduced by Dr Jordan. His subject was international peace and such splendid attention was paid Him! Not a murmur not a distracting move – during the hour and fifteen minutes that he addressed them. When He finished they cheered and cheered until he arose – and then the whole audience rose – and the students gave the college yell! It was perfectly splendid.[19]

Mahmúd reported that there were '1,800 students and 180 professors from the university, many civic leaders and prominent people from the area'.[20] There were 30 others in attendance, as well. Professor Ernest Rogers, a Bahá'í who ran the Montezuma Mountain School for Boys near Los Gatos, brought 30 of his students to hear the Master. To get there, the professor and the boys had to walk five miles to the train station before they could go to Palo Alto, where Stanford was located.[21] After His talk, the Master had lunch with Dr Jordan and then spent the rest of the afternoon with him touring the university campus.

Dr Harry Rathbun began attending Stanford University in September of 1912, just a month before 'Abdu'l-Bahá's talk. In 1986, the San José Bahá'í Community presented its Peace Award to the long-time Stanford professor and cofounder of a group called Beyond War, whose aim was to convince people that war was no longer a feasible way to settle international differences and whose motto was 'Man is One'. At the award ceremony, Dr Rathbun mentioned that he had first gotten the idea for Beyond War when he heard 'Abdu'l-Bahá speak at Stanford in 1912.[22]

Some excerpts from 'Abdu'l-Bahá's talk may reveal why people were so affected:

> For all created things except man are subjects or captives of nature; they cannot deviate in the slightest degree from nature's law and control. The colossal sun, center of our planetary system, is nature's captive, incapable of the least variation from the law of command. All the orbs and luminaries in this illimitable universe are, likewise, obedient to nature's regulation. Our planet, the earth, acknowledges nature's omnipresent sovereignty. The kingdoms of the mineral, vegetable and animal respond to nature's will and fiat of control. The great bulky elephant with its massive strength has no power to disobey the restrictions nature has laid upon him; but man, weak and diminutive in comparison, empowered by mind which is an effulgence of Divinity itself, can resist nature's control and apply natural laws to his own uses.
>
> According to the limitations of his physical powers man was intended by creation to live upon the earth, but through the exercise of his mental faculties, he removes the restriction of this law and soars in the air like a bird. He penetrates the secrets of the sea in submarines and builds fleets to sail at will over the ocean's surface, commanding the laws of nature to do his will. All the sciences and arts we now enjoy and utilize were once mysteries, and according to the mandates of nature should have remained hidden and latent, but the human intellect has broken through the laws surrounding them and discovered the underlying realities. The mind of man has taken these mysteries out of the plane of invisibility and brought them into the plane of the known and visible.
>
> It has classified and adapted these laws to human needs and uses,

this being contrary to the postulates of nature. For example, electricity was once a hidden, or latent, natural force. It would have remained hidden if the human intellect had not discovered it. Man has broken the law of its concealment, taken this energy out of the invisible treasury of the universe and brought it into visibility. Is it not an extraordinary accomplishment that this little creature, man, has imprisoned an irresistible cosmic force in an incandescent lamp? It is beyond the vision and power of nature itself to do this. The East can communicate with the West in a few minutes. This is a miracle transcending nature's control. Man takes the human voice and stores it in a phonograph. The voice naturally should be free and transient according to the law and phenomenon of sound, but man arrests its vibrations and puts it in a box in defiance of nature's laws. All human discoveries were once secrets and mysteries sealed and stored up in the bosom of the material universe until the mind of man, which is the greatest of divine effulgences, penetrated them and made them subservient to his will and purpose. In this sense man has broken the laws of nature and is constantly taking out of nature's laboratory new and wonderful things. Notwithstanding this supreme bestowal of God, which is the greatest power in the world of creation, man continues to war and fight, killing his fellowman with the ferocity of a wild animal. Is this in keeping with his exalted station? Nay, rather, this is contrary to the divine purpose manifest in his creation and endowment . . .

If the animals are savage and ferocious, it is simply a means for their subsistence and preservation. They are deprived of that degree of intellect which can reason and discriminate between right and wrong, justice and injustice; they are justified in their actions and not responsible. When man is ferocious and cruel toward his fellowman, it is not for subsistence or safety. His motive is selfish advantage and wilful wrong. It is neither seemly nor befitting that such a noble creature, endowed with intellect and lofty thoughts, capable of wonderful achievements and discoveries in sciences and arts, with potential for ever higher perceptions and the accomplishment of divine purposes in life, should seek the blood of his fellowmen upon the field of battle. Man is the temple of God. He is not a human temple. If you destroy a house, the owner of that house will be grieved and wrathful. How much greater is the wrong when man destroys a building planned and erected by God! Undoubtedly, he deserves the judgment and wrath of God . . .

Praise be to God! I find myself in an assemblage, the members of which are peace loving and advocates of international unity. The thoughts of all present are centered upon the oneness of the world of mankind, and every ambition is to render service in the cause of human uplift and betterment. I supplicate God that he may confirm and assist you, that each one of you may become a professor emeritus in the world of scientific knowledge, a faithful standard-bearer of peace and bonds of agreement between the hearts of men . . .

Bahá'u'lláh especially emphasized international peace. He declared that all mankind is the one progeny of Adam and members of one great universal family. If the various races and distinct types of mankind had each proceeded from a different original paternity – in other words, if we had two or more Adams for our human fathers – there might be reasonable ground for difference and divergence in humanity today; but inasmuch as we belong to one progeny and one family, all names which seek to differentiate and distinguish mankind as Italian, German, French, Russian and so on are without significance and sanction. We are all human, all servants of God and all come from Mr Adam's family. Why, then, all these fallacious national and racial distinctions? These boundary lines and artificial barriers have been created by despots and conquerors who sought to attain dominion over mankind, thereby engendering patriotic feeling and rousing selfish devotion to merely local standards of government. As a rule they themselves enjoyed luxuries in palaces, surrounded by conditions of ease and affluence, while armies of soldiers, civilians and tillers of the soil fought and died at their command upon the field of battle, shedding their innocent blood for a delusion such as 'we are Germans,' 'our enemies are French,' etc., when, in reality, all are humankind, all belong to the one family and posterity of Adam, the original father. This prejudice or limited patriotism is prevalent throughout the world, while man is blind to patriotism in the larger sense which includes all races and native lands. From every real standpoint there must and should be peace among all nations . . . [23]

The *Palo Altan*, in its editorial of 1 November, wrote of 'Abdu'l-Bahá:

A crowded Assembly Hall, holding nearly two thousand people, awaited with eager expectancy the appearance last Tuesday morning of Abdul-Baha, Abbas Effendi, the world leader of the Bahai movement. The venerable prophet, with his long gray beard and Persian cloak and turban, gave a true impression of the reincarnation of a Far Eastern prophet of old. He spoke in Persian and his remarks were translated by Dr Ameen Fareed, a graduate of the University of Illinois and also of John Hopkins University.

Abdul-Baha is revolutionizing the religion of Asia, bringing Mohammedans, Jews and Christians together on the basis of the laws of Moses, which they all ratify. He already has a vast host of followers and has aroused great interest by his present tour of America and England.

A pilgrimage through England and America undertaken by Abdul-Baha has created great interest in the Bahai movement. The knowledge of this movement has been brought home to thousands of people who are willing and eager to spread its beneficent teachings. On this far western shore of America the seeds of peace and welfare find fertile ground and abundant fruitage. At Stanford there is a keen interest taken in International Peace on account of the prominent part taken by Dr Jordan, one of the trustees of the Carnegie Peace Endowment . . .

It seemed to be a notable day when Abdul-Baha from the far country of the Orient met Dr David Starr Jordan of the far western shore, both carrying the standard of international peace and universal brotherhood. It was Persia, the oldest nation of the world, indeed the fabled country of the Garden of Eden and birthplace of the human race, bringing a message to America, the youngest great nation of the world.[24]

The following day, 'Abdu'l-Bahá had been invited by the Mayor of Berkeley to give a public address in that city.

Many dignitaries and University people were to gather . . . 'As the appointed hour for departure approached, the hostess went upstairs to warn 'Abdu'l-Bahá . . . He smiled and waved her away, saying "Very soon! Very soon!" She left Him with some impatience . . . After some time she went up again, for the automobile was honking at the door . . . At last her patience was quite exhausted for she knew that they could not possibly arrive . . . in time. Suddenly there was a ring at the door bell. Immediately 'Abdu'l-Bahá's step was on the stair, and when the door was open he was beside the maid, pulling over the threshold a dusty and disheveled man whom no one had ever heard of, but whom 'Abdu'l-Bahá embraced like a long lost friend.' He had read of 'Abdu'l-Bahá in the newspapers and felt he must see Him, but as he did not have enough money for the car fare, he walked the fifteen miles into San Francisco.[25]

Juliet Thompson related a story that Lua Getsinger told her. Lua and Georgia Ralston were out driving with 'Abdu'l-Bahá and the Master appeared to have gone to sleep. Lua and Georgia talked about their own concerns until He suddenly opened His eyes, laughed and said, 'I, me, my, mine: words of the Devil!'[26]

'Abdu'l-Bahá was walking in Golden Gate Park on 10 October with Dr Woodson Allen and Lua Getsinger. They were talking about life after death. 'Abdu'l-Bahá said:

> Man must not imagine disease but must ever trust God. Anyway, a man's life here in this world is temporary. He is in a world that is like a house, susceptible to every invasion, and God must protect man – man must be submissive to God . . . The spiritual life of man is important. The everlasting life of man is of the utmost importance. A man must be thinking of that . . .
>
> Dr Allen: Why should we pay attention to the everlasting life? We give up all of our time to this, and why should we be thinking about the rest of it?
>
> Mrs [Lua] Getsinger: You mean why should we not wait until we get there and take it up then?
>
> 'Abdu'l-Bahá: Because whatsoever a man soweth here he reapeth there. This world is like a school. He must learn lessons here so that when he issues from this school he may become learned. He must not be ignorant.
>
> For phenomena in general, there is one virtue. It is innate virtue. For example, this tree: its verdure is innate; its flowers are innate; they are creational. It does not interfere with them. It has no will of its own. As to animals, all their virtues are innate. The sun, its

virtues are innate; therefore, there is no credit to be given it . . . Are you grateful to any of these? Not especially, as they are innate, involuntary virtues. But the virtues of man are acquired . . . Therefore, for man there is need of the acquiring of virtues.[27]

Later that day, 'Abdu'l-Bahá addressed the Open Forum. Since this group was composed primarily of agnostics, freethinkers, and philosophers, He began by saying that since He'd heard that the group was investigating reality and claimed to be free from blind imitation, He had decided to speak on the subject of philosophy. He then examined the unreliability of the senses. Sight sees the mirage, which doesn't actually exist; sight sees planets and stars revolving around the earth whereas the truth is that the earth spins and the celestial bodies are still. He concluded by saying:

> . . . some of the sagacious men declare: We have attained to the superlative degree of knowledge; we have penetrated the laboratory of nature, studying sciences and arts; we have attained the highest station of knowledge in the human world; we have investigated the facts as they are and have arrived at the conclusion that nothing is rightly acceptable except the tangible which alone is a reality worthy of credence; all that is not tangible is imagination and nonsense.
>
> Strange indeed that after 20 years of training in colleges and universities man should reach such a station wherein he will deny the existence of the ideal or that which is not perceptible to the senses. Have you ever stopped to think that the animal already has graduated from such a university? Have you ever realized that the cow is already a professor emeritus of that university? For the cow without hard labor and study is already a philosopher of the superlative degree in the school of nature. The cow denies everything that is not tangible, saying, 'I can see! I can eat! Therefore, I believe only in what is tangible!'
>
> Then why should we go to the colleges? Let us go to the cow.[28]

Writing about this, Maḥmúd-i-Zarqání commented, 'When the Master uttered these words, everyone burst into laughter. This kind of humour, delivered in such a light-hearted manner, is popular and accepted by the Americans and so brought smiles and joy to the audience'.[29] His assessment seems to have been correct, for Lua wrote to Agnes Parsons about the story: 'We are laughing yet!'[30]

Also on the 12th, 'Abdu'l-Bahá visited Charles Tinsley, a black employee of Phoebe Hearst who probably came into the Faith through Robert Turner, Mrs Hearst's long-time butler and the first African-American Bahá'í. Charles was laid up at home with a broken leg when the Master arrived. When 'Abdu'l-Bahá asked how he was, Charles replied that he was fine except for the broken leg that kept him from working for the Cause. 'Abdu'l-Bahá told him to

> Cheer up! Praise be to God, you are dear to me. I will tell you a story: –
>
> A certain ruler wished to appoint one of his subjects to a high office; so, in order to train him, the ruler cast him into prison and caused him to suffer much. The man was surprised at this, for he expected great favors. The ruler had him taken from prison and beaten with sticks. This greatly astonished the man, for he thought the ruler loved him. After this he was hanged on the gallows until he was nearly dead. After he recovered he asked the ruler, 'If you love me, why did you do these things?' The ruler replied: 'I wish to make you prime minister. By having gone through these ordeals you are better fitted for that office. I wish you to know how it is yourself. When you are obliged to punish, you will know how it feels to endure these things. I loved you so I wished you to become perfect.'
>
> [To Mr. Tinsley] Even so with you. After this ordeal you will reach maturity. God sometimes causes us to suffer much and to have many misfortunes that we may become strong in His Cause.
>
> You will soon recover and be spiritually stronger than ever before. You will work for God and carry the Message to many of your people.[31]

On 11 October 'Abdu'l-Bahá spoke to a group of physicians on the use of diet to cure diseases. He then expanded the subject to include the need for a Divine Physician to cure intellectual diseases. He told them that:

> . . . one of the chief reasons for irreligion among people is that the leaders of religion, such as the Catholic priests, take a little bread and wine, blow a breath over it and then say that the bread is the

flesh of Christ and the wine is the blood of Christ. Of course, a man of understanding would not accept these dogmas and would say that if this bread and wine turned into the flesh and blood of Christ by the breath of the priest, then the priest must be superior to Christ. Thus, Bahá'u'lláh has said, 'Every matter that is contrary to sound reason and science and is opposed to the fundamental principles of the divine religions is an obstacle to progress and a cause of people avoiding and rejecting the laws of God.'[32]

Later that afternoon, the Master was driven to Mrs Goodall's house in Oakland for the observance of Children's Day. A large group of children had gathered and when the Master arrived they greeted Him by the singing of a song by Louise Waite, *Softly His Voice is Calling Now*. He gave candy and flowers to the children, speaking to each in short English sentences, and to everyone there He gave an envelope containing rose leaves.[33] After the children's meeting, 'Abdu'l-Bahá went for a walk and visited a neighbour. The lady brought Him a chair and they sat together for a while. The Master was pleased with the woman's reverence and thoughtfulness.[34]

On Saturday 12 October 'Abdu'l-Bahá delivered a powerful talk at the Jewish Temple Emmanu-El. The Master was introduced by Rabbi Martin Meyer who somewhat naively introduced the Centre of the Covenant by saying, "Abdu'l-Bahá is the representative of one of the religious systems which appeals to us Jews, because we feel that we have fathered that idea throughout the centuries. This morning He will speak to us . . . on "The fundamental unity of religious thought".' About 2,000 people then heard Him demonstrate the truth of Christ.[35] To Ramona Allen, the audience appeared to be spellbound. Willard Hatch, who was sitting on the floor in the balcony, described the scene as

> . . . dramatic. The young, highly intelligent, and somewhat heavy-set Rabbi wiped the perspiration from his forehead, although the autumn day was not warm. Not a Jew objected.
>
> Then briefly, the wonderful 'Abdu'l-Bahá showed that the Prophet Muhammad was the upholder of Moses and Christ . . . It was the quarrelling followers of these great Prophets who diverged from the Message of the Founders of their religion and swept into mutually accusing fanaticism.

... Profoundly moved the huge audience poured from the synagogue out upon the street and slowly dispersed to its respective homes.[36]

The effect of 'Abdu'l-Bahá on those who heard Him that day became obvious within a short time. The Christian church located diagonally across the street from the synagogue decided to build a new building, necessitating the demolition of the old one and leaving the Christians temporarily without a place to worship. Rabbi Meyer, with the support of the Jewish community, offered them the use of the synagogue each Sunday. For the next nine months, Christian and Jew shared the same building. When 'Abdu'l-Bahá was told of this, He wrote that 'this action and this deed will become eternal, and in the future ages and cycles, the good intention of the Reverend Rabbi will be recorded in the books and works of universal history and will be on the lips of all men without end.'[37]

On 1 November the *Palo Altan*, edited by H.W. Simkins, devoted its entire issue to a presentation of 'Abdu'l-Bahá's visit. On the first page, with a six-column headline, was a portrait of 'Abdu'l-Bahá and an article about His visit to Leland Stanford University. On page 2 was the editorial, 'The New Evangel', and the Stanford address delivered by 'Abdu'l-Bahá. The third page carried the Master's 'Message to the Jews', while page 4 contained His address at the Unitarian Church. The paper also included a reproduction of the Master's original Tablet, with translation, written to Mr Simkins to thank him for his 'cordiality' and to send him the complete transcript of his address at Temple Emmanu-El, suggesting that he might like to print it 'without abbreviation . . . so that others of the Jews may read it. Perchance this may prove an impetus for their respect for, and belief in Christ, that this strife and contention that has lasted between the two nations for two thousand years may disappear, and the oneness of the world of humanity be unveiled.'[38]

## Pleasanton, California

Phoebe Hearst had invited 'Abdu'l-Bahá to her mansion near Pleasanton, the 'Hacienda', and on 13 October Helen Goodall provided her car and her Bahá'í chauffeur to take Him there.[39]

## Phoebe Hearst

Phoebe Apperson Hearst, widow of Senator George Hearst and mother of William Randolph Hearst, the newspaper magnate, heard of the Faith from Edward Getsinger in 1898, and was instrumental in setting up the first Bahá'í study classes in San Francisco given by Lua Getsinger. She had led the first pilgrimage of Americans to visit 'Abdu'l-Bahá in the Holy Land in 1898–99 and on her return had powerfully defended the Faith against the machinations of Ibrahim Kheiralla, sending Anton Haddad back to the Holy Land to report to 'Abdu'l-Bahá what was going on in America.

However, in the decade between about 1902 and 1912 Phoebe had kept her distance from most of her fellow Bahá'ís. Her devoted servant Robert Turner, a member of that first Western pilgrimage, said that 'dust had been thrown in her eyes'.[40] This was partly due to lack of wisdom on the part of some of the friends, partly due to her adored son William Randolph Hearst's political ambitions, and partly because of the actions of unspiritual people, including Ibrahim Kheiralla, who had hounded her for money. However, she never gave up her belief, kept Bahá'í literature in her bedroom to the end of her life and continued to associate with close Bahá'í friends and to correspond with the Master, often through Ali-Kuli Khan.

Phoebe was a generous benefactor to many worthy causes, particularly those that advanced women and the Faith. Her financial assistance built hospitals, supported medical research, aided women's groups and helped deserving but poor students advance their education. She also was a firm supporter and backer of Green Acre. Her help also allowed Lua and Edward Getsinger to travel extensively across the United States promoting the Faith during the two years following that history-making pilgrimage, and provided a base for May Bolles in Paris from which she lit the lamp of the Faith in Europe during the same time.

When Ella Cooper wrote to 'Abdu'l-Bahá in 1919 to inform Him of Phoebe's passing and of her last days, the Master replied that 'in the future her name shall be uplifted and her fame spread abroad', and revealed a prayer in her honour which includes the following words:

> O my God! Endowed with a seeing eye, she beheld the rays of the Sun of Truth and endowed with a hearing ear, she hearkened to the

call of the Kingdom. Possessing a keen sense of smell, she inhaled the fragrant scent of the Paradise of Abha, and gifted with a pure heart she overflowed with Thy love.[41]

In earlier years, he had sent His greetings 'particularly to that one who has proved that it is possible for a camel to pass through a needle's eye', a clear reference to Phoebe and to the saying of Christ that it is easier for a camel to pass through the eye of a needle than for a rich man to enter the kingdom of God.[42] Phoebe had done it, despite all her wealth (much of which she used philanthropically), but others were not so detached. One of those 'unspiritual people' was at that moment a member of 'Abdu'l-Bahá's party, Dr Amin Fareed, who had already tried to fraudulently get money out of her. And it was probably during 'Abdu'l-Bahá's stay at the Hearst residence that His signet ring disappeared. That theft and some other activities of Dr Fareed were described by Marzieh Gail in her book, *Arches of the Years*:

> 'Abdu'l-Bahá's signet ring disappeared during His Western journey. The Master had confided his loss to Florence and Khan, and named the thief, but He did not wish them to speak of it. We in the family always thought that it took place during His stay at the Hacienda . . . Thereafter the Master signed all His Tablets instead of using a seal, capitalizing neither 'Abdu'l- nor 'Abbás, but only Bahá.
> 
> Fareed's efforts to destroy the Master (who had seen to his education from childhood) make a page of triple darkness . . . Fareed was capable of whispering to the rich in the United States that although 'Abdu'l-Bahá needed funds He would not openly accept them, but if they would pass over the money to him, Fareed, he would deliver it to the Master . . . After returning to the Holy Land 'Abdu'l-Bahá sent Dr Baghdadi a Tablet, and directed that copies be distributed to every community so that all could read it.
> 
> The Master wrote here that during His stay in America He had forgiven a certain member of His suite four times, but that He would forgive the man's misdeeds no longer . . .[43]

When 'Abdu'l-Bahá returned to Haifa, He proceeded directly to the room of His wife, Munírih Khánum, and said in a feeble voice, 'Doctor Fareed has ground me down!'[44]

'YOUR LOVE DREW ME TO YOU'

\* \* \*

On the morning of 14 October, with an American presidential election imminent, 'Abdu'l-Bahá described the sort of person who should be elected to the position:

> The president must be a man who does not insistently seek the presidency. He should be a person free from all thoughts of name and rank; rather, he should say, 'I am unworthy and incapable of this position and cannot bear this great burden.' Such persons deserve the presidency. If the object is to promote the public good, then the president must be a well-wisher of all and not a self-seeking person. If the object, however, is to promote personal interests, then such a position will be injurious to humanity and not beneficial to the public.[45]

Later someone asked: 'How is it that the desires of some people are achieved while others are not?' 'Abdu'l-Bahá replied:

> What conforms with divine decree will be realized. In addition, good intentions and sound thoughts attract confirmations. The desires of human beings are endless. No matter what level a human being reaches, he can still attain higher ones, so he is always making effort and desiring more. He can never find peace but through effort and resignation, so that, notwithstanding all efforts in worldly affairs, the human heart remains free and happy. He neither becomes proud on attaining wealth and position nor becomes dejected on losing them. This station can be attained only through the power of faith.[46]

'Abdu'l-Bahá also touched on the topic of the presidency in Washington, DC, asking Florence Khan with a smile, 'What would you say if a woman were to become President of the United States?' Florence later wrote that 'In 1912, the remark came like a bombshell.' The Master then said, 'The time will come when the Presidency will go begging, so advanced will civilization have become that no one will want to leave his social and humanitarian tasks take the time to assume the Presidency.'[47]

Mrs Hearst had arranged a large house party while the Master was there. She still remembered how the prayers chanted in Arabic had affected her in 'Akká, so she asked if He would chant a prayer. 'Abdu'l-Bahá's powerful voice resounded throughout the mansion as He chanted an Arabic prayer, all to the amazement of the other guests.

The next day, Mrs Hearst invited 'Abdu'l-Bahá to tour her house and gardens. The Master spent considerable time in the nursery examining some of the rare specimens. He asked that seeds from some be sent to the Holy Land for use around the Shrines of the Báb and Bahá'u'lláh.

Mrs Hearst had not spoken openly to her relatives about the Faith, but at this time she encouraged 'Abdu'l-Bahá to speak about the teachings of the Cause. 'Abdu'l-Bahá promptly gave an overview of the Faith and its principles. When He finished, Mrs Hearst told stories of her time in 'Akká.

When 'Abdu'l-Bahá was about to leave the next day, He called for all the servants of the household, the maids, cooks, orderlies and the butler. He thanked each one for their services and gave each two guineas. This act of generosity and majesty left Mrs Hearst's wealthy guests humbled. Mrs Hearst asked to be allowed to accompany Him back to San Francisco and He gave His assent, using the time to tell her:

> The Cause of God is sanctified from all political power and worldly affairs. Among the divine teachings are trustworthiness, detachment and sanctity. So if you should see a man coveting property and evincing greed toward the wealth of others, know that he is not of the people of Bahá. The people of Bahá are they who, should they happen to come upon a valley of gold and silver, would pass by it like lightning in utter disregard.[48]

It was a warning against men like Dr Fareed.

## San Francisco, California

That night, back in San Francisco, Mrs Goodall and Mrs Cooper hosted a Feast at their home in Oakland. While 'Abdu'l-Bahá was upstairs writing a letter to Ḥájí Mírzá Ḥaydar-'Alí, the Bahá'ís waited for his arrival, playing the piano and singing songs of praise. Hearing the melodies, the Master wrote to this believer who had suffered so much for the Faith, the 'Angel of Carmel':

O thou who art partner and co-sharer with 'Abdu'l-Bahá in servitude to the Threshold of Bahá! It is evening and these wandering birds are nestled in the home of the maidservant of God, Mrs Helen Goodall . . . It is the Nineteen Day Feast . . . All the delicacies are spread and ready and the table is exquisitely arranged. Oh, how thou art missed! Severed from all else, they sing a new song and with a new voice repeat spiritual notes. They are in a state of absolute love and supplication. Oh, how thou art missed! Oh, how thou art missed![49]

'Abdu'l-Bahá had heard that the Bahá'ís in Oregon and Washington were unhappy that He was not going to visit them. In answer, He said, 'They are upset that I am not going there. However, in spite of the great distance, they have come to see us . . . Had it been but a one- or two-day trip, I would have gone to Portland and Seattle but the distance is too great. I would not visit Los Angeles were it not for the purpose of visiting the tomb of Mr Chase.' Later He continued, saying 'On the way here we were saying that it never occurred to us that we would come to California and meet with the friends in this manner . . . '[50]

During the evening, 'Abdu'l-Bahá wandered through the rooms of the big house, speaking with the Bahá'ís and every now and then placing a piece of fruit or a sweet on someone's plate. Florence Khan and Ramona Allen were seated together and 'Abdu'l-Bahá placed a candy on each of their plates. Following Persian custom when receiving a precious gift, Florence raised the candy to her heart, her lips and then her forehead before eating it.[51]

At one point, the Master was speaking about Bahá'u'lláh's Revelation and spiritual susceptibilities. Touching a young man named Mr Robinson, 'Abdu'l-Bahá said 'Because of these susceptibilities, this radiant youth is seated here, and in the utmost of love I am patting him on his shoulder.' Ramona Allen wondered why the Master had chosen to specifically bless the youth. Later, she found out. Seated at the same table as Mr Robinson was John Matteson, who was on a search for spiritual truth. 'When Mr Matteson saw the Master put His hands on a young man's shoulder, Mr Matteson thought to himself, "If 'Abdu'l-Bahá did that same thing to me, I would believe." However, the Master strolled into the other rooms. Presently He returned to that room, walked straight to Mr Matteson, and placed His hands upon the young man's shoulders. From that moment Mr Matteson became one of the most faithful followers of Bahá.'[52]

Howard Colby Ives wrote about an illiterate miner who walked a great distance to meet 'Abdu'l-Bahá while He was in San Francisco:

> This man, though uneducated, had great spiritual capacity. He attended a meeting at which 'Abdu'l-Bahá spoke. He seemed enthralled as the measured, bell-like tones fell from the Master's lips. When the interpreter took up the passage in English this miner started as if awakening. 'Why does that man interrupt?' He whispered. Then again 'Abdu'l-Bahá spoke, and again the visitor was lost in attention. Again the interpreter translated as the speaker paused. At this the miner's indignation was aroused. 'Why do they let that man interrupt? He should be put out.'
>
> 'He is the official interpreter,' one sitting beside him explained. 'He translates the Persian into English.'
>
> 'Was He speaking in Persian?' was the naive answer, 'Why anyone could understand that.'[53]

The next day, 17 October, Ramona Allen's cousin Cathryn O'Reilly asked 'Abdu'l-Bahá, 'Have I any special work? I have no home . . .' The Master replied, 'What do you want? A placeless person is better off . . . The whole world belongs to you.'[54]

## LOS ANGELES, CALIFORNIA

Thornton Chase, although longing to see the Master, had been ill and unable to travel East. It was on the very day, 30 September, when 'Abdu'l-Bahá's train passed from Nevada into California at the very end of its long cross-country journey that this devoted believer had passed away, unable to fulfil his longing.

### Thornton Chase

Thornton Chase was in the first group of people who were taught the Faith by Ibrahim Kheiralla in 1894 in Chicago. He quickly accepted the Station of Bahá'u'lláh and played an important role in organizing the Chicago Bahá'í community. As a travelling salesman, he had great opportunities to teach the Faith in many areas. When Kheiralla broke the Covenant, Chase remained firm in the Faith and was an anchor in that troubled time. In 1907, he visited 'Abdu'l-Bahá in 'Akká and wrote a small book about his experiences called *In Galilee*. Two years later, he wrote an introduction to the Faith. The Master learned of Thornton Chase's passing when He arrived in San Francisco and immediately spoke of him:

> This revered personage was the first Bahá'í in America. He served the Cause faithfully and his services will ever be remembered throughout future ages and cycles . . . He travelled once to Acca and there we associated with each other for several days. Indeed he became free from the troubles of this world. No matter how long he might have remained here, he would have met nothing else but trouble. The purpose of life is to get certain results; that is, the life of man must bring forth certain fruitage. It does not depend upon the length of life. As soon as the life is crowned with fruition then it is completed, although that person may have had a short life. There are certain trees which come to fruition very quickly, but there are other trees which attain to fruition very late; the aim is fruit. If the tree brings forth its fruit young, its life is short; it is praiseworthy. How regretful it is that any may live a long life and yet his life may not be crowned with success . . . Praise be to God! the tree of Mr Chase's life brought forth fruit. It gave complete fruit, therefore he is free.[55]

Shoghi Effendi later declared him to be a Disciple of 'Abdu'l-Bahá.

\* \* \*

Thornton Chase's funeral in Los Angeles had been held while the Master was so heavily occupied further north, and so on 18 October He went to the train station in San Francisco accompanied by several Bahá'ís, including Mrs Goodall. They arrived in Los Angeles in the early evening and stayed at the Hotel Lankershim where the Master met informally with the friends.

The room was small and very crowded, with Wilfred Cline having to sit in an awkward position, unable to see the Master although quite close to Him. 'Abdu'l-Bahá spoke about flowers and gardens, describing all the varying colours, sizes and shapes. Concluding His talk, He suddenly turned toward Wilfred Cline and smilingly said, 'Our friend, Mr Cline here, is a very beautiful flower.'[56]

Upon His arrival, many people asked Him to speak at their churches or to their organizations, but He said, 'I have absolutely no time. I have come here to visit Mr Chase's grave and to meet the friends. I will stay here one or two days and then I must leave.'[57]

The next morning, 'Abdu'l-Bahá and a group of 25 friends took the tram to the cemetery. When they arrived at 1 o'clock, 'Abdu'l-Bahá walked directly to the grave 'with dignified solemnity and serenity', asking no one for directions. 'He stood there for a few minutes leaning against a nearby tree', and told the Bahá'ís of San Francisco and Los Angeles to visit Thornton Chase's grave every year on the same day that He Himself visited it. He then spread flowers over the grave and chanted the Tablet of Visitation of Bahá'u'lláh, all standing 'in solemn reverence behind Him'.[58] 'Abdu'l-Bahá concluded the service with these words:

> Mr Chase was of the blessed souls. The best time of his life was spent in the path of God . . . In reality this personage was worthy of respect. This personage is worthy of having the friends visit his grave. The traces of this personage will ever shine. This is a personage who will not be forgotten. For the present his worth is not known but in the future it will be inestimably dear . . . The people will honour this grave. Therefore, the friends of God must visit this grave and on my behalf bring flowers and seek the sublimity of the spiritual station for him . . . This personage will not be forgotten.[59]

Before he left, 'Abdu'l-Bahá placed his forehead on the grave as the believers wept. Harriet Cline wrote: 'As 'Abdu'l-Bahá knelt and kissed the soil which covered all that was mortal of Thornton Chase, I felt he had made holy all the soil of my native state.'[60]

When 'Abdu'l-Bahá returned to the hotel from the cemetery, many people were there to see Him, including reporters. To one reporter He said:

> In this world of existence, civilization is found to be of two kinds: material civilization and spiritual civilization. Philosophers founded the former while the divine Prophets established the latter . . . Material civilization is the cause of worldly prosperity but divine civilization is the means of eternal prosperity. If divine civilization . . .

is established, then material civilization will also attain perfection. When spiritual perfection is attained, then physical perfection is a certainty. Material civilization alone does not suffice and does not become the means of acquiring spiritual virtues. Rather, it leads to an increase in wars and disputes and becomes the cause of bloodshed and ruin. Despite all this, it is surprising that divine civilization has been completely forgotten and the people are constantly submerged in a sea of materialism. This is why night and day they have no peace and are engaged in war and killing.[61]

On 20 October the hotel was crowded with people who hoped to catch a glimpse of the Master. There were too many for private interviews so a public meeting was arranged. One of 'Abdu'l-Bahá's topics was Covenant-breaking. 'Abdu'l-Bahá specifically brought up this topic because Shu'á'u'lláh, the son of 'Abdu'l-Bahá's half-brother and arch-breaker of Bahá'u'lláh's Covenant, was living in California at that time. Shu'á'u'lláh had written to the *Kenosha Evening News* in May denouncing 'Abdu'l-Bahá, accusing Him of subverting the teachings of Bahá'u'lláh and proposing a meeting. 'Abdu'l-Bahá ignored him.

When 'Abdu'l-Bahá arrived in Los Angeles, Shu'á'u'lláh told people about Bahá'u'lláh and his own blood relationship with Him, saying that he was Bahá'u'lláh's grandson. One newspaper editor published two misleading stories in which Shu'á'u'lláh said that because of his biological relationship to Bahá'u'lláh, he would inherit the station of Prophet. 'Abdu'l-Bahá basically ignored Shu'á'u'lláh's ramblings until one particularly persistent journalist kept demanding an answer. 'Abdu'l-Bahá then said:

> I will tell you one thing and it will suffice once and for all. Beyond this neither question me nor will I reply. And that is the words of Christ when told that 'your brothers have come to see you'. He said, 'They are not my brethren but you are my brethren and kindred.' Christ attached no importance to the original relationship with His brethren. Notwithstanding this, my house is open to all. He who wishes may enter and he who wishes to go out may leave.

The editor published the Master's exact words and Shu'á'u'lláh, who had boasted that he would speak out 'In the court of the King of the

Covenant' and make his wishes known, was not heard from again.[62] Both Shuʻáʻuʻlláh and Kheiralla had spread lies and calumnies during ʻAbduʻl-Baháʼs American visit. In summary, ʻAbduʻl-Bahá said, 'These two persons have disgraced themselves once again . . . If they have good intentions for the Cause of God, they must render some service and they must go out to teach the Cause . . .What will they reap by sowing doubt and disbelief? They will get nothing but manifest loss in this world and the next.'[63]

All morning of 21 October the Master's hotel suite was full of people. Frances Allen asked ʻAbduʻl-Bahá, 'I want to consecrate my life to the service of Baháʼuʻlláh. Have I the capacity?' ʻAbduʻl-Bahá replied, 'Because you have this intention, that is capacity. The intention is capacity. If you did not have this intention, you would not ask for the capacity.'[64]

Harriet and Wilfred Cline brought Grandfather Cline and their children, Wilfred Jr. and Frances, to the meeting. As they entered, ʻAbduʻl-Bahá called young Frances and Helen Frankland to come and stand on either side of Him as He spoke. After the meeting, the Master and His Persian attendants were waiting for an elevator when suddenly ʻAbduʻl-Bahá turned and walked over to Grandfather Cline, giving him a fervent embrace. Looking at him, the Master said, 'I hope you will live ten years longer.' That afternoon, as he greeted all the people individually, he said to Grandfather Cline, 'You are my ancient companion, my ancient companion.' Nine years later, in November 1921, ʻAbduʻl-Bahá ascended and Grandfather Cline followed Him a few months later, fulfilling ʻAbduʻl-Baháʼs hope.[65]

Some time while He was in California, ʻAbduʻl-Bahá saw a cardinal, whom he described as

> walking with pomp and ceremony in front of a procession. Inquiring about the occasion, I was told that a new church had been built and the cardinal was to officially open its doors to the public. I said, 'This show and ceremony of the cardinal is like that of Christ. However, there is a slight difference. Christ opened the gate of heaven; this cardinal is going to open that of a church. Christ had a crowd following Him but they were there to hurl contempt and abuse at Him. This cardinal had a crowd with him but they are there to help. Christ had a crown but it was made of thorns, while this cardinal

wears a crown set with lustrous jewels. Christ had clothes but they were made of old, coarse cloth, while this man's robe is made of the finest brocade of the day. Christ spent His days in sorrow, while this cardinal's days are spent in security and comfort. Christ's home was a desert, while this cardinal's home is a splendid building, like that of a king. Christ's throne was upon a cross, while this man's place of rest is a throne of ease and comfort. The adornment of Christ's banquet was the blood of that beloved countenance, while the ornament of this man's court is the goblet of coloured wine. So, this cardinal's display is similar to that of Christ, with only the slightest differences.[66]

## SAN FRANCISCO, CALIFORNIA

'Abdu'l-Bahá returned to San Francisco during the night of 21–22 October. Mrs Goodall had reserved sleeper accommodation, but He was too tired to sleep. In the morning, He said, 'I did not sleep at all last night but was deep in thought.'[67]

During the day, He gave two talks and in the evening had a relaxing walk. Later that evening in response to a commonly asked question, 'Abdu'l-Bahá spoke of the coming of war:

A great war and commotion shall inevitably take place in the world. Things will come to such a pass that the generality of mankind will rise against the statesmen of the world and say, 'You sit in your palaces in perfect comfort; you eat and drink sumptuously; you sleep blissfully; you eat delicious food and relax in gardens with beautiful views. But for the sake of your name and worldly fame, you throw us, your subjects, into war, shed our blood and tear our bodies to pieces. But no thorn ever pricks your hands and not for a moment do you leave your rest and comfort.'[68]

During the war that came only two years later, the Hohenzollern dynasty in Germany fell, the Romanov dynasty in Russia fell and the Hapsburg dynasty in Austro-Hungary fell.

* * *

At one meeting of the Baha'i youth in Oakland, someone asked about how to teach. 'Abdu'l-Bahá told them that they could teach:

> ... in two ways. One way is limited teaching; another way is unlimited teaching. Teaching in a limited way consists of the following, namely: explaining the proofs and evidences in regard to the principles of Bahá'u'lláh, quoting prophecies ... Moreover the intellectual proofs and evidences are this and this, etc. The principles of Bahá'u'lláh have been set forth with such potency and penetration that no one can deny them ... While in prison He withstood two despotic kings, and He gained victory over both. In prison He raised His Banner, He spread His Teachings and spiritually defeated two despotic kings. They could not prevent the spread of His Teachings ... There are many instances of such, and when a person explains these things, He is guiding, he is teaching, He is crying out. This is teaching in a limited sense.
>
> Teaching in an unlimited sense consists of the following and is very good, very great; the teacher himself (or herself) becomes the standing proof of Bahá'u'lláh – that he (or she) may become a miracle of Bahá'u'lláh with such power and such knowledge and desire, such actions and such words and character, and such heavenly powers, that you may live amongst the people, that you may be a proof, undeniable proof, of Bahá'u'lláh.
>
> If someone ask: 'What is the proof of Bahá'u'lláh?' one may say such a person – there is the proof; look at her. Bahá'u'lláh has educated this person. he has awakened this soul. He has quickened this life ... He has made her a sun.
>
> This is the unlimited teaching.[69]

On the morning of 23 October, Ramona Allen took two of her best friends, Marie Barr and Betty Vent, to see 'Abdu'l-Bahá at Mrs Goodall's home. The Master warmly welcomed them and proceeded to speak about teaching the Faith. Marie told Him that she had not gone to college and therefore did not feel qualified to teach. 'Abdu'l-Bahá simply told her, 'When you wish to teach, turn your heart to Bahá'u'lláh, and say what enters your mind.' A short while later at a meeting, He looked at the three ladies in the audience, smiled 'as though we had a little joke between us' and said, 'These young ladies have asked Me how to teach and the method of teaching.' He then proceeded to give a discourse on teaching. Just as the Master was about to leave, Ramona asked Him what she should teach. He smiled and replied, 'Memorize the talk I gave at Stanford University.'[70]

On 24 October 'Abdu'l-Bahá returned to San Francisco from Oakland for His final day in the area and visited a few schools. That evening He was back in the Goodall home for His farewell address. He spoke of how happy He was to have been able to visit the friends in California. Then He talked about the life and suffering of Bahá'u'lláh:

> One felt His great humility as He told of Bahá'u'lláh's life and suffering, His banishment with His Family from Iran . . . Tears filled His eyes and ran down His cheeks, and with a catch in His voice He told of the deprivations and hardships endured by His beloved Father and Family and the little band of followers who accompanied them . . . The Master seemed to be reliving those days of heartbreak. Sadness filled our hearts; tears streamed down our faces while He told us of the cruelties and great injustices inflicted upon His Father. In that quiet room one felt the love and deep sympathy pouring from our souls to our blessed 'Abdu'l-Bahá.
>
> All at once His voice became strong and firm, His eyes luminous, and with great authority He told of the Declaration of Bahá'u'lláh in the Garden of Ridván . . . He told how later, in 'Akká, Bahá'u'lláh gave the Principles of His Revelation and explained that the establishment of His Covenant would forever safeguard His Cause . . . His Father had written: 'I have appointed one who is the Center of my Covenant. All must obey him; all must turn to him; he is the expounder of my book . . .'
>
> Suddenly the atmosphere in the room became electrified. 'Abdu'l-Bahá rose majestically from His chair and in a powerful voice declared: 'I am the Center of that Covenant! I am the Center of that Covenant!.' The friends stood up. They seemed stunned by this great announcement and filled with indescribable emotion. Wonder, joy and happiness showed in their faces. Gradually we became aware in Whose presence we stood: 'The Mystery of God' . . . [71]

It was time for the Master to leave. He was to go to Sacramento and from there to start the long journey back East. Early the following morning, 25 October, 'the Master's residence was full to capacity with a multitude of friends . . . When they heard the Master coming downstairs, everyone rose reverently . . . the Master was deeply moved.' He said:

> This meeting and assemblage are very moving. This is the last draught in the goblet! . . . I am greatly moved because I saw the love of Bahá'u'lláh in you, I witnessed the light of Bahá'u'lláh in your beings. I am so moved that I cannot speak. I leave it to your hearts to feel what I feel . . . When I reach the Shrine of Bahá'u'lláh, I shall lay my head on the Sacred Threshold and beseech confirmation for every one of the friends. These days of our meeting were blissful days . . . There cannot be better days. Do you not forget them and I shall not . . .[72]

The Bahá'ís gathered at the Mole train station in Oakland. Ramona Allen and her cousin Cathryn were standing by the Master's seat on the train and suddenly decided to go with Him to Sacramento. As the inspiration hit them, the train began to move, so they were happy they had no further choice.

## SACRAMENTO, CALIFORNIA

The train arrived in Sacramento at noon. When 'Abdu'l-Bahá stepped off the train, an elegant lady, Christine Fraser, was there to meet Him. Mrs Fraser operated a 'Home of Truth', a place based on New Thought teachings developed by Emma Curtis Hopkins. Mrs Fraser had arranged with Helen Goodall and Ella Cooper that there would be a luncheon at her home, though without the knowledge of the Master, so it was a surprise to Him.[73] After lunch, Helen and Ella arrived. The Master went into another room to rest, then called Ella and asked, 'What have you done? The friends are waiting for me at the hotel!' At this chastisement, tears flooded down Ella's face. 'Abdu'l-Bahá then added, 'Never again arrange anything for 'Abdu'l-Bahá without first consulting Him.' With His point made, He compassionately soothed her with 'No tears! No tears! Be happy! Be happy!'[74] They then joined the friends at the hotel.

That afternoon, a reporter interviewed the Master at the Hotel Sacramento. The *Sacramento Union* newspaper wrote, 'The novelty of seeing American women prostrate themselves before the Bahá'í leader, clad in long flowing robe and turban, was a sensation for the patrons of the hotel. They stood in open-mouthed amazement at the proceeding.' 'Abdu'l-Bahá Himself watched people shopping in the hotel boutiques and noted:

> Regard how negligent these people are! All the insignificant objects are considered by them as means of happiness. How negligent they are! Like unto animals, they eat, they sleep, they walk, they sing, they dance, and, according to their belief, they think they are having a good time.[75]

That afternoon 'Abdu'l-Bahá took a walk in Capitol Park, and in the evening gave a talk about the Faith and His mission to America in the hotel Assembly Hall, following a long introduction and Bahá'í prayer by Christine Fraser. Later yet, He gave an informal talk about materialism.[76]

Next morning, 26 October, 'Abdu'l-Bahá spoke with the chambermaids, anointing them with violet water and giving them fruit.[77] He then addressed a large audience in the Hotel Sacramento, saying:

> Inasmuch as the Californians seem peace loving and possessed of great worthiness and capacity, I hope that advocates of peace may daily increase among them until the whole population shall stand for that beneficent outcome. May the men of affairs in this democracy uphold the standard of international conciliation. Then may altruistic aims and thoughts radiate from this centre toward all other regions of the earth, and may the glory of this accomplishment forever halo the history of this country. May the first flag of international peace be upraised in this state.[78]

Ramona Allen sat in the audience when 'Abdu'l-Bahá spoke these words. She was also in the audience on 26 June 1945 in San Francisco, at the Conference of the United Nations when the United Nations Charter was signed, and was delighted to be there to see the fulfilment of 'Abdu'l-Bahá's wish. But the creation of the United Nations wasn't all that happened. After various speeches and at the moment of the official signing, a new flag was unfurled – the flag of the United Nations. The first flag of international peace had just been upraised in California.[79]

After the Master's last talk, Harriet Cline had to leave for Northern California. When 'Abdu'l-Bahá finished speaking, He quickly gathered some fruit and gave it to her, saying in English, 'Here, take this fruit; you will be hungry, and you must eat.' Mrs Cline was soon on the train, her mind filled with her last moments with the Master. After a while, she grew hungry and asked the conductor about lunch. He informed her that there was no diner on the train and that all the other passengers had gotten off at a station two hours previously to eat. He had announced it, he said, twice. Mrs Cline sat there hungrily, since it had been eight hours since she had eaten, but suddenly remembered the fruit given her by the Master. She didn't have to go hungry.[80]

At lunch that day, fifty Bahá'ís had a final bounty of sharing the meal with 'Abdu'l-Bahá. The hotel manager said in astonishment, 'What I have seen of the majesty of this holy being is that although no one knew him in this city, yet in the course of one day and one night he has created a stir in the city and a spiritual yearning in the hearts of its people.' As 'Abdu'l-Bahá left to catch the train, He was heard to say: 'A spiritual commotion has for the time being been created in this city. Let us see what God desires.'[81]

As the train passed through the Californian countryside, the Master noticed that there were many Greeks on the train, and was told that they were going home to fight against the Turks. When a salesman came through the train selling school pennants, the Master said, 'Tell him to bring the banner of universal peace if he has it. We want such a flag under which the whole world may find rest and peace.'[82]

# 14

# THE LAST DAYS IN AMERICA
## *27 October–5 December*

### To Chicago, Illinois

The passengers on the train quickly discovered 'Abdu'l-Bahá. Some heard His discourses while others saw His unusual dress. But always they gathered around 'Abdu'l-Bahá to listen to His every word. One Jewish lady was particularly impressed. The Master told her, 'It is obvious that you have a pure character, so I want you to become aware of the truth of divine matters. At the time of each Manifestation of God the people were heedless and ignorant of the truth except for a few who investigated and understood the divine words.'[1]

When He went to get tea the next morning, the Jewish lady returned saying that she accepted the teachings of Bahá'u'lláh.

Someone asked the Master about His purpose in travelling across America. 'Abdu'l-Bahá said:

> I have come to America to raise the standard of universal peace and to promote the unity of mankind. My aim is to create love and harmony among the religions. But some people ask me, 'Is your country developed? Is it prosperous and has it good trees, sweet fruits, beautiful animals and swift Arabian horses?' But I speak to them of the trees of the world of existence, of the fruits of human virtues and of heavenly morals and traits and call people to the Kingdom of God.[2]

That night, His assistants tried to persuade the Master to take a sleeping compartment, but He said 'The seats are comfortable. We can lean back and sleep.'[3]

'Abdu'l-Bahá's manner and the love that the other passengers could feel drew them to Him, so by the third day of the trip He was commonly surrounded by interested people and all heard about the teachings and sufferings of His Father. In the afternoon, a party of fifty Turks discovered the Master. The Turks were going to take part in the war against Greece. Since 'Abdu'l-Bahá already knew that there were many Greeks on the train headed east to fight in the same war, He therefore ordered tea and soup for them, then told the Turks about universal peace. The train arrived at the Denver station at midnight and 'Abdu'l-Bahá stayed the night in a nearby hotel.

The next morning, 29 October, the local Bahá'ís quickly learned of His presence and soon appeared at His hotel. The reporters, too, appeared. That afternoon, 'Abdu'l-Bahá gave two public talks. After the second, 'Abdu'l-Bahá and His party returned to the hotel and He ordered everyone to pack for departure. Again, He refused a sleeping compartment, saying, 'We must be equal to the hardships of travelling like a soldier in the path of truth and not be slaves to bodily ease and comfort.'[4] Fujita remembered, 'Long ride in America. We were so tired . . . Hard journey, on the train, coaches, wooden benches.'[5]

On 30 October the Master wrote an account of His travels in America for the friends in the East. As usual, He spoke with the other passengers and informed them of universal peace, divine civilization and the unity of humankind. A Sufi sat with 'Abdu'l-Bahá and learned about the station of a Manifestation. Then a minister came and the Master told him to abandon dogmatic imitation and described the true meaning of baptism.

On this last night of the journey, none of the servants brought up the possibility of the sleeper compartment, but 'Abdu'l-Bahá suddenly told them to reserve six berths because 'We slept in our seats last night and that is enough. Let us not suffer any more hardship.' When they suggested that He alone take a compartment, the Master said, 'No, we must share equally.'[6]

## CHICAGO, ILLINOIS

'Abdu'l-Bahá and His party arrived in Chicago shortly after dawn on 31 October. One station before Chicago, Albert Windust, the young editor of *Star of the West*, joined the group. They were met at the Chicago train station by the friends. The Master again stayed at the Plaza Hotel and

## THE LAST DAYS IN AMERICA

was quickly besieged by people who wanted His attention. Many ministers hoped He would speak from their pulpits, and He accepted a few of the invitations, but apologized to the rest because He did not plan to stay long. That evening, 'Abdu'l-Bahá warned the Bahá'ís in Chicago against the activities of the Covenant-breakers, saying:

> . . . Bahá'u'lláh has not left any possible room for dissension. Naturally, there are some who are antagonistic, some who are followers of self-desire, others who hold to their own ideas and still others who wish to create dissension in the Cause. For example, Judas Iscariot was one of the disciples, yet he betrayed Christ. Such a thing has happened in the past, but in this day the Blessed Perfection has declared 'This person is the Expounder of My Book and all must turn to Him.' The purpose is to ward off dissension and differences among His followers . . .[7]

On 1 November 'Abdu'l-Bahá again met with many people. One prominent man in the city kept inviting the Master to see his private museum. Finally, 'Abdu'l-Bahá went and looked at his collection of antique art, pictures and drawings. After returning to the hotel, 'Abdu'l-Bahá said, 'This man took us to his house to show pictures and other objects. I was greatly surprised to find that people go to view things which are nothing more than children's toys but they fail to examine this divine system.'[8]

The next day, 'Abdu'l-Bahá addressed a gathering of black people and told them about Bahá'u'lláh's faithful servant Isfandíyár. He said, 'If a believer in God prays for piety, it does not matter whether he is robed in black or white.'[9]

On His last day in Chicago, 'Abdu'l-Bahá spoke at four gatherings. That evening, He was visited by a number of people, including a group of engineers who wanted to know more about the Mashriqu'l-Adhkár. He told them:

> The Mashriqu'l-Adhkár is circular in shape. It has nine paths, nine gardens, nine pools with fountains and nine gates. Each path will lead to a centre such as an orphanage, a hospital, a school, a university and other buildings that are dependencies of the Mashriqu'l-Adhkár.[10]

## Cincinnati, Ohio

Before leaving Chicago on 4 November, 'Abdu'l-Bahá telegraphed to the Bahá'ís of Cincinnati, telling them of His coming. He specifically told them that He would only be there for one night in order to visit the believers. When He arrived He was met by the Bahá'ís, who took Him to the Grand Hotel where fifty of the friends, including Sarah Farmer, awaited Him. 'Abdu'l-Bahá was delighted with the gathering and sat at the head of the table for the banquet. Forty of those present chose to stay at the hotel that night so as not to miss a minute of His precious visit.

The next morning, 5 November, 'Abdu'l-Bahá had planned to leave early, but the many seekers and Bahá'ís kept Him there until noon. He told a group at the Grand Hotel that He had come 'to associate here with those who are the standard-bearers of international conciliation and agreement'. He had travelled 'from coast to coast . . . attended many meetings where international peace was discussed' and was 'happy to witness the results of such meetings' because Bahá'u'lláh taught the establishment of agreement between all people. The Master said that because His Father had 'proclaimed international unity, summoned the religions of the world to harmony and reconciliation and established fellowship among many races, sects and communities', that 'today in Persia . . . there are many people of various races and religions who have followed the exhortations of Bahá'u'lláh and are living together in love and fellowship without religious, patriotic or racial prejudices'. 'Abdu'l-Bahá concluded by saying that Bahá'u'lláh had called for the parliaments of the world 'to send their wisest and best men to an international world conference which should decide all questions between the peoples and establish universal peace. This would be the highest court of appeal, and the parliament of man so long dreamed of by poets and idealists would be realized.'[11]

## Washington, DC

Because of leaving Cincinnati later than He had planned, 'Abdu'l-Bahá arrived in Washington, DC only at 8.45 the next morning. Agnes Parsons, the Hannens and others gathered at the station at 6.30, His scheduled arrival time, but the train was late. Some of the friends had passes that allowed them onto the platform to meet the train, but Mrs Parsons did not. When she asked the gatekeeper if she and some others could go through and meet the train, he asked if she was there to meet 'the great poet'. When she replied that she was there to meet 'Abdu'l-Bahá, the gatekeeper allowed them all through. Mrs Parsons took the travel-weary Master in her carriage to the house rented for Him.[12]

At the house, 'Abdu'l-Bahá spoke with the friends, then retired to rest. Later in the afternoon, Mrs Parsons returned and took the Master for a drive around Washington, together with Helen Hillyer Brown, who had been a member of the first historic pilgrimage in 1898–99. That same evening 'Abdu'l-Bahá gave a talk at the Universalist Church.

On 7 November 'Abdu'l-Bahá had a long visit with the Turkish ambassador, Díyá Páshá. Lunch was a quiet affair that day with only Mrs Parsons, Sallie Stockton, Mírzá 'Alí-Akbar, Ahmad Sohrab, Mírzá Mahmúd and Fareed. The Master joked with Ahmad Sohrab about his good appetite. He gave a talk in the afternoon at which Rabbi Abram Symon, a Dutch minister, and General Adolphus Greely were present. Rabbi Symon approached the Master and asked Him to speak in the synagogue. The Master later recalled that:

> I was invited by the Jews to speak. As they had strong enmity, it was now the time to prove the validity of Christ. The Jewish Rabbi came to me and protested that I had spoken in churches, so why not speak in a Synagogue. I told him: 'Maybe you will find my talk against your ideas. If so will you stamp and whistle?' He assured me they would make no disturbance. I replied: 'You may do whatever you like at the end of the service, but do not disturb me until I finish speaking.'[13]

So it was that the following day 'Abdu'l-Bahá spoke at the Eighth Street Temple Synagogue about the oneness of the foundation of spiritual truth. He spoke of the great achievements of Abraham and Moses, and gave a summary of Jewish history, 'leading up to the coming of another great Prophet of God. "His Holiness Jesus Christ!"'[14]

> Let me ask your closest attention in considering this subject. The divine religions embody two kinds of ordinances. First, there are those which constitute essential, or spiritual, teachings of the Word

of God. These are faith in God, the acquirement of the virtues which characterize perfect manhood, praiseworthy moralities, the acquisition of the bestowals and bounties emanating from the divine effulgences – in brief, the ordinances which concern the realm of morals and ethics . . .

Second, there are laws and ordinances which are temporary and nonessential. These concern human transactions and relations. They are accidental and subject to change according to the exigencies of time and place. These ordinances are neither permanent nor fundamental . . .

It has been shown conclusively, therefore, that the foundation of the religion of God remains permanent and unchanging. It is that fixed foundation which ensures the progress and stability of the body politic and the illumination of humanity. It has ever been the cause of love and justice amongst men. It works for the true fellowship and unification of all mankind, for it never changes and is not subject to supersedure. The accidental, or nonessential, laws which regulate the transactions of the social body and everyday affairs of life are changeable and subject to abrogation.

Let me ask: What is the purpose of Prophethood? Why has God sent the Prophets? It is self-evident that the Prophets are the Educators of men and the Teachers of the human race. They come to bestow universal education upon humanity, to give humanity training, to uplift the human race from the abyss of despair and desolation and to enable man to attain the apogee of advancement and glory. The people are in darkness; the Prophets bring them into the realm of light. They are in a state of utter imperfection; the Prophets imbue them with perfections . . .

For example, let us review the events connected with the history of Moses – upon Him be peace! He dwelt in Midian at a time when the children of Israel were in captivity and bondage in the land of Egypt, subjected to every tyranny and severe oppression. They were illiterate and ignorant, undergoing cruel ordeals and experiences. They were in such a state of helplessness and impotence that it was proverbial to state that one Egyptian could overcome ten Israelites. At such a time as this and under such forbidding conditions Moses appeared and shone forth with a heavenly radiance. He saved Israel from the bondage of Pharaoh and released them from captivity. He led them out of the land of Egypt and into the Holy Land. They had been scattered and broken; He unified and disciplined them, conferred upon them the blessing of wisdom and knowledge. They had been slaves; He made them princes. They were ignorant; He made them learned... Through the guidance and training of Moses these slaves and captives became the dominating people amongst the nations. Not only in physical and military superiority were they renowned, but in all the degrees of arts, letters and refinement their fame was widespread. Even the celebrated philosophers of Greece journeyed to Jerusalem in order to study with the Israelitish sages, and many were the lessons of philosophy and wisdom they received. Among these philosophers was the famous Socrates...

Inasmuch as Moses through the influence of His great mission was instrumental in releasing the Israelites from a low state of debasement and humiliation, establishing them in a station of prestige and glorification, disciplining and educating them, it is necessary for us to reach a fair and just judgement in regard to such a marvellous Teacher. For in this great accomplishment He stood single and alone. Could He have made such a change and brought about such a condition among these people without the sanction and assistance of a heavenly power? Could He have transformed a people from humiliation to glory without a holy and divine support?

None other than a divine power could have done this. Therein lies the proof of Prophethood because the mission of a Prophet is education of the human race such as this Personage accomplished, proving Him to be a mighty Prophet among the Prophets and His Book the very Book of God. This is a rational, direct and perfect proof...

I now wish you to examine certain facts and statements which are worthy of consideration. My purpose and intention is to remove from the hearts of men the religious enmity and hatred which have fettered them and to bring all religions into agreement and unity. Inasmuch as this hatred and enmity, this bigotry and intolerance are outcomes of misunderstandings, the reality of religious unity will appear when these misunderstandings are dispelled. For the foundation of the divine religions is one foundation. This is the oneness of revelation or teaching. But, alas, we have turned away from that foundation, holding tenaciously to various dogmatic forms and blind imitation of ancestral beliefs. This is the real cause of enmity, hatred and bloodshed in the world – the reason of alienation and estrangement among mankind. Therefore, I wish you to be very just and fair in your judgement of the following statements.

During the time that the people of Israel were being tossed and afflicted by the conditions I have named, Jesus Christ appeared among them. Jesus of Nazareth was a Jew. He was single and unaided, alone and unique. He had no assistant. The Jews at once pronounced Him to be an enemy of Moses. They declared that He was the destroyer of the Mosaic laws and ordinances. Let us examine the facts as they are, investigate the truth and reality in order to arrive at a true opinion and conclusion. For a completely fair opinion upon this question we must lay aside all we have and investigate independently. This Personage, Jesus Christ, declared Moses to have been the Prophet of God and pronounced all the prophets of Israel as sent from God. He proclaimed the Torah the very Book of God, summoned all to conform to its precepts and follow its teachings . . . through Christ, through the blessing of the New Testament of Jesus Christ, the Old Testament, the Torah, was translated into six hundred different tongues and spread throughout the world . . . Through Him the name of Moses was elevated and revered. . . . Which of the kings of Israel could have accomplished this? Were it not for Jesus Christ, would the Bible, the Torah have reached this land of America? Would the name of Moses be spread throughout the world? Refer to history. Everyone knows that when Christianity was spread, there was a simultaneous spread of the knowledge of Judaism and the Torah . . . so that today the Holy Bible is a household book . . . It is evident, then, that Christ was a friend of Moses, that He loved and believed in Moses; otherwise, He would not have commemorated His name and Prophethood. This is self-evident. Therefore, Christians and Jews should have the greatest love for each other because the Founders of these two great religions have been in perfect agreement in Book and teaching. Their followers should be likewise.

We have already stated the valid proofs of Prophethood. We find the very evidences of the validity of Moses were witnessed and duplicated in Christ. Christ was also a unique and single Personage born of the lineage of Israel. By the power of His Word He was able to unite people of the Roman, Greek, Chaldean, Egyptian and Assyrian nations. Whereas they had been cruel, bloodthirsty and hostile, killing, pillaging and taking each other captive, He cemented them together in a perfect bond of unity and love. He caused them to agree and become reconciled. Such mighty effects were the results of the manifestation of one single Soul. This proves conclusively that Christ was assisted by God. Today all Christians admit and believe that Moses was a Prophet of God. They declare that His Book was the Book of God, that the prophets of Israel were true and valid and that the people of Israel constituted the people of God . . . And now it is time for the Jews to declare that Christ was the Word of God, and then this enmity between two great religions will pass away. For two thousand years this enmity and religious prejudice have continued. Blood has been shed, ordeals have been suffered. These few words will remedy the difficulty and unite two great religions. What harm could follow this: that just as the Christians glorify and praise the name of Moses, likewise the Jews should commemorate the name of Christ, declare Him to be the Word of God and consider Him as one of the chosen Messengers of God?

A few words concerning the Qur'án and the Muslims: When Muḥammad appeared, He spoke of Moses as the great Man of God. In the Qur'án He refers to the sayings of Moses in seven different places, proclaims Him a Prophet and the possessor of a Book, the Founder of the law and the Spirit of God . . . In a certain súrih of the Qur'án He mentions the names of twenty-eight of the prophets of Israel, praising each and all of them. To this great extent He has ratified and commended the prophets and religion of Israel. The purport is this: that Muḥammad praised and glorified Moses and confirmed Judaism. He declared that whosoever denies Moses is contaminated and even if he repents, his repentance will not be accepted . . . In this way Muhammad has praised the Torah, Moses, Christ and the prophets of the past. He appeared amongst the Arabs, who were a people nomadic and illiterate, barbarous in nature and bloodthirsty. He guided and trained them until they attained a high degree of development. Through His education and discipline they rose from the lowest levels of ignorance to the heights of knowledge, becoming masters of erudition and philosophy. We see, therefore, that the proofs applicable to one Prophet are equally applicable to another.

> In conclusion, since the Prophets themselves, the Founders, have loved, praised and testified of each other, why should we disagree and be alienated? God is one. He is the Shepherd of all. We are His sheep and, therefore, should live together in love and unity. We should manifest the spirit of justness and goodwill toward each other. Shall we do this, or shall we censure and pronounce anathema, praising ourselves and condemning all others? What possible good can come from such attitude and action? On the contrary, nothing but enmity and hatred, injustice and inhumanity can possibly result. Has not this been the greatest cause of bloodshed, woe and tribulation in the past?[15]

The mention of Christ created a stir among the audience and the Rabbi tried to get Dr Fareed, who was interpreting, to stop the address,

> but the Master went blandly on, asking for their closest attention. After having finished His message, he went quickly out . . . and the Rabbi arose to make a few closing remarks.
>
> He said[:] 'We are not accustomed here to the mention of other prophets than our own, but people of culture all over the world listen to others with ideas different from their own. They may be right and we may be wrong.'[16]

Many had felt that some might take exception to His talk and object. "'If the Jews will not speak,' they said, 'the Christians, at least, will not remain silent.'"[17] Mrs Parsons said that some people left the synagogue and many of those who remained were 'restless and disturbed. The atmosphere was electrical. That Abdul Baha was able to complete His message to this conservative congregation was the greatest demonstration of Spiritual Power that I have ever witnessed.'[18] 'Abdu'l-Bahá later said:

> Many of those present came up and shook me by the hand, and a certain Jew came to me as I was leaving the synagogue and said, 'I am ashamed to be prejudiced any longer.' And, again, as I was walking one day in the street another Jew came to me and said, 'We were neglectful and heedless, and you enlivened us; we slept and you awoke us. It behooves us to remain steadfast now and to look to true knowledge, and forget our 2,000-year-old differences.[19]

The following day, 'Abdu'l-Bahá went to visit the Rabbi, 'showered him with kindness and countless blessings, and spoke to him regarding peace and harmony among the Jews, Christians and Muslims'. The Rabbi 'left His presence with humility and respect'.[20]

The Master continued to meet the friends every day at Mrs Parsons' house, and in the afternoon of His last day in Washington, 10 November, Mrs Parsons took Him, Mírzá 'Alí-Akbar and Ahmad Sohrab on a drive. As they were entering the carriage, Ahmad Sohrab tried to close the window for the Master with the result that the window came out and fell on Mrs Parsons' head, which was, she wrote, luckily protected by 'my "helmet"! of a hat. Abdul-Baha asked with concern about me, and insisted that I should take off the hat, that he might make sure I was not injured. When I removed it He blessed me three times, putting his hand upon my head.'[21]

That evening, 'Abdu'l-Bahá gave His last talk in the city at the home of Joseph Hannen. He again emphasized the unity of the races:

> This is a beautiful assembly. I am very happy that white and black are together. This is the cause of my happiness, for you all are the servants of one God and, therefore, brothers, sisters, mothers and fathers. In the sight of God there is no distinction between whites and blacks; all are as one. Anyone whose heart is pure is dear to God – whether white or black, red or yellow . . .
>
> I hope you will continue in unity and fellowship. How beautiful to see blacks and whites together! I hope, God willing, the day may come when I shall see the red men, the Indians, with you, also Japanese and others. Then there will be white roses, yellow roses, red roses, and a very wonderful rose garden will appear in the world.[22]

After the talk, 'Abdu'l-Bahá gave the friends His instructions:

> O ye revered people! I leave you in charge of Mrs Parsons. Let her be your advisor. Just as I have been kind to you, she will be kind to you. She will be tender to you. As she is a very busy person, she will not be able to associate and meet with you as often, but she can be looking after you. She can think of you and exercise kindness toward you. And I bear testimony to the effect that she is ideally kind; and you must be most grateful for having such a benefactress in your city.[23]

## Baltimore, Maryland and Philadelphia, Pennsylvania

Originally, the Bahá'ís of Baltimore had expected 'Abdu'l-Bahá to visit shortly after His arrival in America. The *Baltimore Sun* even announced that He would speak at the Unitarian Church on 21 April. But the Master didn't make plans that far in the future, so some of the Baltimore Bahá'ís went to New York to see Him. According to oral traditions, Edward Struven did what Fred Mortensen later did and rode the rails to New York. When he arrived, dishevelled like Fred, 'Abdu'l-Bahá sat him down and fed him bowls of Persian rice.[24]

But when 'Abdu'l-Bahá left Washington on the morning of 11 November, He got off the train in Baltimore, arriving at 11 a.m. After a short rest at the Hotel Rennert, He gave a talk at the Unitarian Chapel. In the hall, which had been filled well before 'Abdu'l-Bahá arrived, sat the Bahá'ís, professors from John Hopkins University, and many business and professional people. The *News American* newspaper reported, in three paragraphs, the parts of the talk about the unity of religion, but ignored His comments about the talk He had given in Washington at the Jewish synagogue.[25]

The *Sun* newspaper included several illustrations of 'Abdu'l-Bahá under the headline 'PERSIAN PHILOSOPHER IN STRIKING POSES' followed by another headline stating 'WOMEN KISS HIS HAND'. The article noted:

> At the lecture he wore a robe of black with a triangular insert of light tan in front reaching from hem to neck.
>
> A striking-looking man of about 70 years, he's of average height, with a strong rugged face covered with a short white beard. His cheekbones are high, his eyes bright and flashing.
>
> The lecture was delivered in Persian in an impressive manner. His voice was low-pitched, but at times increased in volume . . . He used frequent gestures, the favourite one being an inclusive swing of both arms to show the universality of the doctrine he propounded. He also frequently leaned over the reading desk and looked at his hearers.[26]

After the talk, 'Abdu'l-Bahá went to the home of Howard and Hebe Struven and gave a short talk in the courtyard. Maud Thompson missed the talk because she was out getting food for the luncheon. When she returned, 'Abdu'l-Bahá called her to join the crowd, but when she entered the living room, there were no chairs available. With a twinkle in His eye, Maud saw Him point to the floor near His feet. Unable to pass up the offer, Maud, though stout and wearing a tightly-laced corset, did as He bade.

Ursula Shuman Moore, who was living with the Struvens at the time, described the luncheon in a letter to a friend:

> Yesterday, the 11th he came over to our house in Baltimore and had dinner with us at our table! Did you ever dream that this would come to pass. He came to Baltimore about twelve o'clock and spoke at the Unitarian Church, and then they came out to our house and we had dinner for him. Many of the Washington believers came over too and many of the Baltimore believers came up. We had about 55 or 54 to feed. Had a grand chicken dinner, with rice and celery, peas, ice cream and cake, and vegetable soup. He said we had given him a *good* dinner, a *fine* dinner, and that he ate much. When I brought in the big platter of chicken and set it before him at the table, he said, 'Oh, chicken!' and seemed to be much pleased with it ... We had him and the Persians in his party sit down first, 12 at the table, and served them, and then we had four relays and every body had something. They all seemed so glad to be there and enjoyed themselves so much. I was so glad for Mother could be near him and see him. I introduced Mother to him, and he took her hand and said, 'Oh, your Mother!' and looked at her very kindly ... They did not stay very long, as they left on the (3 o'clock) train.[27]

The train arrived in Philadelphia at 6 p.m. and 35 friends gathered at the Baltimore & Ohio station to see Him. Some boarded the train and rode with the Master to the Wayne Junction station. Many brought gifts of fruit and candy. The crowd around 'Abdu'l-Bahá was so great that the conductor could hardly pass when he came to collect the fares. One of the group was a Jewish woman who had recently lost both her husband and another relative. 'Abdu'l-Bahá sat next to her and poured His love out to her. As they approached Wayne Junction, 'Abdu'l-Bahá gave Mary Revell a rosary He had, asking that she distribute the beads among the friends.[28]

## New York, New York

When 'Abdu'l-Bahá arrived in New York at 1 a.m., only Juliet Thompson was there to meet Him, due to a confusion of arrival time and location. Mírzá 'Alí-Akbar had come up from Washington early to go house-hunting with Juliet for 'Abdu'l-Bahá. Originally, the Master had been due to arrive at 10 p.m. and the house-hunters thought they had plenty of time to look and to inform the other Bahá'ís. Then they received a telegram announcing that 'Abdu'l-Bahá would arrive at 8 p.m. This threw Juliet and Mírzá 'Alí-Akbar into a panic. Not knowing exactly where 'Abdu'l-Bahá would be arriving, Mírzá 'Alí-Akbar sent Juliet with Mr Mills' chauffeur to the Twenty-Third Street station while he went to the Liberty Street station. Juliet arrived just as the ferry was pulling in and saw Dr Fareed and the Master on the deck.[29]

Later that day, Juliet was in trouble with 'Abdu'l-Bahá. She had asked her mother if she could bring Mírzá 'Alí-Akbar to the house and then to lunch, considering his very late arrival. Mrs Thompson had lived in luxury before her husband died, but since had lived in rather desperate circumstances and was very conscious of the change, so she said no. This greatly upset Juliet who raged about her mother's '"false pride" and stamped out of the house'. When she arrived at the Master's house, he refused to look at her, asking only, 'How is your mother? Is she happy?'[30]

During His last stay in New York, 'Abdu'l-Bahá spoke at few public meetings. Most of His time was spent with the Bahá'ís, educating them about their Faith and their responsibilities as Bahá'ís. In one of His talks, He explained how He was preparing them for their task ahead:

> Through my training you must become so fitted to spread the Glad-Tiding of the Abha Kingdom that you will follow in the footsteps of these blessed ones in gladness. In Persia there is a wonderful breed of horses which are trained to run long distances at very great speed. They are most carefully trained at first. They are taken out into the fields and made to run a short course. At the commencement of their training they are not able to run far. The distance is gradually increased. They become thinner and thinner, wiry and lean, but their strength increases. Finally, after months of rigid training, their swiftness and endurance become wonderful. They are able to run at

full speed across rough country many parasangs of distance [parasang, or farsang is the distance a laden mule can walk in an hour]. At first this would have been impossible. Not until they become trained, thin and wiry, can they endure this severe test.

In this way I shall train you . . . (little by little, little by little), until your powers of endurance become so increased that you will serve the Cause of God continually, without other motive, without other thought or wish. This is my desire.[31]

The wealthy and powerful constantly requested that 'Abdu'l-Bahá visit them in their homes, but He almost always refused, saying, 'I deal with the poor and visit them, not the rich. I love all, especially the poor. All sorts of people come here and I meet them all with sincere love, with heart and soul. Yet I have no intention of visiting the homes of the rich.' He did make an exception for Andrew Carnegie, who was one of America's richest men.[32] Carnegie was greatly attracted to the teachings of the Bahá'í Faith and had offered a large donation for the construction of the House of Worship in Chicago. The Bahá'ís could not accept the donation because only Bahá'ís had the privilege of contributing to the project, but as a result, Mr Carnegie received both a visit and a Tablet from 'Abdu'l-Bahá, in which the Master described him as an 'illustrious soul', 'the lover of humanity and one of the founders of universal peace'.[33]

On the anniversary of the Birth of Bahá'u'lláh on 12 November, the Bahá'ís held a celebration at the home of Dr and Mrs Krug. When 'Abdu'l-Bahá arrived, He powerfully called out *'Yá Bahá'u'lláh!'* Juliet was overwhelmed at the power released with those words; she felt as though Bahá'u'lláh Himself was present.[34]

Next day, 'Abdu'l-Bahá told a gathering of the friends:

One reason that people despair of the world of religion is this very matter of superstitions and imitations practiced by religious leaders. When intelligent and learned people see these imitations and customs as being contrary to reason and knowledge they forsake the divine religion and are not aware that these are idle fancies of the leaders and have nothing to do with divine principles. The foundations of divine religion do not negate sound reason and true science. The principles of divine religion do not contradict knowledge and insight . . . Of course, the second or social laws suited to the Mosaic dispensation and useful for the Jewish people at that time are now purposeless and ineffective and seem futile, but they were pertinent and useful at the time.[35]

During the evening of 14 November, 'Abdu'l-Bahá spoke to a woman who was a Christian Scientist and fanatical in her beliefs. She had questioned his assertion that there is no evil in existence. His reply was:

> By saying there is no evil in existence is meant that what has come from the Origin of existence and being is good and useful. It is good in its time and place and not evil. For example, I can say that there is no darkness in the sun because darkness is the absence of light and has no existence in itself. Oppression is the absence of justice and ignorance is the lack of knowledge. Hence, the imperfections and defects of the world of creation, the contingent world, are merely the absence of virtues and the lack of perfections. These defects have not come from the Source; rather, the essential properties of the world of matter which are change and transformation cause the training of all things and the manifestation of perfections of realities and spirits.[36]

On 15 November 'Abdu'l-Bahá was tired of people saying that they did not see any difference between Christianity and the Bahá'í Faith, or that they did not understand what a new Dispensation was. While going to Juliet Thompson's house, the Master suddenly said, 'The time has come for Me to throw bombs!' That evening, to a full house, 'Abdu'l-Bahá powerfully explained the greatness of this Dispensation and the amazing victories of Bahá'u'lláh over the kings and rulers of His time.[37]

> I have spoken in the various Christian churches and in the synagogues, and in no assemblage has there been a dissenting voice. All have listened, and all have conceded that the teachings of Bahá'u'lláh are superlative in character, acknowledging that they constitute the very essence or spirit of this new age and that there is no better pathway to the attainment of its ideals. Not a single voice has been raised in objection. At most there have been some who have refused to acknowledge the mission of Bahá'u'lláh, although even these have

admitted that He was a great teacher, a most powerful soul, a very great man. Some who could find no other pretext have said, 'These teachings are not new; they are old and familiar; we have heard them before.' Therefore, I will speak to you upon the distinctive characteristics of the manifestation of Bahá'u'lláh and prove that from every standpoint His Cause is distinguished from all others . . .

When Bahá'u'lláh appeared in Persia, all the contemporaneous religious sects and systems rose against Him. His enemies were kings. The enemies of Christ were the Jews, the Pharisees; but the enemies of Bahá'u'lláh were rulers who could command armies and bring hundreds of thousands of soldiers into the arena of operation. These kings represented some fifty million people, all of whom under their influence and domination were opposed to Bahá'u'lláh. Therefore, in effect Bahá'u'lláh, singly and alone, virtually withstood fifty million enemies . . . Although they were determined upon extinguishing the light in that most brilliant lantern, they were ultimately defeated and overthrown, and day by day His splendour became more radiant. They made every effort to lessen His greatness, but His prestige and renown grew in proportion to their endeavours to diminish it. Surrounded by enemies who were seeking His life, He never sought to conceal Himself, did nothing to protect Himself; on the contrary, in His spiritual might and power He was at all times visible before the faces of men, easy of access, serenely withstanding the multitudes who were opposing Him . . .

But Bahá'u'lláh upheld the banner of the Cause of God while He was in a dungeon, addressing the kings of the earth from His prison cell, severely arraigning them for their oppression of their subjects and their misuse of power. The letter He sent to the Sháh of Persia under such conditions may now be read by anyone. His Epistles to the Sulṭán of Turkey, Napoleon III, Emperor of France, and to the other rulers of the world including the President of the United States are, likewise, current and available . . . Whatever is recorded in these Epistles has happened . . .

While addressing these powerful kings and rulers He was a prisoner in a Turkish dungeon. Consider how marvellous it was for a prisoner under the eye and control of the Turks to arraign so boldly and severely the very king who was responsible for His imprisonment. What power this is! What greatness! Nowhere in history can the record of such a happening be found. In spite of the iron rule and absolute dominion of these kings, His function was to withstand them; and so constant and firm was He that He caused their banners to come down and His own standard to be upraised . . .

First among the great principles revealed by Him is that of the investigation of reality. The meaning is that every individual member of humankind is exhorted and commanded to set aside superstitious beliefs, traditions and blind imitation of ancestral forms in religion and investigate reality for himself . . .

A second characteristic principle of the teachings of Bahá'u'lláh is that which commands recognition of the oneness of the world of humanity. Addressing all mankind, He says, 'Ye are all the leaves of one tree.' There are no differences or distinctions of race among you in the sight of God. Nay, rather, all are the servants of God . . .

Bahá'u'lláh teaches that religion must be in conformity with science and reason . . . that religion must be the source of unity and fellowship in the world. If it is productive of enmity, hatred and bigotry, the absence of religion would be preferable. This is a new principle of revelation found only in the utterances of Bahá'u'lláh.

Again, Bahá'u'lláh declares that all forms of prejudice among mankind must be abandoned . . . Another teaching is that there shall be perfect equality between men and women . . . Bahá'u'lláh has announced the necessity for a universal language which shall serve as a means of international communication . . . He has also proclaimed the principle that all mankind shall be educated . . . He teaches that it is incumbent upon all mankind to become fitted for some useful trade, craft or profession by which subsistence may be assured, and this efficiency is to be considered as an act of worship. The teachings of Bahá'u'lláh are boundless and without end in their far-reaching benefit to mankind. The point and purpose of our statement today is that they are new and that they are not found in any of the religious Books of the past. This is in answer to the question, 'What has Bahá'u'lláh brought that we have not heard before?' . . .

Bahá'u'lláh, speaking of these very ones who were attacking and decrying Him, said, 'They are My heralds; they are the ones who are proclaiming My message and spreading My Word. Pray that they may be multiplied, pray that their number may increase and that they may cry out more loudly. The more they abuse Me by their words and the greater their agitation, the more potent and mighty will be the efficacy of the Cause of God, the more luminous the light of the Word and the greater the radiance of the divine Sun. And eventually the gloomy darkness of the outer world will disappear, and the light of reality will shine until the whole earth will be effulgent with its glory.'[38]

On 22 November a 'just and fair-minded' Christian minister asked 'Abdu'l-Bahá, 'What are the new teachings in this Cause?' The Master patiently replied, 'The fundamental principles of all religions are one. They are unchangeable and do not differ. This what Christ meant when He said, "I am not come to destroy the law of the Torah but to promote it."'

The minister then asked, 'Yes, I understand. Do you mean that at the beginning the followers of all the religions were pure and undefiled but grew polluted and negligent?'

The Master said, 'If there is no change or alteration, then there is no renewal. Not until night falls will a new day dawn. If the religion of Moses had not changed, Christ would not have appeared.'[39]

In these final days of 'Abdu'l-Bahá's stay in America 'there was a great rush of visitors. There was not one moment when people were not present'. When the Master became too tired, he would 'go alone to the nearby gardens along the bank of the river to rest.'[40] In these days, too, one issue was giving Him particular cause for concern – the controversy over Howard MacNutt, which was causing disunity in the New York community.

## Howard MacNutt

Howard MacNutt was one of the most active Bahá'ís, but like many of those who had been pupils of Kheiralla, he had difficulty understanding the station of 'Abdu'l-Bahá. He began attending Kheiralla's classes in about 1898, quickly became one of his primary teachers, was elected to the first Bahá'í 'Board of Counsel' in New York in 1900 and later served on the Brooklyn Board of Counsel and the Bahá'í Temple Unity. He edited Mírzá Abu'l-Faḍl's *Bahá'í Proofs* in 1902 and also Ali-Kuli Khan's translation of the Kitáb-i-Íqán in 1904. The following year he went on pilgrimage to 'Akká and on his return wrote a booklet called

*Unity Through Love.* As a result of his pilgrimage he also introduced the Nineteen Day Feast to the American Bahá'í community and in the first decade of the 20th century travelled widely all over the United States as an extremely effective Bahá'í teacher.[41]

'Abdu'l-Bahá had visited the MacNutts in Brooklyn earlier in the year; the short film made of Him was taken at the MacNutt home. Howard MacNutt's misunderstanding of the station of 'Abdu'l-Bahá, however, was a cause of controversy in the community. It came to a climax on 18 or 19 November:

> ... the Master put Howard MacNutt through a severe ordeal, an inevitable ordeal ... In Chicago there are some so-called Bahá'ís who are still connected with Kheiralla, the great Covenant-breaker, and last week the Master sent Mr MacNutt to Chicago to see them and try to persuade them to give up Kheiralla; otherwise he was to cut them off from the faithful believers. He – Mr MacNutt – wrote Zia Bagdadi that he had found these people 'angels', and did nothing about the situation.
>
> He had just returned to New York and was to meet the Master at the Kinneys' house that evening, November 18, for the first time since his unfruitful trip. I was in the second-floor hall with the Master and Carrie Kinney when he arrived. The Master took him to His own room.
>
> After some time they came out together into the hall.
>
> An immense crowd had gathered by then on the first floor, which is open the whole length of the house.
>
> I heard the Master say to Mr MacNutt: 'Go down and tell the people: 'I was like Saul. Now I am Paul, for I see.'
>
> 'But I *don't* see,' said poor Howard.
>
> '*Go down* and say: 'I was like Saul.'
>
> I pulled his coattail. 'For God's sake,' I said, 'go down.'
>
> 'Let me alone,' he replied in his misery.
>
> 'GO DOWN,' commanded the Master.
>
> Mr MacNutt turned and went down, and his back looked *shrunken*. The Master leaned over the stair rail, His head thrown far back, His eyes closed, in anguished prayer. I sat with Carrie on the top step, watching Him. This is like Christ in Gethsemane, I thought.
>
> We could hear the voice of Howard MacNutt stumbling through

his confession: 'I was like Saul.' But he seemed to be saying it by rote, dragging through it still unconvinced. Nevertheless when he came upstairs again, the Master deluged him with love.

By that time the Master was back in His room and as Mr MacNutt appeared at the door, He *ran* forward to meet him. Our Lord was all in white that night and as He ran with His arms wide open He looked like a great flying bird. He enfolded Howard in a close embrace, kissed his face and neck, welcomed with ecstasy this broken man who, even though bewildered, had obeyed Him. [42]

The Master then called distinguished members of the community, 'asked them to embrace Mr MacNutt and exhorted them to have the utmost love and unity among themselves.' Next day he called them again and 'asked them to show kindness and love to Mr MacNutt and to be patient with him.'[43]

That wasn't the end of it, though, and it wasn't until the following year that Howard MacNutt finally understood the station of 'Abdu'l-Bahá as the Centre of the Covenant.[44] By then his reputation had been seriously damaged in the Bahá'í community. It was redeemed through his compiling 'Abdu'l-Bahá's American talks.

In 1919 'Abdu'l-Bahá wrote, 'Name the book which Mr MacNutt is compiling "The Promulgation of Universal Peace". As to its Introduction, it should be written by Mr MacNutt himself when in heart he is turning toward the Abhá kingdom so that he may leave a permanent trace behind him.' And to Howard MacNutt the Master wrote, 'This service shall cause thee to acquire an effulgent face in the Abhá kingdom and shall make thee the object of praise and gratitude of the friends in the East as well as the West.'[45]

Marzieh Gail writes of Howard MacNutt that he 'served the Bahá'í Faith from its earliest days in America for a total of twenty-six years, and was serving when he died. His was a distinguished career, marred only by one brief aberration, from which he was saved by the firm hand of 'Abdu'l-Bahá.'[46]

Howard MacNutt was later named by Shoghi Effendi as a Disciple of 'Abdu'l-Bahá.

\* \* \*

On 23 November 'Abdu'l-Bahá went to Montclair, New Jersey, thereby missing the booking deadline for the *S.S. Mauritania*, the ship He had planned to sail on to England. This delighted the friends because it meant He had to stay longer.

That evening, the Day of the Covenant was celebrated with a banquet at the Great Northern Hotel. More than 300 Bahá'ís were there from Washington, Philadelphia and Boston, including a few special guests such as Mr Topakyan, the Persian Consul General. Before dinner, 'Abdu'l-Bahá went among the guests, anointing everyone with attar of rose according to Persian custom, then gave a short talk.

One group that had been invited, but did not attend, however, were the black Bahá'ís. The manager of the Great Northern Hotel had absolutely refused to allow them into his hotel, saying 'If the people see that one colored person has entered my hotel, no respectable person will ever set foot in it and my business will go to the winds.'[47]

Because of the hotel manager's insult and the loss of being with the Master that night, the white Bahá'ís organized an interracial feast at the home of the Kinneys the following day, with the white ladies serving the meal to their black friends. The Master was very pleased, saying, 'Today you have carried out the laws of the Blessed Beauty in your actions and have truly acted according to the teaching of the Supreme Pen.'[48]

'Abdu'l-Bahá was supposed to meet Dr Percy Grant on 25 November and was late. He had addressed the Women's Club of New York and when He arrived, He apologized saying, 'I am very, very sorry to have kept you waiting, very sorry. But I was captured by *three hundred women* this afternoon. Is it not a dreadful thing to be captured by so many women? The women in America dominate the men.'[49]

On 28 November the Master talked about the spiritual capacity of the Americans. He said:

> Although they are engrossed in material civilization and physical pursuits, still, unlike people in some European countries, they are not wholly devoid of spiritual susceptibilities. They are seekers and desire to investigate reality. They wish for peace and tranquillity and they desire fellowship and love among humanity.[50]

The next day, 'Abdu'l-Bahá moved to the home of the Emery family. During this time, many of the friends kept trying to give money to the

Master to support His travels. In every case, however, He declined to accept it. He finally said, 'Distribute it among the poor on My behalf. It will be as though I have given it to them. But the most acceptable offering to me is the unity of the believers, service to the Cause of God, diffusion of the divine fragrances, and adherence to the counsels of the Abhá Beauty.' The friends did not like this answer, however; they had collected gifts for the women of the holy household and continued to supplicate the Master, asking the Persians to intercede.

Then, on 30 November, some of the believers came up with a plan to try to force 'Abdu'l-Bahá to accept their donations and presents – they would take hold of His 'abá and not let go until He agreed. But though they clung to the hem, 'Abdu'l-Bahá still would not take their offerings. He told them:

> I am most grateful for your services; in truth you have served me . . . Now you have brought presents for the members of My family. They are most acceptable and excellent but better than all these are the gifts of the love of God which remain preserved in the treasuries of the heart. These gifts are evanescent but those are eternal; these jewels must be kept in boxes and vaults and they will eventually perish but those jewels remain in the treasuries of the heart and will remain throughout the world of God for eternity. Thus I will take to them your love, which the greatest of all gifts. In our house they do not wear diamond rings nor do they keep rubies. That house is sanctified above such adornments.
>
> I, however, have accepted your gifts; but I entrust them to you for you to sell and send the proceeds to the fund for the Ma<u>sh</u>riqu'l-A<u>dh</u>kár in Chicago.[51]

As His time in America drew to its close, 'Abdu'l-Bahá spoke with Mrs Tatum. Later, she told Juliet Thompson of the conversation. 'The Master said such a strange thing to me just before He left America. I had been saying how sorry I was that I had left my car in Boston and couldn't put it at His disposal as I had done last spring. He answered: "Soon, Mrs Tatum, you will not need your car, for you will be riding in a chariot of fire." I wonder, Juliet, what He meant by that!' Within a few weeks, Mrs Tatum suddenly passed away, riding the chariot into the next world.[52]

'Abdu'l-Bahá announced His departure from America while at the Kinney home on 2 December. He told the gathered friends, 'These are the days of my farewell to you.' So it was official, He was finally leaving the shores of America. Though everyone had known that it must happen, it was still a very distressing announcement. The Master told the friends yet again that they must promote unity and concord:

> These are the days of my farewell to you, for I am sailing on the fifth of the month. Wherever I went in this country, I returned always to New York City. This is my fourth or fifth visit here, and now I am going away to the Orient. It will be difficult for me to visit this country again except it be the will of God. I must, therefore, give you my instructions and exhortations today, and these are none other than the teachings of Bahá'u'lláh.
>
> You must manifest complete love and affection toward all mankind. Do not exalt yourselves above others, but consider all as your equals, recognizing them as the servants of one God. Know that God is compassionate toward all; therefore, love all from the depths of your hearts, prefer all religionists before yourselves, be filled with love for every race, and be kind toward the people of all nationalities. Never speak disparagingly of others, but praise without distinction. Pollute not your tongues by speaking evil of another. Recognize your enemies as friends, and consider those who wish you evil as the wishers of good. You must not see evil as evil and then compromise with your opinion, for to treat in a smooth, kindly way one whom you consider evil or an enemy is hypocrisy, and this is not worthy or allowable. You must consider your enemies as your friends, look upon your evil-wishers as your well-wishers and treat them accordingly. Act in such a way that your heart may be free from hatred. Let not your heart be offended with anyone. If some one commits an error and wrong toward you, you must instantly forgive him. Do not complain of others. Refrain from reprimanding them, and if you wish to give admonition or advice, let it be offered in such a way that it will not burden the bearer. Turn all your thoughts toward bringing joy to hearts. Beware! Beware! lest ye offend any heart. Assist the world of humanity as much as possible. Be the source of consolation to every sad one, assist every weak one, be helpful to every indigent one, care for every sick one, be the

cause of glorification to every lowly one, and shelter those who are overshadowed by fear.

In brief, let each one of you be as a lamp shining forth with the light of the virtues of the world of humanity. Be trustworthy, sincere, affectionate and replete with chastity. Be illumined, be spiritual, be divine, be glorious, be quickened of God, be a Baha'i.[53]

Howard MacNutt recorded 'Abdu'l-Bahá's answer to a comment from one of the Bahá'ís who noted that:

> What we expected in connection with your visit has not happened and what we did not expect to happen has indeed come to pass. We expected an attitude of hostility toward you by the clergy and theologians. Instead of this they have welcomed you in the spirit of fairness and sincerity. We did not expect the churches and religious societies would open their doors, but they have done so and most of your important public addresses have been delivered from pulpits of various denominations.

'Abdu'l-Bahá replied:

> According to the record of three Gospels, His Holiness Jesus Christ went into the Temple of Jerusalem, rebuked the Jews for the degeneracy of their worship into materialistic forms and delivered the Message of Divine Glad-tidings. For nineteen hundred years this has been pointed out by Christians as a most wonderful event, – that His Holiness without opposition from the Jews was permitted to enter their most sacred place of worship and proclaim the Word of God. Consider what has happened in this century. During the past year we have been welcomed in churches and pulpits of Europe and America by different denominations, – upraising the Divine Standard of Unity, summoning mankind to the Glad Tidings of the Most Great Peace, proclaiming the Reality of the Kingdom of ABHA. And this has been accomplished not only without opposition but by invitation, and in a spirit of the utmost love and fragrance. Consider therefore the wonderful influence and importance of this in the future.[54]

Agnes Parsons and Mariam Haney arrived in New York on 3 December and went to see 'Abdu'l-Bahá. Soon thereafter, Grace Krug and her daughter, Louise, and Ali-Kuli Khan joined them. The Master introduced Mrs Parsons and Mrs Krug, saying pointedly that He wished them to get to know each other very well. After repeating that point, He also told them that they should correspond because they would work with each other in the future. Mrs Haney then noted that she remembered Him saying in Los Angeles that some souls would arise in America who would be like the Persian believers. 'Abdu'l-Bahá replied, 'I testify that all those who are in this room now are just the same as the Persian believers.' [55]

Spreading the teachings of Bahá'u'lláh was something that 'Abdu'l-Bahá constantly stressed, but while many could easily talk about the principles and teachings of the Faith, some had difficulty giving the source of those teachings. Howard Colby Ives was not one of them. Mírzá Maḥmúd asked Howard whether he spoke about the Cause of Bahá'u'lláh from his church pulpit. 'Yes, not as often as I might wish, but I quote frequently from the Writings in illustration of my subject.'

Mírzá Maḥmúd then asked, 'When you quote do you mention the Author?'

Howard answered, 'Certainly. I naturally give my authority.'

Mírzá Maḥmúd then noted, 'It must require some courage, does that not arouse criticism?'

Howard thought and then said, 'I had not thought of the matter in that light. Why should it require courage to speak of truth without regard to sources?'

When 'Abdu'l-Bahá heard of Howard's answer, however, He said that it took a great deal of courage.[56]

'Abdu'l-Bahá's last day in America was as busy as any other. In the morning, He spoke with a rabbi about the Torah and explained the meanings of several verses:

> The verse 'God created heaven and earth in six days' has reference to the Day of God and the spiritual creation, for there was no day or night before the creation of this heaven and earth. And the meaning of 'the water' in the verse of the Torah 'The spirit of God moved upon the face of the water like a bird' is the water of knowledge which is the source of heavenly life. It is written that God said, 'Let

us make man in our image'; this means in the image of divine names and attributes, for God is holy above all physical images and is pure and sanctified above all forms or likenesses. [57]

Later in the day, the Master talked about understanding the Holy Books:

> The object of reading and reciting is to understand the inner significance of the verses and mysteries of the Book. Had reading sufficed, all the Jewish people should have acknowledged Christ but as they lacked understanding of the mysteries and inner meanings, they were deprived of the bounty of believing in Him. They interpreted the book in a literal or outward manner and did not find the appearance of Christ to conform to their traditions, imitations and the prevailing customs of their people, so they denied and rejected Him.[58]

'Abdu'l-Bahá dined with Edward and Carrie Kinney the evening before He departed. Later, a story about Edward and the Master was told:

> The day before He was to take ship to leave He asked Mr Kinney if there was something amongst His belongings that He might offer as a gift of farewell. At first, Mr Kinney was reluctant to choose, but finally he admitted that well, might he be given a pair of Abdu'l-Bahá's boots? Those boots that had sheltered the feet that walked with such serene certainty upon the Path of God? Mr Kinney would cherish these above all else.
> So, with smiling love, 'Abdu'l-Bahá gave a pair of His boots to Edward Kinney. Reverently and joyfully, Mr Kinney laid them in a bureau drawer in his bedroom, carefully wrapped in a nest of tissue paper. Very rarely – since the boots were such an intimate and precious thing, were they shown to anyone though Mr Kinney touched them frequently as he prayed.
> Then one day, he did wish to show them to someone. He went to the bureau, pulled out the drawer – and the boots were gone – completely gone. No sign of them in the tissue paper, no sign of them in any other drawer, no sign of them in any part of the room which was searched carefully. There simply were no boots anywhere.

So Dad Kinney (he became 'Dad' to all the hundreds who loved him) began to pray and he prayed, shaken, from the depths of his troubled soul. Why had the beloved boots been taken from him? Where had they gone? What could have happened? Was he, had he become – unworthy to possess them? And, at last, he knew this was it. He was no longer worthy to hold the precious boots. Then why was he no longer worthy? What had he done between the time when he had last held the boots in his hands and the moment when he had discovered their absence?

It had been, he estimated, some two, possibly three weeks. So in deepest meditation, he went back, day by day, hour by hour, moment by moment over this period. He remembered his actions; he analysed his motives; he reviewed his thoughts. And suddenly, in a blaze of illumination, he knew what it was. Deeply selfish materialism; clouded hypocritical motives; unjust actions. He had been guilty of all these. But he had deluded himself by calling them such fair and pretty names. No wonder the boots had been taken away. In all justice he had proved himself in no way worthy to hold such treasure. Humbled and ashamed, he prayed abjectly for forgiveness – and then, mournfully, he went to the bureau drawer – just to touch the tissue paper that once had protected the boots. And lo! the boots had returned. They were there, real and tangible; the leather soft beneath his fingertips, the well-worn soles smooth to his touch. They were there, but the warning was never forgotten – the lesson was well learned. [59]

Finally came 5 December. Mrs Parsons and Mrs Haney went to see the Master early and found Him on His bed with Mírzá Maḥmúd and Siyyid Asadu'lláh massaging His limbs. After a breakfast of bread and cheese, everyone climbed aboard Mountfort Mills' auto for the trip to the dock.[60]

The New York dock alongside the *S.S. Celtic* was crowded with Bahá'ís, many in tears. Young and old were affected by 'Abdu'l-Bahá's departure from America after eight months. Juliet Thompson and a hundred others boarded the ship to spend those last minutes in His presence. They gathered in a large, low-ceilinged room.

> Juliet and some of the friends . . . all went to the large first class lounge, packed with Bahá'ís from various parts of the country.

Walking back and forth, a familiar action when speaking to the friends, 'Abdu'l-Bahá gave them His last exhortation in the City of the Covenant, while all the friends were weeping quietly.

He reminded the friends that they were standing for the unity of all nations and for world peace while a war raged in the Balkans. Then He said, 'As to you, your efforts must be lofty. Exert yourselves with heart and soul that perchance through your efforts the light of Universal Peace may shine and this darkness of estrangement and enmity may be dispelled from amongst men.

'You have no excuse to bring before God if you fail to live according to His command, for you are informed of that which constitutes the good pleasure of God.

'It is my hope that you may become successful in this high calling, so that like brilliant lamps you may cast light upon the world of humanity and quicken and stir the body of existence like unto a spirit of life.

'This is eternal glory. This is everlasting felicity. This is immortal life. This is heavenly attainment. This is being created in God's image and likeness. And unto this I call you, praying God to strengthen and bless you.'

The passengers and officers of the Celtic were astonished at the scene: 'Their surprise was beyond expression,' noted Mahmud. 'The Master was seated in a corner of the lounge, while the believers flocked around Him for the last minutes left.' Juliet lamented, '. . . It was death to leave that ship. I stood on the pier with May Maxwell, tears blurred my sight. Through them, I could see the Master in the midst of the group of Persians waving a patient hand to us. It waved and waved, that beautiful hand, till the Figure was lost to sight.'[61]

From the ship, Mírzá Mahmúd could see the friends on the pier: 'The throng of believers, stretching as far as the eye could see, waved farewell to the Master, now far in the distance. And He said:

> Observe how the power of the Cause of God has created a tumult in the hearts and what a revolution it has produced. See how the aid and assistance of the Abhá beauty have reached us constantly and invariable the lights of victory have shone from the supreme horizon. These have been from the promised confirmations of the

Kingdom of God and the assistance of the invisible sovereignty of the Abhá beauty, which He has promised clearly in the verse, 'Verily We behold you from Our realm of Glory, and shall aid whosoever will arise for the triumph of Our Cause with the hosts of the Concourse on high and a company of Our favored angels.'[62]

Howard Colby Ives was there as well:

> We slowly passed in front of Him. To each He gave a handful of the flowers massed near Him . . . When my own turn came I again forgot all but His nearness and the overwhelming fact that never again in this world would I see Him, or hear that beloved voice. I impulsively dropped to a knee, raised His hand with mine and placed it upon my head . . .
>
> The friends gathered on the wharf looked up at the figure of their Master as the ship slowly moved into the river. 'Abdu'l-Bahá stood at the rail, His white hair and beard moved by the breeze, His erect, majestic figure outlined clearly. In His hand I noticed the rosary which was His constant companion. His lips were moving. I could easily read those lips. 'Alláh'u'Abhá! Alláh'u'Abhá!'[63]

The *Celtic* sailed at noon.

# 15

# RETURN TO THE UNITED KINGDOM

## 13 December 1912–21 January 1913

The *Celtic* took eight days to reach Liverpool. On 7 December the weather was as warm and pleasant as spring and the sailors were surprised because this was usually the time for storms. The Captain visited 'Abdu'l-Bahá and expressed his pleasure in having him on the ship. 'Abdu'l-Bahá said He would like to see a big storm and said, 'In future people will cross the Atlantic in airships; steamers will only carry freight' (this was fifteen years before the first transatlantic flight). Two days later, the sea began to get rough, as though in answer to 'Abdu'l-Bahá's desire. 'Abdu'l-Bahá stayed on the deck watching the growing storm. He said, 'Look at that imperial wave, how it mounts high and devours the smaller waves! It is a wonderful sight. This is the best day. I am enjoying it.'[1]

### LIVERPOOL, ENGLAND

When the steamer approached the dock at Liverpool on 13 December 1912, there were a dozen Bahá'ís from Manchester, Liverpool and Leeds waving handkerchiefs and welcoming 'Abdu'l-Bahá to England. The group, including Hippolyte Dreyfus-Barney, who had come from Paris, Elizabeth Herrick, Isabel Fraser, E. T. Hall, John Craven and John Downs, watched the *Celtic* come slowly toward the dock at 9 p.m. Isabel Fraser wrote that they

> watched the great liner come slowly up the stream literally out of the dark night. Suddenly we caught sight of Abdul-Baha in the ship's bow, and as she hove to he walked slowly down the long deck till he stood quite alone, in the very center of the center deck. All eyes were riveted upon him as he peered over the ship's side into the rain and gloom of Liverpool.[2]

To the Bahá'ís on shore, it seemed to take forever before 'Abdu'l-Bahá came down the gang-plank. Before He descended, the second and third-class baggage was taken to customs. At last, the group saw His 'white-turbaned head' as He came slowly down. One of the Persians carried a tiny Japanese orange tree from California. 'Laden with fruit, it looked like an offering from the tropics . . .'[3]

'Abdu'l-Bahá stayed in Liverpool two days, at the Adelphi Hotel, 'the most beautiful hotel in the city'.[4] He gave two talks while in the city, the first to the Theosophical Society and the second to the congregation at the Reverend Donald Fraser's Pembroke Chapel. On 14 December, the President of the Theosophical Society, Mrs Amour, made the mistake of introducing 'Abdu'l-Bahá by saying that He needed no introduction. The Master, therefore, immediately began speaking about searching for the truth:

> When I was in America, I had many opportunities of addressing the Theosophical Society there . . . The Theosophists are very dear to me, for they have abandoned all prejudice. They do not abide in the confines of dogma, but are seeking truth in a spirit of freedom. All the religions of the world are submerged in prejudice. A Jew is a Jew because his father was before him. A Christian is such for the same reason, and it is the same with a Musselman. All follow the precepts of their fathers, refusing to go forth and seek for themselves.
>
> We both (Theosophists and Bahais) have abandoned all dogmas in our earnest search for truth. But look at the tribes and nations of the world – why are they seething with contention? Because they are not seeking truth . . .
>
> All the different religions of God that have risen on the face of the earth have one purpose: to educate man and to inform him of the spiritual, the luminous, the divine, so that he may partake of heavenly spirit and find eternal life, show forth the virtues of mankind, and from a world of darkness enter a world of light . . .
>
> All the religions, all the prophets, all the great teachers had no other purpose than to raise mankind from the animal to the divine nature. Their purpose was to free man and to make him an inhabiter of the Realm of Reality. For although the body of man is material, his reality is spiritual; although his body is darkness, his soul is light; although his body may seem to imprison him, his soul is essentially

free. To prove this freedom, the prophets of God have appeared and will continue to appear, for there is no end to divine teachings and no beginning.[5]

The next night, the Reverend Donald Fraser welcomed 'Abdu'l-Bahá to Pembroke Chapel as a herald of peace and expressed his appreciation, saying that His visit was a great honour. When Reverend Fraser indicated that the Master should ascend the elevated pulpit to speak, 'Abdu'l-Bahá hesitated, saying that he did not like to have to look down on people. He finally ascended the steps after Reverend Fraser told him that the people in the gallery would be higher than He and everyone would be able to hear Him better from the pulpit. 'Abdu'l-Bahá spoke about unity:

> What benefit do we ever draw from separating ourselves one from another? Why should we wrangle and battle to kill each other? God is kind. Why are we unkind?
>
> The first separating principle is religion. Every sect and community has gathered around itself certain imitations of Reality in ceremonies and forms, and as these imitations differ, contentions follow. Each division is encompassed with thick clouds through which the Sun of Reality cannot penetrate. If these divisions should forget the differences in imitations and seek for the underlying Reality, all would be united and agreed and fellowship would be established between the organizations of mankind.[6]

At the conclusion of the talk, 'Abdu'l-Bahá wrote a blessing for Reverend Fraser in the church book: 'O Thou Kind Almighty, confirm Thou this servant of Thine, Mr Fraser, in the service of Thy Kingdom. Make him illumined; make him heavenly; make him spiritual; make him divine . . .'[7]

On the morning of 16 December the Master and His attendants walked to Lime Street Station, where they were to take the train to London. To Elizabeth Herrick and Isabel Fraser, who were travelling in the same compartment with Him along with Hippolyte Dreyfus-Barney and Ahmad Yazdi, He said, 'I am most pleased with you. You are real servants of the Covenant.' And commenting on Isabel Fraser's indefatigable efforts to place articles in the newspapers, he said:

I will never forget these services of yours. You must become like a burning torch so that you may be able to melt mountains of snow. Europe is filled with mountains which are snowcapped all the year around. May you attain to such a degree of heat that you may melt the snow. Europe is submerged in materialism. People are not thinking of God. All their attention is turned toward matter and nature. Like unto the cows they graze in the meadows which are overgrown with grass. They can see nothing beyond their noses. America is much better. People in that country are investigating the Reality. They are more susceptible to spiritual life. [8]

## LONDON, ENGLAND

At 1.40 p.m. the train reached Euston Station, where about fifty Bahá'ís welcomed 'Abdu'l-Bahá to London, including Lady Blomfield with her two daughters. Lady Blomfield had brought her car for the Master to ride in, and took him to her apartment at 97 Cadogan Gardens, which she had once more offered to Him during His stay in London. The ladies accompanied the Master in the car without an interpreter and He spoke English to them all the time.

Ahmad Sohrab was very impressed with Lady Blomfield, describing her as 'a remarkable woman, a most sincere Bahai, an active worker, and an enthusiastic speaker; really a wonderful woman'.[9] 'Abdu'l-Bahá added to this the following day, in calling attention to 'how quickly the Paris and London addresses delivered last year were printed, and this was done through one woman, Lady Blomfield'. 'Abdu'l-Bahá wished to see the addresses he had delivered in America printed as well; 'At present, he declared, they are all scattered and not collected.' When someone suggested the name of a prominent wealthy woman, he said, 'One of these poor, sincere and honest women is more beloved by me than a thousand millionaires; just now this Lady Blomfield is dearer to me than all the queens of the world.'[10]

After resting a while, 'Abdu'l-Bahá met newspaper reporters and later gave a talk to the Bahá'ís. The following day a Bahá'í from Belfast, Ireland, who had travelled all day and all night, arrived to see 'Abdu'l-Bahá. This may have been Joan Waring.[11] 'Abdu'l-Bahá warmly welcomed her and told her, 'You must become the cause of illumination in Ireland . . . now you must ignite four thousand lamps in one year . . .' The lady replied that many people were afraid of a new religion, to which He responded:

> They are like unto those souls who say: 'We don't like fresh flowers but we are satisfied with withered and decayed flowers.' Decayed flowers do not have sweet fragrance; their odour is not good; they have no freshness and charm. The fresher the flower the sweeter it is and the more charming. If old and decayed flowers were good enough then the Adamic flower would have been sufficient. Every new year needs a new flower, new fruits are necessary, fresh and gentle breezes are needed. [12]

Marion Jack was also present that day. 'Abdu'l-Bahá told her:

> Those souls who consider themselves as imperfect, they are the people of the Kingdom. Those persons who prefer themselves above others are egotists and worshippers of self; they are deprived of the graces of the Lord of mankind.[13]

Since His arrival, 'Abdu'l-Bahá had taken many opportunities to talk in glowing terms about his experiences in the United States and to praise the American people, and to a professor of Arabic he now said:

> The American people investigate everything. Their minds are open, their ears are listening . . . They are a mighty nation, a noble people, They love the Reality. They are not limited . . . They listen to every discussion with dignity, urbanity and politeness. If it is in accord with reason they will accept it, if they do not understand they ask questions.[14]

That afternoon a large number of people gathered at Caxton Hall in the heart of Westminster to welcome the Master, and again 'Abdu'l-Bahá spoke of America, 'emphasizing the love and unity which exists between the two countries'. [15]

On 18 December 'Abdu'l-Bahá gave a talk at which Edward Granville Browne, the noted Orientalist, was present. In April 1890 'Abdu'l-Bahá had hosted Browne at Bahjí when he met Bahá'u'lláh, one of the few Westerners to have done so and who left a memorable description of that interview. It was also Browne who had published the book purporting to be an early history of the Faith, the *Nuqtatu'l-Káf*, a few years before (see p. 43 above). After the Master's talk, Browne greeted Him with, 'The last time I met you was twenty-two years ago in Acca under different environment, but now I have the pleasure of seeing you in London.'[16] He would come to see the Master several times during this second visit to London.

After a walk and a taxi ride through Hyde Park and Regent's Park, 'Abdu'l-Bahá met a minister from one of the churches in 'the suburbs of the great Metropolis' . . . the Counsellor of the Persian Embassy . . . the president of the Esperantists of England' and several Persian Bahá'ís, including Ḥájí Amín, who had just arrived from that country and had been waiting in Paris for the Master's arrival.[17]

Ḥájí Amín had had a rather confusing journey from Paris to London. He spoke neither French nor English and carried letters with names and addresses to help him reach his destination. Somehow, after leaving Paris and crossing the English Channel, he inexplicably found himself back in Paris. His second effort to reach London was successful, but 'Abdu'l-Bahá joked that the Ḥájí 'could not forsake the delights of Paris' and had to hurry back there'.[18]

The next day, Ḥájí Amín visited 'Abdu'l-Bahá in the morning. Ahmad Sohrab described what happened when Ḥájí Amín opened his handkerchief, in which he carried letters from Persian Bahá'ís:

> What caught my eyes at first glance were two small loaves of bread and an apple which were sent from a Bahai from far off Russia. This was all this poor man could send to the Beloved with his devotion and love. 'Abdu'l-Bahá looked at this love offering with such tenderness, with such joy and kindness in his eyes, that I shall never forget it. He ate a piece of the stale bread and gave the rest to Said Assadullah for him to serve the rest at the table.[19]

'Abdu'l-Bahá then met with many visitors, including a militant suffragist. A number of suffragettes came to see him during His two visits to England. One, the famous Emmeline Pankhurst, called 'Abdu'l-Bahá a 'prophet', whereupon He said, 'Oh no! I am a man, like you.'[20] Apparently Mrs Pankhurst was 'much cheered by her interview, for the Master told her to continue her work steadfastly, for women would very shortly take their rightful place in the world.'²¹ He advised the militant who visited him on 19 December that women who were campaigning for the right to vote should refrain from any acts of violence in their efforts, but should 'use the power of intelligence, with scientific accomplishments, with artistic attainments. Unseemly deeds would rather retard the realization of their cherished hope. In this age a weak person resorts to frightful measures, but an intelligent person used the superior power of intelligence and wisdom.'²²

The following day, 20 December, visitors again flocked to see 'Abdu'l-Bahá. With Mr Lorge, a well-known English educator, He discussed America. Ahmad Sohrab wrote that he had 'never seen 'Abdu'l-Bahá so enthusiastic about the wonderful possibilities of America. "Europe", He said, "is steeped in a sea of materialism. People are either agnostics or full of religious superstition."' Americans, said the Master, 'are more spiritual, they seek the knowledge of God . . . In brief, they are a nation of independent investigators.'²³

Later in the day, the Persian Ambassador, Mushíru'l-Mulk, came to visit the Master. 'Abdu'l-Bahá told him about 'winning everlasting victories which will bring unfading glory to the peoples of the East'. Dúst-Muḥammad Khán, the son-in-law of Náṣiri'd-Dín Sháh, the archenemy of Bahá'u'lláh, also came to speak with the Master. He was very attached to 'Abdu'l-Bahá and came as often as possible.²⁴

That evening, it was time for 'Abdu'l-Bahá's first public talk since his arrival in London. It took place at the Westminster Palace Hotel. According to Isabel Fraser's article in *The Christian Commonwealth*, it was 'a remarkable cosmopolitan gathering' composed of scientists, diplomats, and leaders of great movements of the day, including a number of Orientals. They had all come to listen to 'Abdu'l-Bahá talk about a topic that was 'agitating many of the thinking minds of to-day – the vast subject of Peace'. Sir Thomas Barclay introduced the Master by saying, 'If I have understood Bahaism, it has a singularly good Christian ring, and I should interpret it to mean: Be a real Christian and you will be a good Bahaist. But I am merely presiding, not proselytizing. I am proud to have been asked to preside at a meeting of those who have come together to do honour to one who deserves it so richly.'²⁵

'Abdu'l-Bahá then proceeded to talk about love, describing how matter was made up of 'constellations' of molecules, each composed of atoms held together by the law of affinity:

> As in the material so in the spiritual world, love is the attracting force that welds together the constituent elements into a composite unity and holds them firm against disintegration . . . Love is the cause of the illumination of whole of humanity; discord and dissension are the cause of the destruction of the human race . . .
>
> The foundation of all religion as taught by all the divine messengers has been love and affinity. A hundred thousand pities, alas, that the divine message has become the means of warfare and strife! In the Balkans blood has been freely and copiously shed, lives are being destroyed, houses are pillaged, cities are razed to the ground – and all this through religious prejudice . . .[26]

The Master had referred to the conflict in the Balkans frequently during his American talks, and also spoke of it to the newspaper reporters on his arrival in London. An international conference was being held just then in London to try to negotiate a peace settlement, and 'Abdu'l-Bahá took the opportunity of mentioning this:

> I am very pleased that I am living in London during these days. I supplicate that the conference may be crowned with success . . .
>
> As the English government is a just Government, and as the British nation is a noble nation and they accomplish what they undertake, it is my hope that in this matter they will show their utmost wisdom and sagacity, so that the sun of peace may dawn on the horizon of the Balkans . . . and whenever in the future there is any difficult problem a conference may be called for its settlement, for through these various conferences all the troubles of humanity may be solved.[27]

The Master's address was listened to 'in tense silence', and when 'Abdu'l-Bahá at the end of the meeting gave the blessing, 'a deep hush fell on the people'. After He had finished speaking, Mrs Despard, President of the Women's Freedom League, said a few words in appreciation; she was 'perfectly convinced' that everyone who had heard him felt 'deeply privileged to have had his presence here in our western isle'. Hippolyte Dreyfus and Alice Buckton also spoke.

Alice Buckton was a London Bahá'í who had spent much time in America during the Master's visit there. She was also a writer of poetry and plays. On 21 December 'Abdu'l-Bahá attended her play *Eager Heart*, which Lady Blomfield described as 'a very interesting Christmas mystery play'. Her daughter Mary played the part of Eager Heart before an audience of 1,200;[28] it was the first time the Master had attended a theatre. 'In one of the scenes in which, despite all her longings and all the preparations she had made to receive the Messiah, Eager Heart failed to recognize the Infant Jesus and would not admit the Holy Family to her home, fatigued and hungry though they were, 'Abdu'l-Bahá was seen to be weeping.'[29]

Afterwards, 'Abdu'l-Bahá met the actors in what Lady Blomfield described as 'an arresting scene. In the Eastern setting the Messenger, in His Eastern robes, speaking to them in the beautiful Eastern words of the Divine significance of the events which had been portrayed.'[30] *The Christian Commonwealth* quoted 'Abdu'l-Bahá as telling the actors:

> The people in the play thought they were waiting for Christ; they thought they were his intimate friends. Some there were who used to cry day and night, saying 'O Lord, hasten the day when he will manifest himself on earth.' When he came they knew him not; they persecuted him and finally killed him, for they said, 'This is not the true Messiah whose coming is to be under special conditions.'[31]

'Abdu'l-Bahá was a guest of Lady Blomfield for dinner on Christmas Eve. When He sat down to dinner on that night, 'He said, playfully, that He was not hungry, but He had to come to the dinner table because Lady Blomfield was very insistent; two despotic monarchs of the East had not been able to command Him and bend His will, but the ladies of America and Europe, because they were free, gave him orders.'[32]

Many people brought gifts for 'Abdu'l-Bahá on Christmas Day. One person brought an expensive gift which 'Abdu'l-Bahá accepted lovingly. He then handed the gift back, saying, 'And now, you see I have accepted your beautiful present, and it has made me very happy. I thank you for it. And now I am going to give it back to you. Sell it, and give the money to the poor. The rich in England are too rich, and the poor too poor.' As the man left, he seemed to have a new understanding of the world.

'Abdu'l-Bahá laughed at gifts that showed 'Yankee ingenuity'. When one American girl heard the Master say that on His travels He had learned to wash His handkerchiefs and to sew, she quickly dashed to a nearby shop, bought a small leather sewing kit and laughingly presented it to 'Abdu'l-Bahá saying she found it impossible to visualize a prophet sewing on His buttons. 'I will accept the sewing case with gratitude, and will keep it,' He said, but then added with a laugh the same words He had spoken to Emmeline Pankhurst, 'I am not a prophet. I am a man – like you.' All laughed at that since the girl was also known as a suffragette. 'He accepted it!' she exclaimed, as she left overjoyed.[33]

That night, 'Abdu'l-Bahá visited the Salvation Army Shelter in Westminster. The shelter provided food and shelter for the homeless of London and each year provided a Christmas dinner 'for those who have no homes and no friends, and but for the shelter would have no lodgings . . . many of the hungry men forgot to eat and listened intently'. That night there were 1,000 men present. 'Abdu'l-Bahá's message was particularly uplifting:

> I feel tonight great joy and happiness to be in this place, because my meetings and callings have ever been mostly with the poor, and I call myself one of them. My lot has ever been with those who have not the goods of this world. When we look at the poor of humanity, we behold a world of brothers. All are the sheep of God; God is the real shepherd. The poor have ever been the cause of the freedom of the world of humanity; the poor have ever been the cause of the upbuilding of the country; the poor have ever laboured for the world's production; the morals of the poor have ever been above those of the rich; the poor are ever nearer to the threshold of God; the humanitarianism of the poor has ever been more acceptable at the threshold of God.
>
> Consider His Holiness Christ: He appeared in the world as one of the poor. He was born of a lowly family; all the apostles of Christ were of humble birth and His followers were of the very poorest of the community . . .
>
> All the prophets of God were poor, His Holiness Moses was a mere shepherd . . . All the tyranny and injustice in this world comes from accumulation. The poor have ever been humble and lowly; their hearts are tender. The rich not so.
>
> Sorrow not, grieve not. Be not unhappy because you are not wealthy. You are the brothers of Jesus Christ. Christ was poor;

Baha'o'llah was poor. For forty years he was imprisoned in poverty. The great ones of the world have come from a lowly station. Be ever happy; be not sad! Trust in God and if in this world you undergo dire vicissitudes I hope that in the Kingdom of God you will have the utmost happiness.[34]

As He left, 'Abdu'l-Bahá left twenty golden sovereigns and many handfuls of silver with Colonel Spencer for a similar dinner on New Year's Eve. When the Colonel announced this, the men leaped to their feet 'and waving their knives and forks gave a rousing farewell cheer'.

During the week after Christmas, 'Abdu'l-Bahá gave a number of talks in His drawing room, speaking on the birth and advent of Christ and of the significance of baptism. He also walked in Hyde Park and Kensington Gardens. On 29 December, the Maharajah of Jhalawar, who was very devoted to the Master, visited. In the afternoon, 'Abdu'l-Bahá spoke at the home of Miss Annie Gamble.[35] In the evening, He spoke at the King's Weigh House Methodist Church. The Reverend E. W. Lewis introduced the Master and explained that the Bahá'í Faith was not 'a new sect, and that it had not committed itself to any form of organisation; it was essentially a spiritual movement, very much on the lines of what Jesus wanted his movement to be.' When 'Abdu'l-Bahá entered, the whole congregation stood until He was at the chancel where He began to speak

> animatedly and impressively, the interpreter translating as the address proceeded. The Master appeared to be quite at home, pacing backwards and forwards in the intervals between sentences. 'I praise God,' he began, 'that a number of reverent souls are gathered in this congregation to serve the Almighty. Their hearts are cemented together. Their faces are joyous with the glad tidings of the Kingdom of God.'[36]

## Oxford

On 31 December, 'Abdu'l-Bahá went to Oxford to gave a talk at Manchester College, where clergymen were trained. He first visited Dr T. K. Cheyne, who had organized the talk but who was in poor health; the Master went to his home in North Oxford. The following year Cheyne would publish his book on the Faith, *The Reconciliation of Races and Religions*. The meeting was, as described by Lady Blomfield,

> fraught with pathos. It seemed almost too intimate to describe, and our very hearts were touched, as we looked on, and realized something of the sacred emotions of that day.
>
> 'Abdu'l-Bahá embraced the Doctor with loving grace, and praised his courageous steadfastness in his life's work, always striving against increasing weakness, and lessening bodily health. Through those veiling clouds the light of the mind and spirit shone with a radiant persistence. The beautiful loving care of the devoted wife for her gifted, invalid husband touched the heart of 'Abdu'l-Bahá. With tears in His kind eyes He spoke of them to Mrs Thornburgh-Cropper and myself on our way back to London:
>
> 'She is an angelic woman, an example to all in her unselfish love. Yes, she is a perfect woman. An angel.'
>
> This lady was Elizabeth Gibson Cheyne, the very specially gifted poetess.[37]

The two men talked and Cheyne showed the Master what he had written about the Faith. 'His attitude of belief and attentiveness so moved the Master that He, several times, kissed him on the head and face, and kept caressing His head.' 'Abdu'l-Bahá called Dr Cheyne His 'spiritual philosopher'.[38]

At Manchester College the Principal, Dr J. Estlin Carpenter, introduced 'Abdu'l-Bahá to the student clergymen with an eloquent tribute to His life and work. The Master then gave a talk on the place of science in our lives and about the supernatural. Interestingly, there were no questions afterwards.[39]

## LONDON

The 1 January 1913 issue of *The Christian Commonwealth* contained several pages about 'Abdu'l-Bahá, including the whole talk He had given to the Jewish congregation at Temple Emmanu-El in San Francisco in October 1912. Like many other publications, the writer began with a pen-portrait:

Even the Western stranger coming into the Master's presence for the first time acknowledges an emotion akin to awe, and after a few minutes speech with him, feels the stirring of a deeper spirit of devotion than the ordinary amenities of social intercourse are calculated to arouse. For 'Abdul Baha, whose mission of peace and universal brotherhood is like the coming of the four winds into the valley of dry bones, in Ezekiel's vision is much more than a picturesque Eastern figure in the romantic setting of Western civilisation. He is a prophet. A venerable figure, of rather less than medium stature, clothed in long, flowing Persian garments, his white beard lying upon his breast, silver-grey plaited hair falling over his shoulders, dark, brooding, pitiful eyes that yet light up when a smile or singular gentleness and sweetness passes across his face, and a low mellow voice whose tones are charged with a strange solemnity – that is the Master as the stranger sees him. But to the Bahais he is the 'Servant of God', the symbol of the unity of religions and races which it is his mission to promote. Although nearly seventy years of age, he has undertaken this tour of the Western world to proclaim his message of universal peace, and to recall the nations from their armed madness to the forgotten simplicities of the spirit. For nine months he travelled in America, crossing the continent from coast to coast, from east to west, addressing large audiences in churches, synagogues, temples, halls, drawing-rooms, hotels, and in some of the universities. Wherever he spoke, it was at the invitation of the heads of the institution or movement which organised the meetings. He was a guest at the National Conference of Peace Societies held recently. The subject of his discourses everywhere was the same – an exposition of the teachings of Baha'o'llah, the source of the present-day Bahai faith . . .

'Abdul Baha rose to receive me with a gentle courtesy and a murmured Persian sentence, which his interpreter, Mirza Ahmad Sohrab, explained meant that the Master was pleased to welcome a representative of *The Christian Commonwealth*, which had done much to promote the progress of his mission. The stir and movement beyond the threshold of the room where 'Abdul Baha held his audience seemed to die away, and the familiar roar of London's traffic through which I had passed a little earlier receded into immense distance as we talked . . .

In America, he said, many societies are organised, whose purpose is the furtherance of universal peace. He has spoken before many of these organisations 'and they have harkened to my addresses with the greatest interest. And now I have returned to Europe. I observe that, praise be to God, in this capital a conference of peace is sitting . . . Therefore I hope that the rays of universal peace may radiate from this great metropolis to all parts of the world, and that the noble nation of England and its just Government, like the people of America, will strive their utmost in promoting the principles of international peace and brotherhood...'

In answer to a question regarding the Master's impressions of America, he said that material civilisation had advanced greatly, and he hoped that divine civilisation would be likewise established. The American universities were carrying on a most profitable and encouraging work, and he spoke of Dr Jordan, the head of the Stanford University, in Oakland, whose guest they had been, as 'as a very wise and erudite man, whose mind is full of thoughts of peace'.[40]

On 2 January 'Abdu'l-Bahá went to the Cedar Club House, a place run by the Women's Service League that provided food for the poorest working mothers and ensured that their youngest children were well fed.

'Through an insistent rain and blustering wind, the motor bore us across the Albert Bridge to the borough of Battersea. We turned from one of the important highways into a dark, narrow, drizzling street, to stop before an inviting open door.'[41] The Master arrived to find sixty women and over one hundred children gathered at two large tables festively decorated with Christmas cheer. Though given a formal, elevated platform from which to speak, 'Abdu'l-Bahá rather, 'as the real friend of the poor . . . walked straight among them, into the body of the room. This at once established the charm of comradeship.' As He walked 'with light characteristic step' between the tables beaming with happiness and love, He told them:

> I am very glad to be among you, who are blessed in God's name with children. They are the true signs of his spiritual love. The most divine gifts of God. These little ones will grow to be fruitful trees. We must look to them for the founders of many beautiful families.

Let their education be directed in the ways of purity and useful service. Here are the seeds of the future race and upon them may be granted God's blessing.[42]

'Abdu'l-Bahá then walked among the women and children giving encouraging words, 'pausing for a few moments to bless each little upturned face, and bestow a silver coin. The remarkable tender hands caressed a baby's cheek or chin. One could hear him pronounce distinct words of comfort to the tiniest members of the audience.' One mother held sleeping twins. The Master placed a coin under the chin of each, whereupon 'two pairs of deep blue eyes opened wide in the spell of wonder'.

Those who were accompanying 'Abdu'l-Bahá commented on 'the thoughtful gaze of the women as they watched the distinguished visitor in white turban and brown burnous, moving in their midst. It is often too true that the very poor are keenly suspicious of foreigners, especially if their mission is a religious one, but Abdul-Baha brings into every environment a profound truth and sympathy that seems to crush the barriers . . .'

As He left, 'Abdu'l-Bahá said,

> I am truly happy when among the gatherings of the poor. It brings full joy to my heart. I come in contact with those in high stations of life, and those rich in worldly possessions, but my joy is in being with those who are in material poverty, for their sufferings draw them nearer to God . . .[43]

In the January 1913 issue of *The International Psychic Gazette*, Felicia R. Scatcherd wrote of the great attraction she had to 'Abdu'l-Bahá, but also her fear of coming too close. Her first contact with the Master was in London in 1911:

> When Abdul Baha first came to England, I refused all invitations to visit him. I had met those who made pilgrimages to his prison-home in Akka, and they talked so much about 'The Blessed Perfection' and 'The Manifested Splendour' that, though interested in what seemed a useful enough form of hero-worship for those to whom it appealed, I had no desire to see Abbas Effendi for myself . . .

... a dear friend compelled me to accompany her to a reception of Abdul Baha, then, as now, the guest of Lady Blomfield ... The submissive sweetness with which the venerable man received the homage of his followers affected me strongly. I wondered whether, like the gifted Heinrich Heine, he ever shrank from the burden of an enforced role of divinity. And an impulse seized me to see him in converse with an intellectual and spiritual peer. But when I cast about to find such a one, I realised the true greatness of the man in whose presence I found myself. I did not go forward with the rest to greet him on this first occasion. I stood at the door busy with my thoughts. And as if he knew these thoughts, as he passed out, he gave me a playful slap on the arm, as one would administer reproof to a wilful child, and his eyes danced with merriment.

Again and again I have noticed evidence of his awareness of the mental states of those around him. And I am assured that this keen intuition has been observed in his correspondence. Those whom he has never seen have been amazed to receive, from the Prophet in Akka, correct perceptions of conditions pertaining to them in America.[44]

On 21 January 1912, Felicia had visited 'Abdu'l-Bahá in Ramleh, Egypt in the company of Dr and Mrs Platon Drakoulès. Dr Drakoulès was a Greek political scientist living in Oxford, and according to Lady Blomfield 'had invited the first Bahá'í gathering in England to meet at his chambers in Oxford'.[45] In her notebook, Felicia wrote:

We found him in a villa, opposite the new Victoria Hotel, Ramleh. Although only 10 a.m., he had been astir for hours, attending to his enormous correspondence, and receiving visitors. Again, in his presence, the old sense of goodness and simplicity overwhelmed one. The venerable figure in its Persian costume, was just as unique in its Eastern setting, as in London.

Of middle-stature, and broadly-built, he yet strikes one at times, as if he were tall, and is undoubtedly imposing. Oval-faced, and large-featured, with heavy eyebrows, a nose resembling that of General Booth, he has the compelling personality of all born leaders of men. His grey eyes are unusually expressive. In moments of excitement they become dark and deep in the piercing intensity of their gaze. I have seen them slash as if generating a kind of lightning, and then they soften and brighten and change expression with all the varying moods of his active mentality. But whether under the influence of sorrow or joy, indignation or pity, they are always surcharged with sympathy. One who knows no word of Persian can share the emotions of his soul by watching the lights and shadows in his eyes. When, as often, he closed them, then one need only follow the movements of his no less wonderful hands.[46]

Felicia saw 'Abdu'l-Bahá once more, on 2 January 1913, this time with Mr Lewis and Mr Child, a well-known palmist from whom she wished to hear his impressions of 'Abdu'l-Bahá's hands. Mr Lewis asked about reincarnation and the immaculate conception. In answering Mr Lewis's question about the latter, the Master concluded by saying that those who accepted the creation of the first man without any human parent should have no difficulty accepting the birth of a person with only one human parent![47] Felicia was so impressed with 'Abdu'l-Bahá that she travelled in Turkey trying to teach the Faith, and in 1914 wrote a book, *A Wise Man from the East*, about her efforts.

One day, two ladies from Scotland, who had requested an evening with 'Abdu'l-Bahá, arrived and were welcomed warmly by the Master. But as Lady Blomfield remembered:

> Not more than a half an hour passed, when, to our consternation, a persistent person pushed past the servitors, and strode into our midst. Seating himself, and lighting a cigarette without invitation, he proceeded to say that he intended writing an article for some newspaper about 'Abdu'l-Bahá, superciliously asking for 'some telling points, don't you know'. He talked without a pause in a far from polite manner.
>
> We were speechless and aghast at the intrusion of this insufferable and altogether unpleasant bore, spoiling our golden hour!
>
> Presently 'Abdu'l-Bahá rose and, making a sign to the man to follow Him, went to His own room.
>
> We looked at one another. The bore had gone, yes, but alas! so also had the Master!
>
> 'Can nothing be done?' Being the hostess, I was perturbed and perplexed. Then I went to the door of the audience room and

said to the secretary: 'Will you kindly say to 'Abdu'l-Bahá that the ladies with whom the appointment has been made are awaiting His pleasure.'

I returned to the guests and we awaited the result.

Almost immediately we heard steps approaching along the corridor. They came down the hall to the door. The sound of kind farewell words reached us. Then the closing of the door and the Beloved came back.

'Oh, Master!' we said.

Pausing near the door, He looked at us each in turn, with a look of deep, grave meaning.

'You were making that poor man uncomfortable, so strongly desiring his absence; I took him away to make him feel happy.'

Truly 'Abdu'l-Bahá's thoughts and ways were far removed from ours! [48]

On 5 January 'Abdu'l-Bahá had dinner with the Maharajah of Jhalawar. The Maharajah spoke fluent English and they discussed the elevation of the women in India, aviation, dispelling prejudices in India, and the Aryan race. The Maharajah stayed till 10.30 p.m. Later, on 18 January, he hosted the Master, Lady Blomfield and her daughters for dinner.[49] The Maharajah was also at the railway station when 'Abdu'l-Bahá departed for Paris.[50]

## EDINBURGH, SCOTLAND

'Abdu'l-Bahá planned to visit Edinburgh, and on 1 January the Bahá'ís of Edinburgh sent a schedule they had devised for Him. Ahmad Sohrab wrote in his diary, 'The plan of Edinburgh is presented to the Master. He says I have not been there yet, and they have already planned what I must do in every hour. Then He jokes with them about these . . . customs, and date-fixing of this so far ahead . . .' [51]

At 8 a.m. on 6 January, Ahmad Sohrab, Mírzá Maḥmúd, Ḥájí Amín and Siyyid Asadu'lláh-i-Qumí left for the station, followed by the Master. Lotfullah Hakím (who later was elected to the first Universal House of Justice) joined the party at the station. The train left at 10 o'clock and at about 5 p.m. pulled into the Waverley Station in Edinburgh. The group was met by Jane Whyte, Isabel Fraser (who had come up from London to help) and several other friends. 'Abdu'l-Bahá stayed at the home of Mrs Whyte and her distinguished husband, Dr Alexander Whyte, Moderator of the General Assembly Free Church of Scotland and principal of the Divinity Faculty of Edinburgh University, who were instrumental in 'Abdu'l-Bahá's visiting Edinburgh.

## Jane Whyte

Jane Elizabeth Whyte, formerly Jane Barbour, may have been the first Scottish Bahá'í. She was married to Reverend Alexander Whyte, Moderator of the General Assembly of the Free Church of Scotland, professor of New Testament literature and principal at New College, Edinburgh. Jane was a good friend of Mrs Thornburgh-Cropper and in March 1906 they had visited 'Abdu'l-Bahá for two brief days in 'Akká. On her return, she wrote:

> The pilgrim to 'Akká is asked many questions on his return. Is this a prophet? A manifestation of divinity . . . Is it enough of Divinity to see love made perfect through suffering a life-long patience, a faith which no exile or imprisonment can dim, a love which no treachery can alter, a hope which rises a pure clear flame after being drenched with the world's indifference through a lifetime? If that is not Divinity enough for this world, what is? . . . What greater sign can you ask than the power to flood this old world with love and aspiration, with patience and courage? . . . His life, as the prisoner of the Sultán, was in continual danger by any sudden pressure from Constantinople and at that time it was not considered wise that visitors from the west should be too much in evidence. So it came that we could not have the farewell conversation we had promised ourselves. Instead I left a letter for him. In due time an answer came . . .[52]

In 'Abdu'l-Bahá's reply to her letter, He called Jane a 'captive of the love of God' and an 'honoured lady'. She had written, 'I am a Christian.' The Master responded with, 'O would that all were truly Christian! It is easy to be a Christian on the tongue, but hard to be a true one.' 'Abdu'l-Bahá wrote that 'the unity of truth, through the power of God, will make these illusory differences to vanish away'. At the end of this Tablet, 'Abdu'l-Bahá listed the seven candles of unity: unity in the political realm, unity of thought in world undertakings, unity in freedom, unity in religion, unity of the nations, unity of the races, and unity of language. These would all, He stated, 'inevitably come to pass'.[53]

Upon her return from 'Akká, Jane Whyte spread the Bahá'í teachings to her family and friends. She was able to see 'Abdu'l-Bahá in London in 1911, and wrote to Him the following year saying, 'If the time should come for him to visit Edinburgh, the Outlook Tower Society will welcome him warmly.'[54] He accepted her invitation.

\* \* \*

'Abdu'l-Bahá would have preferred to stay at a hotel, but Mrs Whyte was insistent that He stay in her home at 7 Charlotte Square, so 'Abdu'l-Bahá and His interpreter Ahmad Sohrab stayed in the Whytes' home while the others in His party were accommodated in a nearby hotel. One Edinburgh resident remembered the three who stayed in the hotel:

> His company consisted of three people, and they were entertained in a hotel within a stone's throw of the house where he was . . . the most personal attendant was called, in translation, the 'Lion of God' [Asadu'lláh], an old man, picturesque in appearance and of a most attractive spirit, whose after-dinner stories were a great delight. There was a young man, an interpreter, who was not of the inner company, I think, and who had a more or less permanent home in London [Lotfullah Hakim]. Then there was a very handsome, cultured man, who was a poet of some distinction, according to the interpreter, and whose talk, even in translation, was deeply interesting, spiritually discerning and beautifully expressed [Mírzá Mahmúd].[55]

At 8.30 on the morning after their arrival, Ahmad Sohrab heard a bell:

> When I went down to the Library I saw principal Whyte with the members of the family standing on one side and all the maids which were seven I think, standing on the other side, each having a hymn book in the hand. Mrs Whyte gave me one of these books and she went to the organ. All of us [sang] the songs and afterward Rev. Whyte prayed while all of them knelt down. It was a very new

experience to me. Of course this is their daily custom for the Master and the servants to pray to God every morning before starting their daily labors. This is a very lovely custom and affords one a few moments whereby to commune with his Creator. After the prayer we had breakfast and I carried up Our Beloved's tea to his room.[56]

Some of the Edinburgh Bahá'ís were worried about how 'Abdu'l-Bahá would handle the cold of a Scottish winter. Surprisingly to the locals, when the Master arrived in Edinburgh, the city experienced four days of sunny weather with mild temperatures. Even so, 'Abdu'l-Bahá was not well-dressed for the climate and did suffer from the cold. He did not mention it to anyone, but one of His attendants informed Mrs Whyte and she took Him out and 'a forenoon was spent in providing for His greater comfort – to the interest and admiration of several shopkeepers unaccustomed to oriental dress and speech'.[57]

The Whytes had managed to publicize 'Abdu'l-Bahá's coming with an article in a local newspaper on 13 December, and articles in two different papers on 3 January, so when 'Abdu'l-Bahá arrived, the reporters were there to ensure that His visit was well reported.

After dinner with the Whytes, 'Abdu'l-Bahá met with the Secretary of the Esperanto Society, the general Secretary of the Theosophical Society, several professors and many clergymen with their wives. 'Abdu'l-Bahá then spoke about his trip from Alexandria to New York and how some had insisted that he sail on the *Titanic* instead of the older and smaller *Cedric*. He talked about his address to the Jews at Temple El-Emmanuel in San Francisco, which 'created a tremendous effect, because most of these people are very devoted Christians', wrote Ahmad Sohrab, adding that 'An old scotch song was sung after the Master's address which was very sweet and effective. The Master bade them good bye and went to his room.'[58]

Florence Altass met the Master in Edinburgh and recalled:

Of course when I saw Him I knew who He was. Oh, you couldn't mistake Him. And that heavenly smile! It was a perpetual smile, and yet it wasn't, if you can imagine; it looked as though He smiled at everyone, and yet the smile seemed always to be there. And His eyes looked as if they were looking through you. He had the most gentle voice; I've never heard a voice like it . . . He embraced a good many people; He didn't me, He just shook hands. Several of us He just shook hands with. When 'Abdu'l-Bahá shook hands with me, He seemed to transmit something to me, and I've never been the same since.

There was an interpreter – who spoilt the whole show! It wasn't that His voice didn't suit me, it was that although 'Abdu'l-Bahá spoke in Persian, you *understood*; you knew what He was saying, somehow. One was so enamoured of His voice that one sort of *felt* what He was saying.[59]

On the morning of 7 January 'Abdu'l-Bahá visited the Outlook Tower, which had a panoramic view of Edinburgh. He was met by the Outlook Tower Society President Sir Patrick Geddes, who escorted 'Abdu'l-Bahá up the five flights of stairs to the top of the tower. After they had admired the view of the city, Geddes showed 'Abdu'l-Bahá the 'Camera Oscura' which projected an image of the city down onto a large table top. Geddes, along with his nephew, Sir Frank Meres, later developed a design in the 1920s for a Bahá'í temple they hoped, futilely as it worked out, would be built in Allahabad, India.[60]

After viewing the various displays and galleries in the Outlook Tower, the Master had a drive down Edinburgh's famous Royal Mile, past Holyrood Palace and on to Arthur's Seat. He then met some of the foreign students at Edinburgh University, who had come from Japan, India and Egypt. 'Dear and honoured Sir,' said Dr Whyte as he introduced the Master, 'I have had many meetings in this house, but never have I seen such a meeting. It reminds me of what St Paul said, "God hath made of one blood all nations of men . . .".' 'Abdu'l-Bahá then spoke to the students on the oneness of religion.

That evening, the Freemasons' Hall, newly rebuilt and 'one of the largest and most beautiful public buildings in the city', was the site of the Master's first public address in Scotland, hosted by the Edinburgh Esperanto Society. 'That evening it was packed, leaving standing room only. A crown of three hundred, failing to gain admission, remained outside.'[61] 'Abdu'l-Bahá spoke about the need for an international language; his talk was later published in *Star of the West* with the Esperanto translation. As usual, the Master made his audience laugh, sweetening a serious subject with a touch of his ineffable humour:

> There were two friends who did not know each other's language. One of them got sick; the other one called upon him, but he could not express his sympathy, so by making a sign he asked him, 'How are you?' By making another sign, the sick man answered, 'I am almost dying,' and the friend . . . thinking that he had told him that he was feeling much better, said, 'Thanks be to God.' By such incidents you realize that the best thing in this world is to be able to make yourself understood by your friends, and also to understand them . . .[62]

But after the meeting, 'Abdu'l-Bahá was exhausted. George S. Stewart commented, 'he was a very weary man. I saw him at Dr Whyte's just after the meeting. He was lying back in an arm-chair, while his personal attendant massaged his legs. He was an exhausted man.'[63]

'Abdu'l-Bahá's schedule was brutal for His much-abused physical body. In Edinburgh Lady Blomfield saw the spiritual power that could overcome physical exhaustion. Before He addressed another gathering two days later, the Master looked very tired. 'He remained seated in silence for a few moments after Mr Graham Pole had reverently introduced Him. Then, seeming to gather strength, He arose, and with voice and manner of joyous animation, and eyes aglow, He paced the platform with a vigorous tread, and spoke with words of great power.'[64]

Lady Blomfield also witnessed a similar remarkable recovery in London one day, when the Master arrived home very tired after a long day.

> We were sad at heart that he should be so fatigued, and bewailed the many steps to be ascended to the flat. Suddenly, to our amazement, the Master ran up the stairs to the top very quickly without stopping.
> 
> He looked down at us as we walked up after Him, saying with a bright smile, from which all traces of fatigue had vanished: 'You are all very old! I am very young!'
> 
> Seeing me full of wonder, 'Abdu'l-Bahá said:
> 
> 'Through the power of Bahá'u'lláh all things can be done. I have just used that power.'
> 
> That was the only time we had ever seen him use that power *for Himself*, and I feel that he did so then to cheer and comfort us, as we were really sad concerning his fatigue.[65]

## 'ABDU'L-BAHÁ IN THEIR MIDST

On 8 January, 'Abdu'l-Bahá continued to receive visitors. One medical student, a 'Mohamadan Hindu', asked Him to perform a marriage between him and a 'Scotch lassie'. Unfortunately, it was discovered that it would take ten days to get a licence from the city Registrar, making it impossible for 'Abdu'l-Bahá to do so since He was to leave in just three days.[66]

The newspapers had reported the meeting of the previous evening, and were looking forward to the next one, to be held that afternoon at the Rainy Hall, part of New College, the Divinity Faculty of Edinburgh University. One of 'Abdu'l-Bahá's common themes was the futility of war. The *Edinburgh Evening Dispatch* wrote: 'He is endeavouring to do what Foreign Secretaries, and Peace Conferences, and Ambassadorial Conversations have been striving to do with cannon on their backs . . . it would be well to listen attentively to what this Persian has to say. His coming is at least opportune, when Europe is full of armed men with murder in their eyes.'[67]

During His talk at Rainy Hall on 8 January, the Master said, just nineteen months before the outbreak of the world war:

> What is this native land, this fatherland that we glory over so much? We live but a few years on the surface of the earth; afterwards it becomes our eternal cemetery, as is has been the cemetery of all men and women that have lived since Adam. In the circumstances, is patriotic prejudice worth all the division it has caused? [68]

After 'Abdu'l-Bahá's presentation, Reverend A. B. Robb thanked Him, saying:

> We have been in the habit of sending missionaries from the West to the East to preach the Gospel. Today we have a missionary from the East to preach the old Gospel in a new and original way. After all, it is not the words which have impressed us so much as the life. He has a right to speak, for He has spent forty years of His life in prison for the sake of the truth which was revealed to Him.[69]

Miss E. C. H. Pagan remembered 'Abdu'l-Bahá saying that 'the Federation of Europe would actually come about in the present century . . . Little did we then think from what terrible suffering this Federation would begin to emerge.'⁷⁰ This prediction came 39 years before the first step was taken in the formation of the European Common Market in 1951, later to develop into the European Union.

Later, 'Abdu'l-Bahá went to St Giles Cathedral for a charity performance of Handel's *Messiah*. When the group entered the Cathedral, 'Abdu'l-Bahá took His seat in the front row of the gallery looking down on the rest of the audience. Ahmad Sohrab wrote:

> All the eyes involuntarily turned to Him with wonder and respect. Then the chorus with delightfully trained voices raised the exultant tone 'And the Glory of the Lord shall be revealed, and all flesh shall see it together; for the mouth of the Lord hath spoken it.' Was not this a wonderful prophecy which had they wisdom and perception they could see the Glory of the Lord revealed before their own eyes!⁷¹

Next day, 9 January, 'a stream of visitors and enquirers made their way to the manse in Charlotte Square'. 'Abdu'l-Bahá spent the entire morning answering their questions, and in the afternoon spoke to a large meeting on women's rights, attended both by suffragettes and those who opposed votes for women. Speaking on the principle of the equality of men and women, the Master 'stressed the necessity of education for women, but also the importance of motherhood. He encouraged women to train themselves by studying every kind of science, art and social service. "Fit yourselves for responsibility, you will inevitably have it thrust upon you,"' He said.⁷² Although He was very tired, 'Abdu'l-Bahá then went to the headquarters of the Theosophical Society to give an address.

After the meeting, 'Abdu'l-Bahá met privately with individuals and groups. One group He met with was the Pagan family. Miss J. M. Pagan, a sister of E. C. H. Pagan, remembered 'Abdu'l-Bahá's happy, friendly manner. When she, her mother, her six sisters and several grandchildren met with the Master, He laughed heartily at the long procession. When the group had literally encircled 'Abdu'l-Bahá, He told Miss Pagan's mother that He hoped she would have as many descendants as Father Abraham.⁷³

'Abdu'l-Bahá left Edinburgh the following day. As they were about to leave, the Master asked to see the maids. When they were all gathered, He said, 'For the last few days you have served me. I am very pleased with you. I will never forget you. I will pray for you that you may become confirmed and assisted and that your heads be crowned with the diadems of eternal glory.'[74] He gave each a guinea and they were so overwhelmed that they had tears in their eyes.

Two cars then took the party to the station, where they met Mr Page, the Secretary of the Esperanto Society, the general secretary of the Theosophical Society, a Persian student and two ministers plus several ladies and gentlemen. The train left shortly before 11 o'clock and Ahmad Sohrab remembered see the waving hands and handkerchiefs of those still on the platform.

As the train headed south, 'Abdu'l-Bahá told the story of a competition between Chinese and Roman artists:

> The king appointed a large hall where both of them could paint. The Chinese asked for a curtain to be hung in the middle of the Hall – so that their competitor may not see what they are doing. The Chinese artists worked for 6 months day and night but the Roman artists did not work and everybody thought they are going to lose. Just one day before the King's coming to give the award, the Roman artists set to work and polished the wall like a mirror. The King's ministers and courtiers came. First they saw the Chinese paintings. They were marvellous and beautiful. The curtain then was put aside so they could see also the Roman works. The wall polished by the Roman Artists was so transparent that the Chinese paintings on the opposite wall were entirely reflected therein.
>
> The award went to the Romans. Now, may your heart be as pure and as transparent so that the pictures and images of the Kingdom of Abhá may be reflected therein.[75]

'Abdu'l-Bahá and His party arrived back in London at 7 p.m. where Marion Jack and several other friends were there to meet them. From the station, they took a taxi to Lady Blomfield's house at 97 Cadogan Gardens where others were waiting for them. After only a few minutes, 'Abdu'l-Bahá said they should move to a hotel and have the meetings there. Lady Blomfield, her daughters and Miss Platt pleaded, the latter on her knees, until 'Abdu'l-Bahá consented to stay.

While still on the train, 'Abdu'l-Bahá had said that it was important that Bahá'í teachers should go to Edinburgh as soon as possible to capitalize on the interest following the Master's visit. Alice Buckton was suggested since she was familiar with speaking to Church people. When Miss Buckton and Annet Schepel arrived the next day, 'Abdu'l-Bahá told her, 'Thou must go to Scotland. The people are immensely interested. Edinburgh has great capability. There are many people who are interested. You must go there and teach in churches, in societies, everywhere. We have scattered good seeds in that soil; now souls who can water this cultivation must go there.'[76]

## LONDON

'Abdu'l-Bahá spoke at Caxton Hall, Westminster, on 11 January. Two distinguished Persians who were present were greatly impressed 'at the powers which 'Abdu'l-Bahá had at His command, and at the appreciation and devotion displayed by the Westerners all around them'.[77] After the talk, 'Abdu'l-Bahá walked back to His apartment, but had no respite as it quickly filled up with people. The Master told them the story of how Bahá'u'lláh had been imprisoned and all His worldly goods pillaged. He told how His Father had been threatened with death but saved, stories described by those who heard Him as 'the most thrilling incidents'.[78]

The next day, 'Abdu'l-Bahá attended a dinner party at the home of Sir Richard and Lady Stapley, after which the Master gave a talk. Following the talk, many people asked questions, including 'whether unruly children should receive corporal punishment. His answer was very clear: not even the animal should be beaten.'[79]

Fog enveloped London on the 13th and 'Abdu'l-Bahá took advantage of the gloomy weather to speak about 'the darkness of superstitions and imitations which cloud the Sun of Truth'. On the 14th, the Master spoke in the East End of London at a Congregational Church, leaving the congregation 'spell-bound by the power which spread like an atmosphere from another, higher world'.[80]

At some point during His stay in London, a man came to the door asking for the lady of the house. When Lady Blomfield asked if he wanted to see her, he responded, saying 'I have walked thirty miles for that purpose.' Lady Blomfield invited the man, who she described as 'an ordinary tramp', and gave him some refreshment. Then the man began his story:

'I was not always as you see me now, a disreputable, hopeless object. My father is a country rector, and I had the advantage of being at public school. Of the various causes which led me to my arrival at the Thames embankment as my only home, I need not speak to you.

'Last evening I had decided to put an end to my futile, hateful life, useless to God and man!

'Whilst taking what I had intended should be my last walk, I saw "a Face" in the window of a newspaper shop. I stood looking at the face as if rooted to the spot. He seemed to speak to me and call me to him!'

'Let me see that paper, please,' I asked. It was the face of 'Abdu'l-Bahá.

'I read that he is here, in this house. I said to myself, "If there is in existence on earth that personage, I shall take up again the burden of my life."

'I set off on my quest. I have come here to find him. Tell me, is he here? Will he see me? Even me?'

Lady Blomfield assured the man: 'Of course he will see you. Come to Him,' then went and knocked on the Master's door. 'Abdu'l-Bahá opened the door Himself and went directly to the poor man as though He had been expecting him.

'Welcome! Most welcome! I am very much pleased that thou has come. Be seated.'

The pathetic man trembled and sank on to a low chair by the Master's feet, as though unable to utter a word.

The other guests, meanwhile, looked on wonderingly to see the attention transferred to the strange-looking new arrival, who seemed to be so overburdened with hopeless misery.

'Be happy! Be happy!' said 'Abdu'l-Bahá, holding one of the poor hands, stroking tenderly the dishevelled, bowed head.

Smiling that wonderful smile of loving compassion, the Master continued:

'Do not be filled with grief when humiliation overtaketh thee.'

'The bounty and power of God is without limit for each and every soul in the world.'

'Seek for spiritual joy and knowledge, then, though thou walk upon this earth, thou wilt be dwelling within the divine realm.'

'Though thou be poor, thou mayest be rich in the Kingdom of God.'

As 'Abdu'l-Bahá continued to pour out His love and compassion, the man slowly brightened and, when he finally arose to leave, he had 'a new look . . . on his face, a new erectness in his carriage, a firm purpose in his steps'. As he left, he told Lady Blomfield that he had found everything he had hoped for and now planned to go work in the fields until he had enough to start a small business. With that, he departed, saying finally, 'As He says "Poverty is unimportant, *work is worship*."'[81]

## Bristol

'Abdu'l-Bahá returned to the Clifton Guest House in Bristol on 15 January, this time accompanied by the Persian Ambassador, Dúst-Muḥammad Khán. At a meeting that evening with many outstanding people in attendance, Mírzá Maḥmúd was struck by the sight of the Ambassador, whose tears flowed down his face as he watched people of all walks of life bowing and curtseying. 'That moved me so much that I was greatly affected, and wept and rejoiced too', wrote Maḥmúd:

> In Britain, at large gatherings, I had noticed time and again the same reaction from men of his standing . . . who kept saying: 'What great glory God conferred upon us . . . what a Sun of grandeur and felicity rose from the horizon of the East, but alas, alas, we did not heed it . . .'[82]

In the evening, 'Abdu'l-Bahá met a group at the Guest House. Interspersed in the crowd, 'Here and there was seen a scarlet fez which denoted the presence of eastern students, some of whom He had met there in 1911.' 'Abdu'l-Bahá greeted them by raising His palms to His forehead, then told them that He had 'come to Clifton this time via Los Angeles and Chicago'. Although the Master began His talk seated, He was soon on His feet 'occasionally walking to and fro, and sometimes emphasizing a fact with upraised hand or standing still with eyes closed and his silver voice low'.[83]

In the *Clifton Chronicle and Directory* of 22 January it was reported that 'Abdu'l-Bahá told Wellesley Tudor-Pole that of all the places He had visited in Europe and America, He found the climate to be the most pleasant in Denver and Clifton. He also complimented the people of Clifton and encouraged them to 'become the means of creating good fellowship between the children of men. May they relinquish those blind dogmas which have created strife in the world of humanity. May they become instrumental in putting into practice the Heavenly teaching.'[84]

## LONDON

Back in London the next day, Lady Blomfield showed 'Abdu'l-Bahá a statement she had written about the Bahá'í Faith and 'Abdu'l-Bahá in London that she hoped, because of her high-level connections, to show to King George V. The Master, after praising the effort, advised her not to carry out her plan because it might be misunderstood by some. Besides, He had come to visit the poor and had little interest in visiting the rich and powerful.

Later He gave a talk to the Bahá'ís gathered at 97 Cadogan Gardens. It was a unique talk that focused on two points: (1) the great diversity of people entering the Faith and the difficulty of administering such a diverse group, and consequently (2) what should happen at Bahá'í meetings. It is here that the Master states that we must abandon the important for the most important.

> The Cause has become very great. Many souls are entering it – souls with different mentalities and degrees of understanding. Complex difficulties constantly rise before us. The administration of the Cause has become most difficult. Conflicting thought and theories attack the Cause from every side. Now consider to what extent the believers of God must become firm and soul-sacrificing. Every one of the friends must become the essence of essences; each one must become a brilliant lamp. People all around the world are entering the Cause; people of various tribes and nations and religions and sects. It is most difficult to administer to such heterogeneous elements. Wisdom and Divine insight are necessary. Firmness and steadfastness are needed at such a crucial period of the Cause. All the meetings must be for

teaching the Cause and spreading the Message, and suffering the souls to enter into the Kingdom of Baha'o'llah. Look at me. All my thoughts are centered around the proclamation of the Kingdom. I have a Lamp in my hand searching throughout the lands and seas to find souls who can become heralds of the Cause. Day and night I am engaged in this work. Any other deliberations in the meetings are futile and fruitless. Convey the Message! Attract the hearts! Sow the seeds! Teach the Cause to those who do not know.

. . . I enter all meetings, all churches, so that the Cause may be spread. When the MOST IMPORTANT work is before our sight, we must let go the *Important* one.

If the meetings or Spiritual Assembly has any other occupation, the time is spent in futility. All the deliberations, all consultation, all the talks and addresses must revolve around one focal center, and that is: TEACH THE CAUSE! TEACH! TEACH! Convey the Message! Awaken the souls! Now is the time of laying the foundation. Now must we gather brick, stone, wood, iron, and other building materials! Now is not the time of decoration. We must strive day and night and think and work. What can I say that may become effective? What can I do that may bring results? What can I write that may bring forth fruits? Nothing else will be useful, today. The interests of such a Glorious Cause will not advance without such undivided attention. While we are carrying this load we cannot carry any other load![85]

On the 17th, 'Abdu'l-Bahá visited the Woking Mosque in Surrey, one of only two mosques in England at that time, where He spoke on the unity of religion. After lunching with Muslim and Christian notables, the Master was ready to speak to the people. The mosque was not large enough for the numbers who came so He spoke in a court outside.[86]

That evening 'Abdu'l-Bahá was talking with Gabrielle Enthoven and told her, 'I will give you a play. It shall be called the Drama of the Kingdom.' He then spoke without notes or pause, except for translation. The play describes the world and its people when the Herald of the Kingdom appears and blows His trumpet:

The curtain rises. The stage is crowded with men and women. All are asleep. At the sound of the trumpet they begin to wake.

Suddenly the music breaks forth. The people hear and wonder. They rise and question one another, saying: 'What is this? Whence comes the music?' Some return to their occupations, unheeding. First a few talk together, then one ceases his work, and proceeds to make enquiries. A merchant, leaving his stall, comes to ask the meaning of the eager group. A soldier, who is practising arms, withdraws from his comrades and joins those who are wondering.

People from all walks of life hear the music and act in one of two ways:

First those who, having heard the music of the Coming of the Promised One, frown and shrug their shoulders, returning to their work, scoffing and disbelieving. The second type are those who hear the music, strain their ears to catch the meaning of the Message, and their eyes to discern the Mystery.

The people who hear the music are ecstatic, but those who do not demand to know where the proof is, cry 'But we await the signs.' One person arises and explains that the signs aren't material ones but spiritual signs and that they must use spiritual eyes to see them. Instead of real earthquakes, unrest and the darkening of the sun and moon, all the signs actually foretell the 'humiliation of those whom the world considers great'. Then a grand procession of all the rulers, kings, and priests passes by covered with fine clothes and jewels, yet all unhappy. When one falls, the others ignore him.

The scene then changes to a sumptuous banquet hall with tables covered with delicious foods. Around the tables sit many people, all poor and with torn clothes, but exceedingly happy. An Oracle announces that 'The Kingdom of God is like a feast! Remember what Christ said! Here we see the Kingdom! The greatest and the worldly wise are not here, but the poor are here.'

Then comes temptation; a man with a sack of gold enters, but is ignored. He is followed by other people: a gifted teacher who used to be ignorant; then a man who had been blind, but can now see; a man once deaf, but who can now hear the beautiful music. Again, a person arises and asks, 'You know the cause of these miracles? It is the Heavenly food!' Then the poor who have eaten the Heavenly food are crowned with crowns of the Kingdom.

The last scene of the play shows several believers being judged by those who do not believe. The prosecutor says they will die, but they simply cry, 'O God, make me ready!' Two die this way and only a beautiful girl dressed in white with a heavenly crown remains. She is offered riches by the king, but she is not tempted, saying, 'Can you say there is not sun, when you have seen the light? I have seen the sun. You are blind. Awake! The sun is shining! Awake!' The king then offers her marriage and jewels, but again she refuses, saying of the jewels, 'These to me are so many pebbles. The jewels I treasure are the jewels of the Knowledge of God.' Then the prosecutor threatens:

'We shall imprison you.'
'I am ready'
'We shall beat you.'
'I am ready.'
'You shall be killed.'
'Is that true? Do you mean it? Good news! Good news! For then shall I be free. Now I am in chains. These bonds shall be broken. Kill me!'

After her death, people enter in awe and watch as lights appear and shine upwards from their bodies. 'These are the spirits of those martyred ones, freed from their bodies. Now they enjoy eternal liberty. See, they ascend to the Kingdom.'[87]

\* \* \*

Finally, came 'Abdu'l-Bahá's last day in London, 21 January 1913. Everyone was ready to leave for the railway station – except 'Abdu'l-Bahá, Who was busy writing. One of His secretaries reminded Him of the time and the train, but He simply said, 'There are things of more importance than trains,' and continued to write. Then abruptly, a man carrying a large garland of fragrant white flowers rushed in and bowed deeply before the Master, saying, 'In the name of the disciples of Zoroaster, The Pure One, I hail Thee as the Promised Sháh Bahrám!' The man then placed the garland of flowers around 'Abdu'l-Bahá, and anointed all present with rose-scented oil. When this amazing ceremony concluded, 'Abdu'l-Bahá carefully removed the flowers and departed for the train.[88]

'Abdu'l-Bahá had gone. Lady Blomfield wrote:

We stood bereft of His presence.

Of the friends who gathered round Him at the train, one had been a constant visitor, a charming Eastern potentate, dignified and picturesque in his jewelled turban. He was an example of earthly kingship, one of the many other great personages of the world, all of whom, absent and present, were so small, so insignificant, when compared with the Ambassador of the Most High, as He stood, clad in a simple garment, speaking courteous words of farewell, smiling that love-laden smile which comforted all hearts.[89]

# 16

# FROM PARIS TO BUDAPEST AND BACK

## *21 January –12 June 1913*

### PARIS, FRANCE

In Paris, 'Abdu'l-Bahá moved into an apartment at 30 Rue St. Didier, rented for Him by Hippolyte Dreyfus-Barney. During His first few days in the city and indeed for much of His time there, the Master was not well. He gave relatively few public talks, but continued to meet His many visitors, particularly prominent Persians and once-high members of the defunct Ottoman Empire, as well as many Bahá'ís who had made the journey from Persia and Egypt in order to meet Him. It was during this visit that the well-known photograph was taken of the Master with a group of these friends at the Eiffel Tower.

On 27 January the Persian Minister visited 'Abdu'l-Bahá even though the Master had a fever and was not sleeping well, and two days later 'a visitor was announced whose presence there was most astonishing'.[1] This was Rashíd Páshá, formerly the Válí of Beirut, who had been very hostile towards 'Abdu'l-Bahá in 'Akká.

Describing this episode later, 'Abdu'l-Bahá said of Rashíd Páshá that he 'must have been bad even before Adam and Eve'. He had used any excuse to extort money for those under his dominion. He also acted as a spy for the Sultan, sending in ugly fabrications about honest citizens in order to enrich himself through bribery or extortion. At one time, a secretary of the Turkish Embassy in Paris met Madame Jackson, a devoted Bahá'í, who told him about 'Abdu'l-Bahá's unjust incarceration in 'Akká. The secretary happened to be a relative of Rashíd Páshá and also fond of money, so he told Madame Jackson that it would require £3,000 to free 'Abdu'l-Bahá. She said that she was willing to pay the sum if 'Abdu'l-Bahá was freed. The secretary reported this to Rashíd Páshá, who immediately began scheming.

Meanwhile, 'Abdu'l-Bahá learned of this from the Mutasarrif of 'Akká, who explained to Him the whole story. 'Abdu'l-Bahá immediately cabled Madame Jackson: 'Beware! Beware! lest you pay one cent for my freedom. In prison I am feeling happy!' When Rashíd Páshá heard of this, he was furious, having expected to make some easy money. Thinking that 'Abdu'l-Bahá couldn't possibly wish to remain in prison any longer than necessary, he had his secretary write the Master a letter saying that he was anxious to see Him freed. 'Abdu'l-Bahá did not reply. Another was sent saying that a petition was being drawn up requesting the Sultan to grant 'Abdu'l-Bahá His freedom. Again 'Abdu'l-Bahá did not answer. There followed another letter saying that the petition was ready to be mailed. Still 'Abdu'l-Bahá did not answer. Yet another letter was sent saying that the Governor had read the petition and ordered that it not be sent. 'Abdu'l-Bahá remained silent.

As a last resort, Rashíd Páshá sent his son to persuade 'Abdu'l-Bahá. When the son arrived in 'Akká, the Mutasarrif hosted a lavish dinner to which he also invited 'Abdu'l-Bahá. After dinner, the son tried to convince the Master to accept His freedom and said, 'I am sorry to see you in prison.' 'Abdu'l-Bahá replied, 'Here I am happy.' The next day, as the son prepared to return to his father, he bade farewell to 'Abdu'l-Bahá saying, 'I hope, my Effendi, that I shall see you next time in Haifa.' 'Abdu'l-Bahá 'waved the matter aside'.

When Rashíd Páshá heard his son's report, he felt humiliated. Everyone else in Syria trembled in fear of him and his decrees were law. One word from him to the Sultan would bring the Sultán's wrath down upon anyone, regardless of position or power. But he couldn't forget the £3,000.

Finally, 'Abdu'l-Bahá called the Mutasarrif to His house and bluntly told him:

> Do not make any more intrigues; you shall fail in all your secret machinations. There is a destined period for my imprisonment. Before the coming of that time, even the kings of the earth cannot take me out of this prison, but when the appointed moment arrives, all the emperors of the world cannot hold me a prisoner in Acca. I shall then go out. Rest thou assured of this.[2]

The Mutasarrif realized that 'Abdu'l-Bahá was not to be moved and wrote that Rashíd Páshá should abandon his hope of gaining the money.

Now that Rashíd Páshá's power was gone, he was very reverential and contrite and the Master received him warmly, returned his visit that very evening. Rashíd Páshá made several more visits.[3]

As the days passed, more and more Persian and Egyptian Bahá'ís arrived and filled the apartment. Day after day, more seekers came to see the Master. The constant meetings took their toll on 'Abdu'l-Bahá's health. He noted that earlier in the journey, He had been able to get up at night and take care of His correspondence, but now He could not, so it remained unanswered.

He did get out to some public meetings. A banquet at the Hôtel Moderne was held by the Esperantists on 12 February. 'Abdu'l-Bahá addressed the meeting that night and the following evening spoke to the Theosophists. On 17 February he spoke at three meetings during the day and then visited Pasteur Monnier's Theological Seminary that evening. He also visited Versailles and a children's home, where he deplored the contrast between 'the many magnificent buildings kept solely for entertainment, while the poor were abandoned to such misery and wretchedness'.[4]

The Paris Bahá'í community, unlike those in London and Stuttgart, where the Master was to go next, had relatively few native believers. The Master spoke of the 'dismal materialism overshadowing Paris'.[5] Years later, after the First World War, he said of his visit, 'in Paris no one would mention the name of God. I used to speak about God to many people and they would ask me to take another topic.'[6]

There was, of course, the unparalleled Hippolyte Dreyfus-Barney with his American wife Laura, and 'Abdu'l-Bahá addressed several meetings at their home, as well as in the homes of Americans such as Edwin Scott, the painter, and Edith Sanderson. But there were also a number of other devoted French believers, and many were interested. Charles Mason Remey wrote later about one of these:

> During Abdul-Baha's visits in Paris, souls became attracted to the Cause, and the principles of his teachings became known and produced an effect upon many. Then out from these people there arose a few who recognized the Covenant of God and realized that in Abdul-Baha was the living spiritual Center of this new life in the world. Madame Chéron was of these few. The spiritual atmosphere

of her home was to the hungry and seeking soul as an oasis in the desert to the tired traveller seeking refreshment and rest.

During the weeks prior to the outbreak of the war, which George Latimer and I spent in Paris, we went often to the apartment of Madame Chéron, overlooking the Seine. At times when surrounded by discouragements we went there to talk about The Center of the Covenant and thus revive our spiritual forces; and at other times we went there to meet groups of friends and seekers whom our kind hostess had gathered to hear the wonderful story of the The Cause of God.[7]

At one of 'Abdu'l-Bahá's talks, Doris Pascal (later Holley) was in the audience and it was an eye-opening experience for her:

I was spiritually asleep at the time, but while I was listening to the Master's talk I felt as if Jesus were speaking and I thought that the Master was saying what Jesus would have said. When the meeting was over, instead of following the Master out of the room as the others in the audience had done, I remained in my chair. The Master soon returned. To my natural astonishment He walked straight up to me and kissed me on the forehead.[8]

Stanwood Cobb was also in Paris in the spring of 1913:

I was one of the staff at Porter Sargent's Travel School for Boys. On my first visit He inquired about the school and asked me what I taught. I told Him I taught English, Latin, algebra and geometry. He gazed intently at me with His luminous eyes and said, 'Do you teach the spiritual things?'

The question embarrassed me. I did not know how to explain to 'Abdu'l-Bahá that the necessity of preparing the boys for college-entrance exams dominated the nature of the curriculum. So I simply answered: 'No, there is not time for that.'

'Abdu'l-Bahá made no comment on this answer, But He did not need to. Out of my own mouth I had condemned myself and modern education . . . But 'Abdu'l-Bahá's question and His silent response indicated that from His viewpoint spiritual things should come first . . .

'Abdu'l-Bahá kindly invited me to bring Porter Sargent and the pupils to see Him. Mr Sargent gladly accepted the invitation, and four of the boys did. The others had excuses, like those people in the Bible who were invited to the wedding feast but did not go. One boy had to buy a pair of shoes; another had planned to take afternoon tea at a restaurant where a gypsy orchestra furnished music, et cetera. How many of life's important opportunities thus pass us by, through our own unperceptiveness or neglect!

I was deeply interested and concerned to see what impression 'Abdu'l-Bahá would make on the owner of the school. Porter Sargent ... was a confirmed and positive atheist ... In one intimate discussion with me on the nature of existence ... he had outlined to me his concept of life and the universe. 'What do you think of it?' he asked me ...

'It is splendid!' I said. 'But it only covers half of existence.'

'What is the other half?'

'Spirit.'

But this other half did not exist for Porter Sargent ... So when the golden opportunity came of an interview with 'Abdu'l-Bahá, I had great hopes ...

And so, when we came out ... after a half-hour conference with 'Abdu'l-Bahá, I eagerly asked, 'Well, what do you think of Him?'

I have never forgotten my shattering disappointment at the answer: 'He's a dear, kind, tired old man.'

I was chagrined. But this experience taught me two spiritual lessons. The first was that skeptism must solve its own problems, in it's own way. The second truth ... was that Spirit never forces itself upon the individual. It must be invited.[9]

'Abdu'l-Bahá gave another talk on 20 February. At its conclusion, Horace Holley's young daughter, whom the Master had last seen at Thonon two years previously, ran up and was happily lifted up into His arms. The moment reminded 'Abdu'l-Bahá of His own son, Ḥusayn, who had died as a child.[10]

The hectic pace was wearing on 'Abdu'l-Bahá and by the 26th He was suffering from a severe cold. The illness kept Him in Paris and unable to travel, but it did not stop Him from speaking with the endless visitors..

Edward G. Browne and his wife visited the Master on 9 March.

Other visitors included the Iranian Minister; Alma Knobloch, the 'pioneer teacher' to Germany, and other German friends who had come to beg the Master to visit their country. But it was only towards the end of March that he was well enough to travel.[11]

## Stuttgart, Germany

On 30 March 'Abdu'l-Bahá, along with Siyyid Aḥmad-i-Báqiroff, Mírzá Maḥmúd, Siyyid Asadu'lláh and Ahmad Sohrab, departed for Stuttgart. In a change, the Master told His companions to switch from Eastern clothing to Western and not to wear their fezzes. They reached Stuttgart at 8 p.m. on 1 April and proceeded directly from the train to the Hotel Marquardt. Before their arrival, 'Abdu'l-Bahá told His attendants, 'This is the best thing; we will arrive in Stuttgart, take our rooms in the hotel, settle down and call up the friends. How surprised they will be! Is this not a fine plan? We are going to surprise them. Then when they come they will find us in their midst, and knowing nothing about it at all. Yes! This is the best plan.'[12]

That same evening 'Abdu'l-Bahá sent for Wilhelm Herrigel, Mr Eckstein and Alma Knobloch and arranged with them that the friends would be able to meet Him during the mornings while afternoons and evenings would be reserved for more formal meetings. During His first afternoon in Stuttgart, Mr Herrigel took the Master for a drive through the Royal Park. Later, 'Abdu'l-Bahá had two meetings with the friends at Mr Herrigel's home, and said, 'How attracted and enkindled are the German Bahá'ís! How full of love they are! Love does not need a teacher.'[13]

### Alma Knobloch

One of the three dedicated Knobloch sisters, Alma Knobloch was destined to 'take the Glad-Tidings of the Advent of Bahá'u'lláh to the soul of the German people'. 'Abdu'l-Bahá had approved her going, to help Dr Edwin Fisher, an American dentist and the first Bahá'í in Germany, writing, 'she must stay as long as possible'.

Arriving in Stuttgart in 1907, Alma began to hold meetings and travel tirelessly to teach the Faith.

Soon many young people in Stuttgart, Leipzig, Hamburg, and other cities, visited by Alma, arose . . . The Bahá'í Faith took root in the hearts of these religiously educated souls, and through the effort and constant study Local Spiritual Assemblies were formed in Stuttgart, Esslingen, Zeffenhausen, Leipzig, and Gera . . .The way was not always easy, and Alma, in her fine, soft voice and well-bred manner, fought many a mental battle . . . One could see the Bahá'í spirit at work in her, when some learned gentleman discussed, in not always a gentle way, the different aspects . . . Never once did Alma lose patience, and never once did she falter in her answers . . .

When war was declared in 1914, Alma joined in the sufferings of her German brothers and sisters, descended into the damp cellars with them, hungered and froze with them, renounced her American citizenship . . . in order to be free to travel in the service of our beloved Master; and indeed, the need for spiritual food was great at that time. Many evenings at the fireside meetings, the spiritual food was the only kind of food the friends had that day.[14]

'Abdu'l-Bahá spoke highly of Alma Knobloch. When George Latimer was on pilgrimage in 1919, 'Abdu'l-Bahá said of Alma, 'Consider the power of God. Such a small woman! She is confirmed in service. She is greatly assisted. When a person compares her success with her physical body, a hundred people will not be so assisted as she – this woman is so short. That is why the confirmations of God are necessary . . . Miss Knobloch has attracted the people. There is a large man, Mr Herrigel, very large. She converted him.'[15]

In 1920 Alma returned to America, where she passed away in 1943.

* * *

On 3 April 'Abdu'l-Bahá gave many interviews until 3 p.m. when Albert Schwarz, the Consul for Norway, and a devoted Bahá'í who later served as Chairman of the National Spiritual Assembly of the Bahá'ís of Germany and who was described by Shoghi Effendi as 'Germany's outstanding pioneer worker',[16] drove Him to the famous Castle Solitude. This was followed by 'Abdu'l-Bahá's first public talk at the Burger Museum that evening attended by over 500 people.

'Abdu'l-Bahá had four hours of interviews with people at the hotel on the morning of 4 April. When finished, He said, 'I was most happy to see the believers of Germany so holy, so pure and so united. They are the Angels of the Paradise of Abha.'[17]

At four o'clock in the afternoon, 'Abdu'l-Bahá left for Esslingen, about ten kilometres away, where a large meeting for children had been arranged.

## Esslingen, Germany

The Bahá'ís in Esslingen had secured a hall which they had decorated with greenery, plants and flowers. The hall was filled with about 50 children and 80 adults. To welcome 'Abdu'l-Bahá, the children, each holding a bunch of flowers, formed two lines in the entry hall through which He passed. Each child gave the Master his bunch of flowers as He greeted them. In return, 'Abdu'l-Bahá gave the children small boxes of chocolates and bon-bons. Everyone was radiantly happy.

When 'Abdu'l-Bahá moved into the main hall, Ahmad Sohrab had to clear a path through the eager crowd. 'Abdu'l-Bahá gave a short talk, during which he said, 'These children are of the Kingdom, they are illumined with the Light of God. . . I love them very much. They are mine . . . May God guide and protect them, make of them useful men and women for the advancement of the Kingdom on earth.'

Then everyone shared tea, chocolate and cake. The group then gathered in front of the hall and a group photograph was taken. Finally, 'Abdu'l-Bahá climbed into His car to leave. Ahmad Sohrab wrote that the children were 'crowding around and waving their flowers. Then one after another stepped up and handed their fragrant tokens. O, it looked really beautiful; I cannot describe it, so wonderfully sweet! The children waving their dear little hands, and 'Abdu'l-Bahá in the auto, covered with flowers, waving his blessed hands to them.'[18]

## Stuttgart, Germany

Next morning, back in Stuttgart at the Hotel Marquardt, 'Abdu'l-Bahá said of the children's meeting:

> The effect of last night's meeting will be put on record in the world of eternity. The mentioning of it will be throughout the centuries and

will be recorded in the countries of the Orient. Because these children are tender plants, their hearts are clear and transparent. They have not yet come to the dross of the world; that is why Christ said: "Blessed are the children, for they are of the Heavenly Kingdom."[19]

Later in the day, 'Abdu'l-Bahá had a tour of the Royal Palace of Emperor Wilhelm and in the afternoon gave a talk on women at the specific request of Alma Knobloch, at a Unity Feast hosted by the Frauen Club. About 160 people were present when 'Abdu'l-Bahá arrived at 4 p.m. Everyone was delighted with the results of the Feast, and 'Abdu'l-Bahá said of it, 'The Supreme Concourse of Angels were pleased and rejoiced. It was an illumined meeting, giving eternal life to mankind.'[20] In the evening the Master gave yet another talk, to the Esperantists.

On 6 April 'Abdu'l-Bahá had a pleasant trip through the cherry blossom district, with the trees in full bloom, then continued on into the Black Forest. On several occasions the Master remarked how glad he was to have seen Germany in the spring. 'Truly', He said, 'it is worthy to become a paradise.' The party visited Mr and Mrs Schweizer in Zuffenhausen before returning to Stuttgart for the evening meeting at the Obere Museum. This was the largest public meeting given in the city and was organized by the Bahá'í women. Alma Knobloch wrote:

> The Master asked me to select a subject for the evening and I asked Him to speak on 'Woman'. Smilingly he questioned, 'On the German Woman?' I answered, 'No, on Woman in general.' His face beamed with that radiance that brought divine fragrances and He said, 'Very well, very well' . . . His address was highly appreciated, especially by those noble, esteemed ladies who had so marvelously assisted us in our early work. After the talk he went through the hall shaking hands and giving words of cheer.[21]

## Bad Mergentheim, Germany

On 7 April 'Abdu'l-Bahá travelled to Bad Mergentheim, about 60 miles north of Stuttgart, at the behest of Consul Albert Schwarz, who was later named a Disciple of 'Abdu'l-Bahá by Shoghi Effendi. Bad Mergentheim was a small, quiet town known for its health spa and hotel, both of which Schwarz owned. They drove up in Consul Schwarz's automobiles, and 'Abdu'l-Bahá spent the rest of the day and that night as his guest. The Master commented that he had not heard so many nightingales singing in such a beautiful setting since He had left Persia.

In 1916, the local Bahá'ís commemorated the Master's visit through 'the dedication of a handsome monument . . . It consisted of a life-sized head of 'Abdu'l-Bahá in bronze on a granite stone about six feet in height. It was placed next to a rose arbor and thus had a mass of exquisite roses for a background.'[22] The Nazis removed it in 1937, but it was replaced in 2007.[23]

Before He left the next day, 'Abdu'l-Bahá spoke with the people working at the spa and told them they must be very conscientious, pointing out their great responsibility to alleviate the suffering of people.[24] 'Abdu'l-Bahá then left Bad Mergentheim and returned to Stuttgart. He had lunch with Consul and Mrs Schwarz and met many Bahá'ís before boarding the train at 8 p.m. for Budapest. Wilhelm Herrigel joined the group to act as the Master's translator for German.

## BUDAPEST, HUNGARY

Before 1913, no Bahá'í travel teacher had visited Budapest and no Bahá'ís lived there. 'Abdu'l-Bahá's reputation had washed across the continent, however, and Leopold Stark, and others who lived there, had read of His journey and had written to beg that He might grace Budapest with His Presence. As during most of His epic journey, 'Abdu'l-Bahá made His decisions about where to go and what to do according to the circumstances of the moment. Thus He decided to go to Budapest.

'Abdu'l-Bahá arrived at the train station in Budapest on 9 April, where He was met by the eminent Orientalist Dr Ignatius Goldziher, Professor Julius Germanus, Leopold Stark and others. He was taken to the Ritz Hotel where He had a room with a view of the Danube River.

Only minutes after His arrival at the hotel, the first delegation of visitors arrived to welcome Him. This group included one of the most honoured thinkers and pacifists in the country, Prelate Alexander Giesswein, and Professor Robert A. Nadler, a well-known painter. Reporters, of course, were also present. The group welcomed 'Abdu'l-Bahá:

> In the name of all present we welcome the blessed Presence of 'Abdu'l-Bahá. We admire your great life and we offer You our thanks

and deep gratitude, that at Your age, You take upon Yourself these long journeys for the sake of helping and comforting humanity. Such labours, such sacrifices as 'Abdu'l-Bahá endures are our great examples, that we may know how to live and to serve humanity.'[25]

The next day, 'Abdu'l-Bahá prepared tea for His party and admired the panoramic view of the Danube. He could see the broad river spanned by many ornamented suspension bridges and plied by colourful boats. After tea, He crossed the Chain Bridge to Buda, quickly attracting many curious people who stopped to ask Him questions. One man recognized 'Abdu'l-Bahá from His photograph in the morning's newspaper and hurried over to have the Master autograph the margin of his paper.[26]

During the day, a stream of visitors came to the hotel and He told them that He was grateful to God that the idea of a spiritual life was obvious in Budapest. He told them that 'it was his hope that Budapest might become a centre for the reunion of the East and West, and that from this city the light might emanate to other places.' When people asked Him what He thought of Budapest's ornate buildings, 'Abdu'l-Bahá kindly replied that He had come to Budapest to see 'the objects of interest and buildings of human hearts, and not the buildings of stone and of the city.'[27]

Later that day, Professor Germanus, a young Orientalist, brought a group of Turkish students bearing 'a letter of solemn welcome signed by all students of the Turkish language in Budapest'. 'Abdu'l-Bahá happily conversed with them in flawless Turkish. That evening, 'Abdu'l-Bahá gave a talk to fifty people at the Theosophical meeting, calling them 'a noble, spiritual gathering because they were most diligent in their endeavors for peace and fellowship'.[28]

One morning when 'Abdu'l-Bahá visited the home of Leopold Stark and his wife, Mrs Stark offered Him wine or another refreshment. When 'Abdu'l-Bahá declined, Mrs Stark offered Him some 'fine spring water, a table delicacy since Roman times'. The maid brought in a tray with beautiful crystal glasses and placed it carefully on a table. When the maid saw 'Abdu'l-Bahá standing near the window, she 'slowly and deliberately . . . advanced, knelt before him and begged him to bless her. This very touching scene brought tears to the eyes of those who surrounded the Master . . . When asked later by her mistress why she did this, she said, "I was impelled to, because he seemed to me one of the 'Kings of the East'."[29]

On 11 April 'Abdu'l-Bahá spoke at a meeting in the old Parliament Building. He stood on a high platform directly underneath two white-winged angels holding Hungary's coat of arms. Before His talk, 'Abdu'l-Bahá was very tired and hardly able to speak, but, as He had done at other times, He gathered His strength and He gave a powerful address.[30] As the Master stood on the platform, He was flanked by Prelate Giesswein on one side and Dr Goldziher on the other. The sight of this unity brought forth a tremendous burst of applause: 'They felt, if they did not understand, that 'Abdu'l-Bahá standing between the Catholic prelate and the Jewish orientalist represented the reconciliation of these two great religions.'[31]

Dr Germanus interpreted 'Abdu'l-Bahá's talk into Hungarian for the packed house. All seats were filled and many people crowded into the galleries, aisles and corridors with some even having to listen from outside. The audience was perfect for the Master, being an amazing mix of members of Parliament, university professors, artists, Catholic priests, Protestant clergymen, and representatives of women's groups, Esperantists, and humanitarian societies as well as many nationalities and races. 'All seats were occupied while many stood in the gallery; aisles and corridors were crowded and a line extended even to the street!'[32]

The following morning, Alajos Paikert, the founder of the Hungarian Turanian Society, visited 'Abdu'l-Bahá and invited Him to address his group a few days later. The talk, on 14 April, was at the former House of Magnates in the National Museum Building. Mr Paikert introduced the Master to the 200 prominent men and women. 'Abdu'l-Bahá spoke in Persian, translated into English by Ahmad Sohrab, then Leopold Stark retranslated His words into Hungarian. 'Abdu'l-Bahá spoke of the Turanian culture (one of the early tribes of the Avestan era, east of Iran) and noted that it had been destroyed by religious conflict. He then gave them a plan to create an enduring peace. Afterwards, someone asked where the centre of peace would be located. 'Abdu'l-Bahá responded that it would be established in whichever country where peace was first established.[33]

In the afternoon 'Abdu'l-Bahá visited Professor Arminius Vámbéry, who was 82 years old and ill at the time. Vámbéry was one of the most erudite and interesting scientists and Orientalists of his time, 'whom both Queen Victoria and King Edward of Great Britain distinguished for many years with their friendship'.³⁴ In the Bahá'í Faith, the famous man found his heart's desire. Before meeting 'Abdu'l-Bahá, Vámbéry had not believed in any religion, despite having travelled in and learned the languages of many countries. The Master quoted Vámbéry as saying, 'Because of this, I am amazed and surprised, that I, Vámbéry have not the courage to and cannot mention the name of Christ with reverence in the churches of the Jews. But you have proved with such courage and power, in the synagogues of the Jews, that Jesus Christ was the Word and the Spirit of God.'³⁵

Vámbéry tried to see the Master again the next day, going along the river from his house at 26 Quai Franz Joseph to the Master's hotel in spite of very cold and stormy weather and his illness. But when he arrived, 'Abdu'l-Bahá was out and though he waited for a long time, Vámbéry was forced to return home unsatisfied. After 'Abdu'l-Bahá had returned to Egypt, He sent Vámbéry a Tablet and a rug. In response, Vámbéry wrote back to 'Abdu'l-Bahá:

> I forward this humble petition to the sanctified and holy presence of Abdul-Baha Abbas who is the centre of knowledge, famous throughout the world and beloved by all mankind. O thou noble friend . . . Although I have travelled through many countries and cities of Islam, yet have I never met so lofty a character and so exalted a personage as your excellency and I can bear witness that it is not possible to find such another. . .
>
> . . .every person is forced by necessity to enlist himself on the side of your excellency and accept with joy the prospect of a fundamental basis for a universal religion of God being laid through your efforts.
>
> I have seen the father of your excellency from afar. I have realized the self-sacrifice and noble courage of his son and I am lost in admiration.
>
> For the principles and aims of your excellency I express the utmost respect and devotion and if God, the most high, confer long life, I will be able to serve you under all conditions. I pray and supplicate this from the depths of my heart.³⁶

On the 14th, 'Alí 'Abbás Áqá, a Persian carpet salesman who had become very attached to the Master, invited Him for dinner at his home. One of the guests was the Ottoman Consul-General.³⁷ 'Abdu'l-Bahá also visited the home of Mr Paikert, who lived on a high hill overlooking the city. Afterwards, He visited Professor Robert Nadler, Mr Stark and Count Albert Apponyi.

Professor Nadler, who was a professor of painting at the Royal Academy of Art, asked if he could paint a portrait of 'Abdu'l-Bahá. The Master agreed and went to Nadler's studio on 13 April. Years later, Nadler said to Martha Root:

> When I saw 'Abdu'l-Bahá, He was in His seventieth year. I was so impressed and charmed with His Personality that I had the great longing to paint His portrait. He consented to come to my studio, but said He could not give me much time because He was so busy. I marvelled at His expression of peace and pure love and absolute good-will. He saw everything with such a nice eye; everything was beautiful to 'Abdu'l-Bahá, both the outer life of Budapest and the souls of all. He praised the situation of our city, our fine Danube in the midst of the town, good water, good people. Oh, He had so many beautiful thoughts! I was inspired, and I knew I did not have much time, so I concentrated very much. He gave me three sittings.³⁸

Nadler also talked of the painting in 1937:

> . . . he came three times to my studio, and was a very patient model. I was all too happy to be able to paint him, feature by feature, and to be able to immortalize the earthly temple of so highly developed a soul.
>
> I was glad to hear him and his companions say that they thought the portrait a success. They even asked me what the price of it would be, but at that time I had no desire *to gain financially* by selling the picture, which remains one of my best works. It has been my pleasure to have 'Abdu'l-Baha's portrait in my studio for twenty-four years, and I shall never forget the few hours of his presence there.³⁹

'Abdu'l-Bahá liked the result of Nadler's work. In 1945, the building which housed the painting was heavily bombed and the only part of the building that survived relatively undamaged was the part containing the painting. The painting was purchased by Bahá'ís in 1972 who gave it to the Universal House of Justice.⁴⁰

The Master had a bad cold for two days, 15 and 16 April, but that didn't stop Him from getting up and meeting His many visitors. It did, however delay his travel plans for a few days until 18 April.

At the railway station He was met by 'a great number of devoted friends . . . many Hungarians and also some Turks, Americans, and Indians',⁴¹ thirty of whom had ostensibly accepted the Bahá'í teachings.⁴² Before departing for Vienna, He told the group that 'He had set a flame aglow, and the day would break when its light would shine visibly to everybody. He explained that the origin of a tree is only a small seed, but if it develops and begins to grow, it will bear a beautiful fruit.'⁴³ 'Each one in his own language begged for a blessing in his endeavor to serve. Then as the train moved out, they continued to gaze at His holy countenance with their arms outstretched in longing!'⁴⁴

A few weeks after leaving Budapest, 'Abdu'l-Bahá wrote to Leopold Stark and asked him to 'unite all those in Budapest who are likely to form the first nucleus.' ⁴⁵

## Vienna, Austria

Arriving in Vienna, 'Abdu'l-Bahá stayed at the Grand Hotel. Although still suffering the effects of His cold, 'Abdu'l-Bahá visited the Turkish Ambassador the next day. The Ambassador had previously been fanatically against the Bahá'ís, but after meeting the Master, he was so impressed that he requested He stay for lunch. Later, 'Abdu'l-Bahá went for a walk and passed people taking a collection for charity to which He made a contribution. Later that afternoon, He went to give a talk at the Theosophical Hall. To get there, He had to climb up 120 steps – the building was new and there was no lift yet.⁴⁶ Over a year later the Master referred to this in talking to pilgrims:

> My power consists of the bestowals of the Blessed Beauty . . . From early morning until now I have been reading and writing and I am feeling exceedingly well. Young people like you can only work three or four hours without ceasing . . . At nine in the evening there was a meeting on the top floor of a high building in a remote part of the city. A heavy snow was falling. It was very cold weather. I had this

cold and fever, but notwithstanding this, I went, ascended 120 steps and addressed the people for about two hours.⁴⁷

'Abdu'l-Bahá spoke three times to the Theosophists in Vienna, and one of them, Frau Tyler, called to 'express her newly found devotion'.⁴⁸ Another visitor was Baroness Berthe von Suttner, the novelist and a leading figure for decades in the international peace movement who had won the Nobel Peace Prize in 1905, one of the few women to do so. On 21 April, the Persian Minister paid the Master a call in the morning and in the afternoon, He went for a drive. During His stay in Vienna, 'Abdu'l-Bahá also permitted a sculptor to model him.⁴⁹

## STUTTGART, GERMANY

'Abdu'l-Bahá stayed in the same hotel He had stayed in during His earlier visit, the Hotel Marquardt. The cold He had acquired in Budapest worsened in Stuttgart and by the 25th it had settled into His chest and made it difficult for Him to talk. His physician said He should not go out into the bad weather, but His attendants devised a solution so that the people at a meeting scheduled for that night would not be disappointed. The plan was that Abdu'l-Bahá would be taken to the Museum in an enclosed saloon car, safe from the foul weather. In a room apart from the main hall, 'Abdu'l-Bahá would have His place to meet those who wished to see Him while Wilhelm Herrigel gave a talk in His stead in the main hall. But as soon as 'Abdu'l-Bahá learned of this plan, and how eagerly the audience were expecting Him, He arose. 'Physicians had made Him stay indoors, He said; but His health was for the purpose of serving the Faith.'⁵⁰

No sooner had Herrigel begun speaking than 'Abdu'l-Bahá walked into the surprised hall and, with His full and powerful voice, gave a talk on world peace. Immediately after His talk, 'Abdu'l-Bahá was about be taken quickly back to the hotel to rest. But as they headed for the door, the Master heard someone sobbing and He stopped to find out who was sad. His attendants found a woman who had tried to reach the Master, but had been prevented by the mass of the crowd. 'Abdu'l-Bahá stayed long enough to speak with the lady.⁵¹

On 27 April 'Abdu'l-Bahá greeted a number of children brought to Him. He loved children and they loved Him. One child, when later asked to pray for the Master's health, responded by saying he didn't want 'Abdu'l-Bahá's health to improve because then He would go away.[52]

On 30 April Consul Schwarz had arranged for 'Abdu'l-Bahá to meet the Kaiser, Wilhelm II, at his hunting lodge near Tübingen. When they arrived, however, the king was not there. In the visitor's book at the lodge, 'Abdu'l-Bahá wrote: 'The royal palace is not occupied, because I can not see the face of the king. The green meadow looks cut down because it is not adorned with the glorious figure of the queen.'[53]

By 1 May 'Abdu'l-Bahá was finally well enough to travel to Paris. Before leaving, He met the Stuttgart Bahá'ís in groups at His hotel. On one memorable occasion, He was looking out of his hotel window when he saw a regiment of soldiers marching by. He said:

> They are ready to fight for their fatherland. How barbarous it seems to send men who do not even know each other, to the battlefield in order to shoot each other down. The Bahai Grand Army consists of the invisible angels of the Supreme Concourse. Our swords are the words of love and life. Our armaments are the invisible armaments of Heaven. We are fighting against the forces of darkness. O my soldiers, my beloved soldiers! Forward! Forward! Have no fear of defeat; do not have failing hearts. Our supreme commander is Baha'o'llah. From the heights of glory he is directing this dramatic engagement. He commands us! Rush forward! Rush forward! Show the strength of your arms. Ye shall scatter the forces of ignorance. Your war confers life; their war brings death. Your war is the cause of the illumination of all mankind. Your war means victory upon victory. Their war is defeat upon defeat. Their war is the origin of destruction. There are no dangers before you. Push forward! Fire! Fire! . . .[54]

Just over a year later the conflagration of war would engulf the whole of Europe.

## Paris, France

During His final visit to Paris, 'Abdu'l-Bahá stayed at the Hotel Baltimore. His travels had greatly weakened Him and He was sometimes unable to attend meetings in the homes of the Bahá'ís. Still, He entertained visitors in His hotel room. During a luncheon, He could not sit at the table for long and had to retire to His room. On another day, tired though He was, He called Siyyid Asadu'lláh and, with a laugh in His voice, told him to fear God and get Him a cup of coffee. At one point He said, 'The Blessed Perfection has trained me to shoulder the burdens of others, not to put mine on others' shoulders.'[55]

Rashíd Páshá and the Persian Minister paid the Master another visit. On 22 May He Himself visited a member of the Persian aristocracy, who was overwhelmed, bowing and kissing the Master's hand. This man, very important in other circles, related a story about how he had lost his hostility toward the Bahá'í Faith. He found himself one day sitting next to a woman in London and was intrigued by her inexpensive but beautiful ring. When he asked about it, the woman replied that since he was a Persian, surely he could read the name of Bahá'u'lláh inscribed on the stone. At that, he felt very ashamed, but then quite elated when he realized that here was evidence of Persia's influence in London. At that moment, he realized that he no longer harboured any hostility toward the Faith of Bahá'u'lláh.[56]

The next day was the celebration of the Declaration of the Báb. Many people arrived, however, with flowers to celebrate the Master's birthday. He told them that it was inappropriate to celebrate His birthday on a day of much greater import – the Declaration by the Báb of His Mission to Mullá Ḥusayn.

On 27 May 'Abdu'l-Bahá moved to a new hotel on Rue Lauriston where He was forced to rest for several days. The hotel food did not suit the Master so the Dreyfus-Barneys and Aḥmad Páshá cooked for Him at their homes, though He asked them not to do so.

As always, the poor were just as attracted to 'Abdu'l-Bahá as were the rich, but didn't always have the same reception. This wasn't due to 'Abdu'l-Bahá, but to those around Him. At one of the hotels the Master stayed in while He was in Paris, a poor black man came to see Him. The man was not a Bahá'í, but was completely in love with the Master. When the man tried to enter the hotel, someone told him that the management of the hotel did not want him there because 'it was not consistent with the standards of the hotel'. The man was forced to leave. When 'Abdu'l-Bahá learned of this, He was very unhappy and called for the person responsible, whom He immediately sent off to find the rejected man and to bring him to His Presence. Said the Master, 'I did not come to see expensive hotels or furnishings, but to meet My friends. I did not come to Paris to conform to the customs of Paris, but to establish the standard of Bahá'u'lláh.'[57]

On 1 June Mírzá 'Alí-Akbar Nakhjavání, who had accompanied the Master during his visit to America, arrived from Haifa and told 'Abdu'l-Bahá that there were many pilgrims awaiting His return.

'Abdu'l-Bahá's final days were marked by the humble visits of a number of former enemies. On 6 June He was visited by Aḥmad 'Izzat Páshá, who had been Sulṭán Abdu'l-Hamid's chief counsellor before the Ottoman Empire succumbed to the Young Turks. He had escaped Turkey ahead of the rebellion. Now, he gave a dinner party for 'Abdu'l-Bahá. A couple days later, a Persian prince stopped by 'Abdu'l-Bahá's hotel. The prince acted in an arrogant manner until the very humble Aḥmad 'Izzat Páshá arrived and, by his attitude of complete deference to the Master, taught the upstart an important lesson.[58]

'Abdu'l-Bahá and His party left the hotel at 8 o'clock in the morning of 12 June for the train station. After some final words to His followers, urging them to be united, He departed for Marseilles. Twelve hours later He reached the city, then left the following morning at 9 a.m. aboard the steamer *Himalaya*, bound for Egypt.

## 17

# HOME AGAIN
### *17 June–5 December 1913*

### PORT SAID, ISMAILIA, ALEXANDRIA AND RAMLEH, EGYPT

'Abdu'l-Bahá arrived in Port Said on 17 June 1913. One of the first things He did was to send a telegram to Haifa, instructing the many pilgrims awaiting his return to come to Port Said. His hotel proved too small for the great crowds that appeared to see Him, so a large tent was erected on the hotel roof.[1]

'Abdu'l-Bahá also wrote to the Greatest Holy Leaf saying, 'My eagerness knows no bounds. I have not seen thee for such a long time. My coming to Haifa is somewhat delayed. If possible, come soon to Port Said.'[2]

The Master was very tired after almost three years of travelling. He stayed in Egypt until December, a span of five and a half months, trying to rebuild His physical strength before returning to Haifa, where a large amount of work awaited Him. It appeared He had little rest because '. . . pilgrims arrived constantly and had to be accommodated and entertained. He was never alone or free from demands. He could never refuse one who came to Him for whatever purpose.'[3]

In spite of His exhaustion, 'Abdu'l-Bahá continued to meet anyone who came. The pilgrims from Haifa occupied much of His time and His ever-increasing volume of correspondence consumed most of what was left. Ahmad Sohrab wrote about the Master's endless letter writing:

> The many difficult problems of the Bahai world are solved by him. Now he writes to Persia on how to hold an election, then to far-off America on how to rent a hall. One Bahai desires to know whether she should cook food for her child; another person asks how to proceed to buy a piece of land. There are some misunderstandings in

this assembly to be removed; the feelings of some person are ruffled, and must be smoothed down. One man's mother or father is dead, he requests a Tablet of visitation, another desires to have a wife. To one a child is born, she begs for a Bahai name; another has taught several souls, he asks for Bahai rings for them. This man has had business reverses, he must be encouraged, another has fallen from a ladder, he implores for a speedy recovery. One has quarrelled with his wife, and he wants advice on how to be reconciled; another supplicates for blessings upon his marriage. The Master goes over these one by one with infinite patience and with his words of advice, creates order out of chaos. The sorrows of the world troop along in review before him, and as they pass, lo, the transformation happens! The sorrowful becomes joyful, the ill-tempered good-natured, the lazy active, the sleepy one awakened. With magical words he transmutes iron into gold and darkness into light. At last he rises from his seat and for a while walks to and fro, still dictating Tablets to the philosopher and to the simple; soaring toward the empyrean of spirituality, giving us a vision of sanctity, and of the roses of Paradise, and for a while we roam, guided by him, in those delectable gardens of Abha, intoxicated with the fragrance of God; and then we find ourselves in the streets, walking home upborne on the wings of light.[4]

But not all of 'Abdu'l-Bahá's correspondence was about personal desires. One day Ahmad Sohrab brought a large quantity of letters from Bahá'ís in America and Europe and the Master quite happily began dictating His replies. Ahmad described how 'Abdu'l-Bahá dictated:

> . . . the words of wisdom like unto a sparkling stream flowed from his blessed mouth, he was a transfigured person. He sat immovable on the sofa, his eyes most of the time shut, but his heart a waving ocean of revelation. Now he revealed a Tablet to a believer in Constantinople, and again to a friend in Rangoon, India; Stuttgart and Switzerland, London and Paris, New York and Honolulu, Washington and Boston were represented. How wonderful and significant appears to me this golden network of spiritual correspondence, reaching to the different parts of the earth! This correspondence is not based upon any commercial or material scheme. It is the eternal

plan of God, to diffuse the fragrance of the spiritual rose and scatter the rays of the Divine Sun! Every day an ideal Congress of religions and nations is held in the rather small room of the Beloved and he presides over the proceedings with a dignity and wisdom that is nothing short of miraculous . . . Toward the end, the Master was so moved that he got up from his seat and began to walk to and fro while continuing dictation. I tried to keep up with the rapidity of his uttered words. When I mentioned the name of one of the believers, his whole countenance changed, and he was very happy, saying that he loved him, because he was very sincere in the Cause.[5]

On 24 June a group of rather antagonistic Christian missionaries came and, even though He was quite tired from a very busy day, 'Abdu'l-Bahá went to meet them with His usual warmth and openness. The group quickly began attacking Islam and its followers. 'Abdu'l-Bahá responded saying that their complaints were about distortions and imitations of Islam and were not true of Islam itself. When their complaints continued, the Master proved to them that some of their own expressed beliefs were not supported by the Bible when it was interpreted accurately.[6]

On 28 June most of the pilgrims left, but other cares fell on the Master. Mírzá Abu'l-Faḍl became ill, which concerned Him greatly. On 11 July 'Abdu'l-Bahá took the train to Ismailia in hopes that the change of climate would help improve His health. In spite of the effects of the heat, His sense of humour was undiminished when He wrote to Ali-Kuli Khan: 'Praise be to God you are spending your days in a delectable, verdant and refreshing place. We too are, praise be to God, enjoying ourself in the hot weather of Port Said with its excessive humidity, dust and dirt, while suffering with nerve fever. As the friends are comfortable, Abdul-Baha is in the utmost joy.'[7]

Before He left for Ismailia, He met with his attendants and a few pilgrims and told them of all the meetings He had in America and how He had found the Americans to be very spiritual people. 'Abdu'l-Bahá told His audience about Fred Mortensen who had 'been so anxious to meet the Master that he risked his life by concealing himself under the train till he reached Green Acre, Maine.' 'Abdu'l-Bahá praised Fred's courage. The Master also said that He had again met Fred, along with his wife, when He went to Minneapolis. He called that later meeting a confirmation of the Holy Spirit.[8]

## HOME AGAIN

'Abdu'l-Bahá moved back to Alexandria on 19 July because the climate at Ismailia was not what was hoped. Initially, He stayed at the Victoria Hotel, then moved into a house in Ramleh. Ahmad Sohrab gave his impressions of Ramleh:

> From my room I see the great clock of the New Victoria Hotel, wherein the Beloved stayed from time to time. The manager with much pride shows to the guests the various rooms occupied by the Master. He knows something about the Cause, and recognizes the great honour and blessing bestowed upon him and his hotel . . . The homes of the Pashas are really wonderful specimens of the best Renaissance architecture. They very much resemble the houses and villas I have seen at Nice. Wonderful palaces, furnished with a taste truly magnificent, and are enclosed within gardens, the beauty and charm of which rival the fairy-lands of the artists and the poets. These "villas" are surrounded by walls from two to four yards high. The principal avenues are macadamized and clean and the narrow streets are also very much like the garden paths of Nice. As one walks through them the perfume of the flowers is inhaled, the branches of the trees overhanging the walls give a cool, inviting shade and the climbing vines add to the charming verdancy. A man passing through the streets and observing the houses, sees all the windows tightly shut. The stranger may think that they are not inhabited, but on inquiring about this custom of closing the windows, he is politely informed that as the owner is Mohammedan, the blinds are drawn, so that no foreign eyes may gaze upon the dark beauties of the women.[9]

'Abdu'l-Bahá wanted to have Mírzá Abu'l-Faḍl close to Him so He rented the upper floor of a nearby house for the tireless believer. Isabel Fraser was at Mírzá Abu'l-Faḍl's home one day when:

> . . . there were about twenty sheiks who had come over from Alexandria to visit him. One who seemed to be the leader was a very learned and gorgeously attired young sheik, who said with some pride that he had been educated in the oldest university in the world. He was the editor of a magazine in Alexandria and had come to interview Mirza Abul-Fazl, who for more than an hour had been

listened to with absorbed attention. His talk was interspersed with
an occasional jest and his sharp eye would glance from one face to
another to see if his point was understood . . .

Suddenly Abdul-Baha appeared. Mirza Abul-Fazl . . . stood
with his head bowed, his whole attitude changed. He immediately
became the most humble and respectful of servitors. Then quickly
arranging a chair for Abdul-Baha, he told him . . . the subject under
discussion. Abdul-Baha continued the subject . . . [10]

'Abdu'l-Bahá related another story about Mírzá Abu'l-Faḍl. Apparently Mírzá Abu'l-Faḍl had difficulties with all the questions from American and English women and their persistence in wanting answers. One day a group of women went to Mírzá Abu'l-Faḍl's home and knocked on the door, but there was no answer. Undeterred, they continued to knock until a voice, obvious Mírzá Abu'l-Faḍl's, spoke in English from the other side of the closed door: *"Abu'l-Faḍl not here."* This convulsed the women with laughter so much so that the hidden object of their desire was also heard laughing from the inside.[11]

'Abdu'l-Bahá used the time in Ramleh to start catching up on the huge amount of correspondence He had been unable to answer. In a Tablet to the Persian believers, He wrote of His travels:

After my return from America and Europe, owing to the difficulties of the long voyage and to the innumerable inconveniences of the journey, a physical reaction set in and I became indisposed. Now, through the Favor and Bounty of the Blessed Perfection, I am feeling better; therefore, I am engaged in writing this letter, so that thou mayest realize that the friends of God are never forgotten under any circumstances . . . Now is the time when the believers of God may imitate the conduct and manner of Abdul Baha. Day and night they must engage in teaching the Cause of God but they must be in the same spiritual state which Abdul Baha manifested while traveling in America. When the teacher delivers an address, his words must first of all have a supreme and powerful effect over himself so that everyone may be in turn affected. His utterances must be like unto flames of fire, burning away the veils of dogmas, passion and desire. Moreover he must be in the utmost state of humility and evanescence – so that others may become mindful. He must have attained to the station of renunciation and annihilation. Then and not until then, will he teach the people with the Melody of the Supreme Concourse.

I have tarried in Egypt for a few days because I was weakened by the fatigue of traveling through the cities of Europe; by the variable climates of the American mountains and prairies and by the length and hardships of the voyage. While in Europe one day we were in London and another in Edinburgh; now in Paris and anon in Stuttgart; once in Budapest and again in Vienna. We were almost every hour in another place, delivering lengthy speeches and addresses, and notwithstanding the indisposition of the body, day and night I cried and raised my voice in large meetings and important churches . . . As there were many obstacles, the door of correspondence was closed; but the faces of the illumined friends were manifest at every hour in the Court of Consciousness, and at all times they were present in my memory. As I have now found a little leisure, I address you this letter so that I may occupy myself with the servitude of the believers of God, and become the means of the happiness of the hearts. This is the utmost desire of 'Abdu'l-Bahá.[12]

On 30 July two mullás came to visit. One tried to begin a hair-splitting religious controversy, something they apparently enjoyed, but 'Abdu'l-Bahá quickly silenced His visitors by saying that they should abandon such useless theological discussions because they produce no result. They should, instead, free themselves from any prejudices and search for the Truth. The Master spoke of His talk at Oxford University and His meeting of Alexander Graham Bell in Washington. 'Abdu'l-Bahá concluded by saying that He was only there to rest from His long journey. The greatly humbled mullás begged His forgiveness and said that they had learned a valuable lesson.[13]

Emogene Hoagg was another American Bahá'í who wanted to see 'Abdu'l-Bahá again. When she learned that the Master was in Egypt, she wrote for permission to visit. When the confirmation arrived, she was confined to bed with a severe illness, but left immediately. She was still weak when she arrived in Ramleh, so she asked 'Abdu'l-Bahá for a remedy. He sent her two baked apples, with instructions to eat them at once. She ate them seeds and all then went to bed and slept soundly. The next morning she was quite well.[14]

Lua Getsinger arrived at Port Said on 23 July and was followed shortly by her husband, Edward. 'Abdu'l-Bahá had asked Lua to go to India and said a man should go with her. She asked if her husband, Edward, could go with her. 'Abdu'l-Bahá's words to Lua on 19 August, writes Velda Metelmann, 'can be accepted as a goal for all those who would serve their Lord':

> Thou must be firm and unshakable in thy purpose, and never, never let any outward circumstances worry thee . . . Thou must enter that country with a never-failing spirituality, a radiant faith, an eternal enthusiasm, an inextinguishable fire, a solid conviction . . . let not thou heart be troubled. If thou goest away with this unchanging condition of invariability of inner state, thou shalt see the doors of confirmation open before thy face . . .
>
> . . . Look at Me! Thou dost not know a thousandth part of the difficulties and seemingly unsurmountable passes that rise daily before my eyes. I do not heed them; I am walking in my chosen highway; I know the destination. Hundreds of storms and tempests may rage furiously around my head; hundreds of *Titanics* may sink to the bottom of the sea, the mad waves may rise to the roof of heaven; all these will not change my purpose, will not disturb me in the least; I will not look either to the right or to the left. I am looking ahead, far, far. Peering through the impenetrable darkness of the night, the howling winds, the raging storms, I see the glorious Light beckoning me forward, forward. [15]

On 13 November Edward wrote to Joseph Hannen in America saying, 'Beware of the Ezeles [Azalís] and NyC had several cablegrams and tablets from 'Abdu'l-Bahá concerning these. He said "I tell them to beware and then they go right and receive them with open arms. They dont do what I tell them to do."'[16]

Other westerners also arrived, including Mrs Stannard from England, and Dr Joseph de Bons, a Swiss dental surgeon who lived in Cairo, and his wife Edith, who had been the first to accept the Faith from May Maxwell in Paris. The brother of the Khedive of Egypt, 'Abbás Ḥilmí Páshá, and the Khedive's chamberlain, Uthmán Páshá, who was devoted to 'Abdu'l-Bahá, also paid the Master visits. The stream continued with deputies from the Turkish Parliament and some of the teachers and students from the Syrian Protestant College (later the American University of Beirut).¹⁷

On 1 August Shoghi Effendi arrived with 'Abdu'l-Bahá's sister, the Greatest Holy Leaf, Bahíyyih Khánum. Their arrival would have lifted 'Abdu'l-Bahá's spirits immensely. Bahíyyih Khánum's feelings were described by Shoghi Effendi:

> She was astounded at the vitality of which He had, despite His unimaginable sufferings, proved Himself capable. She was lost in admiration at the magnitude of the forces which His utterances had released. She was filled with thankfulness to Bahá'u'lláh for having enabled her to witness the evidences of such brilliant victory for His Cause no less than for His Son.¹⁸

The Greatest Holy Leaf spent several weeks in Egypt with 'Abdu'l-Bahá.

Two days after Shoghi Effendi's arrival, Ahmad Sohrab arrived at 'Abdu'l-Bahá's house. As they waited for the Master, he heard Shoghi Effendi chanting 'with pathos and sweetness'. When the prayer was finished, Ahmad heard the Master 'teaching Shoghi Effendi how to chant and how to control his voice under various expressions'.¹⁹

Shoghi Effendi told a story about one event that happened when he was with his Grandfather. Shoghi Effendi, 'Abdu'l-Bahá and a Pasha had rented a carriage to go from Alexandria to Ramleh. When they arrived, the Master asked the driver how much He owed. The driver, a very big man, demanded an exorbitant fee, which 'Abdu'l-Bahá simply refused to pay. The burly man became extremely abusive to the point of grabbing the sash around 'Abdu'l-Bahá's waist and yanking Him back and forth. This was very upsetting and embarrassing to both Shoghi Effendi and the Pasha, but it didn't seem to bother the Master at all. When the bully finally released Him, 'Abdu'l-Bahá paid Him exactly what He owed, telling the bemused driver that his actions had cost him his tip.²⁰

'Abdu'l-Bahá's health slowly improved over the summer, but reversed in the autumn, in part due to the activities of two of His recent travelling companions. Tamaddunu'l-Mulk, who had been with the Master in London and Paris, was attempting to split the Bahá'ís in Tehran while Amin Fareed was defying His orders. By the middle of the next year, Fareed was in open defiance of 'Abdu'l-Bahá and was travelling through Europe trying to raise money for himself using the name of the Faith. He arranged one such meeting in London which was prevented by the efforts of Lotfullah Hakim. Mason Remey and George Latimer also toured Europe to counter Fareed's activities. Fareed's appetite for money, which began in America with his efforts to pry money from Phoebe Hearst and Agnes Parsons, led to his expulsion from the Faith.[21]

Slowly, 'Abdu'l-Bahá's health continued to improve. At about 6 o'clock one morning, He went to the house where His secretaries stayed. Even though He had already done considerable work, He arrived to find every one of them still quite asleep.[22]

On the afternoon of 29 October, 'Abdul-Bahá went for a walk. When He reached the telegraph office at the Bacos station, He went in to visit with the chief operator, something He did on occasion. Ahmad Sohrab wrote:

> How wonderful it seems to me, his power of adaptability to all people . . . how he enjoys the free and unimpeded association of men! Here was Abdul-Baha sitting in a small telegraph office of Ramleh, talking heartily in Arabic with an operator and how he listened to him. First he spoke about the brother of the Khedive, and how he met him in America and France, praising his progressive ideas and intelligence. Then he said:
> 
> 'When I was in America I was most busy. Often I addressed three meetings a day, and gave innumerable interviews from early morning till midnight. In Europe I spread certain divine teachings which will insure security to the human world, and taught them that the foundation of the religions of God is one and the same. Now I have returned to Egypt in order to rest from the effects of this arduous journey; but while I am here correspondence is uninterrupted with all parts of the West . . . I have done this, not because I expected the praise of men. Far from it! How foolish are some people who may think that we have accepted all these hardships and undergone forty years of imprisonment by Sultan Abdul Hamid, in order to receive the commendations of men! How thoughtless they are! Neither their adulation or blame shall reach me. I have done my work! I have sown my seeds, and leave it to the power of God to cause their growth! You wait a few years longer and you will then hear the notes of this melodious music!'[23]

Rúhá Aṣdaq was a young Persian pilgrim who went on pilgrimage with her father, Hand of the Cause Ibn-i-Aṣdaq, late in 1913. Her father was required to go to Alexandria and Bahíyyih Khánum requested that he ask 'Abdu'l-Bahá to return sooner 'to allay the anxious hearts of the pilgrims and the members of the Holy Household'. In response to this plea, 'Abdu'l-Bahá smiled and said, 'How clever her ruse.' When Ibn-i-Aṣdaq returned, he announced the joyful news that 'Abdu'l-Bahá would soon return home. The Holy Family and Bahá'ís in Haifa immediately began preparing for the long-awaited return of the Master. 'Abdu'l-Bahá's favourite foods were prepared, clothes sewn and everything organized.[24]

## Haifa

At last, on 2 December, 'Abdu'l-Bahá boarded a ship headed for Haifa. The ship stopped briefly in Port Said and Jaffa, near Tel Aviv, where He met the Bahá'ís. On the afternoon of 5 December He arrived in Haifa.

Though His ship entered Haifa's harbour at 2 p.m., 'Abdu'l-Bahá did not debark until dusk. Emogene Hoagg described His arrival:

> Abdul-Baha did not come ashore until dusk, although the steamship entered the harbour at 2 o'clock p.m. (Strange to say, as the steamer bearing the Lord of mankind entered port, two warships – one French, the other German – came in also. The Messenger of Peace was accompanied by ships of war! Quite a strange coincidence.) While waiting for Abdu'l-Baha, the holy ladies, the eleven Persian pilgrims, as many children, four American pilgrims, and many other Bahais – about forty in all – chanted prayers and Tablets, while the faces beamed with the happiness of expectation.[25]

Rúhá Aṣdaq remembered that the main hall of the house was prepared and all of the pilgrims and members of the household had gathered there. When 'Abdu'l-Bahá descended from His carriage, the Greatest Holy Leaf and His daughters all ran forward to embrace and greet Him.[26] Emogene Hoagg described the homecoming:

> The home coming of Abdul-Baha, after an absence of three years and four months, was a real festival. Such excitement and happiness

as reigned in the holy household can only be imagined . . . In Abdul-Baha's house, there is a very large central room around which are the other rooms, and in it Persian rugs were spread and tables placed upon which were fruits and sweets . . .

When Abdul-Baha's voice was heard as he entered, the moment was intense – and as he passed through to his room, all heads were bowed. In a few moments he returned to welcome all. He sat in a chair at one end of the room, and most of the believers sat on the floor. 'Abdu'l-Bahá was tired so remained but a short time, and after a prayer chanted by his daughter Zia Khanum, went to his room.

Then the ladies vacated so that the men might enter. To see the faces of those sturdy, earnest men – faces that spoke the fervor of their faith, the earnestness and resoluteness of their purpose – was something to remember. I am sure not an eye was dry; old and young, with happiness filling their hearts, could not refrain from exhibiting their emotion. He welcomed them, and seating himself on the floor, spoke to them a short time, after which he retired . . . [27]

After an absence of three years and three months, 'Abdu'l-Bahá was finally home. The day after His arrival, 'Abdu'l-Bahá ascended Mt. Carmel and went to the Shrine of the Báb. And the following day, the Centre of the Covenant went to 'Akká for eight days to commune with His Father and the Source of His Spiritual Being.

Shoghi Effendi wrote:

A most significant scene in a century-old drama had been enacted. A glorious chapter in the history of the first Bahá'í century had been written. Seeds of undreamt-of potentialities had, with the hand of the Centre of the Covenant Himself, been sown in some of the fertile fields of the Western world. Never in the entire range of religious history had any Figure of comparable stature arisen to perform a labour of such magnitude and imperishable worth. Forces were unleashed through those fateful journeys which even now . . . we are unable to measure or comprehend . . .

'Abdu'l-Bahá's historic journeys to the West, and in particular His eight-month tour of the United States of America, may be said to have marked the culmination of His ministry, a ministry whose untold blessings and stupendous achievements only future generations can adequately estimate. As the day-star of Bahá'u'lláh's Revelation had shone forth in its meridian splendour at the hour of the proclamation of His Message to the rulers of the earth in the city of Adrianople, so did the Orb of His Covenant mount its zenith and shed its brightest rays when He Who was its appointed Centre arose to blazon the glory and greatness of His Father's Faith among the peoples of the West.[28]

# BIBLIOGRAPHY

'Abdu'l-Bahá. *'Abdu'l-Bahá in London* (1912, 1921). London: Bahá'í Publishing Trust, 1982.
— *The Promulgation of Universal Peace: Talks Delivered by 'Abdu'l-Baha During His Visit to the United States and Canada in 1912* (1922, 1925). Comp. H. MacNutt. Wilmette, IL: Bahá'í Publishing Trust, 2nd ed. 1982.
— *Tablets of the Divine Plan.* Wilmette, IL: Bahá'í Publishing Trust, 1993.

Afroukhteh, Youness. *Memories of Nine Years in 'Akká.* Trans. Riaz Masrour. Oxford: George Ronald, 2003.

Ahdieh, Hussein, and Eliane A. Hopson. *'Abdu'l-Bahá in New York: The City of the Covenant.* New York: Spiritual Assembly of the Bahá'ís of New York, 1987.

Aṣdaq, Rúḥá. *One Life, One Memory.* Oxford: George Ronald, 1999.

Atkinson, Anne Gordon et al. *Green Acre on the Piscataqua.* Eliot, Maine: Green Acre Bahá'í School Council, 1991.

Bagdadi, Zia. 'Abdul Baha in America: From the account of 'Abdul Baha's daily activities and words while in America, furnished us by Dr. Zia Bagdadi . . .', in *Star of the West*, vol. 19, no. 3 (June 1928); no. 5 (August 1928); no. 6 (September 1928); no. 11 (February 1929).

Bahá'í Community of Austria. *'Abdu'l-Bahá in Budapest.* 1988.

*Bahá'í News.* National Spiritual Assembly of the United States and Canada, 1924–1937.

*The Bahá'í World: An International Record.* Vol. II (1926–1928), vol. III (1928–1930), vol. IV (1930–1932), vol. VI (1934–1936), vol. VII (1936–1938), vol. VIII (1938–1940), vol. IX (1940–1944), vol. XI (1946–1950), vol. XII (1950–1954), RP Wilmette, IL: Bahá'í Publishing Trust, 1980–81; vol. XIII (1954–1963), vol. XIV (1963–1968), vol. XVIII (1979–1983), vol. XX (1986–1992), Haifa: Bahá'í World Centre, 1976–1996.

*Baḥíyyih Khánum: The Greatest Holy Leaf.* Comp. Research Department of the Bahá'í World Centre. Haifa: Bahá'í World Centre, 1982.

Baker, Dorothy. *The Path to God.* New York: Bahá'í Publishing Committee, 1937.

Balyuzi, H. M. *'Abdu'l-Bahá: The Centre of the Covenant of Bahá'u'lláh.* Oxford: George Ronald, 1971.
— *Edward Granville Browne and the Bahá'í Faith.* Oxford: George Ronald, 1970.

Blomfield, Lady (Sara Louisa). *The Chosen Highway*. London: Bahá'í Publishing Trust, 1940. RP Oxford: George Ronald, 2007.

Brown, Ramona Allen. *Memories of 'Abdu'l-Bahá*. Wilmette, IL: Bahá'í Publishing Trust, 1980.

Caton, Peggy. 'The Sacramento Bahá'í Community, 1912–1987', in Hollinger (ed.), *Community Histories*, pp. 241–280.

Chapman, Anita Ioas. *Leroy Ioas: Hand of the Caus of God*. Oxford: George Ronald. 1998.

Clark, Deb. 'The Bahá'ís of Baltimore, 1898–1990', in Hollinger (ed.), *Community Histories*, pp. 111–152.

Cline, Harriet M. Pilgrim Notes. USBNA, Edwin Mattoon Papers, Box 3.

Cobb, Stanwood. *Memories of 'Abdu'l-Bahá*. Avalon Press, 1962.

Dahl, Roger. 'A History of the Kenosha Bahá'í Community, 1897–1980', in Hollinger (ed.), *Community Histories*, pp. 1–66.

Dodge, Wendell Phillips. 'Abdul-Baha's Arrival in America', in *Star of the West*, vol. III, no. 3 (28 April 1912), pp. 3–5.

Dreyfus-Barney, Laura. 'Hippolyte Dreyfus-Barney', article intended for *The Bahá'í World*, ed. Thomas Linard from the Laura Dreyfus-Barney Papers, Centre National Bahá'í, Paris. Available at: http://bahai-library.com/essays/barney.html.

Ford, Mary Hanford. 'The Economic Teaching of Abdul-Baha', in *Star of the West*, vol. VIII, no. 1 (21 March 1917), pp. 3–7, 11–16.

Freeman, Dorothy. *From Copper to Gold: The Life of Dorothy Baker*. Researched by Louise B. Mathias. Oxford: George Ronald, 1984.

Gail, Marzieh. "Abdu'l-Bahá: Portrayals from East and West', in *World Order*, vol. 6, no. 1 (1971), pp. 29–41. Available at: http://bahai-library.com/gail_abdul-baha_portrayals.
— *Arches of the Years*. Oxford: George Ronald, 1991.
— *Dawn Over Mount Hira*. Oxford: George Ronald, 1976.
— 'Juliet Thompson Remembers Kahlil Gibran', in *World Order*, vol. 12, no. 4 (1978), pp. 29–31
— *Summon Up Remembrance*. Oxford: George Ronald, 1987.

Garis, M. R. *Martha Root: To Move the World*. Wilmette, IL: Bahá'í Publishing Trust, 1983.

Gollmer, Werner. *Mein Herz ist bei euch: 'Abdu'l-Bahá in Deutschland*. Hofheim-Langenhain: Bahá'í-Verlag, 1988.

Graham, Edwin. 'Joan Waring and Thomas Fforde', in McNamara (comp.), *Connections*, pp. 57–69.

Gregory, Louis. *A Heavenly Vista, The Pilgrimage of Louis Gregory*. Available at:

http://bahai-library.com/gregory_heavenly_vista, 1997.

— 'Impressions of Abdul-Baha while at Ramleh', in *Star of the West*, vol. II, no. 10 (8 September 1911), pp. 5–6.

Haney, Mariam. Pilgrim Notes, 1912. USBNA, Agnes Parsons Papers, Box 20.

Hannen, Joseph H. Abdul-Baha in Washington, D.C.', in *Star of the West*, vol. III, no. 3 (28 April 1912), pp. 6–24.

Harper, Barron, *Lights of Fortitude*. Oxford: George Ronald, rev. ed. 2007.

Hatch, Willard P. "Abdu'l-Bahá and the Rabbi', in *The Bahá'í World*, vol. III (1928–1930), pp. 361–2.

Hoagg, Emogene. Pilgrim Notes. USBNA, Emogene Hoagg Papers, Box 7.

Hogenson, Kathryn Jewett. *Lighting the Western Sky: The Hearst Pilgrimage and the Establishment of the Bahá'í Faith in the West*. Oxford: George Ronald, 2010.

Holley, H. H. *Religion for Mankind*. Oxford: George Ronald, 1956, 1963.

Hollinger, Richard (ed.). *Community Histories*. Studies in the Bábí and Bahá'í Religions. Vol. 6. Los Angeles, CA: Kalimát Press, 1992.

Honnold, Annamarie (comp. and ed.). *Vignettes from the Life of 'Abdu'l-Bahá*. Oxford: George Ronald, 1982.

Hutchison, Sandra. 'Foreword', in Parsons, *'Abdu'l-Bahá in America : Agnes Parsons' Diary*, pp. vii–xviii.

Ioas, Sylvia. Interview of Sachiro Fujita, 1965. Available at: http://bci.org/pilgrim/fugita.htm.

Ives, Howard Colby. *Portals to Freedom* (1937). Oxford: George Ronald, 1943, 1974.

Jaxon, Honore J. 'A Stroll with Abdul-Baha', in *Star of the West*, vol. III, no. 4 (17 May 1912), pp. 27–29.

— 'Dedication of the Mashrak-el-Azkar Site', in *Star of the West*, vol. III, no 4. (17 May 1912), pp. 5–7.

Johnson, Charles. 'A Ray from the East', in *Harper's Weekly*, no. 59 (20 July 1912).

Khan, Ali-Kuli, and Marzieh Gail. 'Mírzá Abu'l-Faḍl in America', in *The Bahá'í World*, vol. IX (1940–1944), pp. 855–60.

Khursheed, Anjam. *The Seven Candles of Unity: The Story of 'Abdu'l-Bahá in Edinburgh*. London: Bahá'í Publishing Trust, 1991.

Knobloch, Alma S. 'The Call to Germany', in *The Bahá'í World*, vol. VII (1936–1938), pp. 732–45.

Lacroix-Hopson, Elaine. *'Abdu'l-Bahá in New York*. New York: New VistaDesign, 1999.

Latimer, George. *The Light of the World*. Boston, MA: George Orr Latimer, 1920. Available at: http://bahai-library.com/latimer_light_world.

— Pilgrim Notes, 1912. USBNA, Albert Windust Papers. Box 31.

Ma'ani, Baharieh Rouhani. *Leaves of the Twin Divine Trees*. Oxford: George Ronald, 2008.

McNamara, Brendan (comp.). *Connections: Essays and Notes on Early Links Between the Bahá'í Faith and Ireland*. Cork, Ireland: Tusker Keyes Publications, 2007.

Metelmann, Velda Piff. *Lua Getsinger: Herald of the Covenant*. Oxford: George Ronald, 1997.

Morrison, Gayle. *To Move the World: Louis G. Gregory and the Advancement of Racial Unity in America*. Wilmette, IL: Bahá'í Publishing Trust, 1982.

Mortensen, Fred. 'When a Soul Meets the Master', in *Star of the West*, vol. 14, no. 12 (March 1924), pp. 365–7.

Nakhjavani, Violette. *The Maxwells of Montreal*. Oxford: George Ronald, 2011.
— A Tribute to Amatu'l-Bahá Rúḥíyyih Khánum. Toronto: Bahá'í Canada Publications, 2000.

National Spiritual Assembly of the Bahá'ís of Canada. *'Abdu'l-Bahá in Canada*. Toronto: Bahá'í Canada Publications, 1962.

Newhall, Muriel Ives Barrow. *Stories of 'Abdu'l-Bahá as Told by Mother, 1970*. Available at: http://bahai-library.com/ives_mothers_stories_abdulbaha.

Ober, Harlan F. 'Louis G. Gregory', In Memoriam, in *The Bahá'í World*, Vol. XII (1950–1954), pp. 666–70.

Parsons, Agnes. *'Abdu'l-Bahá in America : Agnes Parsons' Diary*. Ed. Richard Hollinger. Los Angeles, CA: Kalimát Press, 1996.
— 'A Few Incidents in Abdul Baha's Washington and Dublin Visits'. USBNA, Agnes Parsons Papers, Box 20.
— Pilgrim Notes, 1912. USBNA, Emogene Hoagg Papers, Box 7.

Paulson, Feny E. Pilgrim Notes. USBNA, cited in Ward, *239 Days*, pp. 259–263.

Penoyer, Justin. *A Masters Thesis on the Life of Fred Mortensen*. Available at: http://www.fredMortensen.org/academic studies.

Perkins, Mary. *Servant of the Glory: The Life of 'Abdu'l-Bahá*. Oxford: George Ronald, 1999.

Pinchon, Florence E. 'On the Borders of Lake Leman', in *The Bahá'í World*, vol. II (1926–1928), pp. 271–3.

Rabbani, Ahang. "Abdu'l-Bahá Meeting with Two Prominent Iranians', in *World Order*, vol. 30, no. 1 (Fall 1998), pp. 35-46. Available at: http://bahai-library.com/articles/qazvini.html.

Rabbani, Rúḥíyyih. *The Priceless Pearl*. London: Bahá'í Publishing Trust, 1969.

Randall-Winckler, Bahíyyih, and M. R. Garis. *William Henry Randall*. Oneworld Publications, Oxford, 1996.

Revell, Ethel and Jessie. Revell Sisters Pilgrim Notes, 1912. USBNA, Jessie/Ethel Revell Papers, Box 7.

Root, Martha. ' 'Abdu'l-Bahá's Visit to Budapest', in *Star of the West*, vol. 24, no. 3 (June 1933), pp. 84–89.

Ruhe-Shoen, Janet. *A Love Which Does Not Wait*. Riviera Beach, FL: Palabra Publications, 1998.

Rutstein, Nathan. *Corinne True: Faithful Handmaid of 'Abdu'l-Bahá*. Oxford: George Ronald, 1987.

Sears, Marguerite. *Bill*. Eloy, AZ: Desert Rose Publishing, 2003.

Sears, William, and Robert Quigley. *The Flame*. Oxford: George Ronald, 1972.

Shoghi Effendi. *Bahá'í Administration* (1928). Wilmette. IL: Bahá'í Publishing Trust, 1968.

— *God Passes By* (1944). Wilmette. IL: Bahá'í Publishing Trust, 1994.

— *The World Order of Bahá'u'lláh* (1938). Wilmette. IL: Bahá'í Publishing Trust, 1991.

Smith, Peter (ed.). *Bahá'ís in the West*. Studies in the Bábi and Bahá'í Religions. Vol. 14. Los Angeles: Kalimát Press, 2004.

Sohrab, Ahmad. *'Abdu'l-Bahá in Edinburgh*. Ed. David Merrick, 2008. Available at: http://bci.org/edinburgh/history/SohrabDiary.pdf.

— *'Abdu'l-Bahá in Egypt*. New York: New History Foundation, 1929. Available at: http://bahai-library.com/sohrab_abdulbaha_egyp, 1929.

*Star of the West: The Bahai Magazine*. Periodical, 25 vols. 1910–1935. Vols. 1–14 RP Oxford: George Ronald, 1978. Complete CD-ROM version: Talisman Educational Software/Special Ideas, 2001.

Stockman, Robert H. *The Bahá'í Faith in America: Early Expansion, 1900–1912*. Vol. 2. Oxford: George Ronald, 1995.

Thompson, Juliet. *'Abdu'l-Bahá, The Center of the Covenant*. Wilmette, IL: Bahá'í Publishing Committee, 1948.

— *The Diary of Juliet Thompson*. Los Angeles, CA: Kalimát Press, 1995.

Towfigh, Nicola. *Die ersten Früchte des Jahres sind die köstlichen: Die Anfänge des Bahá'í-Glaubens in Stuttgart*. Available at: http://www.bahai-studien-de.

Townshend, George. *'Abdu'l-Bahá, The Master*. Oxford: George Ronald, 1987.

Tudor Pole, Wellesley. *Writing on the Ground*. London: Neville Spearman, 1968.

Tussing, Phillip E. *Finishing the Work: 'Abdu'l-Bahá in Dublin*. Available at: http://bahai-library.com/tussing_abdul-baha_dublin.

Van den Hoonaard, Will C. *The Origins of the Bahá'í Community of Canada, 1898–1948*. Waterloo, Ontario: Wilfrid Laurier University Press, 1996.

Ward, Allan L. *239 Days: 'Abdu'l-Bahá's Journey in America*. Wilmette. IL: Bahá'í Publishing Trust, 1979.

Weinberg, Robert. *Ethel Jenner Rosenberg: England's Outstanding Bahá'í Pioneer Worker*. Oxford: George Ronald, 1995.

Whitehead, O. Z. *Some Bahá'ís to Remember*. Oxford: George Ronald, 1983.
— *Some Early Bahá'ís of the West*. Oxford: George Ronald, 1976.
— *Portraits of Some Bahá'í Women*. Oxford: George Ronald, 1996.

Whitmore, Bruce W. *The Dawning Place*. Wilmette. IL: Bahá'í Publishing Trust, 1984.

Whyte, Jane (Mrs Alexander Whyte). 'A Visit to 'Akká', in *The Bahá'í World*, vol. IV (1930–1932), pp. 396–8.

Wise, Harriet. Pilgrim Notes, 1912. USBNA, Edwin Mattoon Papers, Box 3; Jessie/Ethel Revell Papers, Box 7.

Yazdi, Ali M. *Blessings Beyond Measure: Recollections of 'Abdu'l-Bahá and Shoghi Effendi*. Wilmette, IL: Bahá'í Publishing Trust, 1988.
— 'Memories of 'Abdu'l-Bahá', in *The Bahá'í World*, vol. XVIII (1979–1983), pp. 907–11.
— 'Memories of Shoghi Effendi', in *The Bahá'í World*, vol. XIX (1983–1986), pp. 756–9.

Yazdi, Mohammed. 'Abdul-Baha in Egypt: A Call to the American Bahais', in *Bahai News (Star of the West)*, vol. I, no. 17 (19 January 1911), pp. 4–7.

Zarqání, Mírzá Maḥmúd. *Maḥmúd's Diary: The Dairy of Mírzá Maḥmúd-i-Zarqání Chronicling 'Abdu'l-Bahá's Journey to America*. Translated by Mohi Sobhani with the assistance of Shirley Macias. Oxford: George Ronald, 1998.

Zinky, Kay (comp.), and A. Baram (ed.). *Martha Root, Herald of the Kingdom*. New Delhi: Bahá'í Publishing Trust, 1983.

## Archival Collections

Centre National Bahá'í, Paris
    Laura Dreyfus-Barney Papers

United Kingdom Bahá'í National Archives
    *The Christian Commonwealth* (various issues)
    *The Clifton Chronicle and Directory* (22 January 1913)
    *The International Psychic Gazette* (January 1913)

United States Bahá'í National Archives (USBNA)
    Emogene Hoagg Papers
    Edwin Mattoon Papers
    Agnes Parsons Papers
    Jessie/Ethel Revell Papers
    Albert Windust Papers

# REFERENCES

### Preface
1. Rev. T. K. Cheyne, in *The Bahá'í World*, vol. X (1944–1946), p. 483.
2. Metelmann, *Lua Getsinger*, pp. 198–9.
3. Shoghi Effendi, *The World Order of Bahá'u'lláh*, p. 5.

### 1 Who is 'Abdu'l-Bahá?
1. Shoghi Effendi, *The World Order of Bahá'u'lláh*, p. 85.
2. ibid. pp. 133–4.

### 2 'Abdu'l-Bahá Travels to the West
1. Shoghi Effendi, *God Passes By*, p. 280.
2. Lacroix Hopson, *'Abdu'l-Bahá in New York*, p. 36.
3. Khan and Gail, 'Mírzá Abu'l-Faḍl in America', in *The Bahá'í World*, vol. IX (1940–1944), p. 856.
4. Thompson, *Diary*, p. 82.
5. *Star of the West*, vol. II, no. 4 (17 May 1911), pp. 6–7.
6. ibid. vol. II, no. 5 (5 June 1911), p. 13.
7. Sydney Sprague, letter to Isabella Brittingham, 29 August 1910, in *Bahai News*, 16 October 1910; quoted in Balyuzi, *'Abdu'l-Bahá*, p. 134; and in Ward, *239 Days*, pp. 7–8.
8. Quoted in Balyuzi, *'Abdu'l-Bahá*, pp. 134–5.
9. *Bahíyyih Khánum: The Greatest Holy Leaf*, no. 11, p. 13; also quoted in Ma'ani, *Leaves of the Twin Divine Trees*, pp. 171–2.

### 3 A Delay in Eygpt
1. Balyuzi, *'Abdu'l-Bahá*, pp. 135–6.
2. Quoted in Ma'ani, *Leaves of the Twin Divine Trees*, pp. 343–4.
3. Quoted in Balyuzi, *'Abdu'l-Bahá*. p. 135.
4. A. Yazdi, *Blessings Beyond Measure*, pp. 14–19; an earlier version, 'Memories of 'Abdu'l-Bahá', is in *The Bahá'í World*, vol. XVIII (1979–1983), pp. 908–9.
5. Tudor-Pole, *Writing on the Ground*, p. 142.
6. *Bahai News*, 7 February 1911, quoted in Balyuzi, *'Abdu'l-Bahá*, p. 138.
7. A. Yazdi, *Blessings Beyond Measure*, p. 52.
8. Tudor-Pole, *Writing on the Ground*, pp. 148–150.
9. *Star of the West*, vol. 15, no. 4 (July 1924), p. 108.
10. ibid. vol. II, no. 3 (28 April 1911), p. 5.
11. Balyuzi, *'Abdu'l-Bahá*, p. 137.
12. Gregory, *A Heavenly Vista*, pp. 4–5.
13. Gregory, 'Impressions of Abdul-Bahá while at Ramleh', in *Star of the West*, vol. II, no. 10 (8 September 1911), pp. 5–6.

14  ibid. p. 5.
15  *Star of the West*, vol. II, no. 5 (5 June 1911), pp. 7.
16  Gregory, *A Heavenly Vista*, p. 9.
17  ibid.
18  ibid. pp. 7, 9.
19  Mohammed Yazdi, 'Abdul-Baha in Egypt: A Call to the American Bahais', in *Bahai News (Star of the West)*, vol. 1, no. 17 (19 January 1911), pp. 4–7.

## 4 Arrival in the West

1  Ma'ani, *Leaves of the Twin Divine Trees*, p. 344.
2  Thompson, *Diary*, p. 152.
3  ibid. p. 157.
4  ibid. p. 159.
5  See Shoghi Effendi's appreciation in *The Bahá'í World*, vol. III, p. 210.
6  Thompson, *Diary*, pp. 167–8.
7  ibid. pp. 172–3.
8  ibid. pp. 174–5.
9  ibid. p. 176.
10  ibid. pp. 177–8.
11  ibid. pp. 181–2.
12  ibid. p. 184.
13  ibid. p. 186.
14  ibid. p. 190.
15  *Star of the West*, vol. II, no. 18 (7 February 1912), p. 2.
16  Holley, *Religion for Mankind*, pp. 234–5, 236.
17  Harper, *Lights of Fortitude*, pp. 253–63.
18  Dreyfus-Barney, 'Hippolyte Dreyfus-Barney'.
19  Pinchon, 'On the Borders of Lake Leman', in *The Bahá'í World*, vol. II (1926–1928), p. 271.
20  Blomfield, *The Chosen Highway*, p. 149.
21  Weinberg, *Ethel Jenner Rosenberg*, p. 88.
22  ibid. pp. 47, 73, 96, 129, 135, 142, 211.
23  ibid. p. 259.
24  Blomfield, *The Chosen Highway*, pp. 149–50.
25  ibid. p. 150.
26  *Star of the West*, vol. II, no 11 (27 September 1911), p. 3.
27  ibid. vol. II, no. 12 (16 October 1911), pp. 3–5.
28  *'Abdu'l-Bahá in London*, p. 102.
29  ibid. pp. 56–7.
30  *The Christian Commonwealth*, 13 September 1911, reprinted in *Star of the West*, vol. II, no. 11 (27 September 1911), pp. 6–7.
31  *Star of the West*, vol. II, no. 11 (27 September 1911), p. 3.
32  ibid. pp. 7–8.
33  ibid. p. 4.
34  *'Abdu'l-Bahá in London*, pp. 19–20.
35  ibid. p. 18.
36  Blomfield, *The Chosen Highway*, p. 153.
37  Quoted in Balyuzi, *'Abdu'l-Bahá*, p. 146.
38  Blomfield, *The Chosen Highway*, p. 157.
39  ibid. pp. 162, 161.

40  ibid. p. 159.
41  *Star of the West*, vol. II, no. 12 (16 October 1911), p. 10.
42  ibid. p. 7.
43  *Daily Chronicle*, in United Kingdom Bahá'í Archives.
44  *Star of the West*, vol. II, no. 12 (16 October 1911), p. 7.
45  *'Abdu'l-Bahá in London*, pp. 85–6.
46  ibid. pp. 86–98.
47  ibid. pp. 88–90.
48  ibid. pp. 99–100.
49  Weinberg, *Ethel Jenner Rosenberg*, p. 137.
50  *Star of the West*, vol. II, no. 13 (4 November 1911), p. 4.
51  Blomfield, *The Chosen Highway*, p. 163.
52  Balyuzi, *'Abdu'l-Bahá*, p. 155.
53  *Star of the West*, vol. II, no. 13 (4 November 1911), p. 4.
54  ibid. vol. II, no. 14 (23 November 1911), p. 3.
55  *The Bahá'í World*, vol. VI (1934–1936), p. 654.
56  ibid. p. 655; also in Blomfield, *The Chosen Highway*, p. 181.
57  *Star of the West*, vol. II, no. 14 (23 November 1911), p. 4.
58  ibid. pp. 4–5.
59  Balyuzi, *Edward Granville Browne and the Bahá'í Faith*, Chapter 7.
60  A. Rabbani, *'Abdu'l-Bahá Meeting with Two Prominent Iranians*.
61  *Star of the West*, vol. II, no. 18 (7 February 1912), pp. 6–7, 12.
62  A. Rabbani, *'Abdu'l-Bahá Meeting with Two Prominent Iranians*.
63  ibid.
64  ibid.
65  *Star of the West*, vol. II, no. 16 (31 December 1911), p. 6.
66  ibid. vol. II, no. 14 (23 November 1911), p. 15.
67  ibid.
68  Blomfield, *The Chosen Highway*, p. 180.
69  ibid. pp. 183–4.
70  ibid. p. 185.
71  *Star of the West*, vol. II, no. 16 (31 December 1911), p. 6.

## 5 Egypt and an Atlantic Crossing

1  A. Yazdi, *Blessings Beyond Measure*, pp. 20–22.
2  R. Rabbani, *The Priceless Pearl*, p. 19.
3  A. Yazdi, *Blessings Beyond Measure*, pp. 52–3.
4  R. Rabbani, *The Priceless Pearl*, p. 20.
5  A. Yazdí, *Blessings Beyond Measure*, pp. 53–4.
6  *Star of the West*, vol. IV, no. 12 (16 October 1913), p. 210.
7  Ward, *239 Days*, p. 130.
8  Zarqání, *Mahmúd's Diary*, pp. 22, 24.
9  ibid. p. 27.
10 ibid.
11 ibid. p. 28.
12 ibid. p. 30.
13 ibid. p. 32.
14 ibid. pp. 33–4.

## 6 Greeting the Statue of Liberty

1. Parsons, *Diary*, pp. 3, 162.
2. Dodge, 'Abdu'l-Bahá's Arrival in America', in *Star of the West*, vol. III, no. 3 (28 April 1912), p. 3.
3. ibid.
4. ibid. p. 4.
5. ibid.
6. ibid.
7. Cobb, *Memories of 'Abdu'l-Bahá*, pp. 11–12.
8. Thompson, *Diary*, pp. 232–4.
9. Ward, *239 Days*, pp. 15–19.
10. ibid.
11. ibid. pp. 16–19.
12. ibid. pp. 19–20.
13. ibid. p. 198.
14. Shoghi Effendi, *God Passes By*, pp. 386–7.
15. Information in this section from Garis, *Martha Root*, pp. 41–53.
16. 'Abdu'l-Bahá, *The Promulgation of Universal Peace*, p. 3.
17. Whitehead, *Some Early Bahá'ís of the West*, pp. 45–6.
18. ibid. p. 47.
19. Thompson, *Diary*, p. 234.
20. Whitehead, *Some Early Bahá'ís of the West*, pp. 43, 50, 53.
21. Ives, *Portals to Freedom*, pp. 28–33.
22. ibid. p. 37.
23. ibid. p. 140.
24. Ma'ani, *Leaves of the Twin Divine Trees*, p. 345.
25. Ives, *Portals to Freedom*, pp. 47–9.
26. *Star of the West*, vol. III, no. 8 (1 August 1912), p. 8.
27. ibid. p. 6.
28. ibid. vol. III, no. 7 (13 July 1912), pp. 5, 10.
29. Whitehead, *Portraits*, pp. 150–51.
30. Thompson, *Diary*, pp. 241–2.
31. *Star of the West*, vol. 4, no. 12 (16 October 1913), p. 210.
32. 'Abdu'l-Bahá, *The Promulgation of Universal Peace*, pp. 46–8.
33. Thompson, *Diary*, pp. 247–8.
34. ibid. pp. 244–7.
35. Cobb, *Memories of 'Abdu'l-Bahá*, pp. 12–13.
36. Metelmann, *Lua Getsinger*, pp. 151–2.
37. Ahdieh and Hopson, *'Abdu'l-Bahá in New York*, p. 11.
38. Gail, 'Juliet Thompson Remembers Kahlil Gibran', in *World Order*, vol. 12, no. 4 (Summer 1978), pp. 29–31.
39. Metelmann, *Lua Getsinger*, p. 151.
40. ibid. pp. 1–6.
41. ibid. p. 148.
42. ibid. p. 150.
43. ibid. p. 188.
44. ibid. p. 348; see also Sears and Quigley, *The Flame*, pp. 127–31.
45. Sohrab, *'Abdu'l-Bahá in Egypt*, pp. 67–8.
46. Thompson, *Diary*, p. 252.

47  *Star of the West*, vol. III, no. 10 (8 September 1912), p. 8.
48  Gail, *Arches of the Years*, pp. 106–7.
49  Zarqání, *Maḥmúd's Diary*, p. 182.
50  *Star of the West*, vol. 12, no. 19 (2 March 1922), p. 292; Balyuzi, *'Abdu'l-Bahá*, p. 452.
51  Baker, *The Path to God*, pp. 13–17, quoted in Honnold, *Vignettes*, pp. 131–2.
52  'Abdu'l-Bahá, *The Promulgation of Universal Peace*, pp. 24–5.
53  Gail, *Dawn Over Mount Hira*, pp. 203–4.
54  ibid. pp. 206–7.
55  ibid. pp. 209–10.
56  *The Bahá'í World*, vol XI (1946–1950), p. 492.
57  Quoted in Ward, *239 Days*, pp. 27–35.
58  *The Bahá'í World*, vol. XII (1950–1954), p. 920.
59  Ives, *Portals to Freedom*, pp. 64–5.

## 7 'White and Black Sitting Together'

1  Gail, *Arches of the Years*, p. 79.
2  Parsons, *Diary*, p. 9.
3  Hannen, "Abdu'l-Bahá in Washington, DC", in *Star of the West*, vol. III, no. 3 (28 April 1912), p. 6. Also cited in Parsons, *Diary*, p. 9.
4  Gail, *Arches of the Years*, pp. 79–80.
5  'In Memoriam', *The Bahá'í World*, vol. XIV (1963–1968), pp. 351–2. For more information about the Khans see Gail, *Summon Up Remembrance* and *Arches of the Years*.
6  Stockman, *The Bahá'í Faith in America, 1900–1912* (Vol. 2), p. 137.
7  ibid. pp. 224–6.
8  *The Bahá'í World*, vol. VIII (1938–1940), pp. 661–2.
9  ibid.
10  Zarqání, *Maḥmúd's Diary*, p. 441.
11  Newhall, *Stories of 'Abdu'l-Bahá as Told by Mother*, p. 6.
12  'Abdu'l-Bahá, *The Promulgation of Universal Peace*, pp. 36–7.
13  USBNA, Agnes Parsons Papers, Box 20, folder 35: Agnes Parsons Pilgrim Notes. 'A Few Incidents in Abdul Baha's Washington and Dublin Visits'.
14  Ward, *239 Days*, p. 37.
15  Parsons, *Diary*, pp. 19–21.
16  USBNA, Agnes Parsons Papers, Box 20: Agnes Parsons Pilgrim Notes. 'A Few Incidents . . .', p. 11.
17  Hannen, "Abdu'l-Bahá in Washington, DC", in *Star of the West*, vol. III, no. 3 (28 April 1912), p. 7.
18  'Abdu'l-Bahá, *The Promulgation of Universal Peace*, p. 44.
19  Townshend, *'Abdu'l-Bahá, The Master*, pp. 31–2.
20  Ober, 'Louis G. Gregory, In Memoriam', *The Bahá'í World*, vol. XII (1950–1954), p. 668; cited in Morrison, *To Move the World*, p. 53.
21  Morrison, *To Move the World*, p. 53.
22  Parsons, *Diary*, p. 31.
23  Thompson, *Diary*, pp. 269–70.
24  ibid.
25  ibid. pp. 272–3.
26  Ward, *239 Days*, p. 45.
27  'Abdu'l-Bahá, *The Promulgation of Universal Peace*, pp. 49–50.

28  Honnold, *Vignettes*, p. 95.
29  Hutchison, Foreword to Parsons, *Diary*, pp. xv–xvi.
30  *The Bahá'í World*, Vol. XX (1986–1992), pp. 917–18.
31  Gregory, *A Heavenly Vista*.
32  Morrison, *To Move the World*, p. 64.
33  Letter from Louisa Gregory to Agnes Parsons, 18 January 1921, Agnes Parsons Papers, cited in Morrison, *To Move the World*, pp. 66–7.
34  'Abdu'l-Bahá, Tablet to the Gregorys, translated 14 March 1914, quoted in Morrison, *To Move the World*, p. 72.
35  Zarqání, *Maḥmúd's Diary*, p. 58.
36  Gail, *Arches of the Years*, pp. 83–4.
37  Parsons, *Diary*, pp. 46–7.
38  Gail, *Arches of the Years*, pp. 80–81.
39  USBNA, Agnes Parsons Papers, Box 20: Agnes Parsons Pilgrim Notes. 'A Few Incidents . . .', p. 5.
40  Thompson, *Diary*, pp. 277–9.
41  ibid. p. 281.
42  Gail, *Arches of the Years*, p. 82.
43  *Star of the West*, vol. IX, no. 2 (9 April 1918), p. 24.
44  USBNA, Agnes Parsons Papers, Box 20: Agnes Parsons Pilgrim Notes. 'A Few Incidents . . .', p. 6. See also a slightly different version in Parsons, *Diary*, p. 55.
45  Honnold, *Vignettes*, p. 159, from Thompson, '*Abdu'l-Bahá, The Center of the Covenant*, pp. 21–2; see also a slightly different version in Thompson, *Diary*, p. 280.
46  Ward, *239 Days*, pp. 44–5.
47  USBNA, Agnes Parsons Papers, Box 20: Agnes Parsons Pilgrim Notes. 'A Few Incidents . . .', p. 6. See also a slightly different version in Parsons, *Diary*, p. 55.
48  Zarqání, *Maḥmúd's Diary*, p. 66.

# 8 The Mother Temple of the West

1   Ward, *239 Days*, pp. 49–52.
2   ibid. p. 83.
3   ibid. p. 50.
4   Zarqání, *Maḥmúd's Diary*, p. 70.
5   Chapman, *Leroy Ioas*, pp. 23–4.
6   ibid. p. 22.
7   ibid.
8   ibid. p. 23.
9   Whitmore, *The Dawning Place*, p. 31.
10  Rutstein, *Corinne True*, pp. 69, 71, 81–3, 99–101.
11  'Abdu'l-Bahá, *The Promulgation of Universal Peace*, p. 65.
12  USBNA, Edwin Mattoon Papers, Box 3: Harriet M. Cline Pilgrim Notes, p. 1.
13  Whitmore, *The Dawning Place*, p. 61.
14  Jaxon, 'Dedication of the Mashrak-el-Azkar Site', in *Star of the West*, vol. III, no. 4 (17 May 1912), pp. 5–6.
15  ibid. p. 5.
16  Chapman, *Leroy Ioas*, p. 25.
17  'Abdu'l-Bahá, *The Promulgation of Universal Peace*, p. 71.
18  Ward, *239 Days*, p. 51.
19  Jaxon, 'Dedication of the Mashrak-el-Azkar Site', in *Star of the West*, vol. III, no. 4 (17 May 1912), p. 6.

20 Rutstein, *Corinne True*, p. 102, based on Whitmore, *The Dawning Place*, pp. 61–5.
21 Chapman, *Leroy Ioas*, p. 25.
22 Whitmore, *The Dawning Place*, pp. 46–8.
23 USBNA, Jessie/Ethel Revell Papers, Box 7: Revell Sisters Pilgrim Notes, p. 2.
24 USBNA, Edwin Mattoon Papers, Box 3: Harriet M. Cline Pilgrim Notes, p. 2.
25 Chapman, *Leroy Ioas*, pp. 25–6.
26 *Star of the West*, vol. IX, no. 19 (2 March 1919), p. 225.
27 *The Bahá'í World*, vol. XII (1950–1954), p. 685; quoted in Whitehead, *Portraits*, pp. 134–5.
28 Newhall, *Stories of 'Abdu'l-Bahá as Told by Mother*, p. 38.
29 Jaxon, 'A Stroll with 'Abdu'l-Bahá', in *Star of the West*, vol. III, no. 4 (17 May 1912), p. 29.
30 *Star of the West*, vol. III, no. 7 (13 July 1912), pp. 6–7.
31 ibid.
32 Latimer, *The Light of the World*, p. 43.
33 USBNA, Edwin Mattoon Papers, Box 3: Harriet M. Cline Pilgrim Notes, pp. 2–3.
34 *Star of the West*, vol. 13, no. 8 (November 1922), pp. 204–5.
35 Brown, *Memories of 'Abdu'l-Bahá*, p. 33.
36 Metelmann, *Lua Getsinger*, p. 154.
37 *Star of the West*, vol. 13, no. 8 (November 1922), p. 205.
38 USBNA, Jessie/Ethel Revell Papers, Box 7: Harriet Wise, p. 1.
39 Gail, *Dawn Over Mount Hira*, pp. 205–6.
40 Metelmann, *Lua Getsinger*, p. 161.
41 Thompson, *Diary*, pp. 325–6.
42 Metelmann, *Lua Getsinger*, p. 172.
43 Gail, *Dawn Over Mount Hira*, p. 206.
44 Metelmann, *Lua Getsinger*, p. 174.
45 Gail, *Dawn Over Mount Hira*, p. 206.
46 Brown, *Memories of 'Abdu'l-Bahá*, p. 33; see also Harper, *Lights of Fortitude*, pp. 54–5.
47 Ward, *239 Days*, pp. 59–60.
48 Zarqání, *Maḥmúd's Diary*, p. 82.
49 ibid. p. 83.
50 ibid. p. 84.
51 Parsons, *Diary*, p. 61.
52 ibid. p. 65.
53 Zarqání, *Maḥmúd's Diary*, pp. 86–7.

## 9 The City of the Covenant

1 Ward, *239 Days*, p. 83.
2 Zarqání, *Maḥmúd's Diary*, p. 89.
3 'Abdu'l-Bahá, *The Promulgation of Universal Peace*, pp. 116–22.
4 Thompson, *Diary*, p. 285.
5 Ahdieh and Hopson, *'Abdu'l-Bahá in New York*, p. 13.
6 Zarqání, *Maḥmúd's Diary*, p. 99.
7 Ahdieh and Hopson, *'Abdu'l-Bahá in New York*, p. 13.
8 *The Bahá'í World*, vol. IX (1940–1944), p. 604.
9 Zarqání, *Maḥmúd's Diary*, p. 101.

10  Ives, *Portals to Freedom*, pp. 196–7.
11  Zarqání, *Maḥmúd's Diary*, p. 102.
12  Bagdadi, 'Abdul Baha in America', in *Star of the West*, vol. 19, no. 3 (June 1928), pp. 181–2.
13  *The Bahá'í World*, vol. VIII (1938–1940), p. 658.
14  Newhall, *Stories of 'Abdu'l-Bahá as Told by Mother*, pp. 17–19.
15  ibid. p. 20.
16  Thompson, *Diary*, pp. 350–51.
17  Ives, *Portals to Freedom*, pp. 96–9.
18  Thompson, *Diary*, p. 287.
19  *Star of the West*, vol. III, no. 9 (20 August 1912), pp. 5–6.
20  Zarqání, *Maḥmúd's Diary*, p. 107.
21  Ives, *Portals to Freedom*, p. 89.
22  Zarqání, *Maḥmúd's Diary*, p. 108.
23  Gail, *Arches of the Years*, p. 89.
24  Cobb, *Memories of 'Abdu'l-Bahá*, p. 15.
25  Zarqání, *Maḥmúd's Diary*, pp. 104–5.
26  ibid. pp. 116–17, 122.
27  *The Bahá'í World*, vol. XIII (1954–1963), p. 865.
28  Thompson, *Diary*, pp. 298–9.
29  'Will Bahaism Unite All Religious Faiths', in *The American Review of Reviews*, no. 45 (June 1912), pp. 748–50.
30  ibid.
31  Thompson, *Diary*, p. 298.
32  Zarqání, *Maḥmúd's Diary*, p. 121.
33  USBNA, Jessie/Ethel Revell Papers, Box 7: Revell Sisters Pilgrim Notes, Ethel Revell notes, 1/4/49, p. 1.
34  ibid. Jessie Revell notes, p. 1.
35  ibid.
36  ibid.
37  Zarqání, *Maḥmúd's Diary*, pp. 127–8.
38  Thompson, *Diary*, p. 303.
39  Zarqání, *Maḥmúd's Diary*, p. 133.
40  *Star of the West*, vol. III, no. 10 (8 September 1912), pp. 3–4.
41  ibid.
42  Zarqání, *Maḥmúd's Diary*, pp. 135–7.
43  Balyuzi, *'Abdu'l-Bahá*, p. 220.
44  Thompson, *Diary*, pp. 311–12.
45  Balyuzi, *'Abdu'l-Bahá*, p. 220.

## 10 Summer Travels

1  Ahdieh and Hopson, *'Abdu'l-Bahá in New York*, p. 20; see also Zarqání, *Maḥmúd's Diary*, p. 142.
2  Ward, *239 Days*, p. 85.
3  *Star of the West*, vol. III, no. 8 (1 August 1912), p. 16.
4  Thompson, *Diary*, p. 322.
5  'Abdu'l-Bahá, *The Promulgation of Universal Peace*, pp. 213–15.
6  Thompson, *Diary*, pp. 322–3.
7  ibid. p. 324.
8  Zarqání, *Maḥmúd's Diary*, p. 166.

9   ibid. p. 155.
10  Thompson, *Diary*, p. 327.
11  ibid. p. 329.
12  USBNA, Edwin Mattoon Papers, Box 3: Harriet Wise Pilgrim Notes, p. 1.
13  Gail, *Arches of the Years*, p. 97.
14  USBNA, Edwin Mattoon Papers, Box 3: Harriet Wise Pilgrim Notes, p. 2.
15  Cobb, *Memories of 'Abdu'l-Bahá*, p. 20.
16  ibid. pp. 20–21.
17  Zarqání, *Mahmúd's Diary*, p. 171.
18  ibid. p. 177.
19  Garis, *Martha Root*, pp. 53–4.
20  Charles Johnston, 'A Ray from the East', in *Harper's Weekly*, no. 59 (20 July 1912), p. 9, quoted in Ward, *239 Days*, pp. 114–16.
21  *The Bahá'í World*, vol. XII (1950–1954), p. 671.
22  Freeman, *From Copper to Gold*, p. 10.
23  ibid.
24  *The Bahá'í World*, vol. XII (1950–1954), p. 671.
25  Zarqání, *Mahmúd's Diary*, p. 178.
26  Thompson, *Diary*, pp. 354–6.
27  Zarqání, *Mahmúd's Diary*, p. 179.
28  The research of Phillip E. Tussing, *Finishing the Work: 'Abdu'l-Bahá in Dublin* is gratefully acknowledged for information in this section.
29  Quoted in Tussing, *Finishing the Work*, p. 6.
30  ibid. p. 16.
31  Zarqání, *Mahmúd's Diary*, p. 181.
32  Parsons, *Diary*, pp. 76–7.
33  Quoted in Tussing, *Finishing the Work*, p. 4.
34  Parsons, *Diary*, pp. 77–8.
35  Zarqání, *Mahmúd's Diary*, pp. 185–6.
36  Parsons, *Diary*, pp. 76, 95.
37  USBNA, Albert Windust Papers, Box 31: George Latimer Pilgrim Notes, p. 1.
38  ibid. p. 2.
39  Zarqání, *Mahmúd's Diary*, p. 187.
40  USBNA, Albert Windust Papers, Box 31: George Latimer Pilgrim Notes, p. 5.
41  *Star of the West*, vol. III, no. 11 (27 September, 1912), p. 4.
42  USBNA, Albert Windust Papers, Box 31: George Latimer Pilgrim Notes, p. 5.
43  ibid. p. 6.
44  ibid. pp. 4–5.
45  ibid. p. 7.
46  Zarqání, *Mahmúd's Diary*, p. 189.
47  USBNA, Albert Windust Papers, Box 31: George Latimer Pilgrim Notes, p. 7.
48  USBNA, Emogene Hoagg Papers, Box 7: Agnes Parsons Pilgrim Notes, notes taken by Emogene Hoagg, p. 3.
49  ibid. p. 5.
50  Zarqání, *Mahmúd's Diary*, p. 216.
51  Ives, *Portals to Freedom*, p. 117.
52  Zarqání, *Mahmúd's Diary*, pp. 190–91. 'The Conquests of Mecca' is a well-known exposition of Sufi doctrine (see ibid. note 231).
53  ibid. p. 190.
54  Quoted in Tussing, *Finishing the Work*, p. 4.

55 ibid.
56 ibid. p. 10.
57 ibid.
58 ibid. p. 193.
59 Zarqání, *Maḥmúd's Diary*, p. 194.
60 ibid. p. 199.
61 ibid. p. 200.
62 Ives, *Portals to Freedom*, p. 129.
63 Parsons, *Diary*, p. 107.
64 Tussing, *Finishing the Work*, p. 3.
65 USBNA, Agnes Parsons Papers, Box 20: Agnes Parsons Pilgrim Notes, p. 8.
66 Gail, *Arches of the Years*, p. 77.
67 Tussing, *Finishing the Work*, pp. 4, 5.
68 Parsons, *Diary*, p. 120.
69 Atkinson et al., *Green Acre on the Piscataqua*, p. 27.
70 ibid. p. 53.
71 ibid. pp. 57–9.
72 *Star of the West*, vol. III, no. 15 (12 December 1912), pp. 3–4.
73 Zarqání, *Maḥmúd's Diary*, p. 211.
74 'Abdu'l-Bahá, *The Promulgation of Universal Peace*, pp. 261–2.
75 Thompson, *Diary*, p. 359.
76 Mortensen, 'When a Soul Meets the Master', in *Star of the West*, vol. XIV, no. 12 (March 1924), pp. 365–6.
77 ibid. p. 366.
78 ibid.
79 Penoyer, thesis, pp. 4–5.
80 Mortensen, 'When a Soul Meets the Master', *Star of the West*, vol. XIV, no. 12 (March 1924), p. 366.
81 Penoyer, thesis, pp. 18–19.
82 Mortensen, 'When a Soul Meets the Master', *Star of the West*, vol. XIV, no. 12 (March 1924), pp. 366–7.
83 ibid.
84 *The Bahá'í World*, vol. XI (1946–1950), p. 486.
85 Penoyer, thesis, p. 22.
86 *The Bahá'í World*, vol. XI (1946–1950), p. 486.
87 Penoyer, thesis, pp. 23, 27. Shoghi Effendi mentions Fred's visit to 'Abdu'l-Bahá in *God Passes By*, p. 290.
88 Morrison, *To Move the World*, p. 120.
89 Zarqání, *Maḥmúd's Diary*, p. 216.
90 *Bahá'í News*, no. 49, p. 4.
91 Zarqání, *Maḥmúd's Diary*, p. 224.
92 Information in the following paragraphs from Randall-Winkler, *William Henry Randall*, pp. 36–47.
93 ibid. pp. 40–41.
94 ibid. p. 44.
95 ibid. pp. 44–5.
96 ibid. pp. 46–7.
97 Tablet of 'Abdu'l-Bahá to Ruth Randall, 1920, cited in Randall-Winckler, *William Henry Randall*, p. 189.

## 11 North to Canada

1. Shoghi Effendi, cable on the passing of May Maxwell, in *The Bahá'í World*, vol. VIII (1938–1940), p. 631.
2. 'Abdu'l-Bahá, Tablet to May Maxwell, 17 October 1902, quoted in Nakhjavani, *The Maxwells of Montreal*, p. 216.
3. Shoghi Effendi, cable on the passing of May Maxwell, in *The Bahá'í World*, vol. VIII (1938–1940), p. 631.
4. 'Abdu'l-Bahá, *Tablets of the Divine Plan*, pp. 93–4.
5. Zarqání, *Maḥmúd's Diary*, p. 226.
6. Nakhjavani, *A Tribute to Amatu'l-Bahá Rúḥíyyih Khánum*, p. 10. See also Nakhjavani, *The Maxwells of Montreal*, p. 280.
7. Nakhjavani, *The Maxwells of Montreal*, p. 279–80.
8. Zarqání, *Maḥmúd's Diary*, p. 247.
9. ibid.
10. Amatu'l-Bahá Rúḥíyyih Khánum, interview in the Maxwell House by Douglas Martin.
11. Zarqání, *Maḥmúd's Diary*, pp. 227, 250.
12. ibid. p. 228.
13. Ruhe-Schoen, *A Love Which Does Not Wait*, p. 53.
14. Zarqání, *Maḥmúd's Diary*, p. 228.
15. ibid. p. 236.
16. *'Abdu'l-Bahá in Canada*, pp. 31, 32, 36.
17. van den Hoonaard, *Origins of the Bahá'í Community of Canada 1898–1948*, pp. 55–9.
18. *The Bahá'í World*, vol. VIII (1938–1940), p. 637.
19. Honnold, *Vignettes*, p. 86.
20. Amatu'l-Bahá Rúḥíyyih Khánum, interview in the Maxwell House by Douglas Martin.
21. Zarqání, *Maḥmúd's Diary*, p. 238.
22. ibid.
23. Nakhjavani, *The Maxwells of Montreal*, p. 282.
24. ibid.
25. Amatu'l-Bahá Rúḥíyyih Khánum, interview in the Maxwell House by Douglas Martin.
26. Nakhjavani, *A Tribute to Amatu'l-Bahá Rúḥíyyih Khánum*, p. 11. See also Nakhjavani, *The Maxwells of Montreal*, p. 282.
27. Nakhjavani, *The Maxwells of Montreal*, p. 282.
28. ibid. p. 281.
29. Amatu'l-Bahá Rúḥíyyih Khánum, interview in the Maxwell House by Douglas Martin. See also Nakhjavani, *The Maxwells of Montreal*, p. 284.
30. Nakhjavani, *The Maxwells of Montreal*, pp. 281–2.
31. Zarqání, *Maḥmúd's Diary*, p. 241.
32. ibid. pp. 241–3.
33. Nakhjavani, *The Maxwells of Montreal*, p. 283.
34. Zarqání, *Maḥmúd's Diary*, p. 247.
35. Nakhjavani, *The Maxwells of Montreal*, pp. 272–4.
36. Zarqání, *Maḥmúd's Diary*, p. 243.
37. ibid. p. 245. The Archbishop was Msgr. Louis Jospeh Paul Bruchési, see van den Hoonard, *Origins of the Bahá'í Community of Canada 1898–1948*, p. 52.

38  ibid. p. 246.
39  Ward, *239 Days*, p. 136.
40  Zarqání, *Maḥmúd's Diary*, p. 249.
41  Nakhjavani, *The Maxwells of Montreal*, p. 285.

## 12 California Bound
1   Zarqání, *Maḥmúd's Diary*, pp. 247–8.
2   ibid. p. 251.
3   ibid. pp. 252–3.
4   ibid. p. 254.
5   ibid. p. 257.
6   ibid. pp. 257–8.
7   Diary of Keith Ransom Kehler, in *The Baháʼí World*, vol. II (1926–1928), p. 129; recounted in Honnold, *Vignettes*, p. 169.
8   Zarqání, *Maḥmúd's Diary*, p. 258.
9   Ioas, *Interview of Sachiro Fujita*.
10  Zarqání, *Maḥmúd's Diary*, p. 259.
11  Rutstein, *Corinne True*, pp. 105–6.
12  ibid. p. 106.
13  ibid. p. 107.
14  ʻAbduʼl-Bahá, Tablet to the Kenosha Baháʼí community, July 1912, quoted in Dahl, 'A History of the Kenosha Baháʼí Community, 1897–1980', in Hollinger, *Community Histories*, pp. 22–3.
15  Zarqání, *Maḥmúd's Diary*, p. 267.
16  Dahl, op. cit., in Hollinger, *Community Histories*, p. 24.
17  Zarqání, *Maḥmúd's Diary*, p. 268.
18  Rutstein, *Corinne True*, pp. 107–8.
19  ibid. p. 108.
20  ʻAbduʼl-Bahá, *The Promulgation of Universal Peace*, pp. 322–3.
21  Whitmore, *The Dawning Place*, p. 66.
22  Rutstein, *Corinne True*, p. 109.
23  Zarqání, *Maḥmúd's Diary*, p. 270.
24  ibid. p. 271.
25  ibid. pp. 270–1.
26  ibid. p. 272.
27  ibid. p. 273.
28  Ward, *239 Days*, pp. 148–9.
29  ibid. p. 150.
30  Zarqání, *Maḥmúd's Diary*, p. 274.
31  ibid. pp. 276.
32  ibid.
33  ibid.
34  Sears, *Bill*, pp. 2–3, 8.
35  Zarqání, *Maḥmúd's Diary*, p. 278.
36  ibid. p. 280.
37  *Star of the West*, vol. V, no. 8 (1 August 1914), p. 119.
38  Zarqání, *Maḥmúd's Diary*, p. 282.
39  Balyuzi, *ʻAbduʼl-Bahá*, p. 280.
40  *The Daily News*, Denver, Colorado, 25 September 1912.
41  Ward, *239 Days*, pp. 154–7.

42  Zarqání, *Maḥmúd's Diary*, pp. 286–7.
43  ibid. pp. 288–9.
44  ibid. p. 158.
45  ibid. pp. 289–90.
46  ibid. p. 284.
47  ibid. p. 291.
48  *Daily Avalanche*, Glenwood Springs, Colorado, 30 September 1912.
49  Ioas, *Interview of Sachiro Fujita*.
50  Zarqání, *Maḥmúd's Diary*, pp. 292–3.
51  Ioas, *Interview of Sachiro Fujita*.
52  Zarqání, *Maḥmúd's Diary*, p. 293.
53  Ioas, *Interview of Sachiro Fujita*.
54  USBNA, Notes of Feny E. Paulson, cited in Ward, *239 Days*, pp. 159–60.
55  Zarqání, *Maḥmúd's Diary*, p. 296.
56  Ioas, *Interview of Sachiro Fujita*.
57  Zarqání, *Maḥmúd's Diary*, pp. 296–7.
58  Ioas, *Interview of Sachiro Fujita*.
59  USBNA, Notes of Feny E. Paulson, cited in Ward, *239 Days*, pp. 162–3.

## 13 'Your Love Drew Me to You'

1   Zarqání, *Maḥmúd's Diary*, p. 298.
2   See Hogenson, *Lighting the Western Sky*, pp. 199–205, and Chapter 13.
3   ibid. p. 245.
4   *Star of the West*, vol. XIII, no. 8 (November 1922), pp. 205–6.
5   Zarqání, *Maḥmúd's Diary*, p. 299.
6   Brown, *Memories of 'Abdu'l-Bahá*, pp. 37–8.
7   ibid. p. 39.
8   *The Bahá'í World*, vol. XX (1986–1992), pp. 865–6.
9   *Star of the West*, vol. IV, no. 12 (16 October 1912), p. 207.
10  Ward, *239 Days*, pp. 170–71.
11  Zarqání, *Maḥmúd's Diary*, p. 306.
12  ibid.
13  ibid. p. 304.
14  *The Bahá'í World*, vol. XIII (1954–1963), pp. 932–3. See also Whitehead, *Some Bahá'ís to Remember*, pp. 179–83.
15  Afroukhteh, *Memories of Nine Years in 'Akká*, p. 269.
16  *The Bahá'í World*, vol. XIII (1954–1963), pp. 932.
17  ibid. pp. 932–3.
18  *Star of the West*, vol. III, no. 12 (16 October 1912), p. 9.
19  Metelmann, *Lua Getsinger*, p. 176.
20  Zarqání, *Maḥmúd's Diary*, p. 310.
21  Brown, *Memories of 'Abdu'l-Bahá*, p. 41.
22  Richard Rathbun, personal communication, 7 December 2010.
23  'Abdu'l-Bahá, *The Promulgation of Universal Peace*, pp. 351–5.
24  *Star of the West*, vol. III, no. 13 (4 November 1912), p. 13.
25  Mary Hanford Ford, in *Star of the West*, vol. VIII, no. 1 (21 March 1917), p. 6.
26  Thompson, *Diary*, p. 362.
27  Brown, *Memories of 'Abdu'l-Bahá*, pp. 48–9.
28  'Abdu'l-Bahá, *The Promulgation of Universal Peace*, p. 361.
29  Zarqání, *Maḥmúd's Diary*, p. 313.

30   Metelmann, *Lua Getsinger*, p. 176.
31   *Star of the West*, vol. IV, no. 12 (16 October 1913), p. 205.
32   Zarqání, *Maḥmúd's Diary*, p. 314.
33   Brown, *Memories of 'Abdu'l Bahá*, p. 50, and Zarqání, *Maḥmúd's Diary*, p. 314.
34   Zarqání, *Maḥmúd's Diary*, p. 315.
35   ibid. pp. 315–16.
36   Willard P. Hatch, "Abdu'l-Bahá and the Rabbi', in *The Baháʼí World*, vol. III (1928–1930), pp. 361–2.
37   ibid. p. 362.
38   *Star of the West*, vol. III, no. 13 (4 November 1912), p. 8.
39   Hogenson, *Lighting the Western Sky*, p. 259.
40   See Hogenson, *Lighting the Western Sky*, particularly Chapter 16, for information about Phoebe Hearst and the Baháʼí Faith.
41   'Abdu'l-Bahá, Tablet to Ella Goodall Cooper, 2 June 1919, quoted in Hogensen, *Lighting the Western Sky*, pp. 265–6.
42   ibid. p. 199.
43   Gail, *Arches of the Years*, pp. 95–7.
44   Rabbani, *The Priceless Pearl*, p. 19.
45   Zarqání, *Maḥmúd's Diary*, p. 327.
46   ibid. p. 328.
47   Gail, *Arches of the Years*, pp. 87–8.
48   Zarqání, *Maḥmúd's Diary*, pp. 330–31.
49   ibid. p. 333.
50   ibid. p. 332.
51   Brown, *Memories of 'Abdu'l-Bahá*, p. 55.
52   ibid. pp. 55–6.
53   Ives, *Portals to Freedom*, pp. 98–9.
54   Brown, *Memories of 'Abdu'l-Bahá*, pp. 58–9.
55   *Star of the West*, vol. III, no. 13 (4 November 1912), p. 14.
56   USBNA, Edwin Mattoon Papers, Box 3: Harriet Cline Pilgrim Notes, p. 3.
57   Zarqání, *Maḥmúd's Diary*, p. 336
58   ibid. p. 337.
59   *Star of the West*, vol. III, no. 13 (4 November 1912), p. 15.
60   USBNA, Edwin Mattoon Papers, Box 3: Harriet Cline Pilgrim Notes, p. 3.
61   Zarqání, *Maḥmúd's Diary*, pp. 337–8.
62   ibid. p. 339; see also Balyuzi, *'Abdu'l-Bahá*, p. 310.
63   ibid. pp. 340–41.
64   Brown, *Memories of 'Abdu'l-Bahá*, p. 64.
65   USBNA, Edwin Mattoon Papers, Box 3: Harriet Cline Pilgrim Notes, pp. 4–5.
66   Zarqání, *Maḥmúd's Diary*, pp. 356–7.
67   ibid. p. 343.
68   ibid. p. 344.
69   Brown, *Memories of 'Abdu'l-Bahá*, pp. 66–7.
70   ibid. pp. 78–80.
71   ibid. p. 84.
72   Zarqání, *Maḥmúd's Diary*, pp. 348–9.
73   Caton, 'The Sacramento Baháʼí Community, 1912–1987', in Hollinger, *Community Histories*, pp. 245–6.
74   Brown, *Memories of 'Abdu'l-Bahá*, p. 86.
75   Caton, op. cit., in Hollinger, *Community Histories*, pp. 246–7.

76   ibid. pp. 247–8.
77   ibid. pp. 247.
78   'Abdu'l-Bahá, *The Promulgation of Universal Peace*, pp. 376–7.
79   Brown, *Memories of 'Abdu'l-Bahá*, p. 88.
80   ibid. p. 6.
81   Zarqání, *Maḥmúd's Diary*, p. 351.
82   ibid.

## 14 Last Days in America

1   Zarqání, *Maḥmúd's Diary*, pp. 352–3.
2   ibid. p. 354.
3   ibid.
4   ibid. p. 357.
5   Ioas, *Interview of Sachiro Fujita*.
6   Zarqání, *Maḥmúd's Diary*, p. 359.
7   'Abdu'l-Bahá, *The Promulgation of Universal Peace*, p. 382.
8   Zarqání, *Maḥmúd's Diary*, pp. 362–3.
9   ibid. p. 367.
10  ibid. pp. 370–71.
11  'Abdu'l-Bahá, *The Promulgation of Universal Peace*, pp. 388–9.
12  Parsons, *Diary*, p. 127. Mrs Parsons' account differs considerably from Zarqání.
13  Latimer, *The Light of the World*, p. 83.
14  Parsons, *Diary*, p. 131.
15  'Abdu'l-Bahá, *The Promulgation of Universal Peace*, pp. 403–10.
16  Parsons, *Diary*, pp. 131–2.
17  Zarqání, *Maḥmúd's Diary*, p. 380.
18  USBNA, Agnes Parsons Papers, Box 20: Agnes Parsons Pilgrim Notes, p. 10.
19  *Star of the West*, vol. III, no. 17 (19 January 1913), p. 2.
20  Zarqání, *Maḥmúd's Diary*, pp. 380–81.
21  Parsons, *Diary*, p. 136.
22  'Abdu'l-Bahá, *The Promulgation of Universal Peace*, pp. 425–7.
23  USBNA, Mariam Haney Pilgrim Notes, Box 20: Agnes Parsons Pilgrim Notes, p. 7.
24  Clark, 'The Bahá'ís of Baltimore, 1898–1990', in Hollinger, *Community Histories*, pp. 125–6.
25  ibid.
26  ibid. p. 127.
27  ibid. pp. 128–9.
28  USBNA, Jessie/Ethel Revell Papers, Box 7: Revell Sisters.
29  Thompson, *Diary*, pp. 362–3.
30  ibid. pp. 363–4.
31  *Star of the West*, vol. IV, no. 6 (24 June 1913), p. 104.
32  Zarqání, *Maḥmúd's Diary*, p. 387.
33  Garis, *Martha Root*, p. 52; *Star of the West*, vol. VI, no. 11 (27 September 1915), p. 82.
34  Thompson, *Diary*, p. 364.
35  Zarqání, *Maḥmúd's Diary*, p. 389.
36  ibid. p. 392.
37  Thompson, *Diary*, p. 368.
38  'Abdu'l-Bahá, *The Promulgation of Universal Peace*, pp. 431–7.
39  Zarqání, *Maḥmúd's Diary*, p. 404.

40   ibid. pp. 398–9.
41   For information about Howard MacNutt see Stockman, *The Bahá'í Faith in America*, vol. 2; Gail, *Arches of the Years*, pp. 112–126.
42   Thompson, *Diary*, pp. 369–72.
43   Zarqání, *Maḥmúd's Diary*, p. 401.
44   See Gail, *Arches of the Years*, pp. 112–126.
45   'Abdu'l-Bahá, *The Promulgation of Universal Peace*, p. xx.
46   Gail, *Arches of the Years*, p. 126.
47   ibid. p. 407.
48   Zarqání, *Maḥmúd's Diary*, p. 407.
49   Thompson, *Diary*, p. 378.
50   Zarqání, *Maḥmúd's Diary*, p. 413.
51   ibid. pp. 414–15.
52   Thompson, *Diary*, p. 288.
53   'Abdu'l-Bahá, *The Promulgation of Universal Peace*, pp. 452–3.
54   *Star of the West*, vol. IV, no. 1 (21 March 1913), p. 18.
55   USBNA, Agnes Parsons Papers, Box 20: Mariam Haney Pilgrim Notes, pp. 3–4.
56   Ives, *Portals to Freedom*, pp. 197–8.
57   Zarqání, *Maḥmúd's Diary*, p. 422.
58   ibid. p. 423.
59   Newhall, *Stories of 'Abdu'l-Bahá as Told by Mother*, p. 28.
60   USBNA, Agnes Parsons Papers, Box 20: Mariam Haney Pilgrim Notes, p. 5.
61   Ahdieh and Hopson, *'Abdu'l-Bahá in New York*, pp. 26–7.
62   Zarqání, *Maḥmúd's Diary*, p. 432.
63   Ives, *Portals to Freedom*, pp. 227–8.

## 15 Return to the United Kingdom

1    *Star of the West*, vol. III, no. 16 (31 December 1912), p. 2.
2    ibid. vol. III, no. 17 (19 January 1913), p. 2.
3    ibid.
4    ibid. vol. III, no. 16 (31 December 1912), p. 2.
5    ibid. vol. III, no. 17 (9 January 1913), p. 3.
6    ibid. p. 4.
7    ibid. p. 5.
8    ibid. vol. III, no. 19 (2 March 1913), p. 3.
9    ibid.
10   ibid.
11   Edwin Graham, 'Joan Waring and Thomas Fforde', Chapter 5 in McNamara, *Connections*, p. 58.
12   *Star of the West*, vol. III, no. 19 (2 March 1913), pp. 3–4.
13   ibid. p. 4.
14   ibid.
15   ibid.
16   ibid.
17   ibid. p. 5.
18   Balyuzi, *'Abdu'l-Bahá*, p. 347.
19   *Star of the West*, vol. III, no. 19 (2 March 1913), p. 5.
20   Balyuzi, *'Abdu'l-Bahá*, p. 347.
21   Blomfield, *The Chosen Highway*, p. 155.
22   *Star of the West*, vol. III, no. 19 (2 March 1913), p. 5.

23  ibid. p. 6.
24  Balyuzi, *'Abdu'l-Bahá*, p. 347.
25  *The Christian Commonwealth*, p. 262, United Kingdom Bahá'í Archives. An edited version appears in *Star of the West*, vol. III, no. 17 (19 January 1913), pp. 5–10. The version given here is as it appeared in the newspaper.
26  ibid.
27  ibid.
28  *Star of the West*, vol. III, no. 19 (2 March 1913), p. 7.
29  Balyuzi, *'Abdu'l-Bahá*, p. 348.
30  Blomfield, *The Chosen Highway*, p. 154.
31  *The Christian Commonwealth*, United Kingdom Bahá'í Archives.
32  Balyuzi, *'Abdu'l-Bahá*, p. 350.
33  'Christmas Day With Abdul Baha in London', in *The Christian Commonwealth*, United Kingdom Bahá'í Archives.
34  *Star of the West*, vol. III, no. 18 (7 February 1913), pp. 8–9.
35  Balyuzi, *'Abdu'l-Bahá*, p. 352.
36  'Abdul Baha at the King's Weigh House', in *The Christian Commonwealth*, United Kingdom Bahá'í Archives.
37  Blomfield, *The Chosen Highway*, pp. 168–9.
38  *Star of the West*, vol. IV, no. 17 (19 January 1914), p. 286.
39  Balyuzi, *'Abdu'l-Bahá*, p. 354.
40  *The Christian Commonwealth*, 1 January 1913, United Kingdom Bahá'í Archives.
41  *Star of the West*, vol. III, no. 18 (7 February 1913), pp. 9–10.
42  ibid.
43  ibid. p. 10.
44  *The International Psychic Gazette* (January 1913), p. 158, in United Kingdom Bahá'í Archives.
45  Blomfield, *The Chosen Highway*, p. 154.
46  *The International Psychic Gazette* (January 1913), p. 159.
47  ibid.
48  Blomfield, *The Chosen Highway*, pp. 162–3.
49  Sohrab, *'Abdu'l-Bahá in Edinburgh*, p. 3.
50  Blomfield, *The Chosen Highway*, p. 174.
51  Sohrab, *'Abdu'l-Bahá in Edinburgh*, p. 2.
52  Mrs Alexander Whyte, 'A Visit to 'Akká', in *The Bahá'í World*, vol. IV (1930–1932), pp. 396, 398; quoted in Khursheed, *The Seven Candles of Unity*, pp. 48–9.
53  'Abdu'l-Bahá, *Selections*, p. 32.
54  Khursheed, *The Seven Candles of Unity*, pp. 51–3.
55  Letter from Professor G. S. Stewart to the National Spiritual Assembly of the Bahá'ís of the British Isles, 17 July 1943, quoted in Khursheed, *The Seven Candles of Unity*, p. 71.
56  Sohrab, *'Abdu'l-Bahá in Edinburgh*, p. 5.
57  Letter from Professor G. S. Stewart to the National Spiritual Assembly of the Bahá'ís of the British Isles, 17 July 1943, quoted in Khursheed, *The Seven Candles of Unity*, p. 71.
58  Sohrab, *'Abdu'l-Bahá in Edinburgh*, pp. 4–5.
59  *The Bahá'í World*, vol. XVIII (1979–1983), p. 789.
60  Khursheed, *The Seven Candles of Unity*, pp. 185–9.
61  ibid. pp. 74–5.
62  *Star of the West*, vol. 11, no. 18 (7 February 1921), p. 301.

63 Letter from Professor G. S. Stewart to the National Spiritual Assembly of the Bahá'ís of the British Isles, 17 July 1943, quoted in Khursheed, *The Seven Candles of Unity*, p. 76.
64 Blomfield, *The Chosen Highway*, p. 172.
65 ibid. p. 169.
66 Sohrab, *'Abdu'l-Bahá in Edinburgh*, p. 7.
67 Quoted in Khursheed, *The Seven Candles of Unity*, pp. 86–7.
68 ibid. p. 112.
69 Balyuzi, *'Abdu'l-Bahá*, pp. 365–6.
70 Quoted in Khursheed, *The Seven Candles of Unity*, p. 112.
71 Sohrab, *'Abdu'l-Bahá in Edinburgh*, pp. 6–7.
72 Khursheed, *The Seven Candles of Unity*, p. 101.
73 ibid. p. 103.
74 Sohrab, *'Abdu'l-Bahá in Edinburgh*, p. 10.
75 ibid. p. 11.
76 ibid. p. 12
77 Balyuzi, *'Abdu'l-Bahá*, p. 368.
78 *Star of the West*, vol. III, no. 19 (2 March 1913), p. 4.
79 Balyuzi, *'Abdu'l-Bahá*, p. 369.
80 ibid.
81 Blomfield, *The Chosen Highway*, pp. 159–61.
82 Balyuzi, *'Abdu'l-Bahá*, p. 370.
83 *Star of the West*, vol. IV, no. 1 (21 March 1913), p. 4.
84 *The Clifton Chronicle and Directory*, 22 January 1913, in United Kingdom Bahá'í Archives.
85 *Star of the West*, vol. IV, no. 1 (21 March 1913), p. 16.
86 Balyuzi, *'Abdu'l-Bahá*, p. 370.
87 ibid. pp. 497–502, for the complete outline as given by 'Abdu'l-Bahá.
88 Blomfield, *The Chosen Highway*, pp. 173–4.
89 ibid. p. 174.

## 16 From Paris to Budapest and Back

1 Balyuzi, *'Abdu'l-Bahá*, p. 375.
2 Sohrab, *'Abdu'l-Bahá in Egypt*, pp. 132–5.
3 Balyuzi, *'Abdu'l-Bahá*, pp. 374–5.
4 ibid. p. 376–7.
5 ibid. p. 374.
6 Latimer, *The Light of the World*, p. 22.
7 *Star of the West*, vol. VI, no. 19 (2 March 1916), p. 168.
8 *The Bahá'í World*, vol. XVIII (1979–1983), p. 822.
9 Cobb, *Memories of 'Abdu'l-Bahá*, pp. 16–18.
10 Balyuzi, *'Abdu'l-Bahá*, p. 378.
11 ibid. pp. 378–9.
12 *Star of the West*, vol. IV, no. 9 (20 August 1913), p. 162.
13 ibid.
14 *The Bahá'í World*, vol. IX (1940–1944), p. 642. For further information, see Alma S. Knobloch, 'The Call to Germany', in *The Bahá'í World*, vol. VII (1936–1938), pp. 732–45.
15 Latimer, *The Light of the World*, pp. 43–4.
16 *The Bahá'í World*, vol. IV (1930–1932), p. 266.

17  *Star of the West*, vol. IV, no. 9 (20 August 1913), p. 162.
18  ibid. p. 156.
19  ibid.
20  *The Bahá'í World*, vol. VII (1936–1938), p. 741.
21  ibid. pp. 740–41.
22  ibid. p. 743.
23  Bahá'í World News Service, 25 April 2007.
24  Towfigh, *Die ersten Früchte des Jahres sind die köstlichsten*, p. 4.
25  Root, 'Abdu'l-Bahá's Visit to Budapest', in *Star of the West*, vol. 24, no. 3 (June 1933), p. 84; article reprinted in Zinky and. Baram (eds), *Martha Root*, pp. 361–2.
26  Balyuzi, *'Abdu'l-Bahá*, p. 385.
27  Root, 'Abdu'l-Bahá's Visit to Budapest', in *Star of the West*, vol. 24, no. 3 (June 1933), p. 85.
28  ibid.
29  *The Bahá'í World*, vol. VII (1936–1938), p. 38.
30  Balyuzi, *'Abdu'l-Bahá*, p. 386.
31  Root, 'Abdu'l-Bahá's Visit to Budapest', in *Star of the West*, vol. 24, no. 3 (June 1933), p. 86.
32  ibid.
33  ibid. p. 87.
34  ibid. p. 88.
35  *Star of the West*, vol. IX, no. 2 (9 April 1918), p. 24.
36  ibid. vol. IV, no. 17 (19 January, 1914), pp. 284–5.
37  Balyuzi, *'Abdu'l-Bahá*, p. 387.
38  Root, 'Abdu'l-Bahá's Visit to Budapest', in *Star of the West*, vol. 24, no. 3 (June 1933), p. 88.
39  *The Bahá'í World*, vol.VII (1936–1938), pp. 34–5.
40  Smith (ed), *Bahá'ís in the West*, pp. 118, 125.
41  Root, 'Abdu'l-Bahá's Visit to Budapest', in *Star of the West*, vol. 24, no. 3 (June 1933), p. 89.
42  Smith (ed), *Bahá'ís in the West*, p. 120.
43  Bahá'í Community of Austria, *'Abdu'l-Bahá in Budapest*, p. 6.
44  Root, 'Abdu'l-Bahá's Visit to Budapest', in *Star of the West*, vol. 24, no. 3 (June 1933), p. 89.
45  *Star of the West*, vol. IV, no. 5 (5 June 1913), p. 86.
46  Balyuzi, *'Abdu'l-Bahá*, p. 388.
47  *Star of the West*, nol. V, No. 14 (23 November 1914), pp. 217–18.
48  Balyuzi, *'Abdu'l-Bahá*, p. 389.
49  *Star of the West*, vol. IV, no. 9 (20 August 1913), p. 158.
50  Balyuzi, *'Abdu'l-Bahá*, p. 389.
51  ibid. pp. 389–90.
52  ibid. p. 390.
53  Gollmer, *Mein Herz is bei euch*.
54  *Star of the West*, vol. VII, no. 16 (31 December 1916), p. 157; a slightly different version is in *Star of the West*, vol. IV, no. 4 (17 May 1913), p. 72.
55  Balyuzi, *'Abdu'l-Bahá*, p. 391.
56  ibid. p. 394.
57  *Star of the West (The Bahá'í Magazine)*, vol. 16, no. 5 (August, 1925), p. 528.
58  ibid. p. 395.

## 17 Home Again

1. *Star of the West*, vol. IV, no. 7 (13 July 1913), p. 121.
2. Ma'ani, *Leaves of the Twin Divine Trees*, p. 175.
3. Whitehead, *Portraits*, p. 9.
4. Sohrab, *'Abdu'l-Bahá in Egypt*, pp. 136–7.
5. ibid. pp. 175–6.
6. Balyuzi, *'Abdu'l-Bahá*, p. 398.
7. Gail, *Arches of the Years*, p. 124.
8. Sohrab, *'Abdu'l-Bahá in Egypt*, pp. 52–3.
9. ibid. pp. 165–6.
10. *Star of the West*, vol. IV, no. 19 (2 March 1914), p. 316.
11. ibid. vol. IX, no. 3 (28 April 1913), p. 26.
12. Sohrab, *'Abdu'l-Bahá in Egypt*, pp. 121–2.
13. ibid. p. 130.
14. Whitehead, *Portraits*, p. 9.
15. Metelmann, *Lua Getsinger*, p. 188; the quotation from 'Abdu'l-Bahá is in *Star of the West*, vol. IV, no. 12 (16 October 1913), p. 208.
16. ibid. p. 198.
17. Balyuzi, *'Abdu'l-Bahá*, pp. 400–2.
18. Shoghi Effendi, Letter to the Bahá'ís in the United States and Canada, 17 July 1932, in *Bahá'í Administration*, pp. 192–3; also in *Bahíyyih Khánum*, p. 40.
19. Sohrab, *'Abdu'l-Bahá in Egypt*, p. 152.
20. Rabbani, *The Priceless Pearl*, p. 23.
21. Balyuzi, *'Abdu'l-Bahá*, pp. 402, 407–8.
22. ibid. p. 400.
23. *Star of the West*, vol. VII, no. 11 (27 September 1916), p. 105.
24. Aṣdaq, *One Life, One Memory*, pp. 25–6.
25. *Star of the West*, vol. IV, no. 17 (19 January 1914), p. 288.
26. Aṣdaq, *One Life, One Memory*, p. 26.
27. *Star of the West*, vol. IV, no. 17 (19 January 1914), pp. 288, 290.
28. Shoghi Effendi, *God Passes By*, pp. 294–5.

# INDEX OF NAMES

References in **bold** indicate a biographical note.

'Abbás Ḥilmí Páshá 332
'Abdu'l-Ḥamíd, Sultan of Turkey 47, 291, 307-8, 325, 334
'Abdu'l-Ḥusayn, Shaykh 161
Abraham (Prophet) 247
Abu'l-Faḍl, Mírzá 5, 28, 43, 91, 179, 261, 328-30
Afroukhteh, Dr Youness (Yúnis Khán-i-Afrúkhtih) 216
Agnew, Arthur 110-11
Aḥmad-i-Báqiroff, Siyyid 312
Aḥmad 'Izzat Páshá 325
Aḥmad Páshá 324
Alexander, Agnes 162
'Alí 'Abbás Áqá 319-20
Allen, Dr Woodson 222
Allen, Frances 236
Allen, Ramona (Brown) 212, 225, 231, 238-9, 240, 241
Altass, Florence 293-4
Amatu'l-Bahá Rúḥíyyih Khánum 52, 184 *see also* Mary Maxwell
Amín, Ḥájí 278, 290
Amour, Mrs 274
d'Ange d'Astre, Madame 47
Apponyi, Count Albert 320
Arawaka, Viscount 48
Asadu'lláh-i-Qumí, Siyyid 7, 8, 46, 52, 57, 57, 155, 197, 270, 290, 292, 312, 324
Aṣdaq, Rúḥá 335
Ashton, Mr and Mrs 203
Austin, Mr and Mrs 52
Ayáz 183-4

Báb, The 2, 30, 33, 59, 195, 324
  Shrine of the Báb 7, 52, 110, 180, 230, 336
Bagdadi, Dr Zia 62, 83, 108, 124, 132, 228, 262
Bahá'u'lláh
  and 'Abdu'l-Bahá 1, 2, 93, 101, 160, 325, 337
  Birth of (anniversary) 257
  Covenant of 142-4, 196, 239, 245, 337
  imprisonment, exile and persecution of 20, 22-3, 63, 151, 196, 239, 259-60, 299
  life of 28, 1414, 277
  love of nature 22, 189
  power of 113, 143, 161, 178, 196, 201, 216, 238, 257, 258-9, 295
  Shrine of Bahá'u'lláh 209, 230, 240
  station of 15, 27, 62, 72, 140, 205, 232, 312
  teachings of 23, 26, 30, 31, 34, 44, 62, 67, 125, 128-9, 130, 136, 159-60, 172, 173, 186, 220, 225, 235, 238, 243, 346, 260, 266, 268
  Writings of 1, 2, 75, 142, 234
Bahíyyih Khánum (Greatest Holy Leaf) 7, 326, 333, 335
Bahrám Mírzá (Prince Bahram) 21
Bailey, Ella 116, 118
Baker, Dorothy 4, 103, 151
Barclay, Sir Thomas 279
Barney, Alice *see* Hemmick
Barney, Laura *see* Dreyfus-Barney

Barr, Marie 238-9
Barton-Peeke, Dr Pauline 191-2
Bates, John 165
Beckwith, Mrs 81
Beecher, Ellen 151
Beede, Alice R. 44-5
Bell, Alexander Graham 97, 101-2, 331
Birch, Bishop 76-7
Birks, Geraldine 181
Birks, Henry, 181, 182
Bixby, Reverend J. T. 67-8
Blomfield, Mary (Basil Hall) 281
Blomfield, Sara Louisa (Lady Blomfield) viii, 4, 26, **27-8**, 276, 281, 290, 298, 299, 301, 302
   descriptions by 29, 30, 34, 35-6, 41-2, 281, 284, 289-90, 295, 299-301, 306
Boardman, Mabel 105
Bolles, May *see* Maxwell
Booth, General 288
Bosch, John 18, **80-83**, 118, 119, 121-2
Bowditch, Nancy 154, 164-5
Boylan, Annie 22-3, 141
Breakwell, Thomas 18
Breed, Alice Ives 5, 96, 137, 161-2
Breed, Florence *see* Khan
Breed, Francis 137
Brittingham, Isabella 6
Brown, Helen Hillyer 211-12, 247
Brown, Ramona *see* Allen
Browne, Edward Granville 43, 53, 68, 227-8, 311
Brush, George DeForest 153, 154, 165
Bryan, Mary 201-2
Bryan, Ruth 201
Bryan, William Jennings 201-2
Buckton, Alice 28, 37, 149, 174, 280-81, 299
Burbank, Luther 119
Burton, Mrs 159

Cabot, Elise Pumpelly 165
Cabot family 153
Campbell, Reverend R. J. 31-2
Carew, Kate (Mary Williams) 83-8
Carnegie, Andrew 74, 130, 257
Carpenter, Dr J. Estlin 284

Chase, Thornton 4, 5, 110-11, 161-2, 208, **232-4**
Cheyne, Elizabeth Gibson 284
Cheyne, Dr T. K. 283-4
Chéron, Madame, 309-10
Child, Mr 289
Cline, Cordie 159
Cline, Frances 236
Cline, Grandfather 236
Cline, Harriet 115-116, 118, 157, 234, 242
Cline, Wilfred 233
Cline, Wilfred Jr 236
Cobb, Stanwood 56, 73, 137, 149-50, 310-11
Conwell, Dr Russell H. 141
Cook, Captain 97
Cooper, Ella 96, 118-19, 149, **211-12**, 227, 230, 240
Craven, John 273
Culver, Julia 166
Cuthbert, Arthur 14, 40

Dávúd, Yu'hanna 40
D'Evelyn, Dr Frederick 112-13, 211
de Bons, Dr Joseph 332
de Bons, Edith (MacKay) 332
Dealy, Mrs 115-16
Dealy, Paul 116
Dean, Georgiana 115-16
Despard, Mrs 280
Ḍíyá Páshá, Ambassador 96-7, 103, 106, 247
Dodge, Arthur 59
Dodge, Wendell Phillips 55
Downs, John 273
Drakoulès, Dr Platon, and Mrs 288
Dreyfus-Barney, Hippolyte viii, 4, 17, **19**, 20-21, 22, 24-7, 41, 44-5, 47, 89, 273, 275, 280, 307, 309, 324
Dreyfus-Barney, Laura 4, **19**, 22, 24, 44, 47, 309, 324
Duke Lita 97
Dunn, Clara 4
Dunn, John Hyde 4, 122
Dúst-Muḥammad Khán 279, 301

Eckstein, Mr 312

Edsall, Charles 125
Edward VII, King of Great Britain 319
Edwards, Ivy Drew 166
Elijah, Elias 105, 106, 159
Elkins, Mrs 103-4
Emery family 264
Enthoven, Gabrielle 28, 303
Eurithra, 52

Fallscheer, Dr Josephine 8
Fareed, Dr Ameen (Dr Aminu'lláh Faríd) 51-2, 85-6, 89, 100, 124, 177, 195, 197, 204, 214, 217, 221, 228, 230, 247, 252, 256, 333-4
Farmer, Sarah 4, **166-7**, 246
Fisher, Dr Edwin 312
Ford, Mary Hanford 41, 42
Frankland, Helen 236
Frankland, Kathryn 81
Fraser, Christine 240-41
Fraser, Reverend Donald 275
Fraser, Isabel 4, 273, 275, 290-91, 329
Fujita, Sachiro viii, **191-2**, 197, 207-8, 209, 210, 216, 244

Gail, Marzieh viii, 78, 83, 89, 90, 122, 228, 263
Gamble, Annie 283
Geddes, Sir Patrick 294
Germanus, Professor Julius 316, 317, 318
Getsinger, Edward ix, 4, 13, 74, 75, **76**, 81, 89, 96, 100, 135, 227, 332
Getsinger, Lua 4, 51, **76**, 105, 114, 119-22, 133-5, 141, 143-4, 211, 217, 222, 224, 227, 332
Gibbons, Mrs 104
Gibran, Kahlil 18, 74, **75**
Giesswein, Prelate Alexander 316, 318
George V, King of Great Britain 302
Goldziher, Dr Ignatius 316, 318
Goodall, Helen 60, 81, 96, 118-19, 149, **211-12**, 216, 226, 230-31, 233, 237, 239, 240
Grant, Reverend Percy Stickney 18, 72-3, 130, 140, 264
Greely, General Adolphus 247
Greene, Bernard R. 94

Greenleaf, Charlie (Charles) 114
Gregory, Louis viii, 4, 13-16, 92, 96, **99-101**, 108, 161, 172

Haddad, Anton 5, 227
Hakim, Lotfullah 290, 292, 334
Hall, Albert 169-71, 197, 199
Hall, E. T. 273
Haney, Charles 102-3
Haney, Mariam 102-3, 268, 270
Haney, Paul 4, 102-3
Hannen, Joseph 4, 89-90, **91-2**, 95, 157, 253, 332
Hannen, Pauline 4, **91-2**, 99, 156-7
Harmon, Mr 154
Harrison, Cecilia 115
Ḥasan-i-Taqizadeh, Siyyid 45-6
Hatch, Willard P. 122
Ḥaydar-'Alí, Ḥájí Mírzá 230-31
Hearst, George 227
Hearst, Phoebe Apperson 52, 76, 179, 211-12, 224, 226, **227-8**, 229-30, 334
Hearst, William Randolph 227
Hemmick, Alice Barney 19, 89, 104
Henderson, Dr Charles 159
Herbert, Bertha (Holley) 25, 26, 27
Herrick, Elizabeth 30, 273, 275
Herrigel, Wilhelm 312, 313, 316, 322
Hillyer, Helen (Nell) *see* Brown
Hoagg, Emogene 157, 159, 331, 335-6
Holley, Bertha *see* Herbert
Holley, Doris *see* Pascal
Holley, Horace 4, **25-6**
Holmes, Irene 114
Holsti, Katheryn 214
Hopkins, Emma Curtis 240
Hopper, Marie 99
Hopper, Rene 99
Hopson, Elaine Lacroix 3
Hossein, Abdul 7
House, Mrs Colonel 105
Ḥusayn (son of 'Abdu'l-Bahá) 311

Ioas, Joseph 117
Ioas, Leroy 4, **109-10**, 113, 114, 116
Ioas, Maria 108
Ioas, Monroe 108
Ioas, Sylvia 207

Isaiah 106
Ives, Howard Colby 4, **63-7**, 135-6, 162, 268, 272
　descriptions by 67-8, 88, 136, 232
Ives, Muriel 132-3

Jack, Marion 4, 30, 277, 298
Jackson, Madame 307-8
Jackson, Professor William 130
Jesus Christ 15, 20, 31, 33, 48, 62, 66, 68, 70, 73, 104-6, 126, 129, 140, 156, 158, 161, 163, 187, 198, 200, 204, 209, 211, 225-6, 228, 235, 236-7, 245, 247, 250-52, 259, 261, 267, 269, 281, 282-3, 304, 310, 315, 319
Johnston, Charles 150-51
Jones, Musette 117
Jordan, Dr David Starr 217, 221, 286
Judas Iscariot 245

Kanno, Mr 217
Kappes, Lillian 25
Kazahira, Reverend 217
Khan, Ali-Kuli viii, 4, 5, 89-90, **90-91**, 91-2, 96-7, 101, 103, 137, 227, 228, 261, 268, 328
Khan, Florence (Breed) 78, 89-90, **90-91**, 96-7, 101, 103, 228, 229, 231
Khan, Hamideh 90, 102
Khan, Rahim 89, 90-91
Kheiralla, Ibrahim (Ibráhím Khayru'lláh) 4-5, 76, 194,196, 212, 227, 232, 236, 261-2
Khurásání, Mírzá Hassan (Khorassani) 13
Kinney, Carrie (Vaffa) 4, 57, 61, **62-3**, 80, 88, 138, 148, 171, 262, 266, 269
Kinney, Edward (Saffa) 4, 57, 61, **62-3**, 80, 150, 266, 269-70
Kipling, Rudyard 103
Klebs, Margaret 166
Knobloch, Alma 4, 91, **312-13**, 315
Knobloch, Amalie 91
Knobloch, Fanny 91, 156
Krug, Charles 78
Krug, Dr Florian 78-9, 257
Krug, Grace 778-9, 145-6, 257, 268

Krug, Louise 78, 268

Lachenay, Madame 19
La Grange, Margaret 69
Latimer, George 155-6, 157-8, 310, 313, 334
Leadroot, Leo 115
Lee, General Robert E. 198
Lewis, Mr 289
Lincoln, Abraham 117
Lorge, Mr 279
Lunt, Alfred 166, 170

MacNutt, Howard viii, 22-3, 58, 62, 69-70, 73, 143, **261-3**, 267
Maharajah of Jhalawar 283, 290
Maḥmúd-i-Zarqání, Mírzá 52, 106, 180, 192, 197, 214, 247, 268, 270, 271, 290, 292, 301, 312
Maḥmúd, Sulṭán 183-4
Marie, Queen of Romania 61
Mathew, Louisa 13, 15, 52, **99-101**, 161
Matteson, John 231
Maxim, Hudson 68-9
Maxwell, Mary (Amatu'l-Bahá Rúḥíyyih Khánum) 4, 77, 179-80, 180-81, 184-5
Maxwell, May 4, 19, 77, **179-80**, 181, 184-5, 186-7, 188, 271, 332
Maxwell, Sutherland 4, **179-80**, 180-82, 186-7, 188
Mazlúm, Mírzá 115
McClung, Lee 106
McVeagh, Charles 153, 161-2
Meres, Sir Frank 294
Metelmann, Velda 332
Meyer, Rabbi Martin 225-6
Mills, Mountfort 41, 58, 64, 79-80, 82, 86
Monnier, Pasteur 309
Moody, Susan 25
Moore, Reverend 149-50
Moore, Ursula Shuman 255
Morse, Fannie 166
Mortensen, Fred viii, 4, **168-72**, 254, 328
Morten, Marjorie 57-8, 69
Moses (Prophet of God) 105, 126, 129, 163, 173, 221, 225, 247-51, 261, 282

Moto *see* Yamamoto
Muḥammad (Prophet of God) 127, 163, 198, 225, 251
Muḥammad-'Alí, Mírzá 5, 8, 160-61, 194
Muḥammad-Ḥasan, Mírzá (King of Martyrs) 20-21
Muḥammad-Ḥusayn, Mírzá (Beloved of Martyrs) 20-21
Muḥammad Khán-i-Qazvíní, Mírzá 43-4, 46
Mullá Ḥusayn 324
Muníriḥ Khánum 7, 8, 17, 67, 228
Munír-i-Zayn (Moneer Zain), Mírzá 7, 52
Mushíru'l-Mulk, Persian Ambassador 279
Muther, Elizabeth 112, 216

Nadler, Professor Robert A. 316, 320-21
Nakhjavání, Mírzá 'Alí-Akbar 192, 197, 247, 253, 256, 325
Napoleon (I), Emperor of France 156
Napoleon III, Emperor of France 259
Násiri'd-Dín Sháh 20, 259, 279
Newhall, Muriel Ives Barrow viii
Niles, Mrs 106
Nichols, Rhoda 57-8
Nutt, Frederick 194

O'Reilly, Cathryn 232, 240
Ober, Grace Robarts 4, **132-6**, 176
Ober, Harlan 4, 96, **132-6**, 164-5, 174, 176

Pagan, E.C.H. 296. 297
Pagan, J. M. and family 297
Page, Mr 298
Paikert, Alajos 318, 320
Pankhurst, Emmeline 30-31, 278-9, 282
Parent, Miss 185
Parsons, Agnes viii, 4, 70, 74, 75, 89, 90, 91, 94-5, 96-7, 98-9, 102-3, 105-6, 119, 121, 123-4, 152, 153-6, 159-65, 217, 224, 246-7, 252-3, 268, 270, 334
Parsons, Arthur 70, 94, 98-9
Parsons, Jeffrey 94
Pascal, Doris 310

Paul, Saint 183
Paulson, Feny 208, 209-10
Peary, Admiral Robert 97-8
Penoyer, Justin 169, 172
Penshoe, Mr 140
Peter (Apostle of Christ) 183, 211
Perron, Leo 193
Plato 163
Platt, Miss 298
Pole, Graham 295
Ponsonaille, Mr and Mrs 44-5
Pumpelly, Daisy 165
Pumpelly, Raphael, Mrs and family 165
Putnam, Dr Herbert 95

Quant, Ella 69, 87-8

Rashíd Páshá 307-9, 324
Ralston, Georgia 148, 211, 222
Ralston, William 211
Randall, Margaret (Bahíyyih) 177
Randall, Ruth 175-7
Randall, William Henry (Harry) 166, **174-8**
Rathbun, Dr Harry 218
Regina Núr Mahal 40
Remey, Charles Mason 18, 89, 92, 96, 106, 309-10, 334
Revell, Ellwood 141
Revell, Ethel 141
Revell, Jessie 141
Revell, Mary 115, 130, 141-2, 255
Revell, Rebecca 130
Richmond, Celia 166
Robarts, Ella 132
Robb, Reverend A. B. 296
Roberts, Mrs 203
Robinson, Mr 231
Rogers, Professor Ernest 217
Roosevelt, President Theodore 83, 105
Root, Martha 4, **60-61**, 150, 320
Rosenberg, Ethel 27, **28**
Rúḥá Khánum (daughter of 'Abdu'l-Bahá) 67
Rúḥu'lláh 150

Sacy, Gabriel 47
Sadler, Professor Michael 40

Sanderson, Edith 24, 309
Sargent, Porter 310-11
Scatcherd, Felicia R. 287-9
Scheffler, Carl 110-11
Schepel, Annet 299
Schwarz, Albert, Consul 313, 315-6, 323
Schweizer, Mr and Mrs 315
Scott, Edwin 309
Sears, William (Bill) 200
Sears, Marguerite 200
Shoghi Effendi, Guardian of the Bahá'í Faith
  on 'Abdu'l-Bahá xii, 1-12, 3, 150, 333, 336
  life 11-12, 19, 26, 27, 28, 50-52, 67, 83, 180, 191, 333
  on pilgrims' notes ix-x
  and various believers 19, 26, 28, 61, 83, 92, 101, 112, 212, 233, 263, 313, 315
Short, W. H. 68, 130
Shu'á'u'lláh 5, 194, 235-6
Simkins, H. W. 226
Slater, Ida 193
Smiley, Albert 132
Smith, John Linden 164
Sohrab, Ahmad viii, 17, 69, 89, 155, 171, 180, 183, 192, 195, 197, 210, 247, 253, 276, 278, 279, 285, 290, 291-2, 293, 297, 298, 312, 314, 318, 326, 329, 333, 334
Spencer, Anna 130
Spencer, Colonel 283
Sprague, Sydney 6-7
Stannard, Mrs 332
Stapfer, Louise (Bosch) 22, 83
Stapley, Sir Richard and Lady 299
Stark, Leopold 316-18, 321
Steinmetz, Charles 149-50
Stewart, Elizabeth 25
Stewart, George S. 295
Stockton, Sallie 247
Storch, Juanita Marie 213-14
Struven, Edward 254
Struven, Hebe and Howard 254-5
Sulzer, William 105
Symon, Rabbi Abram 247, 252-3

Tamaddunu'l-Mulk 12, 17-18, 24, 44, 46, 195, 333
Tatum, Mrs 159-60, 265
Thompson, Juliet viii, 4, 17, **18-19**, 19-24, 557-8, 63, 71, 74, 75, 77, 96, 97, 103-5, 120, 129, 135-6, 142, 145, 147-8, 152, 222, 256, 257, 258, 265, 270-71
  paints portrait of 'Abdu'l-Bahá 104, 128-9, 143-4
Thompson, Maud 254-5
Thornburgh, Harriet 27
Thornburgh-Cropper, Mary Virginia (Maryam) 4, 17, 28, 30, 36, 40, 284, 291
Tinsley, Charles 224
Tobin, Esther (Nettie) 114-15
Topakyan, Mr, Consul-General 130, 264
True, Arna 193
True, Corinne 4, **110-12**, 113, 114, 115, 191, 192-3, 195, 196-7
True, Davis 111-12
True, Kenneth 112
True, Laurence 112
True, Moses 112
True, Nathanael 112
Tudor-Pole, Wellesley 10-12, 28, 30, 32, 33, 36, 302
Turner, Robert 227
Tussing, Phillip E. 162
Twain, Mark 83, 153
Tyler, Frau 322

Uthmán Páshá 332

Vámbéry, Arminius, Professor 318-19
Varqá, 'Alí-Muḥammad 150
Vent, Betty 238-9
Victoria, Queen of Great Britain 319
Von Suttner, Berthe 322

Wagner, Henrietta 118
Wagner, Pasteur 26
Wainwright, Admiral 106
Waite, Louise 225
Ward, Allan L. vii
Waring, Joan 276-7

Washington, Booker T. 96
White, Ruth 149
Whyte, Alexander, Reverend Dr 291, 292, 294, 295
Whyte, Jane 28, 290, **291-2**, 293
Wiers, Dr Edgar S. 125
Wilberforce, Archdeacon 34-5, 139
Wilcox, Ella Wheeler 74
Wilhelm II, Emperor of Germany 315, 323
Wilhelm, Roy 4, 18, 60-61, 145
Wilson, Maria 173, 176
Wilson, President Woodrow 94, 105, 201

Windust, Albert 192, 193, 195, 244
Wise, Harriet 119, 149
Wise, Rabbi Stephen 130
Woodcock, Percy 41, 52
Woolson, Dr Clement 199-200

Yahyá, Mírzá 68, 195
Yamamoto, Kanichi **216-17**
Yazdi, Ali viii, 9-10, 11, 50-52
Yazdí, Muḥammad 13, 15-16

Zia (Ḍíyá), Mírzá 103
Zillu's-Sultán 20-21

www.ingramcontent.com/pod-product-compliance
Lightning Source LLC
Chambersburg PA
CBHW021759220426
43662CB00006B/119